ARAFURA SEA

ARNHEM
LAND

Gulf of
Carpentaria

Groote
Eylandt

CARPENTARIA HWY Borroloola

Mornington
Is.

Torres Strait
Cape York

CAPE
YORK
PENINSULA

CORAL
SEA

SOUTH

Cooktown
Mossman
Cairns
Mareeba
Innisfail

ewcastle Waters

STUART HWY
TABLELANDS HWY
BARKLY

Camooweal

Lake Nash

SANDOVER HWY

Alice Springs

MPSON DESERT

ulgera

Birdsville

STURT'S
STONY
DESERT

Lake Eyre

Coober Pedy

Marree

Kingoonya

Everard

Ceduna
Lake
Gairdner

Port Lincoln

Kangaroo Is.

OCEAN

ed

Normanton
Croydon
Georgetown
The Lynd

GREAT DIVIDING RANGE

Townsville

Mt.Isa
Cloncurry
LANDSBOURGH
Dajarra
Boulia

Julia Creek
FLINDERS 78
Winton
Middleton

Charters
Towers
Hughenden

BRUCE HWY

Mackay

Clermont

QUEENSLAND

Longreach
Barcaldine
CAPRICORN
Blackall

Emerald

Maryborough

Rockhampton

DAWSON HWY
BURNETT HWY

Augathella

Charleville
Quilpie

Morven
WARREGO HWY
Roma
54 HWY

Injune

Miles

Maryborough

PACIFIC

Cunnamulla
St.George

MITCHELL HWY
CITY HWY

Goondiwindi

Toowoomba

BRISBANE
Ipswich

42

Moree

RANGE HWY

NEW SOUTH WALES
& A.C.T.

Bourke

Wilcannia
Cobar

COBB HWY

Broken Hill
SILVER CITY HWY

Port Augusta

FLINDERS RANGES

LINCOLN HWY

Spencer Gulf

Gulf St Vincent

ADELAIDE

Tailem Bend

Bordertown

Mt.Gambier

Coonabarabran

Nyngan

Dubbo

West Wyalong

Mildura
Ouyen

CALDER HWY

Hay

Narrandera

Wagga Wagga

Bendigo
Echuca
HUME HWY
Ballarat

GLENELG HWY
PRINCES HWY

MELBOURNE

Glen Innes
NEW ENGLAND HWY
PACIFIC HWY

Grafton

DIVIDING RANGE

Tamworth
Port Macquarie

Bathurst
Newcastle

Cowra
SYDNEY
Yass
Wollongong
Goulburn
CANBERRA

Albury

Cooma

Bega

C.Howe

Cann River

VICTORIA

OCEAN

PRINCES HWY

Orbost

GREAT

C.Otway

Wilsons Promontory

Bass
Strait

King Is.

George Town
Devonport

TASMAN SEA

Flinders Is.

Smithton
Burnie
Queenstown

Strathgordon

Southport

Launceston
TASMANIA

HOBART
Storm Bay

Australian ROAD ATLAS

FABER AND FABER

London and Boston

Contents

Symbols

The roads

Maps of large areas

Freeway with Route Number ....
Freeway under construction ....
Highway, sealed, with National Route Number
Highway, unsealed ....
Highway under construction ....
Major road, sealed ....
Major road, unsealed ....
Major road under construction ....
Other road ....
Vehicular track ....

Maps of small areas

Freeway with Route Number ....
Freeway under construction ....
Highway, sealed, with National Route Number
Highway, unsealed ....
Highway under construction ....
Major road, sealed,
    with Metropolitan Route Number ....
Major road, unsealed ....
Other road with one way street indicator .....
Vehicular track ....

Other features

Total kilometres between two main points ... 30
Intermediate kilometres 5
Number of kilometres from GPO 16
Railway with station .... Newcastle
Railway with town .... Eudlo
State boundary ....
Walking track ....
River ....
Rocks ....
Reef ....
Place of interest .... Lookout ■
Other landmark .... Tower ▪
Homestead .... Mooloogool □
Lighthouse .... ★
Mountain tops .... Mt Hayward 441m +
Vineyard .... ●
Aboriginal reserve ....
Prohibited area ....

Airport, landing ground ....
Heliport ....
Beacon .... ▲
Navigation light ....
Park, recreational area ....
Area of interest ....
Building of interest ....
Built-up area ....
Pine forest ....
Orchard ....
Other timbered area ....
Swamp ....
Mangrove ....
Beach ....
Mud ....
Area subject to flooding ....
Lake ....
Intermittent lake ....

The Maps

Every part of Australia is mapped in *Australian Road Atlas,* from cities to the outback. Heavily-populated areas and places of special tourist interest are mapped in greater detail. Distance is shown by black and red markers on the maps and a scale bar at the top of each map.

Continuation of Maps

For easy continuation from one map to another there is always some overlap when maps are at the same scale. The symbol on the edges of the map pages indicates the next map page that should be turned to.

Maps of New South Wales

Location Map

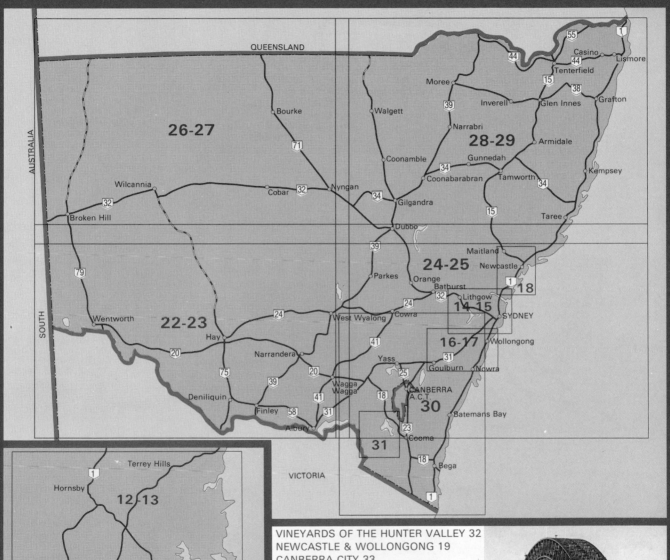

QUEENSLAND

55
1
44
Casino
44
Lismore
Moree
Tenterfield
15
38
39
Inverell
Glen Innes
Grafton
26-27
71
Bourke
Walgett
Narrabri
28-29
Armidale
Coonamble
Gunnedah
Kempsey
34
Coonabarabran
Tamworth
Wilcannia
Cobar
32
Nyngan
34
34
Gilgandra
AUSTRALIA
32
Dubbo
15
Taree
Broken Hill
39
Maitland
24-25
Newcastle
79
Parkes
Orange
1
18
Bathurst
SOUTH
24
32
Lithgow
14-15
22-23
24
West Wyalong
Cowra
SYDNEY
Wentworth
Hay
16-17
Wollongong
41
Narrandera
Yass
31
20
25
Goulburn
Nowra
75
20
18
Deniliquin
39
Wagga
Wagga
CANBERRA
A.C.T.
Finley
58
41
31
30
Batemans Bay
Albury
23
31
Cooma
VICTORIA
18
Bega
1

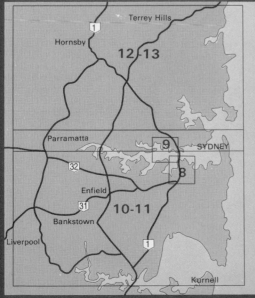

Terrey Hills
1
Hornsby
12-13
Parramatta
9
SYDNEY
32
8
Enfield
31
10-11
Bankstown
Liverpool
1
Kurnell

VINEYARDS OF THE HUNTER VALLEY 32
NEWCASTLE & WOLLONGONG 19
CANBERRA CITY 33
CANBERRA 34
AUSTRALIAN CAPITAL TERRITORY 35
BRISBANE WATER & KU-RING-GAI
CHASE N.P. 20-21

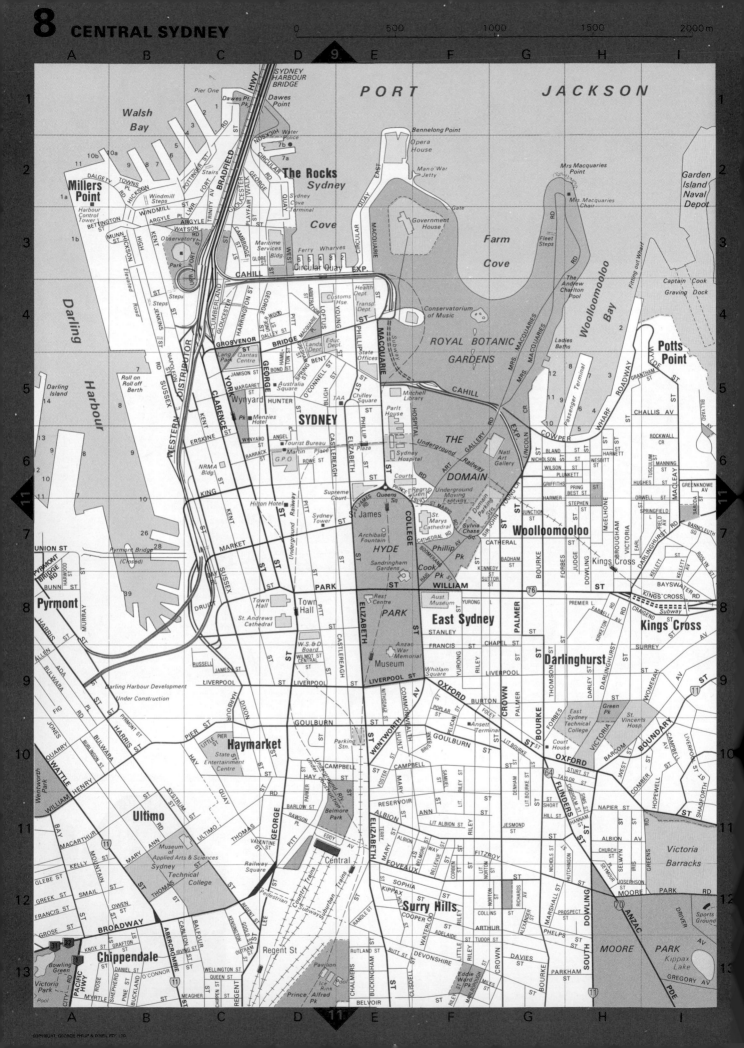

900 900 1000 m

Cammeray

Cremorne

CAMMERAY PARK & GOLF LINKS

Crows Nest

MILITARY RD

ST. LEONARDS PARK

North Sydney Oval

War Memorial Footbridge

Music Shell Oval

North Sydney Bowling Green

North Sydney

Neutral Bay

Nth Sydney Public School

Forsyth Park

Bowling Green

Mater Misericordiae Hosp. Nth Sydney Girls High Sch

Victoria Cross

Anderson Park

Steps Rd

WHALING

Graythwaite Hospital

Nth Sydney Blue St

Lavender Bay

Watt Pk

Clark Pk

Ferry Wharf

Milson Park

Shell Cove

Neutral Bay

Kurraba Wharf

Cremorne Pt

The Hodgson Lookout

Kurraba Point

Careening Cove

Footbridge

Kesterton Park

High St Wharf

Hayes St Wharf

Milsons Point

Lavender Bay

Milsons Point

McMahons Point

Luna Park

McMahons Pt Wharf

McMahons Point

Olympic Pool

Wudyong Point

Royal Sydney Yacht Squadron

Kirribilli

Stanton Lookout

Kirribilli House

Admiralty House

Jeffrey St Wharf

Beulah St Wharf

Milsons Point

Kirribilli Point

Blues Point

Res

SYDNEY HARBOUR BRIDGE

Fort Denison

PORT JACKSON

Maritime Services Board Depot

Millers Point

Pier One

Dawes Pt Pk

Dawes Point

Walsh Bay

To City

To Hornsby

PACIFIC HIGHWAY

WARRINGAH EXPRESSWAY

BRADFIELD HIGHWAY

0 1 2 3 4 5 6 km

J K L M N **13** O P Q R

PACIFIC

1
Boronia Park
Cammeray
Crows Nest
Mosman
Georges Heights
Middle Head
Inner South Head
Obelisk Bay
Lady Bay
Military Reserve

2
Riverview
Linley Pt
Fig Tree
GLADESVILLE
Hunters Hill
Longueville
Greenwich
St Leonards
Wollstonecraft
Neutral Bay
Cremorne
Clifton Gardens
Georges Head
Chowder Bay
Camp Cove
Green Point
Watsons Bay
The Gap
Watsons Bay
Outer South Head

PORT

2
Henley
Woolwich
Woolwich
Waverton
North Sydney
Kirribilli
Cremorne Point
Kurraba Pt.
Robertsons Pt.
Taronga Pk Zoo
Taylors Pt.
Bradleys Head
Shark Bay
Hermit Pt.
Vaucluse
Diamond Bay

3
Chiswick
Drummoyne
Birchgrove
Balmain
Goat Island
Walsh Bay
Blues Pt.
Kirribilli Pt.
Sydney Harbour Bridge
Fort Denison
Garden Island
Clarke Island
Shark Island
Darling Point
Point Piper
Rose Bay
Rose Bay
Dover Heights

4
Russell Lea
Iron Cove
Rozelle
Lilyfield
Pyrmont
The Rocks
Farm Cove
SYDNEY
Bot. Gdns.
The Domain
Potts Point
Elizabeth Bay
Kings Cross
Double Bay
Double Bay
Bellevue Hill
Royal Sydney Golf Course

5
Dobroyd Point
Haberfield
Glebe
Ultimo
Darlinghurst
Rushcutters Bay
Edgecliff
Paddington
Woollahra
Bondi Junction
Bondi
North Bondi
Ben Buckler
Bondi Bay

6
Ashfield
Leichhardt
Annandale
Camperdown
Darlington
Cleveland
Surry Hills
Centennial Park
Bronte
Waverley
Clovelly
Petersham
Stanmore
Newtown
Redfern
Waterloo
Moore Park
RAS Show grounds

7
Summerhill
Lewisham
Enmore
Erskineville
Alexandria
Zetland
Kensington
Randwick Racecourse
Randwick
Clovelly
Coogee

8
Dulwich Hill
St. Peters
Beaconsfield
Rosebery
Australian Golf Course
University of NSW
South Coogee

9
Marrickville
Tempe
Mascot
Eastlakes
Daceyville
Maroubra Junction
Maroubra
Maroubra Beach

9
Undercliffe
Cooks River
Domestic Terminal
SYDNEY AIRPORT
Botany
Botany East
Pagewood
Hillsdale
Anzac Rifle Range

10
Earlwood
Turrella
Arncliffe
International Terminal
Banksia
Kyeemagh
Matraville
Chifley
Malabar
Long Bay

11
Bexley
Rockdale
Kogarah
Brighton-le-Sands
BOTANY
Port Botany
Container Terminal
Phillip Bay
Prince Henry Hospital
Little Bay

12
South Bexley
Carlton
Beverley Park
Ramsgate
La Perouse
Yarra Bay
Frenchmans Bay
Bare Island
Congwong Bay
NSW Golf Course
St Michaels Golf Course

13
Sans Souci
Dolls Point
BAY
Towra Point
Inscription Point
Cape Banks
Kurnell
Captain Cook Landing Place Park

JACKSON

PACIFIC OCEAN

SOUTH

15

J K L M N **15** O P Q R

15

A B C D E F G H I

1 Middle Dural
Galston
Mt.Kuring-gai
HWY
Visitors Centre
Kalkari Wildlife Centre
Koala Reserve

2 PITT TOWN RD
Galston Gorge
Berowra
Mt.Colah
KU-RING-GAI
Hornsby Heights
SOMMERVILLE

3 Kenthurst
KENTHURST
Carters Gully
Rifle Range
Res
PACIFIC
Asquith
The Sphinx
CURAGUL
HEAD

4 ANNANGROVE
Dural
Round Corner
Trunk
Fish
Reserve
Hookhams Corner
BRIDGE RD
Hornsby
Lovers Jump
G.C.

5 GLENHAVEN
Glenhaven
Cumberland S.F. Extension
Georges
Elouéra Bushland Reserve
Hornsby
Waitara
PRETORIA
CLARKE
Wahroonga East
Turramurra North
BOBBIN

6 NORTHERN
OLD
Cherrybrook
Thornleigh
Westleigh
DUFFY
Normanhurst
PACIFIC
Wahroonga
Warrawee
Bangala ST
Turramurra
HWY

7 SHOWGROUND
Showground
Castle Hill
Rogans Hill
CASTLE HILL
Thornleigh
Pennant Hills
Boy Scouts Assn.
Fox Valley
COMENARRA
Pymble

8 PARSONAGE
Castle Hill
State Forest
Koala Park
Pennant Hills West
BEECROFT
Beecroft
Cheltenham
Pennant Hills Park
BOUNDARY
Kissing Point
Avondale G.C.
West Pymble

9 WINDSOR
Rifle Range
State Forest
Royal Deaf & Blind Institute
NORTH
Pennant Hills G.C.
Devlins
PLYMPTON
Epping
EPPING
Macquarie University
LANE COVE NATIONAL PARK

10 Baulkham Hills
North Rocks
CARLINGFORD
Carlingford
Eastwood
Marsfield
North Ryde
Northern Suburbs Cemetery

11 Winston Hills
Northmead
Telopea
Dundas Valley
Denistone
East Ryde
Psychiatric Centre

12 Wentworthville
Westmead
North Parramatta
Dundas
MELROSE PARK
West Ryde
Ryde
Putney

13 Parramatta
Camellia
Rydalmere
Ermington
Meadowbank
Rosehill Racecourse
Silverwater Bridge
Parramatta River
Tennyson

A B C D E F G H I

10

0 1 2 3 4 5 6 km

J K L M N O P Q R

KU-RING-GAI CHASE
NATIONAL
PARK

Bobbin Head

Cowan Creek

Aerodrome
NSW Gun Club
BOORALIE RD
Duffys Forest
Waratah Park
TOORONGA RD
KING RD

CABBAGE TREE
Bayview
G.C.
PARK
DARLEY
BASSETT ST
BARRENJOEY RD
The Basin
Res.
GOLF AV
CICADA GLEN RD
WALTER RD
35
Mona Vale
VINEYARD
ALAN ST
ST
WARRIEWOOD RD
MACPHERSON ST
Mona Vale Beach
Mona Vale GC
Hosp.
PDE

Terrey Hills
30 33 MONA VALE
Ingleside
33
INGLESIDE RD
POWDER WORKS RD
Monash G.C.
Bahai Temple
Elanora
Elanora GC
Narrabeen North
25
Warriewood
Warriewood Beach
Turimetta Head
Turimetta Beach
Narrabeen Head
GARDEN RD
KALANI
ELANORA RD
WOORALA
PITTWATER RD

St. Ives Chase
Ku-ring-gai Wildflower Garden
Showground
Police Driving School
Davidson
Park
MONA VALE 25
FOREST WAY
Deep Ck
Narrabeen Lagoon
Res. Middle Ck
National Fitness Camp
WAKEHURST 22
Camping Area
PARKWAY
Narrabeen
Narrabeen Beach
Wheeler Heights
Collaroy Plateau
EDGECLIFFE BVD
PITTWATER RD
MACTIER ST
OCEAN ST
The Basin
Long Point

St. Ives North
AYERS
WOODBURY RD
DOUGLAS EAST
20
COLLINS RD
MEMORIAL
STANLEY
HORACE ST
Belrose
RALSTON AV
WYATT AV
Snake Ck
OXFORD
Oxford Falls
Oxford Falls
FALLS RD
Wheeler
Cromer
Cromer G.C.
CARCOOLA RD
NARAYA
PARR PDE
McINTOSH
TORONTO AV
PARKES RD
PLATEAU RD
FISHER RD NTH
CAMPBELL
ANZAC
Collaroy
20
Dee Why Lagoon
Long Reef Golf Club
Long Reef Beach
Dee Why Beach

St. Ives
Pony Club
BLACKBUTTS RD
Davidson
Cem.
KAMBORA AV
FRENCHS FOREST RD
GLEN ST
THE ESPLANADE
WEARDON RD
Oxford
PERENTIE RD
HEWS PDE
PRINGLE AV
Davidson Park
Frenchs Forest
WARRINGAH 29
Drive-in
Film Studios
FITZPATRICK
Beacon Hill
Narraweena
BEACON HILL RD
Oval
VICTOR RD
WINBOURNE RD
Dee Why
Pk.
Flora Res.
GRIFFIN RD
HOWARD AV
North Curl Curl
Dee Why Head
Harbord Lagoon
Dee Why Beach

Gordon
ILLEROY AV
Killara
15
East Killara
Lindfield
East Lindfield
WELLINGTON RD
TRYON RD
Roseville G.C.
Roseville Bridge
Killarney Heights
Forestville
Allambie Heights
Warringah
MAXWELL PDE
BANTRY
SALERNO
BROWN
DEAKIN
FERGUSON
CURRIE RD
RATHOWEN PDE
Bates
Manly
WAKEHURST PARKWAY
War Memorial Park
Old Manly Rd
Brookvale
15
Curl Curl
WYADRA AV
North Manly
Harbord
OLIVER ST
EVANS RD
ADAMS ST
BENNETT ST
WILLIAM ST
Curl Curl Head
North Curl Curl
Harbord Beach

KILLARA
ESSEX ST
NORFOLK
SPENCER RD
WERONA AV
WATTLE
STANHOPE RD
LINDFIELD AV
Roseville
Roseville East
Castle Cove
Middle Harbour
BABBAGE RD
EASTERN ARTERIAL RD
Middle Cove
Sugarloaf Bay
North Balgowlah
WOODBINE
Balgowlah
BALGOWLAH RD
Golf Course
Cem.
Manly Vale
North Balgowlah
KENNETH RD
Manly Golf Course
Fairlight
Manly
Manly Beach
Queenscliff
Queenscliff Beach
North Steyne Beach

WHARF RD
PACIFIC HWY
Chatswood West
GROSVENOR
SHIRLEY RD
ARCHBOLD RD
PENSHURST ST
Willoughby North
HIGH ST
BOUNDARY ST
Roseville
26
Middle Cove
North Arm
South Arm
Castlecrag
Sailors Bay
Sugarloaf Point
Seaforth
PONSONBY PDE
SYDNEY RD
22
BALGOWLAH RD
LAUDERDALE AV
Balgowlah Heights
Clontarf
North Harbour
Manly Cove
Marine Pde
Manly Pt.
North Pt.
Inner North Head
Military Reserve
Quarantine Station
Cannae Point
Dobroyd Point
Outer North Head

Lane Cove West
MOWBRAY RD
Chatswood
FULLERS RD
BEACONSFIELD RD
Willoughby
Artarmon
Channel 9
KAKEMUKA
Northbridge
Long Bay
SAILORS RD
STRATHALLEN AV
Golf Course
Fig Tree Pt.
Beauty Point
The Spit
The Spit Bridge
Middle Harbour
Grotto Point
Balmoral
Wy-at-gine Point
Hunters Bay

10
Fullers Bridge
29
Lane Cove River
Gore Hill
PACIFIC HWY
Naremburn
Cammeray
Artarmon
F1
CAMMERAY RD
AMHERST ST
Crows Nest
Neutral Bay
Cremorne
Spit Junction
Mosman
Balmoral
Rocky Point
MILITARY RD
RAGLAN
AVENUE RD
Georges Heights
Georges Head
Middle Head
Obelisk Bay
Inner South Head
Lady Bay
Military Reserve
JACKSON

River
Riverview
Longueville
Greenwich
St. Leonards
Wollstonecraft
Waverton
North Sydney
Cremorne Point
Neutral Bay
Clifton Gardens
Chowder Bay
Chowder Head
Taylors Point
Taronga Pk Zoo
Bradleys Head
PORT
Watsons Bay
The Gap
Green Point
Vaucluse
Vaucluse Bay
Shark Bay
Village Point
Outer South Head
Watsons Bay
CAMBRIDGE
10

Hunters Hill
Fig Tree
Tarban Ck Bridge
Fig Tree Bridge
GLADESVILLE
WOOLWICH RD
Gladesville Bridge

SOUTH PACIFIC OCEAN

N

J K L M N O P Q R

1 2 3 4 5 6 7 8 9 10 11 12 13

A B C D 24 E F G H I

Ben Bullen

994m The Donkey Mtn.

Galah Mtn. 1041m

1

86

11

Wolgan (West branch)

Wolgan

Nayook Ck

Sandy Cave Ck

Ck

Wollangambe River

Angorawa Point Ck

THE PUTTY

69

2

11

Cullen Bullen Rly. Stn.

Cullen Bullen

Wolgan Gap

Angus Place

Wolgan (Eastern Branch) R

Bungleboon

Branch

Rain Ck

Ck

Ck

Wollangambe

Mt. Tootie

Tootie

Wheeny Ck

Little Wheeny Ck

3

Portland

Portland Rly. Stn.

Pipers Flat

Irondale

13 Wallerawang

86

Lidsdale

Tunnel

Marrangaroo

Cox's

Middle River

Nine Mile

Dumbano Ck

Yarramun

Mt. Wilson

Bilpin

18

Comleroi Rda

40 Kurrajong Heights

4

GREAT

GREAT WESTERN

8

Cox's

11 LITHGOW

Clarence

Newnes Junction

Bell Ck

Mt. Wilson

Bell

Bowens Ck

35

40 Berambing

Hungerfords

Bowen Mountain

Ck

31

Kurrajo

Kurrajong North

Grose Vale

Grose Wo

5

Deadmans Ck

Rydal

Bowenfels

Mt. Walker 1187m

Old Bowenfels

Farmers

South Bowenfels 11

32

Hartley

Clwydd

River

Hartley Vale

Hartley Vale Rly. Stn.

11

Victoria Falls

19 BLUE

River

Grose

Vale Lookout

27

Sodwalls

Solitary Ck

Ck

Anartio

11

Mt. Blaxland Monument

Cheethams Flats

Lett

Mt. York

Little Hartley

11

Mt. York Explorers Monument

Mt. Victoria

Perrys Lookdown

MOUNTAINS

Mt. Hay

Wentworth

Hawkesbury Lookout

Yellow Lookout

6

Anarel

16

DIVIDING

River

Lowther

Lowther

Mt. Piddington 1092m

Blackheath

Mt. Blackheath Lookout

Horseshoe Falls

Pulpit Rock

Govetts Leap

The Bridal Vel

Evans Lookout

Beauchamp Falls

Grose

Woodford

Linden

NATIONAL

Springwood

Springwood Nth.

Springwood

Faulconbridge

Valley Heights

7

24

The Meadows

Bonfire Hill 1286m

Hampton

1

3

Marsdens Swamp

Blackheath

Hargreaves Lookout

Medlow Bath

Lake Medlow

18

WESTERN

Minnehaha Falls

WALK

Wentworth Falls

Leura 5

Lawson

32

Hazelbrook

3

Glenbrook

Linden

PARK

32

Warrimoo

Blaxland

21

Riverview Loo

Martins Lookout

8

Duckmaloi

13

27 Jenolan State Forest

Long Swamp

Cullenbenbong

Gibraltar Rocks 1057m

Pulpit Hill

Bonnie Doon Falls

14

Megalong

Katoomba

Katoomba Falls

The Three Sisters

Megalong

Leura Falls

Gordon Falls

Wentworth Falls

Sublime Pt. Lookout

Bullaburra Falls

Cataract Falls

Woodford

Queen Victoria Sanatorium

Bedford

The Oaks Picnic Ground

Nepean

Glenbrook

9

Edith

McKeons

Ti-Tree

Jenolan Ck

24 BLACK RANGE

Harrys River

Little River

Galong

Breakfast Ck

Glenraphael Falls

Cedar

Katoomba Ck

Reedy Ck

Erskine

Ripple Ck

Warragamba

Wala

10

11

13

5 Jenolan Caves

Mumbedah River

River

Mt. Cookum

McMahons Lookout

Silverdale

Lion Park

11

Ginkin

6

Shooters Hill

8

RANGE

32

27

KANANGRA BOYD

Kanangra River

Kangaroo Range

GANGERANG RANGE

GINGRA RANGE

River

SCOTTS MAIN RANGE

LAKE BURRAGORANG

Brimstone Ck

29

Werom

Orangeville

12

16

Tuglow

Tuglow

Tuglow Caves

River

Hollanders

NATIONAL

Kanangra Walls

PARK

Kowmung

Black

Hollow

Green

Wattle Ck

Ck

Lecys

Burragorang Lookout

The Oaks

5

13

Oberon Prison Camp

Banshea State Forest

Burnt Hole

Ck

River

Tonalli

River

Coal Mine

Nattai River

Coal Mine

Werribee

Oakdale

A B C D 16 E F G H I

0   10   20   30 km

J K L M N 18 O P Q R

DHARUG NATIONAL PARK

Colo Heights
WHEELBARROW RIDGE
Comleroy State Forest
Webbs Creek
Wisemans Ferry
Greengrove
Lower Mangrove
Old Sydney Town
Somersby Falls
Strickland State Forest
Narara
Holgate
Matcham
Wamberal
Gosford
Gosford East
Erina
Erina East
Terrigal
The Skillion
Una Voce
Laughtondale
Weavers
Lower Hawkesbury
Leets Vale
Gunderman
Glenworth Valley
Mt. White
Kariong
Koolewong
Point Clare
Brisbane Water
Saratoga
Davistown
Green Pt.
Egyptian Gardens
Kincumber
Avoca Beach
Capacabana

Upper Colo
Morans Rock
Lower Portland
Maroota North
Spencer
Woy Woy
Empire Bay
Bensville
McMasters Beach

Blaxlands Ridge
Kurrajong East
Sackville North
Sackville Reach
Maroota
Canoelands
Brooklyn
Broken Bay
Barranjoey
Bouddi Marine Park

The Slopes
Glossodia
Ebenezer
Marayla
Marramarra
Cattai
Maroota State Forest
Ku-Ring-Gai Chase
Palm Beach
Whale Beach
South Head

Freemans Reach
Wilberforce
Australiana Park
Picnic Gnds
Glenorie
Arcadia
Cowan
Berowra
Cottage Point
Avalon
Clareville Beach
Newport Beach

Richmond
Clarendon
Windsor
McGraths Hill
Mulgrave
Vineyard
Kenthurst
Galston
Mt. Colah
Hornsby Heights
Mt. Ku-Ring-Gai
Terrey Hills
Bayview
Mona Vale
Warriewood

Agnes Banks
Newtown
Hawkesbury Agricult. College
Annangrove
Dural
Round Corner
Hornsby
Asquith
Wahroonga
St. Ives
Elanora
Narrabeen
Collaroy
Long Reef Point

Londonderry
Riverstone
Schofields
Rouse Hill
Glenhaven
Thornleigh
Pennant Hills
Pymble
Gordon
Killara
Belrose
Oxford Falls
Dee Why

Castlereagh
Marsden Park
Quakers Hill
Kellyville
Castle Hill
Beecroft
Cheltenham
Epping
Frenchs Forest
Allambie Heights
Manly North
Queenscliff
Manly

Cranebrook
Castlereagh Upper
Llandillo
Marayong
Baulkham Hills
Carlingford
Eastwood
Chatswood
Northbridge
Seaforth
Balgowlah Heights
Outer North Head

Emu Plains
Penrith
Werrington
St. Marys
Dunheved
Mt. Druitt
Rooty Hill
Plumpton
Doonside
Blacktown
Seven Hills
Winston Hills
North Mead
Dundas
North Ryde
Lane Cove
St. Leonards
Mosman
Middle Head
Inner South Head

Regentville
Kingswood
Orchard Hills
Eastern Ck
GREAT WESTERN
Prospect
Parramatta
Meadowbank
Ryde
Gladesville
Hunters Hill
Drummoyne
Balmain
SYDNEY
Watsons Bay
Dover Heights

WESTERN FWY
Prospect Reservoir
Merrylands
North Auburn
Concord
Mortlake
Russell Lea
King's Cross
Paddington
Double Bay
North Bondi
Bondi

Mulgoa
Erskine Park
Horsley Park
Smithfield
Fairfield
Auburn
Lidcombe
Flemington
Enfield
Ashfield
Leichhardt
Camperdown
Rose Bay

Animal World
Radio Astronomy Centre
Cecil Park
Bonnyrigg
Cabramatta
Bass Hill
Yagoona
Regents Park
Belfield
Marrickville
St Peters
Enmore
Erskineville
Kensington
Clovelly
Coogee

Luddenham
Kemps Creek
Badgerys Creek
Liverpool
Lurnea
Casula
Punchbowl
Lakemba
Earlwood
Canterbury
Sydney Airport
Arncliffe
Botany
Pagewood
Maroubra Junc.
South Coogee
Maroubra

Greendale
Austral
Hoxton Park
Anzac Village
Milperra
East Hills
Revesby
Bankstown
Beverly Hills
Bexley
Rockdale
Banksmeadow
Malabar

Bringelly
Rossmore
Leppington
Glenfield
Holsworthy Barracks
Riverwood
Georges River
Lugarno
Brighton-le-Sands
Beverley Park
Botany Bay
Phillip Bay
La Perouse
Little Bay

Theresa Park
Catherine Field
Oran Park Raceway
Macquarie Fields
Ingleburn
Menai
Sutherland
Como
Oyster Bay
Sylvania
Taren Point
Sans Souci
Towra Pt.
Kurnell
Cape Banks
Inscription Pt.
Henry Hd

Cobbitty
Narellan
Currans Hill
Kenny Hill
Minto
Lucas Heights
Kirrawee
Gymea
Caringbah
Woolooware Bay
Bate Bay
Cronulla
Port Hacking Pt.

Brownlow Hill
Camden
Leumeah
Kentlyn
Engadine
Audley
Royal National Park
Grays Point
Port Hacking
Maianbar
Bundeena

Mt. Hunter
Cawdor
Menangle Park
CAMPBELLTOWN
Military Reserve
Woronora
PRINCES HWY
THE ROYAL NATIONAL PARK
Wattamolla

Menangle
Razorback Mountain
Wedderburn
Picnic Gnd.
Woronora Reservoir
Waterfall
Garie

Helensburgh
Lilyvale
PRINCES F6

PACIFIC OCEAN
SOUTH PACIFIC

J K L M N 17 O P Q R

Porters Retreat
Felled Timber Ck
Burnt Hole Ck
River
Tonalli
Lake Burragorang
Coal Mine
Silent
Ck
Mt. Werong
Murruin
Barrallier Pass
Yerranderie
River
47
Menus
Mt. Armstrong
RANGE
River
26
Ck
Werong Branch
Wiarborough
River
Abercrombie
New Yard Hill
Wollondilly
River
Burra
Burra
Curraweela
Ck
22
12
Lords Mtn
WOMBEYAN
29
Burragorang Lookout
Mt. Wanganderry 835m
High Range
ROAD
61
Golspie
Yalbraith
Broughtons Lookout
Wombeyan Caves
CAVES
Bullio
13
Jellore
Burra
Richlands
10
Ck
Wingecarribee
Tunnel
Burra Burra Lake
8
DIVIDING
Guineacor
Ck
Joadja
Ghost Town Joadja
Mandemar
Mt. Misery 784m
11
Ck
Mt. Penang 795m
MINDEMAR RANGE
Taralga
Taralga
19
Bunnaby
River
Berrima
24
GREAT
Strathaird
7
Kercawary
Ck
River
Wollondilly
Berrima West
Berrima South
28
Currawang
Mt. Rae
Mt. McAlister 1034m
Myrtleville
Belango State Forest
Medway Dam
Belanglo
Sutton Forest
14
Williqam
Myrtle Ck
Cowpers Ck
Black Bobs Ck
Emu Ck
Roslyn
N
Big Hill
Canyon Leigh
Exeter
Kialla
COOKBUNDOON RANGE
35
Greenwich Park
River
HWY
Penrose State Forest
Bundano
Woodhouselee
47
31
Cookbundoon
Brayton
Paddys River
Penrose
Teudts Lookout
Bundanoon
Wingello
Mt. Wayo Ck
14
58
15
Wingello State Forest
Mt. Towrang
Norwood
Towrang
Carrick
Marulan
HUME
Tallong
Mummell
Kingsdale
River
Kenmore
13
HUME
Marulan South
Tallowa
Caoura
MORTO NATION PARK
GOULBURN
Mt. Towrang 867m
Bungonia Lookdown
Parksbourne
Wollondilly
13 HWY
Mulwaree Ponds
Bungonia
Shoalhaven
Yarra
Breadalbane Plain
Gundary
26
HUME
FEDERAL HY
Tirrannaville
Gundary Plains
Bungonia
River
Extrema

0   10   20   30 km

J   K   L   M   N   O   P   Q   R

15

OCEAN

Woronora Reservoir
Garie
Helensburgh 68
Lilyvale
Otford
Blue Gum Forest
Blue Gum Forest
Lawrence Hargraves Memorial and Lookout
Mowbray Park
Douglas Park
Darkes Forest
Stanwell Park
Coalcliff Dam
Coalcliff
Picton
Maldon
Appin
Wedderburn State Forest
Clifton
Scarborough
Lakesland
Thirlmere Lakes Nat. Pk.
Thirlmere
16
Tahmoor
Wilton
Appin Falls
Picnic Gnd.
18
Wombarra
Coledale
Couridjah
Cement Works
Weir
Wollondoola
Cataract Reservoir
Sublime Point Lookout
Austinmer
Buxton
Bargo
39
42
Balmoral
Yanderra
Picnic Gnd.
Picnic Gnd.
32
Bulli Pass
Bulli Lookout
Thirroul
Bulli Point
Bulli
Woonona
Hilltop
Avon Reservoir
Cordeaux Reservoir
Bellambi
Bellambi Point
Nepean Reservoir
Yerrinbool
12
Corrimal
Towradgi
Colo Vale
Mt. Flora 742m
Mt. Keira
Fairy Meadow
Resr. No.2
N. Wollongong
Alpine
Aylmerton
Braemar
Mt. Keira
Mt. Kembla
Flagstaff Point
WOLLONGONG
Welby
Resr.
Mittagong
Kembla Heights
Unanderra
Coniston
Harbour
Bowral
Kembla Grange
Wongawilli
Berkeley
PORT KEMBLA
Big Island
Red Point
Burradoo Rly. Stn.
Dapto
Brownsville
Primbee
Pt. Kembla Beach
14
Burradoo
80
Wingecarribee River
Rileys Peak 827m
Mt. Murray
Avondale
Mullet Ck
Tallawarra Power Stn.
Lake Illawarra
32
Windang
Lake Illawarra South
Warilla
Kangaloon
Kangaloon East
Mt. Marshall
Calderwood
Yallah
Albion Pk Rail
Barrack Point
Glenquarry
Wingecarribee Dam
Ocean View Rly. Stn.
Macquarie Pass Nat. Pk.
Albion Park
18
Oak Flats
SHELLHARBOUR
Moss Vale
ILLAWARRA
11
Robertson
Macquarie Pass
31
Tongarra
HWY
Croom
Bass Point
Yarrunga North
10
Avoca
Fitzroy Falls Dam
St. Anthonys
Yellow Rook
Dunmore
Minnamurra
17
Myra Vale
Belmore Falls
Carrington Falls
Minnamurra Falls
Minnamurra
Bombo
Fitzroy Falls
Fitzroy Falls
Barrengarry Mtn.
Barangary State Park
Jamberoo Pass
Jamberoo
The Blowhole
Jerrara
Kiama
Meryla Pass
Barrengarry
Upper Kangaroo River
Wood Hill
Barren Grounds Fauna Reserve
Saddleback Lookout
Rose Valley
Omega
Werri Beach
Bendeela Pondage
Wattamolla
Brogers
Fox Ground
Willow Vale
26
Gerringong
Kangaroo Valley
37
Bellawongarah
Broughton Vale
Broughton Village
Gerroa
Lake Yarrunga
Beaumont
Berry
Toolijooa
Black Point
Tallowa Dam
Bugong Gap
Cambewarra Mtn.
Good Dog Mtn. Lookout
16
Jaspers Brush
Swamp
SEVEN MILE BEACH NATIONAL PARK
Cambewarra
Meroo Meadow
Mt. Coolangatta 302m
Farmeadow
Shoalhaven
Tapitallie
Bolong
Coolangatta
Shoalhaven Heads
Bight
Bomaderry
Bengalee Scout Camp
Comerong Island
Nowra
Terrara
Worrigee
Greenwell Point
Crookhaven Lighthouse
Crookhaven Heads (Orient Point)
Burrier
Bamarang
Pyree
Curleys Bay
Brundee
Brundee Swamp
Culburra
PRINCES HWY
Wollumboola Lake
Yalwal
HMAS Albatross
Worrain Beach

PACIFIC

SOUTH

J   K   L   M   N   O   P   Q   R

25

0   10   20   30 km

A B C D 25 E F G H I

SINGLETON
Redbournberry
Mitchells Flat
Roughit
Whittingham
Glendon
Eldersли
Stanhope
Patersons
Glen Oak
Dunn's Creek
River
Seaham

Belford Lower
Scotts Flat
Hunter River
Vineyard
Dalwood
Gosforth
Rosebrook
Iona
Woodville
Wallalong
Nelsons Plains
Hinton
Williams
Seaham

NEW ENGLAND
Minimbah
Pothana
Belford
Branxton
Greta
Branxton Rly. Stn.
Greta Rly. Stn.
Lochinvar
Aberglasslyn
Hunter
Largs
Morpeth
Duckenfield
Millers Forest
Grahamstown Lake

HWY 22
Rothbury North
Lochinvar Rly. Stn.
Rutherford
Farley
Telarah
MAITLAND
Swamp
Alanwick Swamp
Raymond Terrace
RAAF Base Williamtown

BACK
Pokolbin State Forest
Rothbury
Keinbah
Bishops Bridge
Allandale
Greta East
20
Thornton
Beresfield
Tarro
Tomago Water Treatment Works
PACIFIC

BROKEN
Mt. Bright Lookout
Vineyards
Pokolbin
Nulkaba
Cessnock State Forest
Kurri Kurri
Weston Kurri
Heddon Greta
Buchanan
JOHN RENSHAW
Hexham
Tomago
Kooragang Island
Stockton Bridge

CESSNOCK
Abermain
Neath
Pelaw Main
Black Hill
Swamp
SANDGATE
MAYFIELD
WARATAH
Stockton
Port Hunter
Nobbys Head

Bellbird
Kearsley
Abernethy
Mt. Sugarloaf TV Towers
West Wallsend
Seahampton
Edgeworth
WALLSEND
LAMBTON
HAMILTON
ADAMSTOWN
NEWCASTLE
MEREWETHER

Crawfordville
Millfield
Greta Main
Pelton
Kitchener
Mulbring
Mt. Vincent
Holmesville
Barnsley
Northville
Boolaroo
Speers Pt.
Warners Bay
Gateshead
Dudley

Sweetmans Creek
Paxton
Ellalong
Quorrobolong
Killingworth
Wakefield
Teralba
Windale
Eleebana
Redhead

Corrabare State Forest
Wollombi
Ellalong Lagoon
Brunkerville
Macleans Lookout
Heaton State Forest
The Gap
Awaba State Forest
Fassifern
Marmong Pt.
Fennell
Valentine

MYALL RANGE
Mootai (Eglinford)
Hunters Lookout
Freemans Waterholes
Heaton Lookout
Ryhope
Blackalls Park
Toronto
Cary Bay
Belmont
Nine Mile Beach

Laguna
Congewai
Flat Rock Lookout
Falls
Awaba
Rathmines
Coal Pt.
Marks Pt.
Blacksmiths

Yango Creek
Yallambie
Watagon
Watagan State Forest
Mt. Warrawolong +637m
Martinsville
Avondale
Dora Creek
Balmoral
Arcadia Vale
Pelican Flat
Skye Pt.
Wangi Wangi
Caves Beach (Mawson)

OCEAN

Bucketty
Mt. McQuoid
Bebeah
Olney State Forest
Wishing Well
Cooranbong
Eraring
Lake View
Balcolyn
Bonnells Bay
Silverwater
Sunshine
Swansea
Nords Wharf
Middle Camp
The Gulf
Catherine Hill Bay

JUDGE DOWLINGS RANGE
PRIESTS RIDGE
Cedar Brush
Muirs Lookout
Mandalong Lookout
Lemon Tree
Morisset
Morisset East
Morisset Park
Brightwaters
Gwandalan
Mannering Park
Vales Pt. Power Station
Chain Valley
Frazer Park
Wybung Head

McPherson State Forest
Ravensdale
Brush Creek
Dooralong
Durren Durren
Vermont
Mandalong
Ramsgate
Wyee
Doyalson
Munmorah Power Station
Elizabeth Bay
Munmorah Lake
Budgewoi

Nevertyre
Yarramalong
Kulnura
Little Jilliby
Jilliby
Charmhaven
Buff Point
Gorokan
Toukley
Norahville
Norah Head

Mt. Baxter
Upper Mangrove Creek
Central Mangrove
Wyong Creek
Fowlers Lookout
Warnervale
Kanwal
Wyongah
Tuggerawong
Lighthouse

Ten Mile Hollow
Mangrove Mountain
Peats Ridge
MILLIGANS RANGE
Ourimbah State Forest
Wyong
Tacoma
Tuggerah
Chittaway Pt.
Tuggerah Beach
Toowoon Bay

DHARUG NAT. PARK
Mangrove Creek
Greengrove
Shakeshaft
Palm Grove
Palm Dale
Somersby
SOMERSBY MOONEY MOONEY STATE FOREST
Niagara Park
Ourimbah
Tumbi Umbi
Berkeley Vale
Killarney Vale
Long Jetty
The Entrance
Shelley Beach
Bateau Bay

Somersby Falls
Strickland State Forest
Old Sydney Town
Narara
Reptile Park
Lisarow
Wamberal North
Holgats
Matcham
Forresters Beach
Gosford
Wamberal

PACIFIC
SOUTH

N

Places of Interest

NEWCASTLE
1	City Hall	6H
2	NRMA	6H
3	Police Station	5I
4	Post Office	5J
5	Railway Station	6H
6	Royal Newcastle Hospital	6J
7	TAA Air Terminal	6H
8	Tourist Information Centre	6H
9	War Memorial Cultural Centre	6H

WOLLONGONG
1	Ambulance Station	11E
2	Coniston Post Office	13D
3	Department of Motor Transport (Registry)	12E
4	Fig Tree Post Office	13A
5	Mt Keira Post Office	8A
6	NRMA	11F
7	Wollongong Court House	11E
8	Wollongong Library	11E
9	Wollongong Police Station	11E
10	Wollongong Town Hall	11F

A B C D 15 E F G H I

Green Point
AVOCA RD
Empire Bay
Pretty Beach
Putty Beach
GOSFORD
Caroline Bay
Davistown
Cockle Channel
Wagstaff
Box Head
BOUDDI STATE PARK
Saratoga
BRISBANE WATER
Rileys Island
110th Mt Pleasant
Booker Bay
Blackwall Mtn Res
Blackwall
Noonan Point
Murphys Bay
Pelican Island
St Huberts Island
WOY WOY
Ettalong
Umina
Lookout
HWY
PACIFIC
Point Clare
Tascott
Koolewong
Woy Woy Inlet
Golf Course
9
Umina Beach
Mt Ettalong
Green Point
Pearl Beach
Lion Island Nature Reserve
Middle Head
Fagans Bay
Eagans Bay
3
Kariong
2
Stables Loop Rd
WOY WOY ROAD
12
NATIONAL
Elvina Bay Swamp
Sanitary Depot
PARK
5
BROKEN
Old Sydney Town
83
Gully
Mt Kariong 251 m
Staples Lookout
BRISBANE WATER
BRISBANE
Creek
Patonga
Patonga
National Fitness Camp
8
Caravan Park
BRISBANE
WATER
Wondabyne
Creek
Muller Creek
HAWKESBURY
Hawkesbury River
Dangar Island
Bridge Pylons
Causeway
Green Point
To Wyong
FREEWAY
HWY
PACIFIC
NATIONAL
Mooney
Creek
Causeway
Oyster Leases
Hawkesbury River Railway Bridge
Brooklyn
Causeway
3
Spectacle Island Nature Reserve
Long Island
287 mtr Air Centre
83
Oyster Leases
Oyster Leases
Peats Ferry Bridge
Peats
Peak Hill
SYDNEY-NEWCASTLE
WATER
PARK
Mooney
Oyster Leases
24
Pearl Island
Milson Island
Prickly Point
MOUGAMARRA
RIDGE
MOUGAMARRA
Bar Point
Bar Island
Peats Bight
HAWKESBURY
Mangrove
RIVER
Berowra Point
Oyster Leases
Oyster Leases
CREEK

A B C D 15 E F G H I

PACIFIC OCEAN

SOUTH

N

Barrenjoey Head
West Head
Lookout
Little Head
Whale Beach
Palm Beach
Beach
Bangalley Head
Careel Bay
Avalon
Bilgola Head
Bilgola
Golf Course
Gas
12
Bungan Head
Newport Beach
Mona Vale
Mona Vale Beach
Turimetta Head
Narrabeen
Narrabeen Beach
Narrabeen Lake
14

Great Mackerel Beach
Soldiers Point
PITT WATER
Taylors Point
Newport
BARRENJOEY ROAD
Church Point
Scotland Island
Marina
Towlers Bay
Refuge Bay
5
Ingleside
Drive-in Theatre
MONA VALE RD
Elanora Heights
Golf Course
Golf Course
PITTWATER RD
14

BAY
Juno Point
Eleanor Bluffs
Gunyah Point
Gunyah Hill
Challenger Head
Shark Rock Point
Bay
WEST HEAD ROAD
12
KU-RING-GAI CHASE NATIONAL PARK
CREEK
COWAN CREEK
McCARRS CREEK ROAD
McCarrs Creek
NATIONAL PARK
The Sugarloaf 196m
Scout Camp
8
5
Duffys Forest
Terrey Hills
3
33

RIVER

NATURE RESERVE
83
SYDNEY-NEWCASTLE FREEWAY
Galstons and Weighing Station
Cowan
HWY
Jerusalem Bay
Coal and Candle Creek
COAL AND CANDLE CREEK RD
Smiths Creek
Cottage Point
COTTAGE CREEK RD
Akuna Bay Marina
CHASE NATIONAL PARK
Police Driving School
MONA VALE ROAD
St Ives Chase
Golf Course

BEROWRA
Berowra Heights
Berowra
6
PACIFIC HWY
Mount Kuring-Gai
KU-RING-GAI CHASE
Bobbin Head
BOBBIN HEAD ROAD
Golf Course

To Hornsby

0 1 2 3 4 5 6 7 8 9 10 km

J K L M N O P Q R

BROKEN HILL

MILDURA

Red Cliffs

Merbein

Wentworth

Menindee

Renmark

Berri

Loxton

Pinnaroo

Swan Hill

Kerang

Balranald

Ouyen

Hopetoun

Birchip

Wycheproof

KINCHEGA NATIONAL PARK

MALLEE CLIFFS NATIONAL PARK

HATTAH-KULKYNE NAT. PK

MUNGO NAT. PK

PINK LAKES + Mt. Cowra STATE PARK

WYPERFELD NATIONAL PARK

LAKE ALBACUTYA PARK

BIG DESERT WILDERNESS

BIG DESERT

SUNSET COUNTRY

Dangali Conservation Park

NEW SOUTH WALES

SOUTH AUSTRALIA

VICTORIA

MANARA HILLS

LANGWELL FLATS

BARRIER HWY

SILVER CITY HWY

STURT HWY

CALDER HWY

HENTY HWY

MALLEE HWY

COBB HWY

Murray River

Darling River

Murrumbidgee

0 50 100 150km

J K L M N 27 O P Q R

Mt.Doris
KARROO RANGE
CORINYA HILLS
Belaraboon Tank
Belaraboon
Paddington
Koonaburra
Kiama
6 Mile Tank
235
Bloomfield
Bellird
Bindi
Durham Park
Taringo Downs
Wiralong
Bedooba
Thule
Priory Tank
Yarrama
Yarranvale
Tin Hat Dam
Hennings Tank
Nymagee
THE BALD HILLS
Five Ways
Bulboroo
Bogan River
Trangie
Mungeriba
Tabratong
Derribong Dam
Dandaloo
Berangabah
Tasman
Wallangarra
Krjuligah
Walenda
Moondine
Morningside
Yallock Amiens
Red Tank
Currajong Tank
6 Mile Tank
Moolah
Tiarri
Karwarn
Ashley Downs
Stanifords Tank
Wirchilleba
Wagga Tank
Gilgunnia
TARRAN HILLS
Eremaran
Marobee
MAROBEE RANGE
Walkers Hill
Nangerybone
Bobadah
Mogal Plain
Tottenham
Kerriwah
Albert
Alagala
100
Mineral Hill
Tullamore
Burra Burra
BOONA MTN.
Kadungle
Fifield
Eribung
Numalla
Dunmore
Terowie
Warge Rock
Wyanga
Mungery
Bulgandramine
87

Marlow
Coombie
KEGINNI RA.
YARRABUNGARA
MAROOBA RA.
Prestons Tank
Mt. Hope
Mt. Solitary
WALTERS RA.
MOONEE RA.
Matakana
Whooey Tank
Euabalong West
Gunebang
Kerein Hills
Melrose
Flamingo
Mowabla Tank
Condobolin North
50
Fairholme
Forbes
Conoble
Trida
Wee Elwah
Roto
One Eye Tank
Euabalong
93
Booberoi
GOOBOTHERY WAY
Condobolin
Derriwong
Ootha
Yarrabandai
Tichborne
Daroobalgie
Trundle
Bogan Gate
Goonumbla
Blow Clear
61

Holey Box Well
50
Willandra
Mossgiel
Boondarra
Moolbong Tank
Polygonum Hut Well
Moolbong
97
WILLANDRA NAT.PK.
Willandra
Willandra Weir
Lowlands
60
Wallanthery
Gunnguildrie
Lachlan
Lake Cargelligo
C'gelligo
Miami
Burgooney
Tullibigeal
Banar Swamp
Bogandillon Swamp
100
105
Bena
Burcher
Lake Cowal
Bird and Animal Sanctuary

St.Andrews
Ravensfield
Culpataro
Alma
82
COBB HWY
Merungle
Creek
Wheahbah
Langtree
Goorawin
Hillston Weir
Lake Brewster
Pine Ridge
LACHLAN RA.
95
Brewer Hall
68
Naradhan
Hannan
119
Weja
Winnunga
Ungarie
Wamboyne
Billys Lookout
Clear Ridge
Lake Cowal
70
Wirrinya
Hullabooka
NEWELL HWY
Garema
Ooma Nth.

Toms Lake
Booligal
79
Lake Gunbar
Gunbar
Merriwagga
60
Allawah
Woodville
Rankins Springs
Marong
Erigolia
Euratha
92
West Wyalong
WESTERN HWY
Wyalong
Girral
Calleen
Marsden
Caragabal
Bogolong
24
Quandialla

Wongalea
Mirrool
Quandong Tank
Sidonia
113
Dry Lake Well
Barren Box Swamp
COCOPARRA NATL PARK
Binya
Yalgogrin Sth.
Barellan
71
Tallimba
Buddigower
Alleena
Bellarwi
Barmedman
69
Reefton
Morangarell
Thuddungra
Tubbul
Milvale
Bimbi
Bribbaree

Thelangerin
Corong
One Tree
Nine Mile Well
Wyangan
Tharbogang
Bilbul
Yenda
Yoogali
85
Beckom
Mirrool
Ariah Park
Quandary
Gidginbung
Grogan

Hay
114
Illilliwa
Uardry
Carrathool Stn.
Carrathool
Bringagee
Willbriggie
Griffith
Hanwood
Murrumbidgee Irrigation Area
Whitton
Darlington Point
87
Wamoon
Coinroobie
Moombooldool
Kamarah
Ardlethan
Uley
Cowabbie West
72
Temora
Springdale
Stockinbingal
Cootamundra

Maude Weir
Glenhope
Walgrove
Euroli
Four Corners Tank
Paradise Tank
Miranda
Coleambally
Coleambally Irrigation
BLACK RANGE
100
Jung Jung Bore
Mabins Corner Tank
Widgiewa
109
Boree Creek
Leeton
Yanco
STURT HWY
Narrandera
Cuddell
Corobimilla
Berembed Weir
68
Grong Grong
Matong
Methul
64
Dullah
Ganmain
Nth. Berry Jerry
Rannock
Junee Reefs
56
Mimosa
Sebastopol
58
Coolamon
Marrar
Old Junee
40
Junee
Eurongilly
63
Nangus
Gundagai

Steam Plains
Delta Creek Tank
Moombria
Boyd Tank
121
Wanganella
106
Morago
Burraboi
Pakool
Yallakool
Caldwell
Deniboota Irrigation Area
Gulpa
Bunnaloo
Mathoura
Womboota
Echuca
58
Gunnower
Kow Swamp
Moama
Barnes
Nathalia
COBB HWY
Strathmerton
Numurkah
Picola
Katunga
Katamatite
Yarrawonga
Tocumwal
Rennie
Lowesdale
Berrigan
Savernake
Coreen
Daysdale
Oaklands
Urangeline East
Ferndale
106
Walbundrie
Rand
Bulgandry
Brocklesby
Walla Walla
53
Gerogery
Burrumbuttock
Jindera
Bowna
Lavington
52
ALBURY
Wodonga
Rutherglen
Chiltern
MURRAY VALLEY
Lake Hume
Mullengandra
Woomargama
Talmalmo
Jingellic
Corryong
62
Tintaldra
Greg Greg
Towong
Cudgewa

Jerilderie
Urana
Lake Urana
45
Cullivel
Osborne
Pleasant Hills
Henty
OLYMPIC HWY
Yerong Creek
Mangoplah
Kyeamba
Humula
Holbrook
Tumbarumba
Batlow
74
Kunama
Laurel Hill
Courabyra
Rosewood
Wondalga
Oberne
Adelong
Tarcutta
The Rock
Milbrulong
Lockhart
Urana
Morundah
Birrego
Galore
98
Currawarna
Millwood
Downside
Collingullie
Kapooka
Uranquinty
WAGGA WAGGA
Ladysmith
Mt. Adrah
Wambidgee
HUME HWY
Bethungra
Illabo
Frampton
Cootamundra
Brawlin
Mt. +Ulandra
Sangar
Myall Plains
Deniliquin
Blighty
Finley
60
Tuppal
Mulwala
Corowa
Howlong
Culcairn
Morven

N 27 59 62

STURT HWY   MID WESTERN HWY   RIVERINA HWY   NEWELL HWY   OLYMPIC HWY   HUME HWY

CENTRAL EASTERN NEW SOUTH WALES

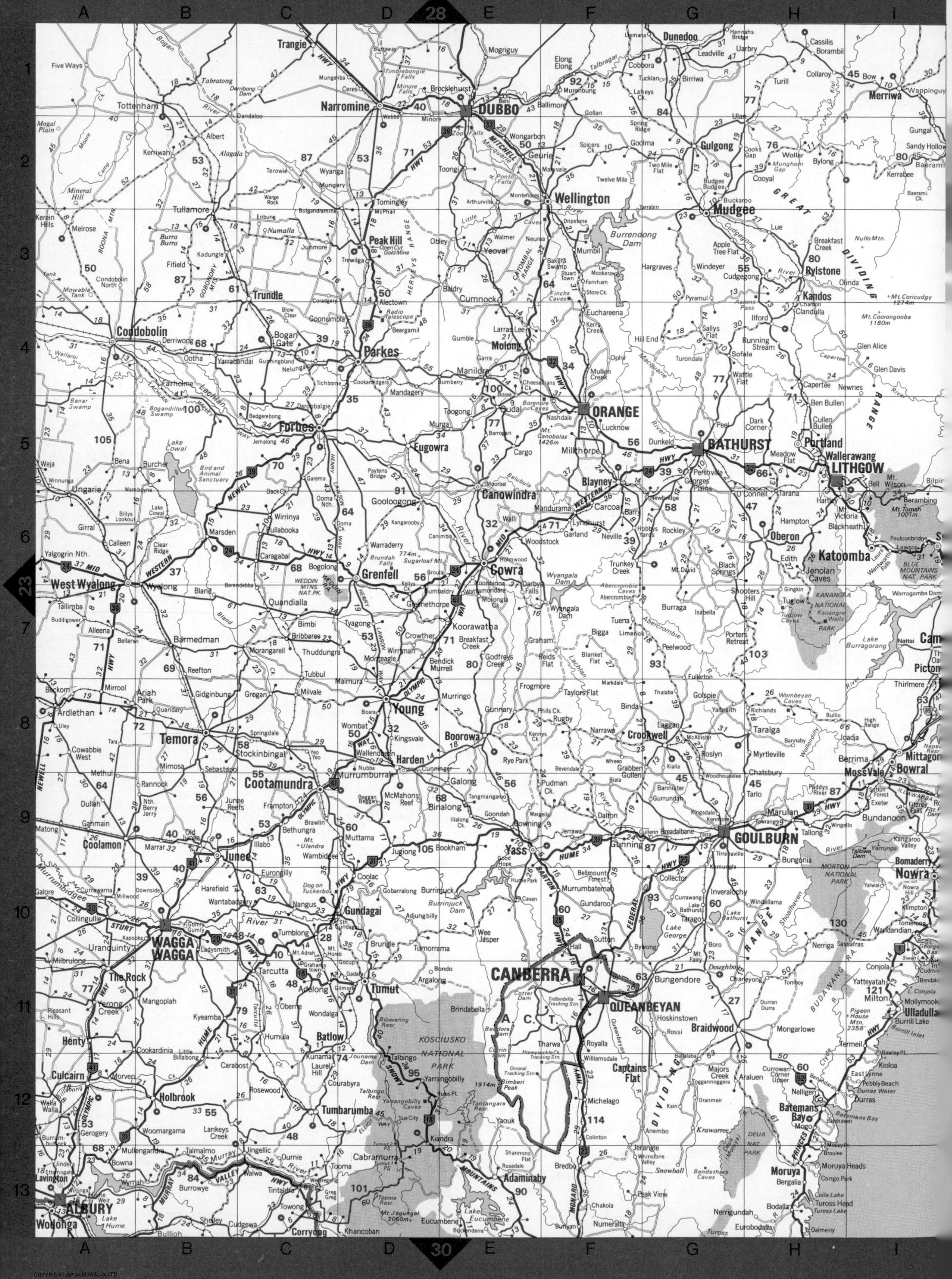

0   50   100   150km

J   K   L   M   N   29   O   P   Q   R

1

Owens Gap Parkville Belltrees Moonan Flat Cobark Upr. Bowman Bundook Kimbriki Tinonee Harrington Manning R.
Bunnan Gundy BARRINGTON TOPS NATIONAL PARK Barrington 42 **TAREE**
Scone 64 Glenbawn Dam Rawdon Vale **Gloucester** 39 Krambach Old Bar
Aberdeen 26 Barrington +Tops 1585m Belbora 27 HWY Halidays Point
Dangarfield Davis Ck. Mt. +McKenzie 1433m Stratford Wang Wauk Nabiac
Rouchel Brook Craven Bunya Tuncurry
Barrington House Salisbury Warra Willina **Forster**
Wybong McCully's Gap Eccleston Chichster Dam Wards River Coolongolook 72 Wallis Lake Pacific Palms
Denman 37 **Muswellbrook** Carrow Brook Halton Weismantels Upper Myall Wootton Elizabeth Bay
Martindale 26 Dawsons Hill Miranie Bendolba Stroud Road 66 Bungwahl Sugarloaf Bay Seal Rocks
Hunter Liddell 48 Hebden Mt. Olive Gresford 24 Stroud MYALL LAKES
Jerrys Plains Ravensworth Camberwell 39 Trevallyn Booral 29 Bulahdelah Myall Lakes The Broadwater
Warkworth Glendon Brook Vacy **Dungog** PACIFIC Tamboy
Mt. Poppong 365m+ Singleton Paterson Clarence Town 19 Broughton Is.
Bulga Branxton 76 Woodville 95 Tea Gardens Hawks Nest
Broke Abermain Largs Limeburners Ck. Seaham 23 Karuah Port Stephens
Adams Peak **MAITLAND** 15 Morpeth **Nelson Bay**
Howes Valley **CESSNOCK** Bellbird Raymond Terrace Williamtown
Mt. Yengo 668m Paynes Crossing Millfield **Kurri Kurri** Wallsend Port Hunter Stockton
Putty Wollombi Toronto Stockton **NEWCASTLE**
232 Macdonald R. Bucketty Cooranbong **Belmont**
Kulnura Morisset L. Macquarie **Swansea**
St. Albans DHARUG NATL. PARK Wyee Doyalson 87
Colo Heights Wyong Budgewoi Wisemans Ferry Norah Head Tuggerah Lake
Kurrajong Heights Calga Durunbah **The Entrance**
Ebenezer Kurrajong **Gosford**
Richmond Wilberforce Pitt Town BRISBANE WATER NAT.
ingwood Windsor Broken Bay Palm Beach
PENRITH KU-RING-GAI CHASE NAT. PK. Mona Vale
Wallacia 88 **HORNSBY** Narrabeen Lagoon Long Reef
PARRAMATTA Port Jackson
LIVERPOOL **SYDNEY**
Catherine Field Botany Bay
61 ROYAL NATL. PK.
CAMPBELLTOWN Garie
Appin 82 Stanwell Park
Cataract Resr. Coledale
Avon Resr. Bulli
Unanderra Corrimal
WOLLONGONG
Dapto Red Pt. Port Kembla
PASS Lake Illawarra
Bass Pt. **SHELLHARBOUR** HWY
Bombo
Jamberoo **Kiama**
80 Gerringong
Berry Shoalhaven Heads
Greenwell Pt. Orient Pt (Crookhaven Heads) Culburra
L. Wollumboola WorrinBeach
Huskisson Currarong
Vincentia Hyams B. Jervis Bay

SOUTH

PACIFIC

OCEAN

N

J   K   L   M   N   O   P   Q   R

A B C D E F G H I

116

STOKES RANGE

GREY RA.

N

QUEENSLAND

Bulloo
Bulloo Downs
Naryilco
Tickalara
Old Naryilco
Bulloo Lake
Lake Wyara
Boorara
Currawinya
Woodburn Lake

Bygrave Range
Warri Warri Gate
Adelaide Gate
Hamilton Gate
Waverley Gate
Hungerford
Weebah
Fortville Tank
Binerah Downs
McDonald Peak
Olive Downs
Onepah
Wompah
Caryapundy Swamp
Swamp
Waverley Downs
Weebah Well
Gumbo
Nangunyah
Glenhope
Fort Grey
Binerah Well
STURT
Narcowla
Connulpie
Teurika
Yarrallee
Bernawinnia
Ourimbah
The Lake Tank
Lake Stewart
Waka
Fromes
NATIONAL
5 Mile Tank
Narriearra
Ram Tank
Thurloo Downs
Budgerygar
93
Lake
Gum Hole Tank
97 23
PARK
Mile Ck.
Wittabrinna
Pinderra Downs
Owen Downs
Kendabooka
Mulganora
Burrajong
Nardoo
Moreland Downs
Yarraburra Swamp
29
13
Tibooburra
Bulloo River Overflow
Lenroy
Hewett Downs
Tilcha Tank
GumVale
Mt. Stuart
Mt. Wood
Mt. Wood Tank
Clifton Downs
Urella Downs
Wonga
Wanaaring
Tilcha
Hewitt Bore
Mt. Sturt
Mt. Poole
Mt. Sturt
Clifton Bore
225
New Osaca Bore
Osaca Bore
Colane
Koridina
Urisino Bore
Nocoleche
Numbarte
Theldarpa
Mt. Poole
Milparinka
Whyjonta
Tinaroo Bore
Salisbury Lake
Baronna Downs
Yamba
Urisino
Wangareena
Yandama
Yandama
MT BROWN RANGE
Yantara
Yantara Lake
Moalie Park
Salisbury Downs
Roela
Bundarra
Myrnong
Garden Vale
4 Mile Bore
Emohruo
Winnathee
Yandaminta
Mt. Shannon
Coally
Lake Ulenia
Yancannia
Bootra
Tero Creek
Petita
The Range
Nagtilla
Hawkers Gate House
Yandaminta South
Mt. Shannon
HWY 72
The Salt Lake
Gumpopla
YANCANNIA RANGE
Yatla Tank
Monolon
Willaroy
Wattle Vale
Troubles Bore
Noonamah
Lake Boolka
Smithville House
83
Lake Wallace
Mt. Arrowsmith
Boullia
Green Lake
Lake Patterson
Calindary
Yancannia
Myro
Wonga Lilli
Gumtree Bore
Chinamans Tank
Lake Muck
Lake Wallace
Pincally
Dalmuir
Cobham
Pulcamurtic
Allandy
Questa Park
Glendara
171
Tongo Lake
Border Downs
Wyarra Tank
CITY HWY
Williams Tank
Milpa
Morden
Pretoria Tank
Pulchra
McCallum Park
Mulga Valley
Purnanga
Tongo
Mullawoolka Basin
Turleys Gate
Pimpara Lake
Lake Windaunka
135
J.K. Tank
Katalpa
Box Vale
Caradoc
Cawnalmurtee
Yanta Bangie
Yantabangee Lake
Napunyah
Sanpah
Swan Lake
Paradise Lake
Yelka
Macs Tank
Wonaminta
Kaynunnera
Oak Vale
Glen Hope
Goodwood
Peri Lake
Olepoloko Lake
Gilpoko Lake
Keelamba
Pine View
Westwood Downs
Pine Ridge
The Veldt
Packsaddle
Nundora
Kara
Nuntherungie
Peak Tank
Williams
Opal Mining
Mandalay
34
Mt. Jack
Polocara
Glenroy
Joulnie
The Selection
Marrapina
Koonawarra
Wertago
Tarella
Glen Gowrie
Momba
Mooratchia Lake
Mt. Pleasant
Wild Duck
Boolpoora Lake
Tilpa
23
Boughams Gate
Avenel
Teilta
Mt. Westwood
SILVER CITY
Floods Creek
Koonawarra
STONY RANGES
Cootawundi
Coonu Coona
Bunker Tanks
9 Mile Tank
Ulolie
Marra
Budda
Dunoo
McDougalls Well
Merphetts Ck.
Corona
BERGORO RA.
BYGLANO RA.
Fowlers Gap
Nucha Lake
Mt. Daubeny
Duntroon
Beefwood Tank
Kopago Tank
Lake Dick
Kalkaroo
Neilia Tank
Cullewie Lake
Thackomble
Kantappa
Sturts Meadows
Mootwingee
Aboriginal Relics
Daubeny
The Sisters
Sisters Tank
Moona Vale
Baymore
97
Kopago Lake
87
Mulga Valley
Wilangee
Langewirra Lake
Jones Lake
Grassmere
McFaddens Tank
Dry Lake Tank
Mt. Murchison
Darling
Wilga
Greenoughs Hill
Mundi Mundi Plain
Mt. Robie 1555'
Mt. Gipps
Gairdners Tank
Fairy Hill
Langidoon
Corega Lake
Comarto
Rainbow Tank
Mena Murtee
Mt. Murchison Hamilton
Talywalka
Wongalaroo Lake
BARRIER
Emmdale
Cuttowa Tank
Umberumberka Resr.
Yanco Glen
Stephens Creek
Stephens Ck. Resr.
Myalla Tank
Coogee Lake
Glenora
Cuthawarra
Devon
Dolo Tank
Blue Lake Swamp
Wilcannia
Murtee
Caltigeena Tank
Lake Poopelloe
Cultowa
64 74
MACCULLOCHS RANGE
Silverton
BROKEN HILL
Rockwell
Stevens
Hazel Vale Hotel
Little Topar
SCOPES RA.
Worungil Tank
Churinga
Cawkers Well
Wilsons Well
Culpaulin
197
Goonalga
Harris Tank
Yoe Bore
Bellavale
Mundi Mundi
Kinalung
Lake Inkerman
Glen Lyon
Treloara Tank
158
Billilla
Fairmount
Moira
Kew
BARRIER HWY
Cockburn
Burns
Inkerman
Caves
Byrnedale
Wintlow Lake
Malta Lake
Burraroo
Teryawynia
Cowary
Yelta
Badon Park
Mingary
Ascot Vale
Redan
Horse Lake
Horse Lake
Box Tank
Quandong Hotel
109
Kars
Lake Menindee
Pine Point
Paamaroo
Tandure
Windale
Bobbies Waterhole
Blantyre
Nyngynderry
Glen Albyn
187
Christmas Bore
Bambilla Tank
KINCHEGA NATIONAL PARK
Menindee
Weir
Lower
Dead Horse Lake
Denian
Teryaweyna Lake
Glen Ora
22

50   100   150km

J   K   L   M   N   O   P   Q   R

1

Dunbourbie
Woolerina
Tuen
Cubbie
Caiwarra
Noorama
Tambingey
Bundaleer
Tinnenburra
Mulga Downs
QUEENSLAND

2

River
Lake Thorlindah
Parragundy Gate
Wambah Lake
Jobs Gate
Hebel
Lake Bokhara
Barringun
55
Brenda
Goodooga
New Angledool
34
Warroo Bore
Brindingbarra
Turrakorang Bore
Sharoon
Eureka
Morton Plains
Ellerslie
Waratah
Culgoa
Glendon Tank
40
19
3
Whim Well
29
Kenmore Bore
Cuttaburra
Belalie Bore
Fairfield
35
Wandella
Weilmoringle
Birrie
Muckerawa
Bangate
Lightning Ridge
48
Willara
56
Comeroo
Wirrawarra
18
Enngonia
Beulah
48
Dalwood
Bora
39
Langboyd
Bomali
Wilby Bore
Opal Mines
4
Yantabulla
21
Back Springs
Stratheame
Ella Vale
37
Lissington
29
Taralba
Talawanta
Bokhara
159
Grawin
Llanillo
CASTLEREAGH HWY
Maureen Joy
Youngerina Bore
Old Kerribree
Native Dog Bore
Bullaroon
Collerina
Mourabilla
19 Mile Tank
Naran Patk
Cumborah
16
5
Minetta
Wampra
Kerribree Bore
217
Fords Bridge
Grass Hut
Grasshut Tank
Dry Lake
Lilyfield
Culgoa
Hospital Tank
Narran Lake
Moramina
43
Lake Burkanoko
Myroolia
Kellys Camp Bore
Lauradale
Tulls Bore
Gidgee Camp Bore
Wattawecna
Mt. Druid
Yambacoona
Brewarrina
Narran Lake
6
Tincheloka Bore
36
Dargle Bore
Goonery Bore
Goombalie
Walkdens
95
Bogan
Tarrion
122
Borooma
River
Walgett
Mullard Tank
193
Yanderoo
Willeroi Lake
Nulty
Paka Tank
Bourke
Hastings
Oakleigh
Charlton
Barwon
54
Salt Lake
Jandra
OXLEYS TABLELAND
Tarcoon
River
Brewon
60
7
Glenora
Opera Bore
Toorale
Ya River
2 Waterholes Tank
Boorindal
Yarrawin
Gongolgon
69
Wangrawally
Utah Lake
Mt. Burragurry
Toorale East
Murrumbarra Dam
79
Dwyers
WaveHill
105
Compton Downs
NEW YEARS RA
Billybingbone
Carinda
Mt. Mulyah
Pelora Lake
100
Gunderbooka
Myrtle Vale
Belah
Ben Lomond
Waddel Tank
Wyuna Downs
Wyuna Downs
Nidgery Downs
60
8
Louth
Lake Arthur
Trilby
Winbar
Mulva
Curraweena
Curraweena Tank
Wilga Downs
Byrock
Glenariff
Colossal
Fairholme
Macquarie Marshes
Canimbia
Campamooka Mtn.
Idalia
RANKINS RA
Davidson
159
Curraweena Hill
Wallangarra
Lyndhurst
Coronga Peak
Mundadoo
Sandy Camp
Tara
Curranyalpah
MT DEERINA RANGE
Kerrigundi Tank
Wilgaroon
Yanta
Helmans Tank
Dijou
Mtn.
Coolabah
Quambone
9
Nangara
Burnamwood
129
Booroondarra Downs
Mookalimbirria Hill
Tindera Tank
Carline
Balgillo
127
Girilambone
Ringorah
Macquarie
Gradgery
Innesowen
Booroondara Tank
Mt. Buckwaroon
Mt. Drysdale
Booroomugga Mtn.
Dowlings Tank
Elmore
Colane
Pirie Ridge
109
10
Tiltagoonah
Mt. Gap
Mt. Grenfell
Cuttygullyaroo Tank
C.S.A. Copper Mines
Sussex
Booroomugga
Summervale
Canonba
Buttaboone
Inglegar
Famous Stud Haddon Rig
Pinchinara
Windara
Springfield Tank
Cobar
Booroomugga Tank
Boppy Mount
Hermidale
Nyngan
Eenaweena
11
Donalds Plain Tank
Barnato Tank
264
Elsinore
10
BARRIER
Florida
133
HWY
23
Miandetta
Miowera
Warren
Bulla Bulla Tank
Barnato
Springfield
Lerida Tank
Double Gate
Lerida
Nurri Mtn.
Canbelego
Mangalore
Wirrina
Mullengudgery
58
Nevertire
Bulla
Noona
Buckwaroon
Hillview
The Rookery
Fairview
Gilgai Tank
Belaringar
Cathundral
Gin Gin
12
Everdale
Tittagara
Wilsons Tank
Bulgoo
64
Shearlegs Tank
Mt. Lewis
Babinda
Pange
Mudall
Budabadah
90
Myall Mundi
Trangie
Mt. Doris
Tittagara Tank
Mt. Buckambool
Killala
Priory Tank
32
Yarrama
Nymagee
THE BALD HILLS
The Range
Five Ways
Bulbodney
HWY
Koonaburra
Belaraboon Tank
Durham Park
Bindi
Ballard
Yarranvale
45
47
Tin Hat Dam
Hennings Tank
Bobadah
Mogal Plain
Tottenham
Derribong Dam
Dandaloo
13
Berangabah
235
Yallock
Kiama
Karwan
Stanifords Tank
Gilgunnia
Bedooba
Notton Peak
Nangerybone
Walkers Hill
TARRAN HILLS
Albert
Kerriwah
Alagala

J   K   L   M   N   O   P   Q   R

QUEENSLAND

Dunbourhie, Woolerina, Whyenbah, Nindigully, BARWON, Toobeah, Goon, Boggabilla

Tambingey, Mulga Downs, Dirranbandi, Noondoo, Cubbie, Daymar, Thallon, Talwood, 163, HWY, 45, North Star, 42

Mungindi, Neeworra, Weemelah, Boomi, Whalan, Caloona, Garah, 122, Croppa Creek, Crooble

Culgoa, Brenda, Goodooga, New Angledool, Old Yerranbah, Jomara, Whyalla, Gundablule, 97, Boomi, Gil Gil Ck, Ashley, Moppin, Camurra, Milguy, Mosquito Creek

Weilmoringle, Birrie, Muckerawa, Glendon Tank, Bangate, Opal Mines, Lightning Ridge, Dungle Ridge Bore, Moongulla Tank, Mogil Mogil, Wongalee, Currigundi, Wandoona, Moree, Pallamallawa, Yagobie

Langboyd, Taralba, Bomali, Wilby Bore, Dunumbril, Bundabarina, Collarenebri, GWYDIR, Gwydir (Mehi), 138, Bullarah, Tycannah, Weah Waa, Gravesend, 82

Talawanta, Bokhara, 159, 140, Borah Tank, Dungalear, 74, Lornay, Pokataroo, Poison Gate, Tellerega, Gurley, Terry Hie Hie, Elcombe, Biniguy

Mourabilla, Naran Park, Grawin, Llanillo, Cumborah, Moramina, Thalaba, Merrywinebone, Rowena, Millie, 98, Bellata, Courada, Rocky Creek

Narran Lake, Hospital Ck Tank, Waminda, Cryon, Bugilbone, Nowley, Doreen, Boolcarrol, Myall Vale, Edgeroi, MT. KAPUTAR NATIONAL PARK, Mt. Kaputar 1524m, Mt. Lindsay

Brewarrina, Barwon, Walgett, Goangra, Burren Junction, Cubbaroo, Merah Nth, WeeWaa, 98, CSIRO Obs, Narrabri West, Narrabri, Turrawan, 95, Baan Baa

Tarrion, 122, Boorooma, Castlereagh, Brewon, Namoi River, Bugilbone, Piliga, Cuttabri, Yarrie Lake, Lucky Flat, PILLIGA SCRUB, 122, Boggabri, Kelvin

Gongolgon, Yarrawin, 69, Wangrawally, Come-by-Chance, Milchomi, 71, Cubbo, Emerald Hill, Gunnedah

Billybingbone, Carinda, Coombogolong, 117, Wingadee, 77, Gwabegar, Merebene, Kenebri, Teridgerie, Warrumbungle, Rocky Glen, 105, OXLEY, Mullaley, Curlewis, Mooki

Nidgery Downs, Macquarie Marshes, 77, Canimbia, Beanbah, Billeroy, Mayfield, Gilgooma, Unawilkey, Pine Grove, Baradine, Borah, BurraBeeDee, Garrawilla, Black Bulga Mt., Lake Goran

Mundadoo, Colossal, Fairholme, Sandy Camp, Quambone, Coonamble, 68, Goorianawah, Brigalow, Gummin Gummin, Siding Spring Obs, Coonabarabran, Ulamambri, Tambar Springs, Spring Ridge, Caroona

Jacksons Flat, Bogan, Ringorah, Tooloon, Combara, 98, 126, Gulargambone, Gular Rail, Tooraweenah, WARRUMBUNGLE NATL PARK, Mt. Cenn Cruaich, Warkton, Deriangulla, Premer, Tamarang, Colly Blue, Pine Ridge

Summervale, Girilambone, Colane, Pine Ridge, Canonba, Buttabone, Inglegar, 109, Famous Stud Haddon Rig, Armatree, 95, Windurong, Curban, Biddon, Bearbung, Wallumburrawang, Binnaway, Ulinda, Bomera, Connemarra, Yarraman Nth, Blackville

Nyngan, Miandetta, Miowera, Mullengudgery, Warren, Collie, Gilgandra, Kamber, Yarragrin, New Mollyann, 90, Weetaliba, Neilrex, The Black Stump

Wirrina, Mudall, Budabadah, Eenaweena, Nevertire, Belaringar, Egelabra, OXLEY, 106, Kickabil, Breelong, Mendooran, Merrygoen, Coolah, LIVER

The Range, 90, Trangie, Bundemar Famous Stud, Gin Gir, Myall Mundi, Cathundral, Balladoran, Eumungerie, Breelong, Lymana, Dunedoo, 47, Hannahs Bridge, Uarbry, Cassilis, Borambil

Five Ways, Tabratong, Derribong Dam, Dandaloo, Albert, Narromine, Webbs, DUBBO, Minore, Brocklehurst, Ballimore, Gollan, Cobbora, Leadville, Birriwa, 77, Collaroy, 45, Merriwa

Mogal Plain, Kerriwah, Alagala, Geurie, Wongarbon, Spicers, Goomla, Ulan, Spring Ridge, Two Mile Flat, Gulgong, Wollar, Gungal, Sandy He

117, 27, 24

0   50   100 km

NEW SOUTH WALES

CANBERRA
A.C.T.
QUEANBEYAN

GOULBURN

WOLLONGONG
Port Kembla
SHELLHARBOUR

PENRITH
PARRAMATTA
CAMPBELLTOWN
LIVERPOOL
Camden
Picton
Katoomba

Kiama
Gerringong
Bomaderry
Nowra
Berry

Cootamundra
Young
Boorowa
Crookwell
Yass
Gunning
Harden
Murrumburrah
Junee
Gundagai
Tumut
Cowra
Grenfell
Temora

Mittagong
Bowral
Moss Vale
Oberon

Ulladulla
Milton
Batemans Bay
Moruya
Narooma
Cobargo
Bermagui
Bega
Merimbula
Eden

Braidwood
Captains Flat
Cooma
Berridale
Jindabyne
Adaminaby
Tumbarumba
Batlow
Corryong

Nimmitabel
Bombala
Delegate
Bombala

VICTORIA
Orbost
Bairnsdale
Lakes Entrance
Buchan
Omeo

SOUTH PACIFIC OCEAN

TASMAN SEA

Cape Howe

N

KOSCIUSKO NATIONAL PARK
SNOWY RIVER NATIONAL PARK
BLUE MOUNTAINS NAT. PARK
MORTON NATIONAL PARK
Mt. Kosciusko 2173m
GREAT DIVIDING RANGE

0 5 10km

To Talbingo

Snowy Mountains Highway

Big Boggy Hill 1623m

Reeds Hill 1573m

Tantangara Mtn 1738m

Kiandra

Three Mile Dam

Pikes Peak

Kings Cross

CABRAMURRA

Tabletop Mtn 1785m

Anglers Reach

MONARO

ADAMINABY

Rosedale

River

Goondae

Muriumbdgee River

Wollumbi Hill 735m

Jagumba Mtn 1677m

ROAD

Young Mtn 1267m

Old Adaminaby

Eucumbene Lookout

RANGE

Mt Tooloon 1663m

The Big Darby 1714m

LAKE EUCUMBENE

Cobrabald 1473m

Braemar

EUCUMBENE

Jagungal Mtn 1757m

STRUMBO RANGE

KOSCIUSKO NATIONAL PARK

Buckenderra

Middlingbank

KHANCOBAN

The Gray Mare 1672m

Round Mtn 1580m

Wattle Hill 1510m

Gungarton 2070m

Kalkite Mtn 1586m

The Grenadiers 1300m

Indi

The Twins 1954m

GREY MARE MOUNTAINS

Pinnacle 1584m

Osens Lookout

ISLAND BEND

Kalkite

PLAINS ROAD

Geehi Road Junction

Guthega

Wilsons Valley Ski Tows

Mt Kosciusko

Snowy Flat

LAKE JINDABYNE

BERRIDALE

Ski Tows

SMIGGIN HOLES

PERISHER

Coolamatong

Mt Twynam 2197m

Carruthers 2147m

Chair lift

Mt Townsend 2210m

The Porcupine 1926m

JINDABYNE

19

The Chalet

Round Hill 1262

SNOWY

Penderlea

N

Mt Kosciusko 2230m

RAMSHEAD RANGE

Moonbah

Dalgety

THREDBO VILLAGE

Ramshead 2192m

Chair Lift

Drift Hill 1933m

Beloka

Dead Horse Gap RIDGE

Tom Groggin

HERMIT MTN

CHIMNEYS

Paupong

Mt Stilwell 1941m

ALPINE WAY

Numbla Vale

Ingebyra

Thatchers Mtn 1390m

VICTORIA

NEW SOUTH WALES

0 1 2 3 4km

Legend:
- Vineyard
- Winery
- Restaurant

N

To Branxton

To Heritage

Creek

Rothbury

DEASEYS

LANE

Terrace Vale

ALLANDALE ROAD

Black

Ck

WILDERNESS ROAD

Old Rothbury

Millstone

McPhersons

John Alder

Broken Back (Rothbury Group)

Tyrrells

PALMERS LANE

The Wilderness

Rothbury

Wollundry

GILLARDS ROAD

Lindemans

Owen Matthews

Hungerford Hill

The Rothbury Estate

Herlstone (Rothbury Group)

BROKE ROAD

Francois

Tyrrells

Cellar Restaurant

Pokolbin Cellars

McWilliams

Rosehill

Tallawanta

Blaxlands Barn Restaurant

Hungerford Hill

Len Drayton

Lake's Folly

ALLANDALE

Allandale

De Beyers

THOMPSONS ROAD

Hungerford Hill

Middle Ck

Mead

Tulloch

Tamburlaine

Pokolbin Estate

DE BEYERS ROAD

Airport

Lovedale

12 ROAD

Oakdale

Tulloch

DE BEYERS ROAD

Pokolbin

Ck

Eric Roberts

Phillips

Deep

Ck

Ben Ean

Maluna

Saxonvale Happy Valley

Nulkaba

6

Tinkler

OAKEY CREEK ROAD

Happy Valley Restaurant

Ivanhoe

Bellevue

Howard

E.B. Drayton

Stevens

Hillside

Mt Pleasant

Oaky

+ Jackson's Hill

MT VIEW ROAD

KURRI RD

To Kurri Kurri

To Sawyers Gully

BROKEN BACK RANGE

Cessnock

WOLLOMBI ROAD

ABERDARE ROAD

Robson

The Cottage Restaurant

To Aberdare

West Cessnock

0   0.5   1 km

A B C D 34 E F G To North Canberra H I

Turner

Braddon

MASSON ST
GREENWAY ST
HAIG PARK
MASSON STREET
Numerous BBQ's
GIRRAHWEEN

McCAUGHEY
NORTH RD
BARRY
Creek
Sullivans

Seventh Day Adventist Church
Lutheran Church
Ukrainian Orthodox Church
Police & Citizens Boys Club
MACLEAY ST
GOULD ST
WATSON ST
McKAY LANE
McKAY GDNS
McKAY LANE
McKAY
MOORE ST

Australian National University

Tennis Courts
Pavilion
North Oval
Toad Hall
Hall
J. Dedman Bldg
Union Bldg
Copland Bldg
A.D.Hope Bldg
Canberra Workmens Club
HUTTON ST
KINGSLEY ST
STREET DRIVE
CLARKE ST
ALINGA
RUDD ST
WEST ROW
Town House Motor Inn
C.W.A. Rooms
Canberra Squash Bowl
Canberra Memorial RSL
City Uniting Church
Gas Industry House
Queen Elizabeth II Coronation Home
Capital Territory Health Commission
Parking
P.O.
Canberra House
TAA
Melbourne Pl
City Mutual Bldg
Tasman House
AMP Bldg
Hobart Pl
CML Bldg
Tamar House
Reserve Bank
National Mutual Bldg
T & G Bldg
Parking

NORTHBOURNE AVENUE
Parkroyal Motor Inn
Kythera Motel
NRMA House
Havelock House
Phoenix House
NZI Bldg
G.I.O
Speros Motel
IBM Bldg
MMI Bldg
City Travelodge
ELOU STREET
MORT ST
LONSDALE ST
TORRENS ST
COOYONG ST
DONALDSON ST
CURRONG ST
Church
FAWKNER
Pavilion
Northbourne Oval
BALLUMBIR
BUNDA ST
City Walk
Radio 2CA
Griffin Centre
Parking
Jolimont Centre
Ansett
Parking
Civic Cinema
Center Cinema
Hotel Civic
Y.W.C.A
Garema Pl
Sydney Pl
EAST ROW
Brisbane Pl
Plaza
Merry-Go-Round
Monaro Mall
Petrie
Perth Pl
AINSLIE AVE
Parking
Canberra Playhouse
Civic SQ
Canberra Theatre
P.O
Capital Savings Centre
Moresby Pl
AKUNA
Caga Centre
Wales Centre
Boulevard Twin Cinemas
Electricity House
Boulevard Shopping Centre
BINARA ST
NANGARI ST
Lombard House
CONSTITUTION
ALLARA ST
CORANDERRK
Picnic Area

Reid

N

UNIVERSITY
CHILDERS
MARCUS
CLARKE
MARCUS AVE
School of Music
City Education Centre
ELERY CIRT
McCOY CIRT
GORDON
Beauchamp House
Academy of Science
EDINBURGH
Hotel Acton
Lakeside International Hotel
KENDALL ST
PARKES WAY
Police Headquarters
ACT Tourist Bureau
ACT Law Courts
LONDON CIRCUIT
VERNON CIRCLE
City
City Hill
Lookout
Derwent House
Parking
STREET
AVENUE
LONDON CIRCUIT
Y.M.C.A
C M F Drill Hall
Olympic Bowl

Acton

1 2 3 4 5 6 7 8 9 10 11 12 13

To Belconnen
To Woden

COPYRIGHT GEORGE PHILIP & O'NEIL PTY LTD

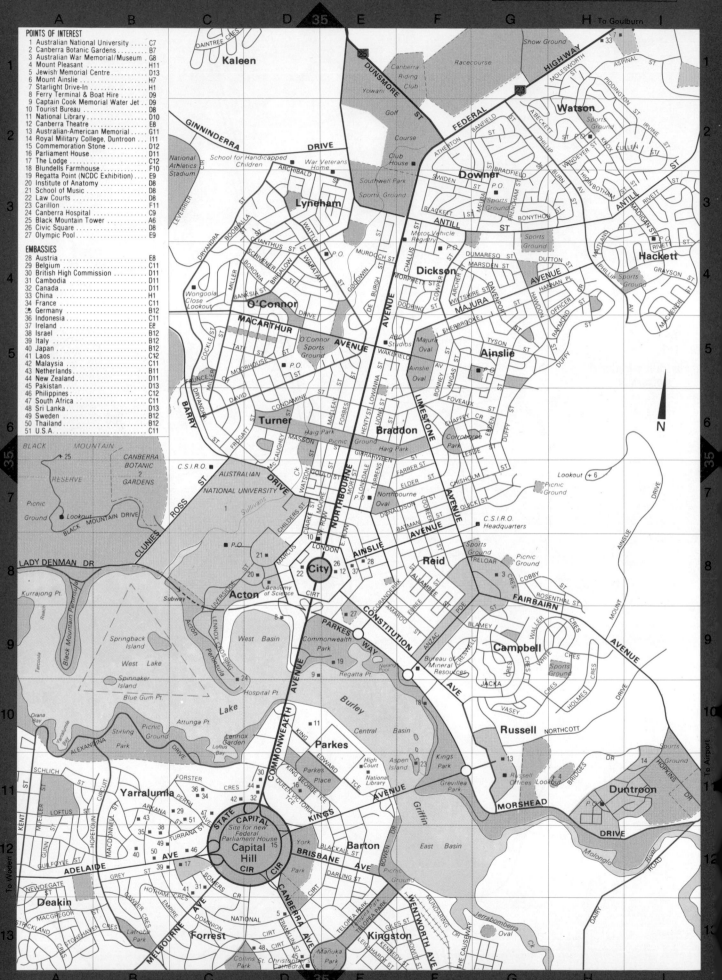

0 4 8 12 16 20 24 28km

BARTON

Talagandra Hill 665m

Lake George

Surveyors Hill 736m

Hall

FEDERAL

HWY

BROOKS

19

GUNDAROO

12   11   9

YASS

Belconnen

Lake Ginninderra

2

North Canberra

Mt Ainsie 843m

NEW SOUTH WALES

BRINDABELLA RANGE

Molonglo River

Black Mountain 812m

Stromlo Observatory

4

Lake Burley Griffin

6   7

Canberra Airport

KINGS

37

Numerous Timber Tracks

Mt Ainslie

Weston Creek

Woden Valley

3   3

Mt Mugga Mugga 813m

Queanbeyan

Balcombe Hill 953m

Tuggeranong

MUGGA LANE

18

Fraser Park Speedway

Googong Dam

Mt Wanniassa 810m

5

12

TIDBINBILLA RANGE

URIARRA

COTTER   8

Murrumbidgee River

15

Tidbinbilla Deep Space Tracking Stn

2   2

20   12

COOMA   8

Royalla

BRINDABELLA RANGE

Bendora Dam

Animal Enclosure

18

Corin Dam

CORIN   RD

19

29   12

Tharwa

Williamsdale

Mt McKeahnie

Honeysuckle Ck Tracking Stn

Gudgenby

8   8

Horseshoe Hill 1143m

GUARRANGORAMBLA RANGE

Mt Bimberi 1911m

Orroral Tracking Stn

4

NAAS   RD

5   6

Mt Michelago 1090m

Mt Woolpack 1227m

Mt Morgan 1874m

SCABBY RANGE

BIMBERI RANGE

Michelago

TINDERRY MOUNTAINS

MONARO   HWY

19

Shanahans Mtn

BOOTH RANGE

NEW SOUTH WALES

32

Numerous Timber Tracks

Numerous Timber Tracks

Colinton

YAOUK BILL RANGE

Mt Brest 1587m

Colinton Hill 1133m

N

Maps of Victoria

Location Map

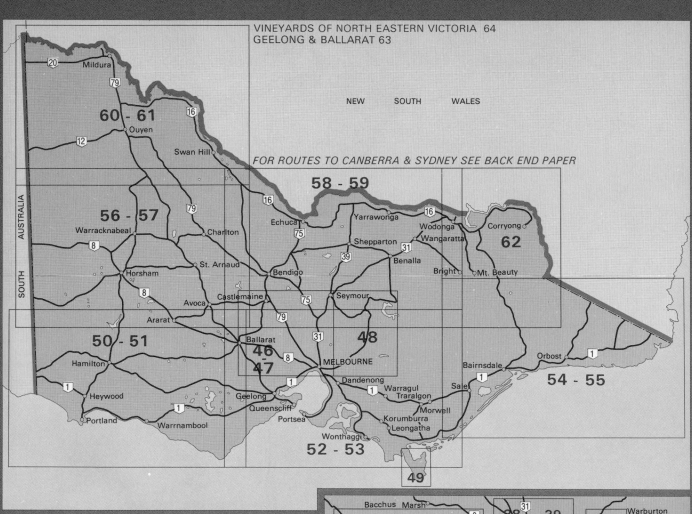

VINEYARDS OF NORTH EASTERN VICTORIA 64
GEELONG & BALLARAT 63

NEW SOUTH WALES

FOR ROUTES TO CANBERRA & SYDNEY SEE BACK END PAPER

SOUTH AUSTRALIA

20 Mildura
79
60 - 61
Ouyen
12
Swan Hill
79
56 - 57
Warracknabeal
Charlton
8
St. Arnaud
Horsham
8
Avoca
Ararat
50 - 51
Hamilton
1
Heywood
1
Portland
Warrnambool

16
58 - 59
Echuca
75
Yarrawonga
16
Shepparton
Wodonga
Wangaratta
Corryong
62
Benalla
Bright
Mt. Beauty
Bendigo
39
31
Castlemaine
75
Seymour
79
31
48
Ballarat
46 - 47
8
MELBOURNE
1
Dandenong
Geelong
1
Warragul
Traralgon
Sale
Bairnsdale
1
Orbost
1
54 - 55
Queenscliff
Portsea
Korumburra
Leongatha
Morwell
Wonthaggi
52 - 53
49

(inset map)

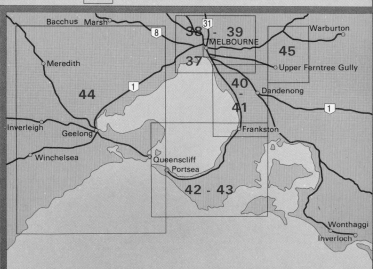

Bacchus Marsh
8
31
38 - 39
MELBOURNE
Warburton
Meredith
37
45
Upper Ferntree Gully
44
1
40 - 41
Dandenong
Inverleigh
Geelong
1
Frankston
1
Winchelsea
Queenscliff
Portsea
42 - 43
Wonthaggi
Inverloch

The centre of Melbourne from Princes Bridge

Places of Interest

1	Botanic Gardens	G10
2	BP House	E11
3	Cook's Cottage	F7
4	City Court	C5
5	Commonwealth Offices	D5
6	Customs House	B7
7	Exhibition Building	E3
8	Floral Clock	D8
9	Government House	F10
10	Hilton Hotel	G7
11	ICI Building	E5
12	LaTrobe's Cottage	F10
13	LaTrobe Library	C5
14	Law Courts	B6
15	Mail Exchange	A7
16	Melbourne Cricket Gnd.	G7
48	Melb. Indoor Sports & Entertainment Centre	F9
17	Melbourne University	C2
18	Myer Music Bowl	E8
19	National Museum	D5
20	Old Melbourne Motor Inn	B3
21	Olympic Park	G9
22	Parliament House	E5
23	Police Headquarters	B5
24	Post Office	C6
25	Princes Gate	D7
43	Regent Hotel	E6
49	Rialto Hotel	B7
26	Royale Ballroom	E4
27	St.Paul's Cathedral	D7
28	St.Patrick's Cathedral	F5
29	Scots Church	D6
30	Shrine of R'embrance	E10
31	Southern Cross Hotel	D6
32	Sporting Centre	D12
33	State Admin. Offices	E6
34	State Library	C5
35	Stock Exchange	C7
36	Tivoli Court	D6
37	Trades Hall	D4
38	Unity Hall	A7
39	Victorian Arts Centre	D8

Transport and Touring

40	Ansett Terminal	C4
41	Flinders St. Railway Stn.	D7
42	Heliport	B8
44	RACV Building	B7
45	Spencer St. Railway Stn.	A7
46	TAA Terminal	C4
47	Tourist Bureau	C7

A B C D 47 E F G H I

1
Sydenham Park
Keilor North
Westmeadows
MELBOURNE AIRPORT
Tullamarine
Broadmeadows
Broadmeadows Military Camp
Commonwealth Property

2
Keilor Public Golf Course
Tullamarine Country Club
Jacana
Glenroy

3
Taylors Lakes
Keilor
Keilor Council Depot
Keilor Pk Rec Res
Oak Park
Fawkner
Northern Golf Club
Fawkner Crematorium & Memorial Park
Edwardes Lake
Keilor Downs
Airport West
Keilor East
Essendon Airport
Coburg North
Pentridge Gaol
Phillip Inst. of Technology
Preston

4
St. Albans
Brimbank Park
SEC Terminal Stn.
Pascoe Vale
Coburg
Tho

5
St. Albans East
Keilor East
Essendon
Strathmore
Glenbervie
Moreland
Croxton

6
St. Albans South
Avondale Heights
C. of A. Dept of Productivity Explosives Factory
Maribyrnong
Moonee Ponds
Moonee Valley R'course
Brunswick
Brunswick East
North

7
Ardeer
Sunshine North
Highpoint West Shopping Centre
Fairbairn Park
Ascot Vale
Showgrounds
Newmarket
Royal Park
Zoo
Melb. Gen. Cem.
Fitzroy North

8
Sunshine
Braybrook
Maidstone
Flemington
Flemington Racecourse
Army Ord. Depot
Kensington
Sth Kensington
Melb. Univ.
Carlton
Collingwood
Abbotsford

9
Brooklyn
Tottenham
Yarraville
West Footscray
Mid Footscray
Footscray
Wholesale Fruit & Veg Market
MELBOURNE
Fitzroy Gardens
Richmond

10
Laverton North
Altona North
Newport
Spotswood
Williamstown
Fishermans Bend
Westgate Bridge
GMH
Port Melbourne
Graham
Sth. Yarra

11
Kororoit Creek
Paisley Park
Paisley
Mobiltown
Newport Railway W'shops
Webb Dock
Princes Pier
Station Pier
Hobsons Bay
Albert Park Lake
Middle Park
Prahran
Windsor

12
Altona
Altona Sports Park
Migrant Centre
Merrett Rifle Range
Launching Ramp
W'town Beach
Nelson Pier
Gellibrand Pier
Breakwater Pier
Williamstown Pier
Williamstown
Altona Bay
St. Kilda
St. Kilda East

13
Former Explosives Reserve
PORT PHILLIP BAY
Elwood Park
Els

A B C D E F G H I

0 1 2 3 4 5 6 7 8km

J K L M N O P Q R

47
52
40

Thomastown
Keon Park
KEON PDE
Reservoir
MMBW Reservoirs
Bundoora
Settlement
Grimshaw
Greensborough
Plenty
Janefield Colony
Aqueduct
St Helena
Eltham North
Research Park
Research
Kangaroo Ground
Diamond Creek
Warrandyte North
Kingsbury
Bundoora Park Public Golf Course
Bundoora Repat. Hospital
Bundoora Park
Larundel Psych. Hospital
Plenty Hospital
Macleod Repat. Hospital
Mont Park Hospital
Watsonia
Montmorency
Eltham
Macleod
Latrobe University
Greensborough
Watsonia Military Camp
Yallambie
Heidelberg Golf Club
Warrandyte Public Golf Cse
Warrandyte Park
YARRA
Rosanna East
Rosanna
Banyule
Warringal Park
Banyule Flats Res.
Rosanna Golf Club
Westerfolds Park
Mullum Mullum
Heidelberg Repat. Hospital
Austin Hospital
Heidelberg
Eaglemont
Templestowe
Templestowe Lower
Park Orchards
Ivanhoe
Darebin Parklands
Ivanhoe Public Golf Course
Bulleen
Bullen Pk
Sentimental Bloke Motor Inn
Doncaster
Doncaster East
Donvale
Fairfield
Greenacres Golf Course
Kew Golf Club
Camberwell Public Golf Course
Balwyn North
Eastern Golf Club
Doncaster Shopping Town
Schramms Reserve
Doncaster Res.
YARRA
Yarra Bend Park
Kew Mental Hosp.
Studley Pk
Kew
Kew East
Belmore
Gordon Barnard Res.
Koonung
Blackburn North
Mitcham
Hawthorn
Burnley
Boulevard
Xavier College
Kew Junct.
Cotham
Whitehorse
Box Hill
Koonung Springfield
Maroondah
Nunawading
Heatherdale
Ringwood
Surrey Hills
Mont Albert
Box Hill Cem
Blackburn
Blackburn Lake
Heatherdale Res.
Riversdale
Camberwell
Canterbury
Canterbury
Prospect Hill
Chatham
Surrey Pk
MMBW Resr.
Box Hill South
Box Hill Golf Club
Blackburn South
Forest Hills Shopping Centre
Forest Hill
Boronia
Scotch Coll
Kooyong
Wattle Park Public Golf Course
Middleborough
Blackburn South
Blind Institute Nursery & School
Burwood
Tooronga Village Gardiner
Burwood East
East Burwood Park
Vermont
Toorak
Armadale
Glen Iris
Rosedale Ashburton
Ashburton
Warrigal
Burwood
Malvern
Caulfield Park
Darling
East Malvern
Gardiners
Holmesglen
Alamein
Riversdale Golf Club Jordanville
Mt Waverley
Valley Res.
Glen Waverley
Waverley Municipal Public Golf Course
Caulfield
Caulfield Racecourse
Carnegie
Glenhuntly
Murrumbeena
Chadstone Shopping Centre
Central Res.
Princes
Mulgrave
Warrigal
Stephensons
Plenty
Diamond Creek
Kangaroo Ground

Wantirna
Knoxfield
Scoresby
Rowville
Mulgrave
Wantirna South
Vermont
Wheelers Hill
Jells Park
Dandenong North
Dandenong
Doveton
Glen Waverley
Burwood East
Mt Waverley
Notting Hill
Monash University
Clayton
Clayton North
Clayton South
Noble Park
Springvale
Springvale South
Keysborough
Burwood
Ashburton
East Malvern
Oakleigh
Oakleigh South
Huntingdale
Heatherton
Kingston
Braeside
Moorabbin Airport
Cheltenham East
Cheltenham
Parkdale
Mentone
Mordialloc
Glen Iris
Carnegie
Murrumbeena
Bentleigh East
Cheltenham North
Beaumaris
Malvern
Caulfield
Glenhuntly
McKinnon
Bentleigh
Moorabbin
Highett
Black Rock
Toorak
Armadale
Elsternwick
Hampton
Prahran
St Kilda East
Brighton
Sandringham

Beaumaris Bay

MULGRAVE FWY
PRINCES HWY
STUD RD
BURWOOD HWY
FERNTREE GULLY RD
NEPEAN HWY
WARRIGAL RD
DANDENONG RD

0 1 2 3 4 5 6 7 8km

J K L M N 52 O P Q R

1

STH. GIPPSLAND RD

Dandenong South

Lyndhurst

Lyndhurst South

HASTINGS-DANDENONG

Proposed SEC Lyndhurst Terminal Station

Eastern Contour Drain

Skye North

FRANKSTON RD

HASTINGS-DANDENONG

PEARCEDALE

2

GREENS RD

Carrum Downs North

Skye

CRANBOURNE-

WARRANDYTE

3

PERRY RD

HAMMOND

BANGHOLME RD

Dandenong RD

Carrum Downs

WORSLEY

Drain

McCORMICKS

McCLELLAND

RD

Lloyd Park

Langwarrin Reserve

MMBW South Eastern Purification Plant

Frankston Sewerage Authority Treatment Works

HALL RD

Keith Turnbull Research Station

Dept. of Agriculture Vegetable Research Station

Karingal Shopping Centre

4

Bangholme

Drain River

Drain

FRANKSTON-DANDENONG

BALLARTO

Bogly

Drain

Frankston North

Karingal

LINDRUM RD

Ballam Park

5

PILLARS RD

Smythes Drain

Springs Drain

Carrum North

THOMPSON

PENINSULA

RD

FWY

9

9

Peninsula Country Golf Club

CRANBOURNE

Frankston Golf Club

Main Drain

Mordialloc

Mornington

WELLS RD

Chelsea Heights

CHELSEA RD

BLVD

Magna

WELLS

AUSTIN

FRANKSTON FWY

KLAUER ST

Long Island Golf Club

Frankston Drive-In

BEACH

FRANKSTON-FLINDERS

6

11

11

11

Patterson River Country Club

Launching Ramps

Drain

RAILWAY

PDE

SEAFORD

FORTESCUE AV

Kananook Ck

McCULLOCH AV

BENTON

9

KARS

JASPER

ROBINSONS RD

43

State Rivers & Water Supply Commn

Frankston Reservoir

Wells Secondary

STATION ST

EDITHVALE

THAMES PROM

30

STATION ST

3

3

HWY

Seaford

Seaford South

40

Frankston

NEPEAN

HWY

HUMPHRIES

OVERPORT

7

Rosedale Golf Club

Aspendale

Edithvale

Chelsea Heights

Chelsea

Bonbeach

Carrum

Chelsea Public Golf Course

NEPEAN

Launching Ramps

Olivers Hill

Daveys Bay

TOWERHILL

ASU Research Home

POWELL RD

BADEN

OLD MORNINGTON

8

3

Pelican Point

Canadian Bay

Tootrak College

CANADIAN RD

Mt. Eliza

PHILLIP

9

N

10

PORT

BAY

11

12

13

J K L M N O P Q R

BELLARINE

PENINSULA

St.Leonards
South Red Bluff

PORT

PHILLIP

Swan

Bay

Edwards Pt.

Schr

Morning

Fisherman
Fisherman
Mother Hic

BAY

Swan
Island

Mari

Fossil

Golf
Bridge
Rabbit Island
Bridge
Pier

Balcombe
Bay

Queenscliff

Lighthouse

Mud
Islands

Mt.Martha

Balc

Balcombe Pt.

MARINE

Passenger Ferry

8

Scout
Camp

THE RIP

Point
Nepean

Nepean
Bay

Ticonderoga
Quarantine
Station

Cheviot
Beach

C'wealth
Territory
Prohibited
Area

Weeroona
Bay

Lord Mayors
Camp

Collins
Bay

Portsea
Golf
Links

Golf
Links

Aquarium

London
Bridge

LONDON
BRIDGE
RD

HOTHAM RD

Sorrento

Portsea
Surf Beach

Cape

Jubilee Pt.
Diamond Bay

Sullivan Bay
"The Sisters"
Settlers Monument
Cameron Bay

Martha Pt.

Mt. Martha
Public Pk

Mt. Marth
160m

CAPEL

SOUND

Dromana
Safety Beach
Bay

NEPEAN

Moats
Corner

Sheepwash

Dromana

"The Rocks"

FWY

3

Red Hill

10

44

Sorrento
Ocean Beach

20

Blairgowrie

"Canterbury"

NEPEAN

McCrae
Lighthouse

Rosebud

Rosebud
West

MORNINGTON PENINSULA

Chairlift
305m
Arthurs Seat
Lookout

ARTHURS SEAT

Higgins
Corner

Musk

Koonya Beach
Pelleys Pt.
Spray Pt.

White
Cliffs

Rye

Tootgarook

JOHNS
WOOD
RD

JETTY

CANTERBURY

DUNDAS
RD

Observation
Hill

TRUEMANS

Drum

Drum

BAY VIEW

Alloc

Golf
Links

Falls

Kings
Waterfalls
Reserve

PURVES

SPLITTERS

MAIN CREEK

MORNINGTON

TUCK

MORNIN

Koreen Pt.
Pearses Beach
Glenn Pt.

The Divide

BROWNS

BROWNS

Boneo

Alloc

11

SHANDS

BARKER

Main
Ridge

PENINSU

BASS

Rye
Ocean
Beach

SANDY

School Hill
184m

Meakin
Junction

Cotton
Tree

11

Hyldberry

Capri
Beach

TRUEMANS

BONEO

Lightwood
CK

Main

North

FLINDERS RD

Double

Double

Boags Rocks
Gunnamatta
Surf Beach

Park

STRAIT

Golf
Course

22

ROSEBUD

MEAKIN

Stockyard

Tea Tree Ck.

South

Cem.

Golf
Lin

N

Rowley
Rocks

Burrabong

Main

FLINDERS

The
Pinnacles
77m

The
Blowhole

Lighthouse
Angel Cave

Cape Schanck

Pulpit
Rock

Bushranger
Bay

Picnic
Pt.

The
Arch

Simmons
Bay

0   5   10   15 km

J K L M N O P Q R

FRANKSTON

CRANBOURNE
Leawarra
Davey Pt.
Daveys Bay
Canadian Bay
Mt. Eliza
Mornington Golf Club
Upper Pt.
Red Bluff
Mills Beach
NEPEAN
13
Mt. Eliza +160m
Baxter Pk.
Baxter
Watson
Baxter
BOUNDARY RD
WARRANDYTE RD
NORTH RD
CENTRE RD
DANDENONG RD
BROWNS RD
SOUTH GIPPSLAND
MOORES RD
MUDDY GATES LA
Five Ways
MANKS RD
Tooradin Rly. Stn.
18
17
ERAMOSA
Mornington Resr.
Wooralla Res.
Disused
Moorooduc Rly. Stn.
Railway
GOLF LINKS RD
ROBINSONS RD
FRANKSTON
Golden Poultry Factory
GRANT
11
Somerville
LWR SOMERVILLE
WEST RD
HASTINGS
CLARKE RD
PEARCEDALE
SMITH LA
CRAIG
FISHERIES RD
TOORADIN
Pearcedale
Cannons Creek
CHONS RD
WARNEET
Warneet
Tooradin HWY
Beach
TYABB
BENTONS
CRAIGIE
BUNGOWER
Tanti Park
Mornington Racecourse
Mooroodue
BOUNDARY RD
BALCOMBE
COOLART RD
STUMPY GULLY
TYABB RD
JONES RD
FLINDERS
BUNGOWER RD
TYABB RD
TOORADIN
McKIRDY
Bembridge
Watson Inlet
Quail Island
Blind Bight
WESTERNPORT BAY
MOOROODUC
Devilbend
13
TUERONG RD
Tuerong Junction
GRAYDEN
Picnic Area
Devilbend Reservoir
Kings Ck
GRAYDEN RD
HODGINS RD
COOLART RD
Tyabb
BAY VIEW RD
Lysaght
CEMETERY RD
Cem.
Liquid Fuel Wharf
Long Island Point
Long Island
Scrub Pt.
McKenzie Junction
Tubbarubba Ck
Bulldog Ck
Foxes Corner
Bittern Reservoir
Warrenquite Ck
BALNARING
MYER RD
Hastings
Pier
Ck
FRENCH ISLAND
Jetty
Mt. Wellington △ 96m
TTERN-DROMANA
12
14
Merricks North
BITTERN-DROMANA
STUMPY GULLY
Emu Plains Racecourse
9
FRANKSTON
DISNEY
Bittern
WOOLLEYS RD
Sandstone Island
Golden Pt.
Crib Pt.
2 10
ST
BP WESTERNPORT OIL REFINERY
Crib Point
Passenger Ferry
STANLEYS
Merricks Ck
Balnarring
FLINDERS
COOLART
SANDY POINT RD
Tulum
Balnarring Beach
Somers Camp
Western Hill +48m
Cem.
HMAS Cerberus
Hann Inlet
Stony Pt.
Passenger Ferry
Tankerton Jetty
Passenger Ferry
Red Hill South
Merricks
Merricks Beach
Coles Beach
Somers
Pt. Sumner
South Beach
Western Park Beach
FLINDERS NAVAL DEPOT
Prohibited Area
Tortoise Head
Peak Pt.
POINT LEO
Reedy Waterholes Ck
FRANKSTON
18
Carlinga Childrens Holiday Camps
Point Leo
Pt Leo Surf Beach
Sandy Pt.
Long Pt.
A
Ck
Shoreham
Shoreham Beach
Cruiser Pt.
WESTERN PORT
Pengiun Rock
Cowes
CHURCH ST
Observation Pt.
Res
Rhyll
Fishermans Pt.
Flinders
Kennon Cove
West Head Area
McHaffie Pt.
Ventnor Beach
Ventnor Res
Picnic Area & Zoo
THOMPSON AV
COWES-RHYLL
Bird Sanctuary
Koalas
NEWHAVEN RD
RHYLL RD
PHILLIP ISLAND
Black Hill +
VENTNOR
66m + Richardson Hill
HARBISON
Koalas
THE GAP RD
RHYLL-
Green Lake
BACK BEACH
Cat Bay
Barrys Beach
Churchill Island
Swan Corner
PHILLIP ISLAND
Newhaven
Woody Pt.
San Remo
Davis Pt.
Pt. Grant
The Nobbies
Seal Rocks
Penguin Parade
Pyramid Rock

J K L M N O P Q R

0 5 10 km

A B C D 46 E F G H I

1

Clarendon
Bungal
Mt. Doran
Ballark
35
Glenmore
Parwan
Rowsley
Pakwan
Melton Sth.
Rockbank
42
MIDLAND
Geelong
421m
The Bluff
Mt. Wallace
Melton Resr.
Exford
WESTERN HWY
52

2

The Tableland
Elaine
Morrisons
Mt. Wallace 514m
Twin Lakes
36
Beremboke
BRISBANE RANGES NAT. PARK
BRISBANE RANGE
Balliang East
33
Mt. Cottrell 204m

3

Cargerie
Woodburne
Meredith
HWY
Durdidwarrah
Upr. Stony Ck. Resr.
Staughton Vale
Balliang
BRISBANE RANGES NAT. PK.
She Oak Hill
Anakie Gorge
Little
Balliang Ck.
One Tree Hill 149m
Werribee
Truganina
Tarneit

4

Yarrowee Ck.
Baronganie
Steiglitz
She Oaks
STEIGLITZ PK.
Maude
Anakie
Anakie Junction
399m Mt. Anakie
Fairy Park
Anakie East
Anakie Gorge
58
THE YOU YANGS FOREST PARK
Flinders Peak 364m
Ford Proving Ground
Little River
Manor
FWY
74
MMBW Sewerage Farm
Werribee Pk
Werribee South

5

Shelford
Teesdale
Lethbridge
Golf Hill 196m
Bannockburn
45
MIDLAND
Sutherlands Creek
31
Hovells Ck.
Lara Lake
Lara
PRINCES
Avalon Airfield
Lake Barrie
Beacon Pt.
Kirk Point
PORT PHILLIP BAY

6

HAMILTON
51
Ellingerrin
Inverleigh
Murgheboluc
Stonehaven
Gheringhap
Moorabool
Batesford
HWY
Corio
Pt. Abeona
Pt. Lillias
Pt. Wilson
Prohibited Area
Pt. Richards
Portarlington

7

Warrambine Ck.
HWY
Barwon
Evansford
NEWTOWN
GEELONG
CITY
EAST GEELONG
Botanical Gardens
ALCOA Works
Pt. Henry
Corio Bay
Clifton Springs
Indented Head
Bellarine
Mt. Bellarine
BELLARINE
St. Leonards

8

Gnarwarre
Mt. Pollock 184m
Barrabool
Highton
BELMONT
Marshall
STH. GEELONG
Mt. Moriac
Waurn Ponds
Grovedale
22
Moolap
Leopold
Wallington
BELLARINE HWY
Swamp
Lake Connewarre
Fenwick
31
Marcus Hill
PENINSULA
Mannerim
22
Edwards Pt
Swan Bay
Duck Is.
Swan Island

9

Winchelsea
PRINCES
Buckley
Lake Modewarre
Moriac
37
HWY
Pettavel
Mt. Duneed
Connewarre
Swamp
18
Ocean Grove
Surf Beach
Barwon Heads
Pt. Flinders
Pt. Lonsdale
Queenscliff
PASSENGER FERRY

10

Wurdiboluc
Wurdiboluc Resr.
Modewarre
Paraparap
Freshwater Creek
22
Breamlea
Bancoora Surf Beach
Portsea
London Bridge
Back Beach

11

Wensleydale
Bambra
48
Boonah
RANGES
Painkalac Ck.
Mt. Ingoldsby
16
Pt. Addis
N

12

Benwerrin
OTWAY
Eastern View
31
Aireys Inlet
Split Pt.
Fairhaven Surf Beach
Cinema Pt.
Big Hill
Urquhart Bluff
Moggs Ck.
Eagle Nest Reef
Anglesea
Surf Beach
Pt. Roadknight
ROAD

13

St. George
Erskine Falls
Erskine R.
OCEAN
Loutit Bay
Lorne
Mt. St. George
The Spit
Surf Beach
Pt. Grey
BASS STRAIT

A B C D E F G H I

0 1 2 3 4 5 6 7 8km

A B C D E 48 F G H I

1

YARRA RD
PAYNES RD
HOMESTEAD RD
BRUSHY PARK RD
SWITCHBACK RD
BERESFORD RD
Golf Course
Chirnside Park
MAROONDAH
EDWARDS RD
VICTORIA RD
Lilydale
ENDS 34
ENDS 32
WARBURTON HWY

2
9
LILYDALE - MONBULK
5
OLD GIPPSLAND RD
SEBIRE AV
WILD CATTLE CK
BURGI HILL RD
HENDERSON RD
Wandin
Seville
MONBULK SEVILLE RD
HWY

Croydon
BELLARA DR
Barngeong Res.
Croydon Golf Club
34
3
MANCHESTER RD
LINCOLN AV
LINCOLN RD
CAMBRIDGE RD
HAWTHORY RD
O'Shannassy
HULL RD
Mooroolbark
Quarry
Olinda Reservoir
Pipeline
BIRMINGHAM RD
YORK RD
National Fitness Camp
7
LILYDALE - MONTROSE RD
MONTROSE RD
Res.
Mt.Evelyn
McKillop
CLEGG RD
Aqueduct
MONBULK RD
HUNTER RD
O'Shannassy
Wandin Yallock
QUAYLE RD
BEENAK RD
3

Sacred Heart RC Monastery
KENT AV
CROYDON RD
WICKLOW AV
Croydon Oval
22
Mun. Offices
Town Pk
MT. DANDENONG RD
KILSYTH
DURHAM RD
CAMBRIDGE RD
6
MONTROSE RD
QUEENS RD
Wandin
Yallock
Wandin East
4

Croydon Main
EASTFIELD RD
32
DORSET RD
3
ICI Merrindale Research Station
CANTERBURY
Bungalook
Bungalook
3
5
Montrose
MT. DANDENONG RD
22
32
Views
Kalorama
Forest Reserve
BARBERS RD
FALLS RD
OLINDA RD
Olinda CREEK
STONYFORD RD
Picnic Area
Silvan
PARKER RD
Conduit
15
5

BAYSWATER
Bungalook
Little Fibremakers Ck
32
Bungalook
COLCHESTER RD
Eastwood Golf Club
RIDGE RD
Mt.Dandenong 633m 'Sky High' Restaurant
GTV9
11
Ricketts Sanctuary
Olinda Falls
OLINDA
MMBW Reserve
Yarra-Silvan
FERNDALE RD
Silvan South
52
Bayswater
1
28
MOUNTAIN
POWELT
BARRY ST
SCORESBY RD
Dandenong Ck
ABV2
HSV7
Burkes Lookout Reserve
ATV10
Mt Dandenong
Olinda
State
Forest
Silvan
Reservoir
Tulip Farm
MONBULK RD
52
7

WOODMASON RD
ALBERT AV
OLIVE GV
MILLER RD
MT. VIEW RD
3
Liverpool Rd Retarding Basin
3
The Basin
Salvation Army Bayswater Youth Training Centre
'Fairyland'
FOREST RD
Rhododendron Gardens
Olinda Public Golf Course
MMBW Reserve
Parkers Corner
SEVILLE RD
Burleigh
SWALES RD
8

Boronia
36
BORONIA RD
3
ENDS 36
BASIN RD
28
ENDS 28
OLINDA
7
HWY
Olinda
22
Sassafras
Perrins Ck
Lookout
Views
OLINDA-MONBULK RD
7
Monbulk
Emerald
OLD EMERALD RD
Whites Corner
Macclesfield
MACCLESFIELD RD
8

BURWOOD
26
22
DORSET RD
2
Blind FRANCIS RD
FOREST RD
One Tree Hill 502m Lookout Tower
Ferny Creek
ONE TREE HILL RD
CHURCHILL DR
TOURIST RD
Nicholas Veterinary Research Farm
Sherbrooke
Giant Tree
Sherbrooke
Sassafras Ck
8
MONBULK RD
Baynes Pk
MICKHAM RD
Monbulk Rec. Res.
DAVID HILL RD
EMERALD-MONBULK
11
9

Ferntree Gully
GLENFERN RD
3
DANDENONG
HWY
22
Tremont
8
FERNTREE GULLY NATIONAL PARK
MT. Ferntree Gully
Monbulk Sherbrooke Falls State Forest
Clematis Ck
Sherbrooke Forest Park
Hardys Ck
Kallista
GRANTULLA RD
EMERALD RD
The Patch
THE PATCH RD
PRIORS RD
Woori Yallock Ck
KALLISTA-EMERALD RD
11
10

Upper Ferntree Gully
26
MONBULK RD
NAPOLEON RD
GLENFERN RD
MORRIS RD
Upwey
5
Ferny Ck
Monbulk Ck
MONBULK RD
Belgrave
Monbulk Ck
BELGRAVE-GEMBROOK RD
11
Menzies Ck
Menzies RD
Railway
Emerald Country Club
11

KELLETTS RD
ENDS 18
WELLINGTON RD
LYSTERFIELD RD
6
MCNICOL RD
Tecoma
Selby
Park
Belgrave Lake Park
Dandenong Reservoir
Puffing Billy
SELBY-AURA RD
SCHOOL RD
MENZIES CK RD
AURA VALE RD
Menzies Creek
MAIN ST
Emerald Gallery
Clematis
Emerald Lake
BELGRAVE-GEMBROOK RD
MACCLESFIELD RD
11

Lysterfield
WELLINGTON RD
Belgrave Heights
COLBY DR
TEMPLE RD
7
Belgrave South
AURA VALE RD
Emerald Park
Emerald Lake
BEACONSFIELD-EMERALD RD
12

N

Lysterfield Lake Park
Lysterfield Lake
LOGAN PARK RD
5
BELGRAVE-HALLAM RD
Muddy Ck
Cardinia
MENZIES CK
11
Emerald
13

WELLINGTON RD
52
MMBW Catchment Area Reservoir

Grid columns: A B C D E F G H I

Grid rows: 1–13

Map of region north-west of Melbourne, showing towns including:

Maldon, Harcourt, Harcourt North, Sutton Grange, Mia Mia, Redesdale, Baringhup, Nuggetty, Porcupine Flat, Walmer, North Muckleford, Muckleford, Castlemaine, Chewton, Golden Point, Faraday, Elphinstone, Metcalfe, Barfold, Sidonia, Taylors Hill 629m, Baynton, Campbells Creek, Campbelltown, Welshmans Reef, Moolert, Joyces Ck, Newstead, Strathlea, Strangways, Guildford, Yapeen, Irishtown, Fryerstown, Taradale, Malmsbury, Green Hill, Langley, Edgecombe, Pastoria East, Sandon, Clydesdale, Tarilta, Vaughan, Glenluce, Drummond North, Drummond, Kyneton, Pipers Creek, Cobaw, Glengower, Eberys, Yandoit, Franklinford, Rocky Hill 443m, Shepherds Flat, Mt Franklin, Porcupine Ridge, Denver, Lauriston, Carlsruhe, The Jim Jim 745m, Newham, Kooroocheang, Smeaton Hill 675m, Glenlyon, Spring Hill, Tylden, Woodend North, Hanging Rock, Lawrence, Smeaton, Kangaroo Hill, Hepburn Springs, Wheatsheaf, Coomoora, Little Hampton, Ashbourne, Woodend, Mount Macedon, Kerrie, Allandale, Kingston, Blampied, Musk Vale, Musk, Daylesford, Eganstown, Lyonville, Fern Hill, Macedon, Broomfield, Newlyn North, Mt Prospect, Bullarto, Bullarto South, Newbury, Trentham, Trentham East, North Blackwood, Gisborne, Creswick North, Springmount, Newlyn, Rocklyn, Leonards Hill, Wombat, Korweinguboora, Barrys Reef, Spa, Blue Mountain, Gisborne Rly Stn, Creswick, Bald Hills, Dean, Barkstead, Spargo Creek, Simmonds Reef, Blackwood, Bullengarook North, Bullengarook, Mt Gisborne 643m, Mt Bullengarook 673m, Couangalt, Mt Aitken 502m, Waubra Junction, Wattle Flat, Clarks Hill, Mollongghip, Mt Hops 779m, Blakeville, Green Hill 705m, Greendale, Mt Blackwood 736m, Poppet Head, White Swan Resr, Glen Park, Pootilla, Bullarook, Claretown, Bolwarrah, Cleevers Hill, Hunts Dam, Mt Steiglitz 638m, Wendouree, Nerrina, Leigh Ck, Springbank, Brown Hill, Bungaree, Wallace, Gordon, Bunding, Korobeit, Djerriwarrh Reservoir, Toolern Vale, Ballarat, Eureka Stockade, Canadian, Warrenheip, Millbrook, Gordon Rly Stn, Ballan, Pikes Ck Resr, Myrniong, Darley, Melton, Sebastopol, Mt Pleasant, Dunnstown, Mt Egerton, Bostock Resr, Mt Gorong 519m, Mt Darriwil, Merrimu Resr, Melton South, Magpie, Mt Clear, Navigators, Lal Lal, Yendon, Mt Egerton, Ingliston, Bacchus Marsh, Parwan, Sydenham West, Cambrian Hill, Mt Helen, Buninyong, Scotsburn, Lal Lal Resr, Fiskville, Werribee Gorge State Park, Lion Ck, Glenmore, Mt Misery 238m, Napoleons, Greenville Hill, Clarendon, Bungal, Ballark, The Bluff 421m, Rowsley, Exford, Garibaldi, Durham Lead, Mt Doran, Ballark, Mt Wallace, Brisbane Range, Balliang East, Mt Cottrell 204m, Grenville, The Tableland, Morrisons, Twin Lakes, Bereemboke, Brisbane Ranges National Park, Balliang, Melton Resr, Mt Mercer, Cargerie, Elaine, Durdidwarrah, Upr Stony Ck Resr, Staughton Vale, Anakie Gorge, One Tree Hill 149m, Mt Mercer 428m, Woodburne, Meredith

Highways/ranges labelled: PYRENEES, MIDLAND HWY, CALDER HWY, WESTERN FWY, GREAT DIVIDING RANGE, BLACK FOREST, BLACKWOOD RANGES, PENTLAND HILLS

0 10 20 30 40 km

J K L M N 58 / 39 O P Q R

1
Dellars Hill 281m | MILITARY TRAINING AREA | Mt.Puckapunyal 413m | Scrub Hill 295m+ | Army Camp | Puckapunyal | Mt.Rose | Tarombe | The Peak +431m | Ruffy

Tooborac | Mt.Koala +574m | Heywoods Hill 320m | 296m+ Stony Creek Hill | Seymour | Whiteheads Creek | Mt.Helen 576m | Mt.Tickatory 604m | Dropmore

2
NORTHERN | Mt.Lookout +487m | Greenshields Hill 336m | GOULBURN | WAGGS RANGE | Mt.Stewart | 60 | Wattle Hill 681m | Highlands | Caveat

3
Emu Flat | Pyalong | Glenaroua | Tallarook | 53 | Trawool | Granite | 43 | Kerrisdale | Mt.Eaglehawk +532m | Mt.Broughton 877m | SWITZERLAND RANGES | 29 | Meadows Hill 611m | Breech Peak 490m | Ghin Ghin | Killingworth | Cottons Pinch

Nulla Vale | High Camp | Moranding | Broadford | Mt.Piper 442m | 806m+ Mt.Tallarook | BROWN RANGE | Mt.Marianne 486m | Homewood | Mt.Charlotte | Yea | Cheviot | Limestone

4
Mt.William 804m | 17 | Willowmavin | Sunday Creek | Tyaak | One Tree Hill 486m | Strath Creek | GOULBURN VALLEY | Mt.Bullamalite +523m | Spion Kopje 486m+

5
Lancefield | BALD HILLS | Kilmore East | Reedy Creek | Murchison Gap 365m | 473m+ Lades Hill | THE YEA SPUR | MINTOS HILLS | Mt.Caroline 515m | River

Kilmore | 22 | 34 | Clonbinane | (Petersons) Flowerdale | Junction Hill 513m+ | Murrindindi

6
Romsey | Springfield | Monument Hill 490m+ | Bylands | Wandong | Hazeldene | 557m+ Flagpole Hill | Break O'Day | 42 | Murrindindi | 48

7
Mt.Eliza 201m | Monegeeta North | Chintin | Darraweit Guim | Pretty Sally | Heathcote Junction | GREAT | Toolangi

32 | Monegeeta | 37 | Bolinda | Deep | Wallan | Wallan East | Upper Plenty | RANGE | Mt.Disappointment 795m | Glenburn | Mt.Klondyke | N

8
Clarkefield | Pentons Hill | HUME FWY | Beveridge | Glenvale | Eden Park | Tooourrong Reservoir | Humevale | Kinglake West | Pheasant Creek | Masons Falls | 39 | KINGLAKE NATIONAL PARK | Wests Bridge | YEA RIVER PK | Gordons Bridge | Castella

9
Sunbury | Emu Bottom Homestead | Konagaderra | Mickleham | Kalkallo | Donnybrook | Woodstock | Whittlesea | Yan Yean Reservoir | SHERWIN RANGES | Howatts Lookout 515m | Strathewen | KINGLAKE | Kinglake Central | Kinglake | Kinglake East | NATIONAL | Mt.Jerusalem | Mt.Slide | PAULS RANGE | 25 | 26 | Toolangi

10
Diggers Rest | Bulla | Yuroke | Mt.Aitken 266m | Craigieburn | Wollert | Mernda | Yan Yean | Doreen | Nutfield | Arthurs Creek | St.Andrews | Mt.Everard +472m | Steels Creek | PARK | Dixons Creek | Healesville West | Healesville

11
39 | Radio Mast | Picnic Area & Lookout | Greenvale | Greenvale Resr. | Oaklands Junction | Somerton | Epping | 40 | Yarrambat | Morang | Hurstbridge | Cottles Bridge | Panton Hill | One Tree Hill 372m+ | Rob Roy | Christmas Hills | Yarra Glen | Tarrawarra | 22 | HWY

40 | Calder Raceway | Organ Pipes National Park | 32 | TULLAMARINE | WESTMEADOWS | Melbourne Airport | BROADMEADOWS | CAMPBELLFIELD | THOMASTOWN | Morang South | Diamond Creek | GREENSBOROUGH | WATTLE GLEN | Watsons Creek | Kangaroo Ground | WARRANDYTE STATE PK | Yering | Coldstream | Gruyere

12
Sydenham | KEILOR | CALDER FWY | GLENROY | PASCOE VALE | PRESTON | FAWKNER | Reservoir | WATSONIA | MONTMORENCY | ELTHAM | RESEARCH | WARRANDYTE | WONGA PARK | PIRIANDA GARDENS | WARBURTON | 18 | Woori Yallock

St.Albans | AVONDALE HEIGHTS | ESSENDON | MOONEE PONDS | BRUNSWICK | NORTHCOTE | IVANHOE | HEIDELBERG | LOWER PLENTY | Yarra | WARRANDYTE SOUTH | CROYDON NORTH | LILYDALE | MOUNT EVELYN | WANDIN | Yellingbo

13
Truganina | DEER PARK | BRAYBROOK | MAIDSTONE | FOOTSCRAY | ASCOT VALE | PARKVILLE | FAIRFIELD | KEW | TEMPLESTOWE | DONCASTER | PARK ORCHARDS | CROYDON | KILSYTH | SILVAN | MAROONDAH | MELBOURNE | YARRAVILLE | WEST GATE | RICHMOND | HAWTHORN | CAMBERWELL | BOX HILL | MITCHAM | RINGWOOD | 40 | MONTROSE | MT DANDENONG | Silvan Resr.

ALTONA NORTH | NEWPORT | Hobsons Bay | ST.KILDA | PRAHRAN | TOORAK | ARMADALE | GLEN IRIS | ASHBURTON | BURWOOD | BLACKBURN | NUNAWADING | FOREST HILL | VERMONT | BAYSWATER | BORONIA | THE BASIN

BURWOOD HWY

J K L M N 40 O P Q R

0   5   10   15   20   25km

Grid columns: A B C D 59 E F G H I

Mt.Rose, CALLEN RANGE, Tarombe, Ruffy, Mt.Budd, Merton, Ancona
The Peak +431m, Terip Terip, HWY, Woodfield, Brankeet Arm, Maindample
Whiteheads Creek, Mt.Helen 576m, Mt.Tickatory 604m, Dropmore, Gobur, Mt.Paradox, Bonnie Doon, Brankeet Inlet
WAGGS RANGE, Kobyboyne, Highlands, Wattle Hill 681m, Caveat, Kanumbra, MAROONDAH 24, Yarck, Delatite Arm, Lake Eildon
Mt.Stewart, Trawool, GOULBURN VALLEY, Mt.Eaglehawk +532m, Mt.Broughton 877m, SWITZERLAND RANGES, Mt.Concord 651m, Cathkin, Fawcett, Mt.Prospect +476m, FRASER NATIONAL PARK
Granite, 39, Kerrisdale, Ghin Ghin, Killingworth, Cottons Pinch, Molesworth, 13 GOULBURN, Koriella, Johnson Ck, EILDON STATE PARK
Homewood, Mt.Marianne 486m, Mt.Charlotte, Yea HWY 19, Mt.Nibo, Mt.Cunningham, Alexandra, VALLEY 13, Eildon, Sugarloaf
THE YEA SPUR, MINTOS HILLS, Cheviot, Limestone, Scrubby Ck, Acheron, Thornton, HWY 11, Snobs Creek Fish Hatchery, Jerusalem Inlet
Strath Ck, 473m +Lades Hill, Mt.Bullamalite +523m, Spion Kopje 486m, HWY, 18, Swamp, 13, Rubicon Terminal Station, EILDON STATE PARK, ROCKY SPUR
Petersons Flowerdale, Junction Hill 513m, Mt.Caroline 515m, Murrindindi, 42, Taggerty, Mt.Cathedral 814m, Rubicon, Rubicon Power Stn, Mt.Torbreck 1514m, TORBRECK RANGE
Hazeldene, 557m +Flagpole Hill, Break O'Day, Devlins Bridge, Murrindindi, Andrews, KNOBBY SPUR, Royston Power Stn, BLUE RANGE
Glenburn, Break-o-Jay Ck, Wilhelmina Falls, Mt.Despair, Mt.Mitchell, CATHEDRAL RANGE NATIONAL PARK, Sugarloaf Peak, Buxton, 26, 22, FEDERATION RANGE, 59, Bullfight, Rough Hill
Kinglake West, Pheasant Creek, KINGLAKE NATIONAL PARK, YEA RIVER PARK, Mt.Klondyke, Bull Ck, Yellowdindi Ck, Robbie Ck, Keppel Ck, Mt.Margaret 1295m, Lake Mountain 1432m, RANGE
Masons Falls, 39, Kinglake Central, Gordons Bridge, Williams, Woods L'out Mt.Gordon, Marysville, 19, Snowy Junc. Mt.Arnold 1310m, Big River Camp
Howqua Lookout 515m, DIVIDING, Kinglake East, Castella, Mt.Tanglefoot, St.Fillans, Steavenson Falls, Nicholls L'out, Snowy Hill, Cambarville, Cumberland Junction
Strathewen, Mt.Jerusalem, Mt.Slide, MELBA, PAULS RANGE, Toolangi, Mt.St.Leonard, Narbethong, Mt.Kitchener 960m, Mt.Observation, Cumberland Falls
Arthurs Creek, NATIONAL PARK, Mt.Everard 472m, 34, Steels Creek, 25, 26, 19, Mt.Monda, Mt.Dom Dom, Mt.Strickland 1219m, POLEY RANGE, 21
St.Andrews, Dixons Creek, Healesville West, Fernshaw, Black Spur, 26, Mt.Vinegar, THE ACHERON WAY, Deep Ck
Cottles Bridge, One Tree Hill 372m, Rob Roy, Tarrawarra, Maroondah Reservoir, Mt.Juliet 1104m, 37, Reefton, Upper Yarra Dam, Upper Yarra Reservoir
Panton Hill, Christmas Hills, Yarra Glen, Healesville, Mt.Riddell, Grace Burn, Mt.Donna Buang 1249m, O'Shannassy Resr., McMahons Creek
Hurstbridge, WATSONS CREEK, Yering, HWY, Healesville Sanctuary, Panton Gap, Badger Ck, Smith Ck, Acheron Gap, Cement Creek, 18 21
KANGAROO GROUND, 22, Coldstream, Gruyere, 16, Mt.Toole-be-wong 792m, HAINING 5 FARM, Mt.Victoria, Warburton, Warburton East
WARRANDYTE STATE PK, WONGA PARK, PIRANDA GARDENS, Lilydale, Launching Place, Woori Yallock, 43, Millgrove, 10, Wesburn, Big Pats Creek, Smoko Hill, Flowerpot Hill
PARK ORCHARDS, CROYDON NORTH, MOOROOLBARK, MOUNT EVELYN, WANDIN, 18, Yelingbo, Yarra Junction, 10, Mt.Little Joe, Mt.Bride +781m, Mt.Tugwell
MAROONDAH, WARBURTON, SILVAN, Silvan Resr., Hoddles Creek, Mt.Thule, Gladysdale, Mt.Myrtalia, Starling Hill Starling Gap, Marney Hill, Roy Hill
RINGWOOD, BAYSWATER, MONTROSE, Mt.Dandenong, THE BASIN, OLINDA, Three Bridges, Black Sandy Ck, Fryer Hill, Gilderoy, Powelltown
WANTIRNA, VERMONT, BORONIA, McCrae

GOULBURN VALLEY HWY

59 / 53 (grid diamonds)

47 / 53 (side diamonds)

53

0 2 4 6 8 km

Doughboy Island

Shelter Cove
Entrance Point
Mt Singapore 145m
Freshwater Cove
Chinaman Beach

Shallow Inlet

Stockyard Hill 35m
Yanakie
Duck Point

Granite Island

Sand Island

CORNER INLET

Hunter Point

Mt Hunter 351m

Bennison Island

Mt Margaret 219m

Lighthouse Point

Park Entrance

Chinaman Knob 62m

Chinaman Long Beach

Bar Ck

Mt Roundback 314m

Three Mile Point

Chinaman

Johnnie Sussie Point

Creek

Lilly Pilly 140m

Creek

WILSONS PROMONTORY

VEREKER

Rabbit Rock
Causeway

NATIONAL PARK

Gravel pit

Emergency landing ground

BASS

N

Black Rock

Mt Vereker

RANGE

Five Mile Beach

Shellback Island

Darby

Tongue Point

River

LA TROBE RANGE

Mt La Trobe 755m

STRAIT

BASS STRAIT

Sparkes Lookout
Darby Saddle

Mt Leonard 356m

Whisky Ck

Sealers Creek

Sealers Cove

Picnic Point
Whisky Bay

Bishop Peak 319m

River

Mt Ramsay 686m

Ruins

Horn Point

Norman Island

Leonard Point

Leonard Bay

N

Tidal

Park Office
Tidal River
Microwave tower
Mt Oberon 558m

Car Park
Telegraph Saddle

Windy Saddle

WILSON RANGE

Smith Cove
Hobbs Head
Refuge Cove
Brown Head

Pillar Point

Norman Bay

Little Oberon 276m

Cove Ck

Bare Back Cove
Kersop Peak 214m

Norman Point
Little Oberon Bay

Mt Wilson 705m

Oberon Bay

North

Waterloo Bay
Little Waterloo Bay

Cape Wellington

Great Glennie Island

Oberon Point

Freshwater Ck

Waterloo Bay

GLENNIE GROUP

PMG hut

Mt Norgate 414m

Mt Boulder 501m

Waterloo Point

Boat Harbour Hill

Dannevig Island

Roaring Meg Ck

BOULDER RANGE

Citadel Island
McHugh Island

Jetty

South West Point

Barry Ck

South East Point

LEGEND

- - - Walking track

N Nature trail

■ Camping area

Anser Island

South Point

Wattle Island

COPYRIGHT GEORGE PHILIP & O'NEIL PTY LTD

56

Struan, Joanna, Langkoop, Kadnook, Powers Creek, Harrow, Glenelg, THE BLACK RANGE, Mt. Becha, Cave of Fishes

Wrattonbully, Connewirricoo, Moree, Culla, Balmoral, Rocklands Reservoir, Glenisla

Glenroy, Poolaijelo, Chetwynd, Pigeon Ponds, Glendinning, CAVE OF HANDS, Woohlpooer

SOUTH, Comaum, Dorodong, 77, Tarrayoukyan, Coojar, Englefield, Caddens Flat, Vasey, Mooralla, GRAMPIANS NATIONAL, The Chimney Pots

Coonawarra, Brimboal, Nareen, Gatum, Mt. Dundas 468m, Mt. Mackersay, HENTY, Mona Park, Victoria Lag.

Penola, Dergholm, Konong Wootong North, Brit Brit, Gringegalgona, Wannon, Cavendish, Victoria Point, Victoria

Krongart, Roseneath, Wando Bridge, Wando Vale, Konong Wootong, Wootong Vale, Melville Forest, Bulart, Mt. Cavendish, Kyup, Karabeal, Victoria Valley

AUSTRALIA, L Mundi, Lake Mundi, 63, Dunrobin, Carapook, Gritjurk, Kanawalla, Moutajup

Nangwarry, Heathfield, Casterton, Coleraine, 63, Parkwood, Hensley Park, Strathkellar, 50, Warrayure

Kalangadoo, 52, Lindsay, Sandford, Hilgay, Paschendale, Wannon, Bochara, GLENELG, Tarrington

Tarpeena, Strathdownie, 69, GLENELG, Henty, Tahara Bridge, Tarrenlea, HAMILTON, Yulecart, Yatchaw, Croxton East, Linlithgow, Tabor

Ardno, Myaring, Merino, Tahara, Branxholme, Buckley Swamp, Mt. Napier 412m

MT. GAMBIER, Glenburnie, Puralka, PRINCES, Marp, Digby, Grassdale, HWY, Wallacedale, Byaduk North, Gazette, Penshurst

O.B. Flat, Yahl, Caroline, Dartmoor, Crawford, Hotspur, Condah, Byaduk, Warrabrook, Minham

25, Mt. Schank, Mumbannar, Winnap, Greenwald, Myamyn, Knebsworth, Macarthur, 82, Hawkesdale W.

Ewans Ponds, Nelson, 89, Drik Drik, Lyons, HIGHWAY, Drumborg, Milltown, Mt. Eccles, L. Condah, MT. ECCLES NATL. PARK, Broadwater, Dunmore, Willatook, Warro

Port Macdonnell, Princess Margaret Rose Caves, Wanwin, Mt. Vandyke, Fitzroy, HENTY, L. Condah, Bessiebelle, Orford

Glenelg, LOWER GLENELG NATIONAL PARK, Kentbruck, Heywood, Homerton, Tyrendarra, Tyrendarra East, St. Helens, Kirkstall

Lake Bungbung, Mt. Kincaid, Surrey, Heathmere, Mt. Clay, 63, PRINCES, Toolong, Killarn, Rosebrook

Mt. Richmond, MT. RICHMOND NAT. PK., Malseed Lake, Gorae West, Gorae, Bolwarra, Narrawong, Codrington, Yambuk, L. Yambuk

DISCOVERY BAY COASTAL, Cashmore, Tarragal, Descartes Bay, Trewalla, Mt. Chaucer, PORTLAND, Aringa, Cape Reamur, PORT FAIRY

Cape Duquesne, Cape Bridgewater, Bridgewater Bay, Cape Bridgewater, Nelson Bay, CAPE NELSON STATE PK, Lighthouse Cape Nelson, Pt. Danger, Lawrence Rocks, Cape Sir William Grant, Lady Julia Percy Is.

Discovery Bay

Portland Bay

N

SOUTHERN

0 10 20 30 40 50km

57

J K L M N O P Q R

52

Ararat **Beaufort** **Creswick** **BALLARAT**

Great Western · Bunjil Caves · Pomonal · Armstrong · Rhymney Reef · Dunneworthy · Eversley · Elmhurst · Amphitheatre · Talbot · Sandon · Campbelltown · Glengower · Dunach · Werona · Ullina · Blampied · Newlyn · Rocklyn

Moora Moora Res. · Cathedral Rock · Mt. William · Jallukar · Norval · Cathcart · Moyston · Warra Yadin · Warrak · Mt. Cole · Ben Nevis · Mt. Lonarch · Lexton · Beckworth · Evansford · Coghills Ck. · Ascot · Lawrence · Smeaton · Dean · Kingston · Springmount

GRAMPIANS NATIONAL PARK · Sugarloaf Hill · Mafeking · Barton · Denicull Ck. · Dobie · Buangor · Middle Ck. · Eurambeen · Raglan · Shirley · Chute · Waterloo · Glenbrae · Mt. Misery 724m · Addington · Learmonth · Windermere · Burrumbeet · Waubra Junc.

SERRA · Bellfield · Langi Logan · Ballyrogan · Maroona · Ross Bridge · Tatyoon · Yalla-y-poora · Nerring · Brewster · Cardigan · Haddon · Carngham · Mt.Emu · Mt.Chepstowe · Lake Goldsmith · Goldsmith · Mena Park · Burrumbeet · Sebastopol

Willaura 48 · Stavely · Calvert · Lake Buninjon · Streatham · Stockyard Hill · Snake Valley · Hillcrest · Mortchup · Smythesdale · Scarsdale · Ross Ck · Napoleons · Buninyong · Durham Lead · Scotsburn · Clarendon · Garibaldi · Lal Lal · Mt. Doran

Glenthompson · Mt. Stavely 326m · Wickliffe · Lake Bolac · Westmere · Carranballac · Skipton · Pittong · Linton · Happy Valley · Piggoreet · Berringa · Enfield · Grenville · Cargerie · Elaine

Nerrin Nerrin · L. Mc Laren · Pura Pura · Vite Vite North · Bradvale · Willowvale · Cape Clear · Illabarook · Dereel · Mt. Mercer · Woodburne · 63

Chatsworth · Woorndoo · Dundonnell · Lake Eyang · Vite Vite · Mt. Bute · Wallinduc · Rokewood Junction · Corindhap · Rokewood · Leigh

Caramut · HAMILTON · Hexham · Darlington · Derrinallum · Mt. Elephant 393m · Lismore · Berrybank · Werneth · Warrambine · Shelford · Teesdale

Mortlake · Kolora · Bookar · Glenormiston North · Gnar-purt · Lake Gnar-purt · Foxhow · Duverney · Cressy · Wingeel · HIGHWAY

The Sisters · Ellerslie · Noorat · Glenormiston South · Boorcan · Lake Bookar · Lake Colongulac · Kariah · Leslie Manor · Lake Corangamite · Cundare · Barpinba · Lake Murdeduke

Woolsthorpe · Ballangeich · Keilambete · L. Gnotuk · Camperdown · Weerite · Dreeite · L. Beeac · Beeac · Eurack · Ombersley · 39 · Winchelsea

Koroit · Mailors Flat · Grassmere · Purnim · Garvoc · Terang · Naroghid · Cobrico · Mt. Leura · Pomborneit Nth. · Pomborneit · Warrion · Alvie · Ondit · Mt.Gellibrand 261m · Coragulac · Armytage · 37

Illowa · Bushfield · Dennington · Wangoon · Panmure · Dixie · Cobden · Bosteck Ck. · Koallah · Purrumbete South · Pomborneit · Stoneyford · Nalangil · Cororooke · Lake Colac · Irrewarra · Warncoort · Birregurra · Bambra · 50

WARRNAMBOOL · Pickering Pt. · Allansford · Mt. Emu · Laang · Ecklin · Mumblin · Jancourt · Jancourt East · Purrumbete South · Carpendeit · Swan Marsh · Bungador · Pirron Yallock · Larpent · Elliminyt · COLAC · Yeodene · Barongarook · Whoorel · Deans Marsh · Boonah

Mepunga West · Naringal · Ayrford · Brucknall · Glenfyne · Scotts Ck · Heytesbury Settlement · Irrewillipe · Kawarren · Gerangamete · Barwon Downs · Murroon · Benwerrin · Eastern View

The Cove · Nullawarre · Timboon · Cowleys Creek · Simpson · Tomahawk Ck. · Gellibrand · Forrest · Wimba · Barramunga · Lorne · Pt. Grey

Nirranda South · Curdie Vale · Paaratte · Newfield · Kennedys Creek · Carlisle River · Charley Ck · Ferguson · Beech Forest · Webster Hill · Olangalah · Tanybryn · 45 · Mt.Defiance · Wye River · Kennett River

Bay of Islands · Peterborough · Curdies Inlet · London Bridge · The Arch · The Sentinel Rock · Port Campbell · Chapple Vale · Weeaproinah · Wyelangta · OTWAY RANGES · Mt.Sabine 583m · Cape Patton · Wongarra

PORT CAMPBELL NATIONAL PARK · The Twelve Apostles · Princetown · Lower Gellibrand · Wangerrip · Lavers Hill · Devondale · MELBA GULLY ST. PARK · Yuulong · Aire Scenic Reserve · Apollo Bay · Little Henry Reef · Marengo · Skenes Creek

Moonlight Head · Pt. Reginald · Johanna · Glenaire · Hordern Vale · OTWAY NATIONAL PARK · Storm Pt. · Pt. Lewis

OCEAN · Lighthouse · Pt. Franklin · Cape Otway

GREAT OCEAN ROAD · SOUTHERN OCEAN

1 2 3 4 5 6 7 8 9 10 11 12 13

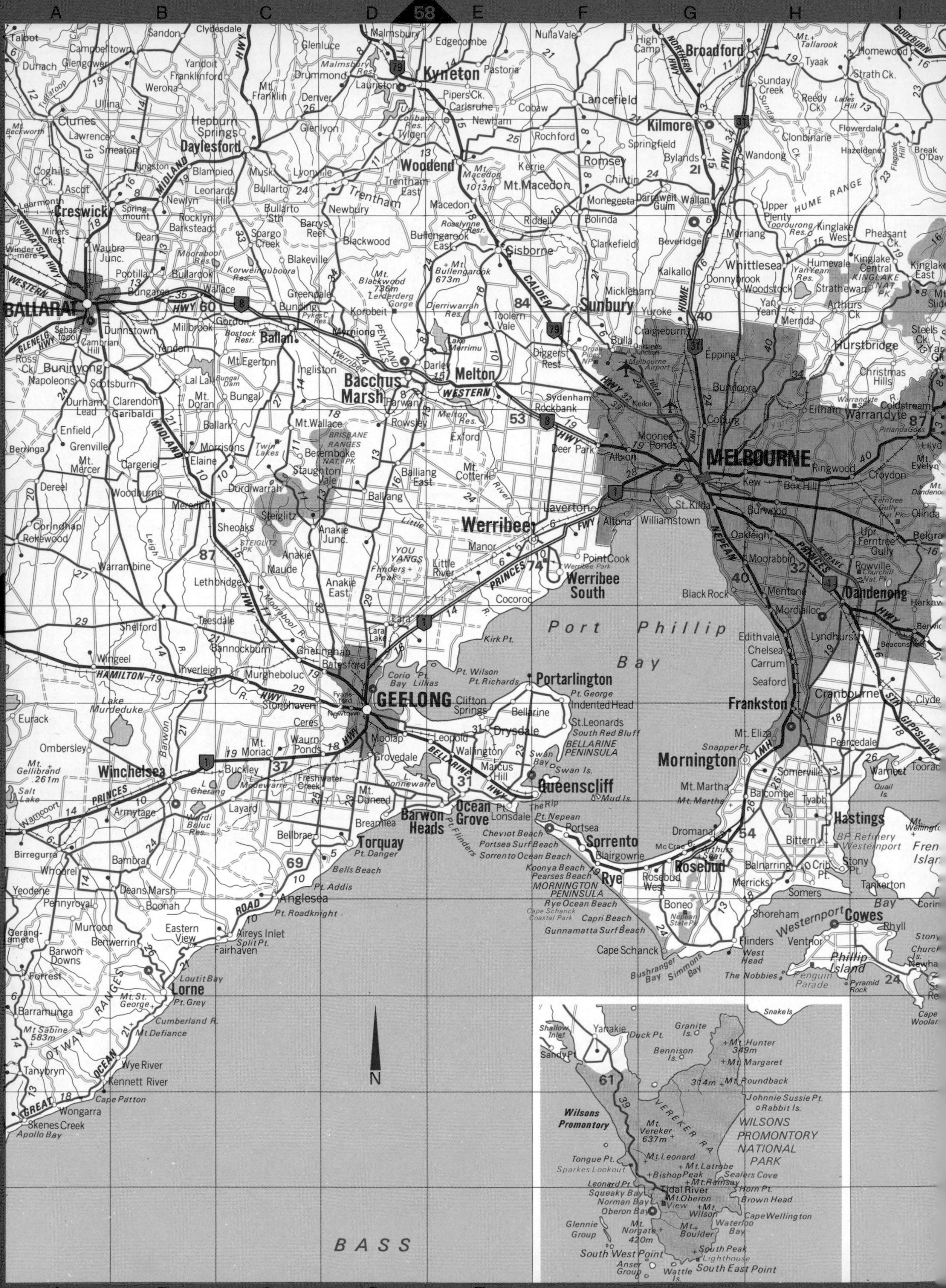

58

A B C D E F G H I

1

2

3

51

4

5

6

7

8

9

10

11

12

13

A B C D E F G H I

BALLARAT
MELBOURNE
GEELONG
WERRIBEE
Port Phillip Bay
BASS
Daylesford
Creswick
Kyneton
Woodend
Sunbury
Melton
Bacchus Marsh
Gisborne
Broadford
Kilmore
Whittlesea
Hurstbridge
Dandenong
Frankston
Mornington
Hastings
Queenscliff
Sorrento
Rosebud
Rye
Torquay
Lorne
Anglesea
Winchelsea
Barwon Heads
Ocean Grove
Portarlington
Cowes
Phillip Island

WILSONS PROMONTORY NATIONAL PARK
Wilsons Promontory
Tidal River

N

0 10 20 30 40 50km

J K L M N 59 O P Q R

Mt Timbertop

Koriella
Molesworth
Alexandra
Gough Bay
Mt. Thorn
+Mt. Howitt 1742m
Basalt Knob

Cheviot
Limestone
Mt. Sugarloaf
Eildon
Thornton
+Mt.Pinniger
Howqua
RANGE
HOWITT
PLAINS
WONNANGATTA

Acheron
Snobs Ck.
Jamieson
+ Mt. Clear
MOROKA
NATIONAL
PARK

Murrindindi
Rubicon
BLUE
FEILDON
STATE
PARK
Bald Hill
Jamieson
Howqua
+Mt. McDonald
SNOWY
Mt. Hart
Mt Cynthia

Glenburn
+Mt
Mitchell
Buxton 43
CATHEDRAL
ST. NAT.PK.
+Mt. Torbreck
Kevington
Mt. Sunday
Mt. Reynard +
Snowy Bluff
Happy Valley
Crooked River

Mt.
Klondyke
YEA RIVER PK
Marysville
1513m
Lake Mountain
Ten Mile
Knockwood
Mt. Skene 1571m
Mt. Arbuckle
Mt Kent +1563m

Castella
Toolangi
St Fillans
+Mt. Margaret
Mt.+Grant
Stockmans Reward
A.I. Mine Settlement
Glencairn
Mt. Tamboritha 1640m
+Mt. Wellington
Trapyard Hill
Castle Hill 1436m

Narbethong
Mt.+Strickland
Mt.+Arnold
Woods Point
+Mt. Margaret
+Mt. Hump
Mt Blomford

Healesville
Mt. Dom Buang
Mt. Observation
Mt Matlock +1375m
Mt. Selma 1459m
Licola
Tarli Karng

Fernshaw
Acheron Gap
McMahons Creek
Matlock
Jericho
Mt. Useful + 1441m
Ben Cruachan 840m
Valencia

Warburton
Upr. Yarra Dam Resr.
Red Jacket
Aberfeldy
Avon
Valencia Ck.
Briagalong

Woori Yallock
Yarra Junction
Gladysdale
Loch Valley
Toorongo
Aberfeldy
Glenmaggie
Upr. Maffra West
Bushy Park
Llowalong

Hoddles Creek
Gilderoy
Powelltown
Tanjil Bren
Mt. Baw Baw 1563m
Glenmaggie Resr.
Boisdale

Monbulk
Nangana
+Mt. Beenak
Noojee
Vesper
Icy Ck.
Alpine Village
Mt Kernot
Walhalla
Seaton
Newry
Maffra
Airly

Emerald
Macclesfield
BLUE RANGE
Nayook
Neerim Nth.
Fumina
Mt Erica
BAW BAW
Erica
Thomson
Heyfield
Dawson
Tinamba

Cockatoo
Gembrook
Neerim Junction
Neerim East
Fumina Sth
Tyers Junction
Bawson
Coopers Ck.
Cowwarr
Bundalaguah
Nambrok
Montgomery
Cobains

Tonimbuk
Jindivick
Neerim Sth.
Hill End
Mt +Tanjil
Moondarra
Toongabbie
Winnindoo
Fulham

Officer
Mt. Tow 354m+
Labertouche
Rokeby
Willow Grove
Mt. Carmel
Moondarra Resr.
Glengarry
Sale

PRINCES
Nar-nar-goon
Tynong
Garfield
Longwarry
Bulln Bulln East
Shady Ck.
Tanjil Sth
Yallourn Nth
Tyers
Latrobe
PRINCES
Kilmany
Wurruk

Drouin
Drouin Sth
Nilma
Darnum
Westbury
New borough
MOE
Yallourn
Loy Yang
Rosedale
Kilmany Sth

Koo-wee-rup
Modella
Yarragon
Trafalgar
Coalville
Traralgon
Flynn
63
HOLEY PLAINS STATE PARK

Lang Lang
Ripplebrook
Ellinbank
Narracan
Flynns Ck.
Traralgon Sth
Stradbroke

Bayles
Catani
Athlone
43
Heath Hill
Seaview
Allambee
Thorpdale
Hazelwood
MORWELL
Gormandale
Hiamdale

The Gurdies
Grantville
Nyora
Poowong East
Strzelecki
Mt Eccles
Childers
Delburn
Cooling Pond
Churchill
Callignee Nth.
Willung
Willung Sth

Bass
Woodleigh
Loch
Bena
Ranceby
Hallston
Boolarra
Yinnar
Callignee
Carrajung
Le Roy
Blackwarry
Carrajung Sth.
Giffard

Korumburra
Krowera
Jumbunna
Ruby
Mirboo Nth
Mardan
Budgeree
Budgeree East
Balook
BULGA NATL. PK
TARRA VALLEY NATL. PARK
Wonwron
Darriman

Leongatha
Kongwak
Leongatha South
Mirboo Brch
80
Ryton
Madalya
Macks Ck.
Devon
Greenmount
Woodside

Woolamai
Anderson
Kilcunda
Dalyston
Dudley
Koonwarra
Meeniyan
Dumbalk
Turtons Ck.
Gupyah
Hiawatha
Jack River
Yarram
Hunterston
Woodside Beach
Reeves Beach

Wonthaggi
Inverloch
Tarwin
Pound Ck.
Stony Ck.
Mt. Fatigue 591m
Wonyip
Binginwarri
Hedley
Gelliondale
Alberton
Taravile
McLaughlins Beach

Cape Patterson
Pt Smythe
Venus Bay
Tarwin Middle
Tarwin Lower
Buffalo
Hoddle
Toora
Woorarra East
Kay Hill
Welshpool
Port Albert
Manns Beach

Cape Patterson
Tarwin Meadows
Fish Creek
Port Franklin
Barry Beach
Agnes
Port Welshpool
Clonmel Is.
Sunday

Waratah Nth
Rock Hill
Yanakie
Corner Inlet
Little Snake Is.
Duck Pt.
Snake Is.

Liptrap
Waratah Bay
Shallow Inlet
Mt. Hunter 349m
+Mt. Margaret

Mt. Liptrap
Walkerville Beach
Waratah South
Sandy Pt.
Bennison Is.
Granite Is.
314m +Mt. Roundback

STRAIT
Cape Liptrap
Lighthouse
Walkerville South Bell Pt
Wilsons Promontory
Mt. Vereker
Johnnie Sussie Pt.
Rabbit Is.
WILSONS PROMONTORY NATIONAL PARK

JOINS INSET AT LEFT

J K L M N O P Q R

1
2
3
4
5
6
7
8
9
10
11
12
13

A B C D 62 E F G H I

KOSCIUSKO

1
Buckland Upr. • Smoko • KIEWA HYDRO ELECTRIC SCHEME • Pyramid Hill • Little Spion Kopje • Spion Kopje • Mt. Nelse • 1760m • Sunnyside • Mt. Fraser • Deep Ck. • Mt. Misery • Mt. Cobberas No. 1 • Mt. Cobberas No. 2 • Willis • Harrietville • Falls Ck. • 13 • Mt. Feathertop +1922m • Mt. McKay • Rocky Valley Resr. • Buckety • Glen Wills • The Knocker • Glen Valley • Porphyry Hill • The Brothers • Big Hill • Mt. Stradbroke • Paddy Hill • Mt. Little Feathertop • Mt. Cope + 1837m • Pl. • 23 • Shannonvale • Morass • 72

2
Mt. Selwyn + • 1524m • Mt. St. Bernard • Mt. Hotham • BOGONG 1862m • Loch • Hotham Heights • NATIONAL • PARK • Cobungra • 37 • Mt. Battery • 39 • Anglers Rest • Lake Omeo • Hinnomunjie • 19 • Benambra • Mt. Tambo • BOWEN • MOUNTAINS • The Brothers • 174 • 10 • 13 • Suggan Buggan • 21 • Suggan Buggan • Little River Falls • MCKillop Bridge • 50

3
53 • Humffray • Wonnangatta • Basalt Knob • Mt. Murray • 1609m • Mt. Blue Rag • DARGO HIGH PLAINS • Mt. Parslow + • Round Hill • 25 • Sams Hill • 9 • Omeo • Days Hill • Mt. Shaw • Bindi • Mt. Nunniong • Mt. Deception • Mt. Statham + • 13 • Gelantipy • SNOW RIVER • WONNANGATTA MOROKA NATIONAL PARK • Mt. Hart • Mt. Phipps • 32 • Tongio • OMEO • Mt. Nugong • 60

4
Mt. Cynthia • 155 • Mt. Birregun + • Cassilis • Tongio West • Swifts Ck. • Doctors Flat • 19 • Mt. Bindi • Green Hill • Timbarra • Gillingal • Wattle Tree • Butchers Ridge • NATIONAL PARK • Mountain • Rodger • Snowy Bluff • Happy Valley • Mt. Grant • Mt. Delusion • Brookville • 23 • Ensay • 27 • Crooked River • Mt. Steve • Notch Hill • Mt. Baldhead • Mt. + Wellington • Buchan • Murrindal

5
Mt. Kent +1563m • Trapyard Hill • Dargo • Waterford • Castle Hill 1436m • Stirling • Ensay Sth. • 96 • Reedy Flat • Tambo • Buchan Caves • 14 • Buchan • Mt. Tab • Tarli Karng • 29 • 9

6
Mt. Hump • Mt. Blomford • Tabberabbera • 25 • 19 • Mt. Hood • Mt. Welcome • Deptford • 32 • HWY • Tambo Crossing • Spanker Knob • Flukes Knob • Buchan Sth. • Mt. Tara 608m • Stringer Knob • Mt. Buck + 507m • Cobbannah • 16 • Mitchell • Bulumwaal • Nicholson • 50 • 32 • 58

7
Davey Knob • Yellowman Knob • GLENALADALE NATIONAL PARK • Mt. Alfred • Mt. Taylor • Waterholes • 24 • 11 • Bruthen • 23 • 29 • Nowa Nowa • Wairewa • Bete Bolong • Waygara • Orbo • 37 • 35 • Newmere • Lake Corringle • Corringle • Mt. + Difficulty • 42 • 56 • 12 • Iguana Ck. • Mt. + Lookout • Mt. + Taylor • 13 • Sarsfield • Mossiface • Tambo Upr. • Johnsonville • Colquhoun • Tostaree • Lake Tyers • Aboriginal Settlement • LakeTyers

8
Upr. Maffra West • Boisdale • Busby Park • Briagolong • 14 • Llowalong • Munro • 13 • 58 • Walpa • 26 • Coongulmerang • Lindenow • Wy Yung • 13 • Lucknow • Nicholson • Swan Reach • 23 • Katimna West • Newry • 11 • Stockdale • 51 • Delvine • 10 • 14 • Bengworden • Forge Ck. • Eagle Pt. • Paynesville • 18 • Bairnsdale • Jones Bay • Lake King • 20 • 34 • Nungurner • Metung • Lakes Entrance • Glenmaggie Resr. • Valencia Ck. • Glenaladale • Fernbank • 1 • 13 • Eagle I. • Raymond Is. • Bunga Arm

9
Heyfield • Tinamba • 11 • Maffra • 10 • Stratford • 24 • Perry Bridge • 29 • Clydebank • Meerlieu • Red Morass • Goon Nure • Lake Victoria • THE LAKES NATIONAL PARK • Bundalaguah • Nambrok • Montgomery • Airly • Hollands Landing • Pt. Wilson • Sperm Whale Head • Ocean Grange • Bunga • BEACH • Mt. Wellington • 18 • 18 • 15

10
PRINCES • Fulham • Kilmany • 18 • Wurruk • Sale • 6 • River • Cobains • The Heart • Lake Wellington • Seacombe • GIPPSLAND LAKES PARK • Loch Sport • Causeway • Stockyard Hill (Good Fishing) • Rosedale • 8 • Kilmany Sth. • Longford • Lake Coleman • NINETY • Reeve • MILE • 13 • HOLEY PLAINS STATE PARK • Dutson • 29

11
Willung • Stradbroke West • 18 • Gas Processing Plant • Letts Beach (Paradise Beach) • Golden Beach • 26 • Stradbroke • 26 • THE • Little Monkey Ck.

12
72 • GIPPSLAND • 27 • Giffard • Seaspray • Lake Denison • N • Brothen • Darriman • Jack Smith Lake

13
Hunterston • Woodside • Woodside Beach • Reeves Beach

A B C D E F G H I

0 10 20 30 40 50km

30

J K L M N O P Q R

1

NATIONAL PARK

Snowy

Candelo 13
37
Wolumla 12
Bibbenluke Wallagoot Lake
HWY 10
Bombala 13 Cathcart
8 32
Tingiringi Merimbula 13

2

TINGARINGY Mt Taylor NAT. PARK
NEW SOUTH Wyndham 1 Pambula
Mt Tingaringy +
Ambyne Rowes 21 WALES 24
Tubbut Bombala Burragate
Delegate River 15 16 PRINCES 20 BEN
Deddick Delegate 11
Dellicknora BOYD

3

32 Haydens Bog MONARO Eden
21 Bendoc Nalbaugh Towamba 7
Bonang 32 NATIONAL 20 Boydtown NATIONAL
Mt Bowen + PARK Kiah 11
Rockton 40 R PARK
Bonang West Mt Tennyson 93 Nungatta Mtn. 938m Pericoe
Narrabarba Wonboyn Lake

4

R Buldah NUNGATTA Mt Merragunegin 29 109 Disaster Bay
Mt Jersey + HWY 23 34 Kowat NATIONAL 1
Goongerah 6 Chandlers Ck. PARK Coopracambra State Park
Errinundra Wroxham Mt Buckle 456m
Mt Ellery +1298m Weeragua Wangarabell NADGEE

5

Martins Creek 13 97 VALLEY CANN Mt Kaye + HWY 13 FAUNA
BONANG 16 Combienbar 27 Noorinbee Nth. Genoa R PARK
River 32 Gipsy Point
Karlo Ck. 8 Cape Howe
Sardine Creek Noorinbee 31 Genoa + Peak
Mt Jack + Mt Drummer + Wingan Gabo Island

6

Mt Rich + Mt Kuark + Club Terrace 1 Mallacoota
Brodribb Mt Puggaree + Tonghi Ck. 21 18 ALFRED NAT. PK. 16 Mallacoota Inlet
Murrungowar 19 Cann River NATIONAL

7

74 LIND NATIONAL PARK Mt Cann Little Ram Head
odribb Bellbird Ck. 16 Thurra 26 PARK
iver 34 PRINCES Lake O' Furnell Mt Everard + Wingan Inlet
Mt Raymond + Cabbage Tree Creek 23 CROAJINGOLONG Ram Head
Curlip Bemm River Tamboon Inlet Lighthouse

8

Tabbara Sydenham Inlet Point Hicks (Cape Everard)
arlo 18
Pt. Ricardo Cape Conran Pearl Pt.

9

10

11

T A S M A N *S E A*

12

13

J K L M N O P Q R

A B C D **60** E F G H I

1

SOUTH AUSTRALIA

VICTORIA

BIG DESERT

BIG DESERT WILDERNESS

Mt. Little Doughboy

Mt. Shaugh +
+ Red Bluff

N

Moonlight Tank

Broken Bucket Tank

WYPERFELD NATIONAL PARK

L. Brambruk Ck
Dattuck
Burroin
Wathe

Hopetoun West
Nypo
LAKE ALBACUTYA
PARK
Lake Albacutya
Yaapeet
Hopetoun
Lake Coorong

Goyura
Hopevale
Rosebery

Albacutya
21
48
Beulah

Ross L. Ck
Kurnbrunin
Pella
Rainbow
77
16 Kenmare
Beulah West
25
Galaquil
Brim
61

Lake Hindmarsh
Werrap
Pullut
Brentwood
Dalmallee
68
22

32
Ellam
Willenabrina
Lah

Perenna
Lake Hindmarsh
Angip
Yellangip
Crymillan
Batchica

Baker
Netherby
Lorquon West
Detpa
Jeparit
Peppers Plain
45
Aubrey
Warracknabeal
18

Yanac
21
Lorquon
22 Allanby
27
Cannum

Broughton
Yanac South
Woorak West
Ni Ni
45
Tarranyurk
Glenlee
37
Antwerp
20
BORUNG

Telopea Downs
Sandsmere
Bleak House
Boyeo
Propodollah
Balrootan North
Woorak
Katyll
Wallup
Ailsa

Yarrock
Diapur
Nhill
13
Salisbury
39
Gerang Gerung
Arkona
42
Kellalac

Yearinga
Miram
Tarranginnie
13 13 HWY
Kiata 10
17
Dart Dart
Murra Warra
Borung

Bordertown
77
Dinyarrak
Lillimur
Mt. Elgin
40
WESTERN
Winiam East
Dimboola
11
Blackheath
60

Wolseley
43
8 13
Kaniva
13
Lawloit
Kinimakatka Winiam
Wail
Kalkee
Byrneville
Kewe

Pooginagoric
Serviceton
Lillimur South
Miram South
Yanipy
LITTLE DESERT
Pimpinio
35
Jung
10

Custon

Bangham
LITTLE DESERT
45
LITTLE DESERT NATIONAL PARK
Polkemmet
Dahlen
Dooen
Longerenor Drung Drung

Lemon Springs
Grass Flat
Lake Wyn Wyn
Natimuk
Quantong
Vectis
Horsham

Wallabrook
Minimay
Goroke
13
Duffholme
Mitre L.
Mitre Mt. Arapiles
Natimuk
Haven
Green Lake
Drung Sth.

Frances
Neuarpurr
Peronne
Mortat
Gymbowen
Tooan
Lwr Norton
McKenzie Creek
Wonwondah East
Mt. Zero

Binnum
Morea (Carpolac)
Booroopki
Dopewarra
Kangawall
Karnak
HIGHWAY 98
Tooan East
Noradjuha
Wonwondah North
Flat Rock Caves
6

Tallageira
Bringalbert
Ozenkadnook
Cooper L.
L. Koynock
L. Karnak
Lake Charchap
Nurrabiel
Mockinya
Lah-Arum

Kybybolite
Patyah
Ullswater
Pine Hut L.
Miga Lake
Lake Bow
Clear Lake
Jallumba
Connangorach
Wartook

Hynam
Jessie
Apsley
53
WIMMERA
Lake Yallakar
Charam
Miga Lake
Clear Lake
Toolondo
77

Naracoorte
Edenhope
Lake Yampitcha
Wallace
Wombelano
North L.
Jeffries
Telangatuk East
Cherrypool
Zumsteins
McKenzie Falls
GRAMPIANS

Koppamurra
Meereek
Lake Kemi Kemi
Scrubby Lake
Douglas
Centre L.
White L.
Telangatuk
Kanagulk
THE BLACK RANGE
Aboriginal Paintings
Cave of Fishes

Joanna
Langkoop
Kadnook
Powers Creek
Harrow
Mt. Evins
Glenelg
Kahaguk
Balmoral
Rocklands Reservoir
Glenisla

Struan
Glenroy
Wrattonbully
Poolaijelo
Connewirricoo
Moree
Culla
Pigeon Ponds
Glendinning
Cave of Hands
NATION PARK

Comaum
A B C D **50** E F G H I

13

0   10   20   30   40   50km

J   K   L   M   N   61   O   P   Q   R

Gama
Lascelles
26
29
Nyallo
Beulah East
40
Galaquil East
6
Challambra
32
Mellis
Sheep Hills
Bangerang
Homecroft
58 10
Areegra
Bodite
Carron
Nullan
29
Minyip
11
Rupanyup Nth.
13
Coromby
21
Murtoa 16
Rupanyup 109
Lallat
24
Marma
6
Lubeck
Ashens
Wal Wal
WESTERN
Wimmera
Glenorchy
dswells Bridge
8
22
Mt. Difficult
Mt. William
1167m
Halls Gap 12
GRAMPIANS NATIONAL PARK
Cathedral Rock
Mt. William 616m
48
Norval
Moyston
Cathcart 16
Ararat
Dobie
Mt. Ararat
Bayindeen
Chute

Boigbeat
Green Lake
19
79
26
8
10
Banyan
Berriwillock
15
Woomelang
Watchupga
16
64
Curyo
Roseberry East
Kinnabulla
11
Karyrie
Ballapur
10
Birchip
9
Wilkur
10
Morton Plains
61
Beyal
Warmur
9
Watchem
32
53
Massey
19
Litchfield
16
Lake Buloke
Buloke
Carron
Lawler
40
Laen Nth.
Donald
Laen
18
Rich Avon
Burrereo
Cope Cope
Swanwater West
39
Swanwater South
27
Avon Plains
Traynors Lagoon
Banyena
Lallat Nth.
Burrum
21
Marnoo
Mitchells Hill
Gre Gre
Marnoo West
Wallaloo
HIGHWAY
Rupanyup Sth.
Warranook
24
Kanya
Wallaloo East
Willaring
Riachella
Callawadda
Morrl Morrl
Campbells Bridge
Greens Creek
Tulkara
Deep Lead
23
Joel Joel
35
Lake Lonsdale
Illawarra
Stawell
14 HWY
24
Bellellen
Bunjil Caves
31
Great Western
Dunneworthy
Pomonal
Jallukar
30
Rhymney Reef
Armstrong
Warra Yadin
Ben Nevis
18
Warrak
Mt. Cole
Mt. Buangor

CALDER
16
Sutton
13
Warnel
16
Jil Jil
Nullawil
Whirily
43 HWY
Narraport
11
Thalia
Wycheproof
79
Chirrup
14
Banyenong
21
Jeffcott North
Jeffcott
26
Dooboobetic
Gooroc
Slaty Creek
16
Navarre
Teddington Res.
63
Redbank
Barkly
Frenchmans
Moonambel
Warrenmang
Percydale
Shays Flat
Joel South
18
Crowlands
Glenlofty
Glenshee
Eversley
63
Elmhurst
PYRENEES
14
Amphitheatre

Meatian
Mumbel
Culgoa
Kalpienung
L. Lalbert
Lalbert
29
Towaninny
18
Dumosa
Ninyeunook
Bunguluke
Fairview
Glenloth
31
Teddywaddy
Wooroonook
Barrakee
Woosang
Charlton
15 HWY
BORUNG 42
BORUNG
Yeungroon
44
Nine Mile
Coonooer Bridge
Berrimal
St.Arnaud
Mooler
13
Koorch
Logan
Carapooee
Emu
39
Rostron
Winjallock
Stuart Mill
Paradise
14
Archdale
Natte Yallock
Tanwood
Rathscar
Glenpatrick
Avoca
Mt. Avoca 750m
Bung Bong
Lamplough

Mystic Park
Lake Charm
Capels Crossing
Myall
Culfearne
Barham
Koondrook
Westby
18
Bael Bael
Lake Bael Bael
Fairley
Teal Point
Koroop
Kerang
Sandhill Lake
Normanville
Dingwall
Langville
Lake Meering
Appin
Macorna
Rowland
47
Mincha
Budgerum
Koorack Koorack
52
Oakvale
Gredgwin
Minmindie
Barraport
Catumnal
Appin South
Loddon Vale
Canary Is. South
Pyramid Hill
Gladfield
19
Yarrawalla
Boort
21
Narrewillock
Lake Marmal
Lake Marmal
27
Mysia
Fernihurst
Jarklin
Calivil
Wychitella
Buckrabanyule
16
Borung
24
Bears Lagoon
Pompapiel
Korong Vale
Wedderburn
Fiery Flat
Serpentine
58
Wedderburn Junct.
Powlett Plains
Glenalbyn
Kurraca West
Kurraca
Kurting
Glenloth
49
Fentons Creek
Wehla
Mt. Kooyoora
Melville Caves
Salisbury West
Inglewood
Bridgewater
Burkes Flat
Kingower
Rheola
Arnold West
Arnold
Derby
79
Leichardt
McIntyres
Llanelly
Moliagul
Murphys Creek
16
Tarnagulla
Newbridge
Woodstock
Marong
Cochranes Creek
13
Bealiba
Goldsborough
Mt. Bealiba
Painswick
14
Dunolly
Laanecoorie Res.
Laanecoorie
Shelbourne
Bradford
Dunluce
Bet Bet
Betley
Eddington
18
Timor West
Havelock
Baringhup East
Wareek
Bowenvale
Carisbrook
Maldon
Alma
26 HWY
Maryborough
Moolort
Welshmans Reef
Amherst
Daisy Hill
Majorca
Strathlea
Cairn Curran Res.
Tullaroop Res.
Strangways
Sandon
Clydesdale
Talbot
Campbelltown
Glengower
Yandoit
Franklinford
Werona
Burnbank
Dunach
Evansford
Lexton
Mt. Lonarch
19
Beckworth
Clunes
Ullina
Lawrence
Smeaton

J   K   L   M   N   51   O   P   Q   R

Grid columns: A B C D E F G H I
Grid rows: 1–13

Major towns and places:

Kerang, Barham, Koondrook, Cohuna, Gunbower, Echuca, Moama, Mathoura, Barmah, Picola, Nathalia, Yalca, Ulupna, Tongala, Kyabram, Merrigum, Tatura, Stanhope, Rushworth, Murchison, Murchison East, Nagambie, Seymour, Bendigo, Eaglehawk, Epsom, Heathcote, Elmore, Rochester, Inglewood, Bridgewater, Maldon, Castlemaine, Maryborough, Kyneton, Daylesford, Kilmore, Broadford, Lancefield.

Other localities (selection):
Lake Charm, Myall, Capels Crossing, Culfearne, Westby, Fairley, Teal Point, Koroop, Gannawarra, Kerang East, South Kerang, Mead, McMillans, Thule, Caldwell, Bunnaloo, Lake Moira, Top Is., Bearii, Dingwall, Langville, Lake Meering, Appin, Appin South, Leaghur, Canary Is., Loddon Vale, Tragowel, Rowland, Macorna, Leitchville, Wee Wee Rup, Kow Swamp, Torrumbarry Weir, Womboota, Barnes, Kanyapella, Narioka, Picola North, Yalca North, Barwo, Waaia, Minmindie, Gladfield, Pyramid Hill, Bald Rock, Mt. Hope, Terrick Terrick, Sylvaterre, Roslynmead, Wharparilla Nth, Wharparilla, Echuca Village, Koyuga, Yambuna, Kotupna, McCoys Bridge, Wyuna, Undera Nth, Kaarimba, Mundoona, Yando, Boort, Canary Is. South, Durham Ox, Yarrawalla, Mologa, Mt. Terrick Terrick, Mitiamo, Kotta, Bamawm Extension, Bamawm, Strathallan, Simmie, Kyvalley, St. Germains, Undera, Zeerus, Mysia, Fernihurst, Jarklin, Calivil, Prairie, Milloo, Lockington, Tennyson, Ballendella, Nanneella, Fairy Dell, Timmering, Cooma, Girgarre, Byrneside, Ardmona, Gillieston, Borung, Bears Lagoon, Pompapiel, Dingee, Warragamba, Diggora, Hunter, Corop, Green Lake, Waranga, Lancaster, Fiery Flat, Serpentine, Tandarra, Drummartin, Kamarooka, Mt. Burrumboot, Runnymede, Burkumboot, Colbinabbin, Colbinabbin West, Wanalta, Mathiesons, Karook, Harston, Toolamba, Dhurringile, Arcadie, Glenalbyn, Powlett Plains, Summerfield, May Reef, Avonmore, Neilborough East, Neilborough, Creek View, Whroo, Waranga, Moora, Kurting, Salisbury West, Raywood, Sebastian, Goornong, Wellsford, Barnadown, Myola, Cornella, Angustown, Goulburn Weir, Reedy Lake, Wahring, Kingower, Arnold West, Arnold, Derby, Leichardt, Woodvale, Huntly, Bagshot, Fosterville, Muskerry West, Toolleen, Redcastle, Moormbool, Graytown, Wattle Vale, Mitchellstown, Bailieston, Mt. Black +318m, L. Nagambie, Longwood, Llanelly, Murphys Creek, Newbridge, Marong, Myers Flat, Maiden Gully, Epsom, Longlea, Axedale, Mt. Camel, Knowsley, Ladys Pass, Costerfield, Gardner Ck., Tabilk, Monea, Locksley, Tarnagulla, Woodstock, Lockwood, Kangaroo Flat, Junortoun, Strathfieldsaye, Eppalock, Derrinal, Mt. Ida +450m, Mitchellstown, Avenel, Mt. Bernard, Tarcombe, Painswick, Laanecoorie Res., Laanecoorie, Lockwood South, Shelbourne, Sedgwick, Ravenswood, Axe Creek, Lake Eppalock, Pilchers Bridge, Argyle, Costerfield, Majors Line, Mt. Puckapunyal +413m, Puckapunyal, Army Camp, Northwood, Dunolly, Betley, Eddington, Bradford, Ravenswood South, Sutton Grange, Myrtle Bridge, Lyal, Mia Mia, Redesdale, Puckapunyal, Whiteheads Creek, Kobyboy, Havelock, Baringhup East, Harcourt, Barkers Ck., Cairn Curran Res., Mt. Alexander +741m, Gowar, Faraday, Chewton, Metcalfe, Barfold, Glenhope, Tooborac, Pyalong, Glenaroua, Tallarook, Granite, Highlands, Carisbrook, Moolort, Welshmans Reef, Campbells Ck., Elphinstone, Taradale, Langley, Sidonia, Edgecombe, Emu Flat, Bayton, Nulla Vale, Mollisons, Kerrisdale, Trawool, Mt. Eaglehawk, Daisy Hill, Majorca, Joyces Ck., Newstead, Yapeen, Guildford, Vaughan, Malmsbury, Pastoria, High Camp, Broadford, Tyaak, Homewood, Tullaroop Res., Strathlea, Sandon, Clydesdale, Glenluce, Drummond, Langley, High Camp, Reedy Creek, Ladys Hill, Duhach, Glengower, Campbelltown, Yandoit, Franklinford, Mt. Franklin, Denver, Kyneton, Piters Ck., Carlsruhe, Cobaw, Lancefield, Springfield, Wandong, Hazeldene, Clunes, Ullina, Werona, Launceston, Malmsbury Res., Coliban Res., Tylden, Newham, Rochford, Romsey, Kilmore, Clonbinane, Lawrence, Smeaton, Hepburn Springs, Daylesford, Glenlyon.

Rivers / features: Murray River, Riverina, Edward R., Tuppal Ck., Bullatale Ck., Goulburn River, Campaspe River, Loddon River, Serpentine Creek, Coliban R., Waranga Res., Great Dividing Range, Warby Range.

Highways / routes: Murray Valley Hwy, Loddon Valley Hwy, Northern Hwy, Midland Hwy, Calder Hwy, McIvor Hwy, Goulburn Valley Hwy, Hume Hwy, Great Dividing Range.

Route numbers shown: 16, 75, 79, 31, 39, 22, 52, 57, 48, 82, 97, 47, 60, 21, 29.

COPYRIGHT SP AUSTRALIA LTD

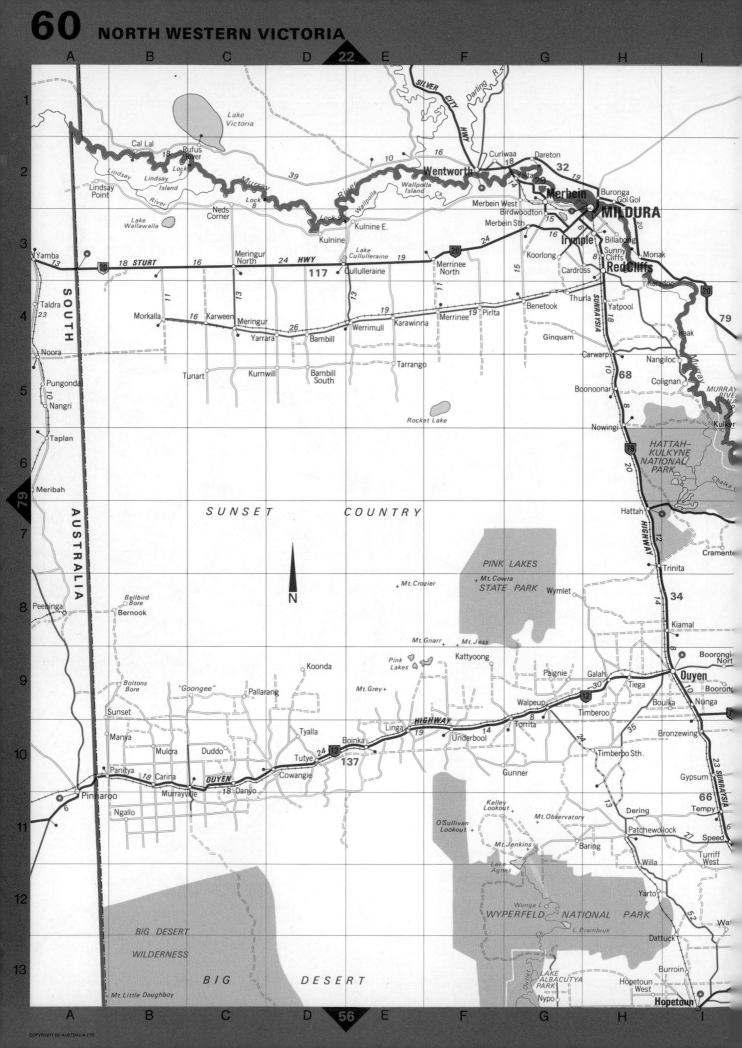

0 10 20 30 40 50km

J K L M N O P Q R

23

Junction Tank

25

Lake Ganaway

Penarie

27

NEW SOUTH WALES

STURT HIGHWAY 77

20

16

Euston Robinvale 22

Balranald

13 17 8 Belcher Is. Lake Powell 27 Murrumbidgee 16

Happy Valley Bannerton Kyndalyn HWY 16 Boundary Bend 74 Murray Condoulpe Yanga Lake 20 75

66 VALLEY 61 Narrung 21 58 23

Wemen Margooya Yungera 18 28 Piambie Kenley 35 80

MURRAY 36 Koorkab Koolonong Haysdale 5 Kyalite 29

Annuello 13 Goodnight Edward River Moolpa 29

Koimbo 19 16 18

Winnambool 36 Bolton Natya Tooleybuc Stony Crossing 42 Moulamein

Kulwin 24 Prooinga 42 Piangil 23 Dilpura 69 31

Wagant Lietpar Manangatang Tudor Towan Wood Wood Koraleigh

Mittyack Cocamba 16 Miralie MURRAY 43 Speewa 16

Woornack 6 24 Yarraby Nyah Vlhifera 16

CALDER Chinkapook 40 Nyah West Beverford Tyntynder Central VALLEY Tyntynder South 13

Pier Millan 90 Day Trap Ryanby Pira Woorinen Swan Hill 19

Nandaly 19 Chillingollah Nowie North 18 6 19 13

Nyarrin 6 Lake Wahpool Waitchie 22 Pental Lake Boga Fish Point Gonn Crossing

Turriff East 24 Lake Tyrrell Tyrrell Downs L. Timboram Long Plains Gowanford 10 Ultima 75 18 Goschen 16 Tresco Benjeroop Murrabit 6

Ninda Sea Lake 24 Lalbert Road Kunat Tresco West 60 Myall Culfearne

34 19 6 Boigbeat 79 19 Meatian Mumbel 25 Mystic Park Lake Charm 16 27 Westby Koondrook

Lascelles 26 Green Lake 10 L. Lalbert Lalbert Beauchamp Bael Bael Fairley Teal Point

Woomelang 16 21 Banyan Berriwillock 13 Culgoa 29 Koorack Koorack Sandhill Lake Kerapg

57

0 10 20 30 40 50km

23

A B C D E F G H I

NEW SOUTH WALES

Cookardinia
Little Billabong
Batlow
Blowering Resr
Carabost
Bago Kumara
Talbingo
Culcairn Morven 31 Talbingo Resr
Holbrook Courabyra
Walbundrie
Wala Walla Gerogery Rosewood
Burrumbuttock 68 Woomargama Tumbarumba
53 Mullengandra Talmalmo Jingellic Ournie
Jindera Bowna Thologolong Walwa 52
Ettamogah Lake Hume Wymah Fy Mt Alfred Welaregang Tooma
Lavington Talgarno Bungil 113 Guys Forest Cudgewa Nth Tintaldra
Barnawartha Mt Talgarno Burrowye BURROWA–PINE MTN. NAT. PARK Towong 23 Kharicoban
ALBURY Hume Weir Granya Mt Firebrace Mt Burrowa Corryong Towong Upr Geehi
Wodonga Huon Hill Bonegilla Mt Lawson Koetong 77 Shelley Cudgewa Wabba Biggara Mt Toolong 1665m
Baranduda Ebden Bethanga Koetong Darbyshire Berringama Colac Colac Thowgla Olsens Lookout
Wooragee Nth Barandula 47 Tallangatta Jarvis Ck The Cascade Lucyvale Thowgla Upr 135 Geehi
Leneva Huon Bullioh Mt Bullioh Tallangatta Valley Nariel Ck. Mt Kosciusko 2173m The Chalet
Indigo Upr Kiewa Sandy Ck. Noorongong Yabba Valley Wyeeboo Mt Cudgewa 1100m Upr. Nariel Tom Groggin
Yackandandah Allans Flat Charleroi Bullhead Ck. Cravensville Bucheen Ck. Mt Tempest WAY Dead Horse Gap
Back Creek Osbornes Flat Kergunyah Connels Peak 949m Pilot Lookout
Hurdle Flat Kergunyah Sth. Sandy Ck. Upr. Mt Benambra 1476m Dartmouth Sassafras Gap Mt Gibbo Mt Pinnabar
Stanley Gundowring Tallandoon Mitta Dartmouth Dam 148 Mt Hope Buckwong
Bruarong Mt Stanley 1051m Glen Gundowring Mitta Granite Flat Dartmouth Reservoir Mt Murphy
Mudgegonga 84 Dederang Eskdale Little Snowy Ck. Granite Peak Lightning Ck. Mt Misery
Barwidgee Ck. The Pinnacles Gundowring Upr. Mt Doorchap Track Mt Pinnabar
Ovens Rosewhite Running Ck. Mt Tawonga Mitta Mt Cooper 1319m Forest Hill
Happy Valley Kancoona Mongans Bridge Mt Bogong 1988m Sunnyside Mt Fraser Mt Cobberas No.1
Eurobin Kancoona Sth. Coral Bank 167 Mt Bogong Central Glen Wills Deep Ck. Mt Cobberas No.2
MT BUFFALO NATIONAL PARK Havilah Mullindolingong Mt Arthur Spion Kopje Glen Valley Porphyry Hill Big Hill Mt Stradbroke
Mt Porepunkah Redbank Mt Emu Junction Dam Mt Nelse The Knocker The Brothers Suggan Buggan
Mt Buffalo Chalet Porepunkah Tawonga Mt Little Emu Little Spion Kopje Mt Wills 1760m Lake Omeo The Brothers
Brookside Bright Tawonga Gap 30 Mt Beauty KIEWA HYDRO ELECTRIC SCHEME Mt Nelse Benambra BOWEN MOUNTAINS Little River Falls
White Hill Wandiligong Freeburgh Big Hill Hollands Knob Marm Pt Mt Misery Wulgulmerang
Mt Buffalo 1721m Buckland Smoko Pyramid Hill Falls Ck Rocky Valley Resr. Sharmonvale Mt Tambo Gelantipy
Buckland Upr. Harrietville Mt Feathertop 1922m Mt McKay Buckety Anglers Rest Hinnomunjie Mt Nunniong Mt Statham
Mt McIvor Paddy Hill Mt Little Feathertop Loch Mt Cope 1837m Grey Hill Mt Battery Sams Hill Mt Shaw Green Hill
BOGONG 1862m Hotham Heights 113 Days Hill Omeo Bindi Mt Deception Butchers Ridge
Mt Selwyn 1524m Mt Hotham NATIONAL PARK Cobungra Round Hill Mt Bindi
BARRY MOUNTAINS Mt St. Bernard DARGO HIGH PLAINS Mt Parslow Mt Livingstone 1227m Mt Phipps OMEO Tongio
WONNANGATTA–MOROKA NATIONAL PARK Mt Hart Basalt Knob Cassilis Mt Nugong Tongio West Swifts Ck. Doctors Flat

RIVERINA HWY OLYMPIC WAY HUME HWY MURRAY VALLEY HWY KIEWA VALLEY OMEO HWY ALPINE HWY KOSCIUSKO NATIONAL PARK

59 30

N

Places of Interest

1 Armytage House E3
2 Belmont Common Railway .. F6
3 Geelong Railway Station F2
4 Hospital G3
5 Memorial Art Gallery F2
6 Police Station F2
7 Post Office F2
8 RACV Branch Office F3
9 Tourist Bureau F2
10 Town Hall F2

Places of Interest

1 Ballarat Base Hospital D12
2 Ballarat Fine Art Gallery F12
3 Ballarat Railway Station F11
4 Eureka Stockade H12
5 Historical Museum G12
6 Montrose Cottage and Museum G12
7 Old Curiosity Shop H12
8 Police Station F12
9 Post Office F12
10 RACV Branch Office E12
11 Regional Tourist Information Office ... E11
12 Sovereign Hill Historical Park G14
13 Town Hall E12
14 Victorian Govt. Tourist Bureau F12

0   2   4   6   8km

A B C D 59 E F G H I

To Berrigan

NEW SOUTH WALES

VICTORIA

Racetrack

Racetrack

Howlong

RIVERINA HIGHWAY

To Albury

Lindemans Cellars

St Leonards Cellars

Flour Mills

All Saints

Ruins

Ruins

Golf Course

MURRAY RIVER

+Mount Ochtertyre

Corowa

Rec. Res.

Wahgunyah

To Wodonga

KILBORN ROAD

10

Numerous Mine Tailings

Abandoned Mine

Fairfield

MURRAY VALLEY HIGHWAY

Morris 'Mia Mia' Winery

Cemetery

Lake Moodemere

COROWA ROAD

Chambers Rosewood

Gold Battery

RUTHERGLEN

Bottle Water Tower

12

Olive Hills

GILLS ROAD

Gehrig Bros

To Wodonga

Seppelt & Sons

Stanton & Killeen's Gracerray

16

Campbell's 'Bobbie Burns'

Racecourse

Jones Winery

Mine Tailings

CORNISHTOWN RD

Rose Hill+

Bullers 'Calliope'

BULLERS ROAD

Rifle Range

Mt Ophir Historic Winery

+Mount Ophir

10

Barnawartha

Golf Course

To Wodonga

WARRENS RD

KINGS ROAD

JACKS ROAD

NORONG ROAD

BRIDGE ROAD

CHANDLERS ROAD

SLAUGHTERHOUSE ROAD

GREAT SOUTHERN ROAD

CHILTERN VALLEY ROAD

Murdering Hut Creek

RUTHERGLEN MAIN ROAD

31

LILLIPUT

PEVITTS ROAD

14

Lilliput

+Terrill Hill

18

7

Magenta Mine

CHAIN

THREE

Black Dog Creek

Mine Tailings

Chiltern Valley

Mine Tailings

Monument

Numerous Mine Tailings

Chiltern

Golf Course

Brickworks

Cem

59

Diddah Creek

Diddah Creek

Racecourse

31

13

HUME HIGHWAY

Gayfers Winery

306m +Skeleton Hill

Black Dog Creek

Ruins

N

Springhurst

Mount Warby +

Yellow Creek

WANGARATTA

Racecourse

Sewage Treatment Plant

Cem

31

Tarrawingee

Hodgson Creek

OVENS HIGHWAY

Cem

Tarrawingee

Taminick Homestead

Booth Bros.

WARBY RANGE

Racetrack

OVENS RIVER

Rec Res

Everton

Taminick

Lake Mokoan

Tower

Ruins

Ruins

Numerous

Tobacco

Monument

Everton

Baileys Bundarra

HUME HIGHWAY

Fifteen Mile Creek

Cem

Kilns

Milawa

Rec.Res

Ruins

Monument

Water Tower

Brown Bros

Ruins

Morris Markwood Estate

Markwood

Monument

Mount Glenrowan +514m

One Mile Creek

To Myrtleford

To Benalla

Ned Kelly Statue

Glenrowan

A B C 59 D E F G H I

Maps of Tasmania

Location Map

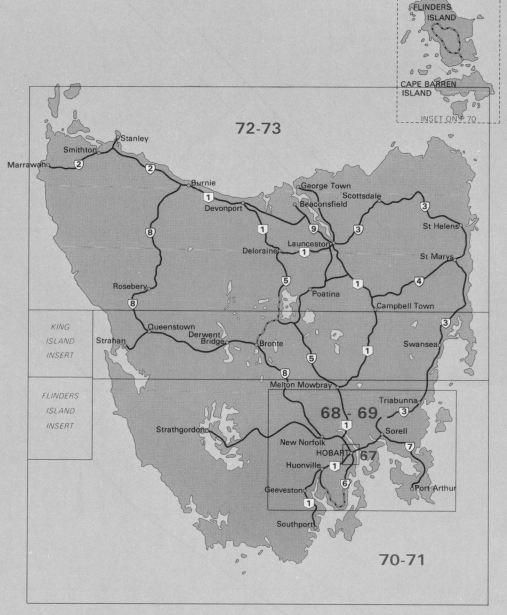

CENTRAL HOBART & CENTRAL LAUNCESTON 66

KING ISLAND

INSET ON P.70

FLINDERS ISLAND

CAPE BARREN ISLAND

INSET ON P.70

72-73

Stanley
Smithton
Marrawah
Burnie
Devonport
George Town
Scottsdale
Beaconsfield
St Helens
Launceston
Deloraine
St Marys
Rosebery
Poatina
Campbell Town
Queenstown
Derwent Bridge
Bronte
Swansea
Strahan
Melton Mowbray
Triabunna
Sorell
Strathgordon
New Norfolk
HOBART
67
Huonville
Port Arthur
Geeveston
Southport

KING ISLAND INSERT

FLINDERS ISLAND INSERT

68 - 69

70-71

Hobart

North Hobart
West Hobart
Glebe
Queens Domain
City
Battery Point

Elizabeth Matriculation College
Holy Trinity Church
St.Andrews Pk
St.Marys Cathedral
St.Marys College
Royal ACT Headquarters
St.Virgils College
Centrepoint Arcade
Ansett Terminal
Hadleys Hotel
State Library
Tourist Bureau
St.Davids Cathedral
Police Headquarters
Royal Hobart Hospital
Post Office
Town Hall
Museum and Art Gallery
Franklin Square
Constitution Dock
Victoria Dock
TAA Term.
Olympic Swimming Pool
Cenotaph
Naval Depot
Macquarie Point
Railway Goods Yard
Railway Depot
Macquarie Wharf
Sullivans Cove
Parliament House
Parlt. Square
St.Davids Park
Salamanca
National Trust Info. Office
Lenna Motor Inn
Princes Park
Princes Wharf
Brooke St. Pier
Elizabeth St.Pier
Ferry Wharf
Castray Esplanade
Folk Museum (Narryna)
Anglesea Barracks
School
To West Point Hotel & Casino

Street names: ARTHUR ST, BURNETT ST, MURRAY, MARY, TASMA, ELIZABETH, CHURCH ST, ARGYLE, CAMPBELL, BROOKER, SCOTT ST, GLEBE ST, SHORT ST, EDWARD, ABERDEEN ST, DAVIES AV, TASMAN HWY, UNION ST, BROWNE, DEVONSHIRE, WINDSOR, PATERNOSTER, BRISBANE, HARRINGTON, WARWICK, WATKINS AV, BARRACK, BATHURST, WATCHORN ST, VICTORIA, MARKET PL, DUNN ST, SACKVILLE ST, SLIN ST, EVANS, HUNTER, WELLINGTON, PATRICK, MELVILLE, MOLLE, LIVERPOOL, COLLINS, MORRISON, FRANKLIN, CAVELL ST, BATHURST, GOULBURN, MACQUARIE, DAVEY, SANDY BAY, HAMPTON, WILMOT ST, GLADSTONE ST, MONTPELLIER RET., SALAMANCA PL, CASTRAY, KELLY, SOUTH, RUNNYMEDE, STOWELL AV, JAMES, HAMPTON RD, FINDLAY ST, AMELIA ST, HUGOS LA, FREDERICK ST, PROSPECT PL, ROBERTS ST, FOREST, BEN ST, FARADAY ST, CANN ST, FRANKLIN WHARF, ESPLANADE, PATRICK

Scale: 0 100 200 300 m — One-way Streets shown →

N

Launceston

Inveresk
City
East Launceston
Trevallyn

Ogilvie Park
Railway Station
N.T.C.A. Ground
Kings Wharf
Charles Bridge
Dry Dock
Town Point
Royal Park
Kings Park
Cataract Gorge
Zig Zag Reserve
Trevallyn Res
Penny Royal Mills
Walking Track
Kings Bridge
Cenotaph
Art Gallery & Museum
Police HQ
Civic Square
Public Library
Town Hall
Post Office
Tourist Bureau
Ansett Terminal
TAA Terminal
Cimitiere
Esk Brewery
Albert Hall
City Park
Launceston Swimming Centre
Windmill Hill Reserve
Brisbane St. Mall
Quadrant
Princess Square
St.Vincents Hospital
Sports Ground
St.Georges Square
To Launceston Gen. Hosp.

River North Esk
River Tamar
Victoria Bridge

Street names: GODERICH ST, LINDSAY ST, TAROONA ST, BATHURST, WILLIAM, CHARLES, ST JOHN, CAMERON, WELLINGTON, PATERSON, THE KINGSWAY, BRISBANE, BATHURST, YORK, MARGARET, MIDDLE, ELIZABETH, FREDERICK, CANNING, SHIELDS ST, GEORGE, ESPLANADE, TAMAR, BRISBANE, VINCENT ST, EARL, WEYMOUTH, FAWKNER ST, BIFRONS CT, INNES ST, LAWRENCE, WILLIS, RACECOURSE, ELPHIN, CLARENCE, ABBOTT ST, HIGH, WELMAN, MY STREET, STEWART, ARTHUR ST, ADELAIDE, SPENCER ST, SCOTT ST, HOPKINS, ANN ST, SQUARE, HORNSEY, LYTTLETON, SANDEN, HOPKINS, PHILLIP ST, UNION ST, WEST TAMAR HWY, TREVALLYN RD, STILLEK RD, PARK RD, BRIDGE, KINGS, LYNDSAY

West Tamar Hwy / Trevallyn
73 / 9 / 3

Scale: 0 100 200 300 m — One-way Streets shown →

N

0 1 2 3 4 km

A B C D E F G H I

68

River Derwent

East Derwent Hwy

Bowens Monument

Bowen Bridge

Bowen Pk

Risdon Cove

Risdon Rd

Saunderson Rd

Gaol

Gardenia Rd

Coobar Rd

Sugarloaf

Risdon Vale

Sugarloaf Hill

Flagstaff Gully Reservoir

Goodwood

Elwick Bay

Elwick Racecourse

Goodwood Rd

Howard Rd

Acton Cr.

Prince of Wales Bay

Risdon

Porter Bay

Wharf

Road to be closed

Zinc Works

Clinton Rd

B32

Brooker Hwy

Grove Rd

King George Pk

Glenorchy RS

Bowden St

Main Rd

Leonard Av

Derwent Pk Junc.

Royal Show ground

Sunderland St

Derwent Park

Lampton Av.

1

Derwent Park Rd

Maple Av.

Bayswater Rd.

Gormanston Rd

Charles St

Amy St

Hopkins St

Albert Rd

Lennox Av.

Ashbolt Av.

Bowen Rd.

Central Av

Springfield

Clydesdale Av.

Barossa Av.

Fourth Av.

Springfield Av.

Garden Av

Second Av

West Moonah

Devines Rd

Tower Rd.

Moonah

New Town Oval

Florence St.

Swanston St.

Risdon Rd

New Town

Bellevue Pde.

Queens Walk

Lutana

Reservoir

Derwent

New Town Bay

Selfs Point

Cornelian Bay Cemetery

Cornelian Bay

Shag Bay

Recn. Res.

Geilston Bay

Golf Links Rd

Fairfield Rd

Karoola Rd

Karoola Rd

Flagstaff Gully

Lindisfarne

Natone Hill 129m

Moirunna St.

Derwent

Talune St.

Lincoln St.

Lime Kiln Point

Koomela Bay

Lindisfarne Rec Res

Res.

Flagstaff Gully

A3

East Derwent Hwy

Kalang Av.

Lenah Valley

Girrabong Rd

Creek Rd

Forster St.

Pedder St.

Montagu St.

Clare St.

Giblin St.

Augusta Rd

Doyle Av.

Gordon Av

Giblin St.

Elphinstone Rd.

Mt. Stuart

Mt. Stuart Rd.

Mt Stuart Reservoir Lookout

Lenah Valley

Lady Franklin Museum

Brushy Creek Rd

Pottery Rd

Rose Bay

Topham

Esplanade

Kaoota Rd

Riawena Rd

Gordons Hill

Gordons Hill Rd

Kangaroo Bay Rvt.

Tasman Hwy

Montagu Bay

Akuna St.

Rosny

Rosny Hill 94m

Kellatie

Ninna

Bastick St.

Rosny Point

Kangaroo Bay

Bellerive

Cambridge Rd

Alma St.

Clarence St.

Beach Rd

Hill St.

Scott St.

Queen St.

King St.

Abbott St.

Victoria

Esplanade

Kangaroo Bluff

Pavilion Point

Tasman Bridge

Botanical Gardens

Govt. House

Nth. Hobart

Nth. Hobart Oval

Athletic Centre

Domain

Queens Domain

Upper Domain

Lower Domain Rd

Glebe

T.C.A. Ground

Tasman Hwy

A3

West Hobart

Knocklofty

Arthur St.

Hill St.

Warwick St.

Woodsn'v't. Cr.

Patrick St.

Faraday St.

Melville St.

Burnett St.

Commercial Rd.

Argyle St.

Federal St.

Campbell St.

Elizabeth St.

Murray St.

Harrington St.

Goulburn St.

Liverpool St.

Collins St.

Olympic Pool

Naval Depot

Macquarie Point

Cenotaph

HOBART

Salvator Rd.

Forest Rd.

Macquarie St.

Davey St.

St.Georges TCA

Napoleon St.

Battery Point

Secheron Point

Slipyards

River Derwent

Cascades

Old Farm Rd

Hobart Rvt.

Cascade Rd.

Brewery

Sth. Hobart

Washington St.

D'arcy St.

Adelaide St.

Davey St.

Philinger St.

Digney St.

Regent St.

Queen St.

Grosvenor St.

Sandy Bay Rd

Sandy Bay

Casino

Wrest Point

Huon Rd

Marlyn Rd

Strickland Av.

Waterworks Rd

Princes St.

Lord St.

View St.

Romilly St.

University of Tasmania

Dynnyrne

A6

Huon Highway

B64

Southern Outlet

Proctors Rd

Tolmans Hill

Olinda Gv.

Nelson Rd

Gv.

Mount Nelson

Hobart Matriculation College

A6

Ridgeway Rd

Chimney Pot Hill

Resr.

Sandy Bay

Red Chapel Av.

Maning Av.

Churchill Av.

Derwent Water Av.

Waimea Av.

Nutgrove Beach

Channel

Sandown Park

Long Point

Long Beach

Lower Sandy Bay

Bathing Sheds

Blinking Billy Point

Lookout

Wayne Av.

N

Ouse
Cluny Power Stn.
A10
Lawrenny
Chiltern Hill
+ Mt. Clark
Repulse R.
Repulse Power Stn.
River
Broad R.
Dunrobin
Langloh
Hamilton
Clyde
Dew Rivt.
Hollow Tree
Black Tier + 775m
Melton Mowbray
Mt. Mercer 548m +
MIDLAND
Kempton
Quoin Mt. 900m +
Weedons Fords
Huntingdon Tier 545m
Meadowbank Lake
13
Espies Crag 667m
Pelham
Mt. Spode 521m
8
5
Dysart
34
Mt. Bethune 508m +
35
TYENT
A10
Allenvale Rvt.
Taylors Tier 640m
13
River
Mangalore Tier
Bagdad
HWY
Butlers Hill 670m
Ellendale
Meadowbank Power Station
Derwent
Tanina
Elderslie
8
Mangalore
Mt. Field East 1269m
Fentonbury
13
Gretna
Broadmarsh
Jordan
Cobbs Hill
Winton Hill 6
Pontville
MT. FIELD NATIONAL PARK
Mt. Field West
L. Webster
Nicholls
16
Westerway
Karanja
Glenora
Rosegarland
Platform Peak
Mt. Dromedary 989m +
Dromedary Upr.
11
Brighton
Tea Tree
Russell Falls C.
National Park 33
Mt. Fenton
Macquarie Plains
3
Black Hills
Dromedary
R
6
Bridgewater
Cove Hill 239m
L. Seal
L. Belcher
L. Dobson
Fenton
Lady Barron C.
Bushy Park
11
A10 12
Plenty
Hayes
Boyer
A10
Granton
10
Claremont
Old Beach
ANM Private Road
Tyenna R.
Tyenna
5
Fitzgerald
Park R.
13
Salmon Ponds
HWY
13
4
Magra
11
Sorell
Berriedale
Mt. + Faulkner 901m
Mt. Directic +448m
GORDON RIVER RD
Barron RD
Maydena
Uxbridge
Feilton
New Norfolk
5 32
Malbina
Dry Ck.
12
Glenlusk
10
Glenorchy
Moonah
21
Risdon
Toll Gate
Styx
Moogara
Glen Fern
Mount Lloyd
Lachlan
Collins Cap
Collinsvale
Collsvale
11
New Town
Mt. Styx
Plenty
Lachlan R.
Mount Rvt.
Collins Cap + 1091m
HOBART
Collins Bonnet + 1260m
Mt. Wellington 1270m The Pinnacle
12
10
N
SNOWY RANGE
Little Denison
Russell
Lonnavale
Blue Hill 756m
Mt. Montagu 1061m
Mountain River
Ferntree
Ridgeway
12
A6
34
Mt. Weld
Neika
10
Taroor Shot Tower
Weld
Judds Ck.
Mt. Misery 695m +
Crabtree
Longley Lower
Longley
11
HWY
Leslie Vale
OUTLET
River
Judbury
Lucaston
A6
Grove
37
SOUTHERN
Sandfly
Kingston
35
15
Ranelagh
Herring Back 747m
Kaoota
Boronia Hill
Kingst Beach
Blackma Bay
Glen Huon
5
Huonville
Sandfly Rvt.
Margate
8
Huon Td.
Woodstock
Nierinna
Howden
25
Mt. Louis 313m +
Irving Pan Ck.
HUON
5
Cradoc
Grey Mt. 827m
Pelverata
Snug
North West Bay
Coningham
Denn Point
Snug Pt.
Huon R.
Franklin
Franklin Sth
5
Sandfly Ck.
13
Kettering
Scott Rivt.
17
A6 23
Glaziers Bay
Oyster Cove
HWY
8
Woodbridge
Oyster Cove
Mt. Picton 1327m +
L. Picton
Castle Forbes Bay
Port Huon
20
Cygnet
Nicholls Rvt.
Birchs Bay
Channel
Roberts Hill 206m
L. Riveaux
Geeveston
Cairns Bay
Wattle Grove
Wattle Grove Upr.
Nicholls Rivt.
15
Gardners Bay
Arve R.
Kermandi R.
5
Waterloo
Petcheys Bay
Lymington
Port Cygnet
13
Birchs Bay
16
Green I.
Waratah Lookout
HARTZ MOUNTAINS NATIONAL PARK
Hartz Mt. 1255m
Huon R.
Tongatabu
Surges Bay
Police Pt.
Garden Island
Garden Island Ck.
CHANNEL
Middleton
48
Simpsons Bay
Cracroft
Picton R.
E'Esperance
Mt. Snowy
Glendevie
A6
Garden Id.
14
Gordon
D'Entrecasteaux
Isthmus Bay
SOUTH WEST NATIONAL PARK
Wobbly Ck.
Surveyors Bay
Huon Pt.
Nine Pin Pt.
Simpsons Bay

71

0 5 10 15 20 25 km

J K L M N O P Q R

Rhyndaston
Eldon
Woodsdale
Mt. Hobbs 821m +
Mt. Douglas +
Blue Tier 593m +
MacLaines Ck
Triabunna
A3
Cape Bougainville
Lords Bluff

Colebrook
Levendale
8
Bluff
152m +
Moreys Hill
Okehampton
Cape Boullanger
Convict Ruins
Isle Du Nord

+ Mt. Bains 334m
8
7
Louisville Pt. Horne
Prosser Bay
Quarry Pt.
Spring Beach
Darlington

nby siding
21
Kangaroo Rivt
White Rivt
16
Boomer Hill
Sand R
Back R.
Orford
Stapleton Pt.
Johnson Pt.
Mt. Maria 709m +
Beaching Bay

Coal R
Lowdina
Historic Church
HWY
18
Three Thumbs 549m +
11
MARIA ISLAND NATIONAL PARK
Mistaken Cape

Brown Mt. 792m +
62
Buckland
A3
Rheban
Prosser
Carrickfergus Bay
Booming Bay

Campania
Runnymede
TASMAN
Burst My Gall Hill
Mt. Gatehouse
Tea Tree Rivt
Griffiths
Lachlan
Shoal Bay
Reidle Bay
MARIA ISLAND

kuna
Native Hut Rivt
10
Brushy
Plains
Prossers S.L. 647m +
Sandspit R
Earlham Hill
Pt. Des Galets
Cape Peron

Longs Hill 315m +
6
8
A3
18
Mt. Morrison 471m +
15
Curryjong Rivt
Nugent
Middle Peak
Jacob Hill
Cockle Bay
Cape Bernier
Mercury
Cape Maurouard

Richmond
Australias oldest bridge
Orielton
6
Pawleena
11
Bream R
Welling Trek
SEA

Mt. Lord 279m + Penna
10
Iron R
8
Wattle Hill
15
Gordon S.L. 415m +
Kellevie
Marion

13
Pitt
12
Water
Sorell
Forcett
Ck R
6
Bream Creek
Bay

disarne
26
A3
Midway Pt.
A9
ARTHUR
16
Copping
Cape Paul Lamanon

Cambridge
378m + Mt. Rumney Fine coastal views
14
Hobart Airport
Lewisham
Carlton
10
Blackman Bay
Tasman Memorial North Bay
Cape Frederick Hendrick

Bellerive
12
Seven Mile Beach
9
Dodges Ferry
Carlton
Tasman Monument
Boomer Id.
Humper Bluff

Howrah
Rokeby
Tiger Hd.
5
Fishing
13
Dunalley
Mt. Forestier 320m +
High Yellow Bluff

River
Lauderdale
3
Frederick
Carlton Bluff
Surfing
Primrose Sands
Primrose Pt.
Dunalley Bay
A9
8
HWY
FORESTIER

Droughty Pt.
yfish Pt.
Sandford
Henry
Green Hd.
Fulham Id.
King George Id.
Murdunna
Cape Surville

llibrand Pt.
Cremorne
Sloping Id.
Smooth Id.
Whitehouse Pt.
PENINSULA

Mt. Augustus 163m +
Pipe Clay Lagoon
Bay
Chronicle Pt.
13
Macgregor Peak 592m +

Opossum Bay
16
Clifton Beach
Cape Deslacs
Sloping Main
6
Convict Coal Mine Ruins
Norfolk
Flinders Bay
Flinders Ck
74

South Arm
5
North West Hd.
Gwandalon
Saltwater River
Bay
Deer Pt.
Eaglehawk Bay
Tessellated Pavement
Pirates Bay

Hope Beach
Cape Contrariety
Premaydena Pt.
Eaglehawk Neck
Blow Hole
Devils Kitchen

Cape Direction
Iron Pot
Betsey Island
Mt. Communication
Premaydena
8
9
Taranna
10
Tasmans Arch
Waterfall Bay

Cape Delasorte
Outer North Hd.
Koonya
Signal Hill
O'Hara Bluff

One Tree Pt.
Auk Pt.
8
TASMAN
11
PENINSULA
Thumb Pt.

Storm
Wedge Bay
Nubeena
Oakwood
A9
Hippolyte Rocks

The Yellow Bluff
Wedge Id.
13
Denman
Fortescue Bay
The Lanterns
Cape Hauy

Trumpeter Bay
Bay
10
Highcroft
Radnor
Port Arthur
Mt. Fortescue

Trumpeter Pt.
Stormlea
Remarkable Cave
Port Arthur
Munroe Bight

NORTH BRUNY ISLAND
Church Hill 178m +
Salters Pt.
Mt. Raoul +
West Arthur Hd.
Black Hd.
Cape Pillar

Cape Queen Elizabeth
Raoul Bay
Maingon
Bay
Tasman Id.

h Museum
Cooks Landing Place
dventure Bay
Cape Raoul

TASMAN

J K L M N O P Q R

1 2 3 4 5 6 7 8 9 10 11 12 13

A B C D 72 E F G H I

KING ISLAND

1
Cape Farewell Cape Wickham
Phoques Bay
New Year Islands
Egg Lagoon Yambacoona Lavinia Pt.
Whistle Pt.
31
Reekara
Looraba
Sea Elephant
Sea Elephant Bay
Naracoopa Fraser Bluff
2
Currie Pegarah 26
Parenna
24
Lymwood
Yarra Creek
Bold Head
Pearshape
Grassy
3
Surprise Bay Seal Bay Stokes Pt.
0 10
kilometres

King Island Flinders Island
Launceston
HOBART

FLINDERS ISLAND

West Sister Id.
Bligh Pt. North Pt.
Palana
Cape Frankland
4
Leeka
29
Lughrata Babel Id.
Marshall Bay
FURNEAUX
Emita
Prime Seal Id. Blue Rocks Memana
Arthur Bay 16 Memana Burnett Lagoon
5
Whitemark Cameron Inlet
East Kangaroo Id.
Trousers Pt. 15 Ranga Loccota Lady Barron
Mt Chappell Id. MT STRZELECKI NATL. PARK Great Dog Id.
Goose Id. Anderson Id. Vansittart Id. Puncheon Pt.
Badger Id. Franklin Sound
Long Id. GROUP
6
Cape Barren Island Cape Barren Island
Kent Bay Cape Barren
Clarke Id.
7
Look Out Heads
0 10
kilometres
Banks Strait

ZEEHAN HWY
A10
Badger R
Henty R
Tully R
LYELL HWY
Margaret Lake Margaret
Yolande R
+1147m Mt.Sedgewick
Mt.Lyell Mine
Mt.Owen
Queenstown 6 Gormanston Linda
LYELL
36 Lynchford
AMH
King Crotty
Mt.Huxley
Straban Regatta Point
LYELL
Ocean Beach
Cape Sorell
Hells Gates
King River Gorge King 1168m + Mt.Jukes
Governor
Cradle Mt. Lake St.Clair NAT PK
Eldon Peak 1439m
Sth Eldon High Dome 1356m Mt Gould 1491m +
Scenic walking tracks
1250m + Pyramid Mt.
Mt Olympus
Mt Hugel 1307m
Collingwood R
Bubs Hill
81
71 Mt Gell 1439m+ Mt Rufus 1402m
A10 HWY
Mt Arrowsmith +981m Derwent Bridge
Alma R
Franklin R
Mt King William I 1324m
Lake King William
A10
Clark Dam
20 26
21 26
Butlers Gorge P.S.
16
Tarrale
Sloop Pt. Mt Fincham
Franklin R
Macquarie Harbour
1031m Mt.Darwin 1144m + Mt.Sorell
Frenchmans Cap 1443m
Mt King William II 1372m
Mt King William III 1158m
Mt Hobhouse 1219m
11
Wayatinah
Gorge Pt. Pillinger
FRANKLIN LOWER GORDON WILD RIVERS
Mt.Lyne Jane R
Erebus R
Elizabeth Pwr Stn
Wayatinah Pwr
Birthday Bay Modder R Sarah Id. (Settlement Id.) Convict Ruins Birch R
NATIONAL PARK Jane R Algonkian Mt.
Wylds Craig 1337m
Gell R Gordon R
4
Cruise
Hibbs R Mt.Humboldt Reeds Pk. 1280m
PRINCE OF WALES RANGE Denison R
Hibbs Bay Sorell R Mt Discovery
Point Hibbs Mt Lee 734m + Innes Peak
KING WILLIAM RANGE
5
Spero Bay Spero R Maxwell R Wings Clear Hill
Endeavour Bay Sprent R Adamsfield
Florentine R
Wanderer R 793m Gordon Power Station Dam Lake Gordon
6
High Rocky Point Mt.Lewis Serpentine Dam 13 Strathgordon Mt Mueller 1234m+
Halas R Mt.Sorent 1058m McPartlan Pass 84 Frodshams Pass
Albert R 40 GORDON RIVER Mt Wedge 1146m Mt Bowes
Ogle R Mt.Anne 1425m
7
Hudson R Double Peak 1060m Lake Pedder 35 Mt.Eliza 1289m Lake Judd
Lewis R Mt.Solitary Lake Anne
Low Rocky Pt. Elliott Bay Scotts Peak Dam
8
Giblin R FRANKLAND RANGE SOUTH WEST
Nye Bay Hardwood R ARTHUR RANGE Arthurs Plains
Deverd R Mt Hayes Track
Mt Hean 747m Creating R NATIONAL
9
Wreck Bay North R Mt Ripple
Payne Bay Mt Norold PARK
Spring R Federation Peak 1224m+
Watts R
10
Pt.St.Vincent Mt Rugby 771m Bathurst Harbour Sally R
Port Davey Old R
Stephens Bay Ray R Louisa R
11
Island Bay 800m Mt Counsel Cox Bight Louisa Bay
Window Pane Bay Mt Melaleuca 695m
South West Cape Ile Du Golf

SOUTHERN
OCEAN
N

12
Flat Witch I. De Witt I. MAATSUYKER GROUP Maatsuyker I.

13

A B C D E F G H I

0 10 20 30 40 50 km

73

J K L M N O P Q R

Campbell Town

MARLBOROUGH HWY

A5 Dam 14 Tods Corner Arthurs Lake
Miena 1158m Barren Tier Pump 952m +Mt Penny 1115m
33 30 Wihareja Auburn Goldsmith 32
Shannon 5 Mt Franklin 1102m Ross Old Bridge Lake Leake Brushy R HWY Apslawn A3
LAKE 12 Waddamana Penstock Lag. Steppes Woods Lake Mona Vale Mt Hobgobbin Cranbrook Moulting Lag.
56 Lake Echo 846m Hermitage Lagoon of Islands Interlaken Lake Sorell Woodbury Tunbridge Mt Connection Wye R Swansea Coles Bay Cape Tourville
HIGHWAY 67 Lake Crescent Old Mans Head Blackman Antill Ponds Macquarie Meredith 18 Great Oyster Bay Sleepy Bay The Hazards Wineglass Bay
33.6 Victoria Valley Osterley Blue Hill Table Mt 1095m Oatlands York Plains Fadden Tier Tooms Lake Mt Tooms Mayfield Bay Buxton Point Cape Forestier FREYCINET NATL. PARK
Strickland Rutland Nala Lemont Little Swanport A3 Mayfield 51 Schouten FREYCINET PENINSULA
Catagunya Pwr. Stn. A10 Dee Lagoon Power Stn Dam Bothwell Mud Walls Parattah Antover Little Swanport Triabunna Isle des Phoques Schouten Island Cape Baudin
Ouse Cluny Hamilton Jericho Stonor Mt Seymour Whiteford Stonehenge Hobbs Lagoon Point Bailly Cape Sonnerat
LYELL 35 Pelham Elderslie Lake Tiberias Baden Tunnack Woodsdale TASMAN Grindstone Bay
MT. FIELD NAT. PK Meadowbank Lake Bagdad Rhyndaston Eldon Bluff R Barrier Orford Prosser Bay Spring Beach MARIA ISLAND NATIONAL PARK
Mt Field East 1269m+ Fentonbury Westerway Tanina Broadmarsh Lowdina Campania Runnymede Buckland Rheban Mt Maria 709m
National Park Glenora Gretna Mangalore Pontville Rekuna 62 Church Oyster Bay MARIA ISLAND
Russell Falls Bushy Park Macquarie Plains Oberlin Dromedary Brighton Tea Tree Oneton Pawleena Nugent Cape Peron
Maydena Plenty Hayes Magra Boyer Granton Old Beach Richmond Penna Wattle Hill Kellevie Marion Reidle Bay
Toll Gate Styx Uxbridge Mooga Claremont Malbina 21 Risdon Vale Midway Pt Sorell Forcett ARTHUR Bream Creek Bay Cape Frederick Hendrick
New Norfolk 32 Glenlusk Cambridge A3 Pitt Water Lewisham Carlton A9 Tasman Memorial
Mt Lloyd Collins Cap Glenorchy Collinsvale 26 Seven Mile Beach Dodges Ferry Carlton Copping Dunalley FORESTIER PENINSULA
HOBART Bellerive Rumney Frederick Henry Bay Lauderdale Sandford Blackman Bay Tasman Monument Cape Surville
Mt Wellington 1270m Ferntree Rokeby Sloping Id Cremorne Green Hd Smooth I Norfolk Bay Murdunna HWY
Mt Montagu Mountain River Taroona Rabbits Bay Opossum Bay Clifton Beach C Deslacs Gwandalan Saltwater River Convict Coal Mine Ruins 74 Eaglehawk Neck
Judbury Lucaston Grove 37 Longley Kingston Blackmans Bay South Arm Betsey Id. Premaydena Koonya Taranna Blow Hole Tessellated Pavement Tasmans Arch Devils Kitchen
Glen Huon Huonville Kaoota Margate Snug Howden Dennes Point Storm Bay Woodbridge Nubeena Oakwood TASMAN PENINSULA Hippolyte Rocks
Franklin Woodstock Pelverata Oyster Cove Kettering Barnes Bay NORTH BRUNY ISLAND Wedge I Port Arthur Highcroft Fortescue Bay The Lanterns Cape Hauy
Castle Forbes Cradoc Grey Mt 17 Nicholls Rivulet Great Bay Isthmus Bay Stormlea Remarkable Cave Munroe Bight
Geeveston Port Huon Cygnet Lymington Gardners Bay Middleton Garden Island Creek Gordon Cape Queen Elizabeth Raoul Bay Maingon Bay Cape Pillar
44 Surges Bay CHANNEL 48 Simpsons Bay Bligh Museum Cape Raoul Tasman Id.
HARTZ MOUNTAINS NATIONAL PARK Glendevie Police Point A6 Dover Huon I. Alonnah Adventure Bay Memorials to early navigators
Hartz Pk 1255m Raminea 21 Ida Bay Rly Luna wanna Adventure Bay Capt Cooks Landing Place
Mt Picton 1327m+ Strathblane A6 Lady Bay Partridge I Mt Mangana Cookville Fluted Cape Cape Connella
Adamsons Pk 1226m Hastings Caves Thermal pool Hastings Gt Taylors Bay SOUTH BRUNY ISLAND
Lune River Ida Bay Southport Cloudy Bay Mt Bruny 506m
Precipitous Bluff +1120m Mt La Perouse Leprena Cape Bruny Boreal Head Tasman Head
New River Lagoon Pindars Peak 1250m Southport Lagoon Actaeon I. Friar Rocks
Catamaran Recherche Bay

Surprise Bay South Cape Bay South East Cape Whale Head South East Cape

T A S M A N   S E A

J K L M N O P Q R

Grid references: A B C D E F G H I (top and bottom)
Row numbers: 1 2 3 4 5 6 7 8 9 10 11 12 13

BASS (Bass Strait)

SOUTHERN OCEAN

Hunter Island
Three Hummock Island
Cape Adansan
Hope Channel
Trefoil I.
Cape Grim
Valley Bay
Walker Channel
Walker I.
Robbins Island
Robbins Passage
Cape Elie
Perkins I.
Studland Bay
Montagu
North Pt
West Pt
Half Moon Bay
Highfield Pt
Stanley
Circular Head
The Nut
Sawyer Bay
Duck B.
Smithton
Mella
Forest
Wiltshire Junction
Black River
Port Latta
Rocky Cape
ROCKY CAPE NATL. PARK
Sisters Beach
Boat Harbour Beach
Table Cape
Marrawah
Redpa
Togari
Christmas Hills
Irishtown
Brittons Swamp
Edith Creek
Alcomie
Menghn
Mawbanna Sdg
Mawbanna
Montumana
Sisters Creek
Flowerdale
Wynyard
Somerset
BURNIE
West Pt
Welcome
Nabageena
Lileah
Roger River
Roger River West
Trowutta
DIP RANGE
Detention
Lapoinya
Moorleah
Myalla
Oldina
Calder
Preolenna
Lwr. Mt. Hicks
Upr. Mt. Hicks
Heybridge
Sulphur Creek
Penguin
Cooee
Mooreville Road
Arthur River
Nelson Bay
Nelson
Frankland
Rapid
Arthur
Meunna
West Ridgley
Yolla
Elliott
Ridgley
Natone
Stowport
Cuprona
Ulverstone
DEVONPORT
Searoad Terminal
Turners Beach
Leith
Forth
Wesley Vale
Temma Harbour
Temma
Balfour
Parrawe
Takone
West Takone
Tewksbury
Henrietta
Cam
Highclere
Natone Upper
Hampshire
Camena
Riana
Sth. Riana
Gunns Plains
Sorent
Spellford
Kindred
Melrose
Abbotsham
Gawler
Latrobe
Sandy Cape
Mt. Norfolk 759m
Mt. Vero
Mt. Cleveland
Mt. Bischoff
Waratah
Guildford
Barrier
Black Bluff 1339m
ARPM Private Roads
St Valentines Peak +1105m
Eucalypt forests
Loyetea
Preston
Lower Wilmot
Castra
Central Castra
Preston Sth.
Nietta
Heka
Wilmot
Nietta South
Roland
Gowrie Park
Kentish West
Sheffield
Nook
Railton
Mersey
Kimberley
Beulah
Paradise
Claude Road
Sth. Wilmot
Weegena
Moltema
Mole Creek
Caveside
Marakoopa Cave
King Solomon Cave
Western Bluff
Lagoon
Interview R.
Donaldson
Savage
White
Pieman Gorge
Rupert Point
Pieman
Corinna
Pieman Head
Hardwick Bay
Ahrberg Bay
Iron-ore project Savage River
Mt. Meredith
Mt. Ramsey 855m
Que
Bulgobac
Burns Peak 660m
1001m Mt. Pearse
Mt. Livingstone
Lake Pieman
Dam
Tullah
Renison Bell
Rosebery
Williamsford
Mt. Murchison 1275m
Mt. Raid
Lake Rosebery
Dundas
Mt. Dundas
Zeehan
Mt. Zeehan
Remine
Trial Harbour
Granville Harbour
Mt. Heemskirk
Mt. Agnew 846m
Old mining town
CRADLE MOUNTAIN
Mt. Pelion West 1564m
Mt. Achilles
Mt. Pelion East 1461m
Mt. Ossa 1617m
Cathedral Mt +1372m
LAKE ST. CLAIR
NATIONAL PARK
Cradle Valley
Cradle Mtn.
Barn Bluff 1559m
Waldheim Chalet
Trailside Museum
Mt. Remus
Mountain scenery +1545m
Lake Mackintosh
Lake Fury
Lake Lea
Daisy Dell
Mayday +1140m
Dove
Cethana
Moina
Lorinna
Liena
WALLS OF JERUSALEM NAT. PK
Mt. Jerusalem +1458m
Lake Rowallan
Rowallan Pwr. Stn.
Clumner Bluff 1490m
Mackenzie
Ironstone Mt +1443m
Augusta
L. Ada
GREAT PINE TIER
Badger
Henty
Lit. Henty
Queenstown
Mt. Lyell Mine
Lynchford
Linda
Gormanston
Mt. Owen
Mt. Huxley
King 1188m
Crotty
Mt. Jukes
Mt. Sedgwick +1147m
L. Margaret
Eldon Peak 1439m
Eldon Bluff 1357m
High Dome 1356m
Last Hill
Sth. Eldon
Pyramid Mt +250m
Bubs Hill
Governor
Mt. Gell 1439m
LYELL HWY
Mt. Arrowsmith +987m
Mt. Gould 1491m
Mt. Hugel 1307m
Mt. Rufus 1402m
Mt. King William I +1324m
Mt. Olympus +1447m
Derwent Bridge
Lake King William
Bronte Park
Bronte Lagoon
Strahan
Regatta Point
Ocean Beach
Cape Sorell
Hells Gates
Macquarie Harbour
King River Gorge
Mt. Strahan
Mt. Darwin
Mt. Sorell 1144m
1031m Mt. Fincham
FRANKLIN LOWER GORDON WILD RIVERS NATIONAL PARK
Frenchmans Cap 1443m
Mt. Lyoe
Collingwood R.
Franklin R.
Mt. King William II +1372m
Mt. Hobhouse 1219m
Butlers Gorge P.S.
Pow. Stat.
Tarraleah
Sloop Pt.
Pillinger
Gordon R.

Highway markers: A2 BASS HWY, 51, 28, A10, 65, 82, A2, MURCHISON HWY, 73, 76, A10, ZEEHAN HWY, 27, LYELL HWY, 36, 81, 71, A10, 26, 31, 54, 14, 22

0 10 20 30 40 50 km

J K L M N O P Q R

STRAIT

N

Cape Barren Island
Sloping Pt
Kent Bay
Snug Cove
Clarke Island
Forsyth I.
Passage I.
Look Out Heads
Moriarty Bay
Moriarty Point
Banks Strait

Cape Portland
Swan I.
Waterhouse I.
Waterhouse Pt
Mussel Roe Bay
Ringarooma Bay
Cape Naturaliste
Croppies Pt.
Poole
Mt William
Tomahawk
Waterhouse
Boobyalla
Gladstone
MT WILLIAM NATIONAL PARK
Eddystone Pt
Ansons Bay
South Mt Cameron
Ansons Bay

West Sandy Cape
East Sandy Cape
Anderson Bay
Stony Head
Noland Bay
Bellingham
Bridport
Commercial Trout Farm
Forester
Winnaleah
Herrick
Moorina
Pioneer
Lottah
Goulds Country
Bay of Fires
The Gardens

Five Mile Bluff
Lulworth
Weymouth
Beechford
Pipers River
Pipers Brook
Scottsdale North
Scottsdale
Telita
Derby
Branxholm
Weldborough
99
HWY
Goshen
Binalong Bay
Grants Pt
St Helens Pt

Low Head Lighthouse
Low Head
Port Dalrymple
West Head
Badger Head
Greens Beach
Kelso
York Town
GeorgeTown
Lefroy
Retreat
Lebrina
Golconda
Nabowla
Scottsdale West
Springfield
Karnona
Warrentinna
Legerwood
Ringarooma
Legunia
Pyengana
St. Columba Falls
George R
Priory
St Helens

Port Sorell
ASBESTOS RANGE NAT. PK
Beauty Point
Bell Bay
Rowella
Sidmouth
Deviot
Hillwood
Robigana
Turners Marsh Lower
Karoola
Lilydale
Bangor
Mt Arthur 1187m
Myrtle Bank
Targa
Springfield South
Talawah
Alberton
Mt Maurice 1120m
Trenah
Mt Victoria
Mt Young 903m
Lottah
18 R
St Helens I.

Christiana
Harford
Beaconsfield
Flowery Gully
Winkleigh
Exeter
Rosevears
Dilston
Turners Marsh
Patersonia
Nunamara
Rocherlea
Didleum Plains
Tayene
Ben Nevis 1367m
Mt. Saddleback
Esk Upper
Mt Barrow National Park
+1413m
St. Helens
Beaumaris
Scamander Upper
37
Scamander

Sassafras East
Frankford
Glengarry
Notley Hills
Notley Fern Gorge
Bridgenorth
Legana
Riverside North
Trevallyn P.S.
LAUNCESTON
St Leonards
Burns Creek
Musselboro
Roses Tier
Mathinna
1277m
Henderson Lagoon
Falmouth

Parkham
Birralee
Rosevale
Selbourne
Westwood
Hadspen
Relbia
White Hills
North Esk
Breadalbane
Blessington
Castle Hill 699m
Skiing
Legges Tor 1573m
Tower Hill
869m
Mt Nicholas 1027m
Cornwall
St Patricks Head
Avenue

Elizabeth Town
Reedy Marsh
Weetah
Deloraine
Westbury
Hagley
Carrick
Western Junction
Evandale
Deddington
Nile
BEN LOMOND NATIONAL PARK
Stacks Bluff 1527m
Storys Creek
Mangana
O'Day
Break
St Marys
Gray
A4
Elephant Pass

Lemana
Exton
48
Whitemore
Oaks
Perth
Toiberry
Longford
Nile
Powranna
Cressy
Delmont
Ben Lomond Rvr
Rossarden
A4
Fingal
74
Ormley
St Pauls Dome 1027m
St Patricks Head
Lagoons
Piccaninny Pt.

Quamby Brook
Cluan
Bishopsbourne
39
Bracknell
Liffey
Drys Bluff 297m
Blackwood Creek
Epping Forest
22
Cleveland
Avoca
St Pauls
Llewellyn Siding
Royal George
Seymour
Long Point

Golden Valley
Quamby Bluff 1226m
Jackeys Marsh
Liffey Falls
WESTERN TIERS
Poatina
21
Macquarie
Isis
51
Conara Junction
11
Campbell Town
Auburn
Goldsmith
South Esk
Mathinna
Douglas River
Maclean Bay

Meander
Breona
Bald Dog Tier
Poatina P.S.
Bradys Lookout 1371m
Millers Bluff 1212m
Snow Hill
Lake Leake
Cygnet
Apslawn
89
Bicheno
Waubs Harbour
Cape Lodi

Augusta
Rats Castle 1393m
Bernacchi
Reynolds I.
41
Mt Franklin 1102m
Ross Old Bridge
Morne Vale
Lake Leake
Brushy
Cranbrook
Moulting Lagoon
31

Liaweenee
Great Lake 1090m
Arthurs Lake 952m
Pump
Woods Lake
Mt Penny 1115m
Auburn
18
Glen Morriston Rvr
Mt Connection
Wye R
Swansea
Coles Bay
Cape Tourville

Miena
Lit. Pine Lag.
Barren Tier
Shannon
Wihareja
Mt Penny
Lake Sorell
Mt Franklin
Barrier
Nine Mile Beach
Sleepy Bay
The Hazards
Wineglass Bay

Steppes
Waddamana
Lag. of Islands
Lake Sorell
Interlaken
Woodbury
Grimes Lagoon
Tunbridge
Barrier
Great Oyster Bay
Cape Degerando
FREYCINET NATIONAL PARK

Lake Echo 846m
Crescent
Old Mans Head
Antill Ponds
Macquarie Nth.
Meredith R
Mt Freycinet +614m
FREYCINET PENINSULA

Dee Lagoon
Hermitage
Table Mt. 1095m
Fadden Tier
Tooms Lake
Mt Tooms
Buxton
Mayfield Bay
Buxton Point
Schouten Passage
Schouten Island
Cape Baudin

Power Stn Dee
Victoria Valley
Blue Hill
Oatlands
York Plains
Nala
Lemont
Barrier
Mayfield
11
Little Swanport
Pontypool
Cape Faure

Osterley
Parattah
Rutland
Andover
18
Promise Bay

MIDLAND HWY
TASMAN HWY
WEST TAMAR HWY
EAST TAMAR HWY
FRANKFORD HWY
LAKE HWY
HIGHWAY
MAIN ROAD

SEA

TASMAN

J K L M N O P Q R

Maps of
South Australia

Location Map

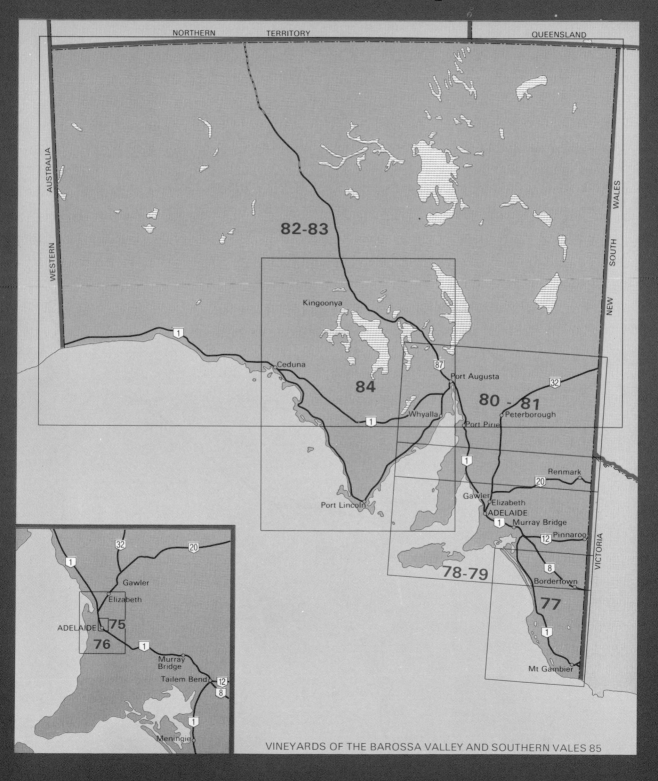

0   0·5   1   1·5   2 km

Places of Interest

1 Art Gallery of South Aust. F6	11 Hotel Adelaide.................E4	24 Victoria Park Racecourse H9
2 Ayers House G6	12 Parliament House E6	25 War Memorial..................F6
35 Casino E6	13 Police Headquarters...........E8	26 Zoological Gardens F5
3 Central Market...............E7	14 Post Office...................E7	
4 Festival Centre Complex E6	15 Public Library F6	**Transport and Touring**
5 Government House E6	16 Rundle Mall F6	34 Adelaide Rail Passenger Terminal. B9
6 Grosvenor Hotel E6	17 St.Francis Xavier Cathedral ... E7	27 Ansett Terminal................E6
33 Hilton Hotel E7	18 St.Peters Cathedral E5	28 Glenelg Tram Terminus E7
7 Lights Vision E4	19 Showgrounds................C10	29 RAA Sth. Aust. Headquarters ..F7
8 Memorial Drive Tennis E5	20 South Terrace Travelodge F9	30 Railway Station E6
9 Mosque....................D8	21 State Administration Centre .. E7	31 TAA Terminal..................E6
10 Museum F6	22 Town Hall E7	32 Tourist Bureau E6
	23 University of Adelaide.........F6	

0 1 2 3 4 5 km

Elizabeth
Salisbury
Port Adelaide
ADELAIDE
North Adelaide
Glenelg
Campbelltown
Payneham
Norwood
Unley
Burnside
Mitcham
Blackwood
Brighton
Marion
Woodville
Grange
Henley Beach
Enfield
Prospect
Walkerville
Hindmarsh
Thebarton
Osborne
North Haven
Largs Bay
Semaphore

GULF ST VINCENT

MOUNT LOFTY RANGES

0 20 40 60 80km

A B C D E 79 F G H I

SOUTHERN

OCEAN

N

Lake Albert
Waltowa
Meningie
Binnie Lookout 170m+
Carcuma
Carcum Con. Pk.
Coonalpyn
Coonalpyn Downs
48
YOUNGHUSBAND
PRINCES
22
16
11
Culburra
Mt. Boothby Con. Park
Magrath Flat
Mt. Boothby 130m
47
Tintinara
Kumorna
Coombe
Gosse Hill
DUKES
Mt. Rescue Conservation Park
+ Mt. Rescue
Ngarkat Conservation Park
Mt. Shaugh +
Mt. Shaugh Con. Park
COORONG
NATIONAL
PARK
21
Coorong
Woods Well
18
Policemans Point
PENINSULA
Salt Creek
146
24
Messent Con. Park
Mt. Charles +
Tauna Downs
Keith
8
Banealla
Brimbago
Wirrega North
Wirrega
11
Inglewood
SOUTH AUSTRALIA
VICTORIA
Bunbury
HWY
24
45
70
Lowan Vale
Cannawigara
Bordertown
Dinyarrak
Monster Mt.+
Brecon
45
Kongal
24
Buckingham
6
13
8
WESTERN HWY
8
Gum Lagoon Con. Park
Willalooka
18
47
Mundulla
Wolseley
Serviceton
Custon
Pooginagoric
Kercoonda
Tilley Swamp
13
JIP JIP NATL. PK.
DESERT CAMP NATL. PK.
23
Swede Flat
Western Flat
45
Bangham
Lillimur South
Water Valley
Padthaway Con. Pk.
Padthaway
21
27
Taratap
35
Myroga
67
66
Keppoch Park
21
80
Wallabrook
13
Frances
Neuarpurr
50
21
Lacepede Bay
29
Blackford
Keilira
27
Mt. Scot Con. Pk.
Fairview Con. Pk.
Drain
14
Lochaber
14
13
Bingum
10
Kybybolite
21
10
Kingston S.E.
3
1
18
Reedy Creek
Bull Island
Cairnbank
Avenue
Fairview
Stewarts Range
13
Hynam
21
Apsley
Cape Jaffa
26
42
21
Avenue Plains
61
13
Lucindale
23
34
Naracoorte
11
NARACOORTE CAVES NATL. PK.
Koppamurra
14
Joanna
Langkoop
Mt. Benson
Mt. Benson 56m+
19
Conmurra
68
Crower
6
26
Big Heath Con. Pk.
Struan
6
11
Bool Lag.
50
Wattonbully
Boatswain
Cape Thomas
GUICHEN BAY NATL. PARK
16
PRINCES
18
47
Greenways
Conmurra
Callendale
Maaoope
Bool Lagoon
Glenroy
Poolaigelo
Comaum
Guichen Bay
Cape Dombey
Robe
L. Hawdon Nth.
Drain
21
19
L. Hawdon South
Chinamans Wells
10
Clay Wells
Mt. Bruce
Reedy Creek
14
19
Drain
Coonawarra
18
L. Robe
Little Dip Con. Park
19
L. Eliza
Bray Junct.
23
29
HWY
13
29
61
CALECTASIA NATL. PARK
Wattle Range
18
Penola
Nora Creina Bay
Lake St. Clair
Lake George
80
Drain
26
Furner
39
Hatherleigh
Mt. Burr
40
Krongart
20
Mundi
39
Nangwarry
Beachport
BEACHPORT NATL. PARK
Cape Martin
PENGUIN IS. NATL. PARK
1
Rendelsham
Mt. Burr
13
Mt. Muirhead
Mt. McIntyre
21
11
Kalangadoo
Wepar
Tarpeena
52
18
Rivoli Bay
Cape Buffon
South End
11
L. Frome
Millicent
16
Mt. Burr+ 241m
Glencoe West
Suttons Glencoe
Dismal Swamp
Wandilo
32
29
18
CANUNDA NATIONAL PARK
Snuggery
Tantanoola
13
Tantanoola Caves
50
21
Burrungule
Compton
GLENELG HWY
Lake Bonney
BUCKS LAKE NATIONAL PARK
16
MT. GAMBIER
Mil Lel
Suttontown
6
Glenburnie
PRINCES HWY
Carpenter Rocks
Cape Banks
Blackfellows Caves
O.B. Flat
21
Yahl
Caroline
Kongorong
Mt. Schank
26
Princess Margaret Rose Caves
Allendale East
6
"Dingley Dell" Home of Adam Lindsay Gordon
Cape Port MacDonnell
Northumberland
Ewens Ponds
10
Nelson
Donovans Landing
Discovery Bay

A B C D 80 E F G H I

EYRE PENINSULA

Cleve · Yabmana · 43 · Cowell · Victoria Pt. · Franklin Harbour · Germein Pt.
Boothby · Carpa · Elbow Hill · Port Gibbon · Pt. Gibbon
Mt. Priscilla · 23 · HWY · 47
Arno Bay · Carpa
LINCOLN · 34 · Arno Bay · Cape Driver
Karinya · Dutton Bay
Port Neill · Cape Burr

SPENCER GULF

Cape Elizabeth
Revesby Is.
Hareby Is. · Roxby Is.
Joseph Banks Group · Spilsby Is.

YORKE PENINSULA

Wardong Island
Reef Pt. · Pt. Pearce Mission · Island Pt. · Pt. Pearce
Port Victoria
Wauraltee
Mt. Rat · Koolywurtie
Port Rickaby
Bluff
Brentwood
Greig Lookout · Souttar Pt. · Hardwicke Bay · Roger Corner · Pt. Turton · Turton
Corny Pt. · Berry Bay · Corny Pt. · Warooka · Yorketown · Oaklands
White Hut · 49 · Moorowie · Fowler · L.
Daly Head · Formby Bay · Pt. Margaret · Carrible · Happy Valley
Foul Bay · Pt. Yorke
INNES NATIONAL PARK · Royston Head · Marion Bay · Hillock Point
Pondalowie Bay · West Cape · Stenhouse Bay · Inneston · Cape Spencer

Tickera Bay · Tickera · Lincolnfields · Illawarra Hill · Snowtown · Barunga Gap · Condowie · Hart
Brucefield · Alford · 74 · Bute · L. Bumbunga · Lochiel
Myponie Pt. · 11 · 16 · 19 · 31 · Mona · 13 · Bumbunga · Boowilta · Watervale
Pt. Riley · Wallaroo Bay · Willamulka · Thomas Plains · Kybunga · SPRING SULLY NATL. PK. · Clare
Wallaroo · Pt. Hughes · **Kadina** · Ninnes · Sth. Hummocks · Everard Cent. · Nantawarra · Stow · Wanappa
Warburto Pt. · Tiparra Bay · Boors Plain · Thrington · Myohres · 10 · Watchman · Halbury · 31 · Undalya
Moonta · Yelta Nth. · Paskeville · Kulpara · Beaufort · Diamond Lake · 15 · Mull
Moonta Bay · Port Hughes · Cunliffe · Melton · 14 · Port Broughton · Whitwarta · Saints · 26 · **Balaklava** · Rhynie
Yelta · 53 · Agery · Sunnyvale · 67 · Kainton · 18 · Port Wakefield · Bowmans · 15 · Salters Springs · Erith
Weetulta · Arthurton · Clinton Centre · **Port Wakefield** · 11 · Kallora · Woods · Alma
Balgowan · 19 · Winulta · 47 · Mary Burts Corner · Inkerman · Avon · 10 · Owen · 16
Maitland · Cunningham · Dowlingville · Price · Mangrove Pt. · Wild Horse Plains · Stockyard Ck.
South Kilkerran · Sandilands · Ardrossan · Windsor · Dublin · 56 · Long Plains · 52 · Hamley Bridge · 69 · Mallala · Wasleys
Urania · Yorke Valley · Pine Point · Port Alfred · Black Pt. · 1 · Light · 26 · 17 · Two Wells · **Gawl**
Curramulka · 84 · Port Julia · Gawler River · Virginia · 39
Minlaton · 134 · 92 · Dowcer Bluff · Port Vincent · Outer Harbour · **Salisbury**
Stansbury · **GULF** · ST. VINCENT · **ADELAIDE**
Wool Bay · Giles Pt. · Salt Creek Bay · Coobowie · Edithburgh · Honiton · Troubridge Is. · Sultana Pt. · Troubridge Pt.
Reynella · Morphett Vale · 34 · Ale · 45
Port Noarlunga · Old Noarlunga · McLaren Vale · Aldinga · Willung
Aldinga Bay · 41 · Mt. Compass · 50 · Myponga
Strait · North Islet · Gambier Islands · Wedge Is. · Normanville · Yankalilla · 37 · 35
Investigator · Yankalilla Bay · Rapid Bay · Second Valley · FLEURIEU · 60 · Vic Har
Athorpe Islands · Deep Creek Con. Park · Newland Head · PENINSULA

KANGAROO ISLAND

Cape D'Estaing · Smith Bay · Mt. Marsden 182m · Pt. Marsden · Emu Bay · Cape Rouge · Vehicular Ferry to Port Lincoln & Adelaide · Vehicular Ferry to Cape Jervis · Cape Jervis · Backstairs Passage
Cassini · Mt. McDonnell · 50 · Wisanger · ROAD · Bay of Shoals · **Kingscote** · Beatrice Pt. · Cape Jervis · Pennaw
Western River Con. Pk. · Stokes Bay · Cape Borda · Salt O Lag · Cygnet River · Nepean Bay · Pt. Morrison · Kangaroo Head · Eastern Cove · Pennershaw
Western River · Middle River · COAST · Woodlana · Cygnet Park · 28 · American River · 18 · Antechamber Bay
NTH. · Buiong · Pioneer Bend · Cygnet · HWY · Muston · 11 · Dudley Con. Pk. · Antechamber Bay
Cape Forbin · Western · 36 · Parndana · Corr Amar · 76 · High Barbaree · Sapphiretown · 80 · Wilson · Cape Willoughby
Cape Torrens Con. Pk. · Middle · PLAYFORD · Birchmore Lag · Macgillivray · Wilson Pt. · 14
Cape Borda · 31 · Gremlin Lodge · Pemobram · 42 · ROAD · Pennington Bay · DUDLEY PENINSULA · Cape Hart Con. Pk.
FLINDERS CHASE NATIONAL PARK · 24 · Binnowie · 27 · Wirrilda · Warrawee · Hawks Nest · Cape Hart
Moreview · WEST END HWY · D'Estrees Bay
West Bay · N.W. · N.E. · Vivonne Heights · Ada · Murray Lag. · Cape Linois
Cape Bedout · STH. · 103 · Vivonne Bay · Seal Bay · Gantheaume Con. Pk. · Cape Gantheaume
Rocky River · Karatta · 39 · Karatta · COAST · Vivonne Bay Con. Pk. · Cape Kersaint
Maupertuis Bay · Kelly Hill Caves · Kelly Hill Con. Pk. · Cape Bouger
Cape du Couedic · Hanson Bay · Cloughsdtband · Youngbusband · Sanderson Bay · Kirkpatrick

GREAT AUSTRALIAN BIGHT

A B C D E F G H I

81

J K L M N O P Q R

1

Pine Camp
New Paradise Dam
Narweena
Sampsons Well
Gluepot
Kulkurna
Stein Hill
Worlds End Creek
Florieton
The Gums
Whites Dam Con. Park
Bungunnia
Chowilla
Murtho Park
Black Springs
Emu Downs
Church Land
Bunyung
Hawks Nest Dam
Cooltong
Renmark West
Renmark
Paringa
Murray
Saddleworth
Morgan
Cadell
Westons Flat
Taylorville
Pooginook Con. Park
Overland Corner
Lock 3
Calperum
Lock 5
Wonuarra
Yamba
Julia
Point Pass
Qualco
Ramco
Kingston O.M.
Lake Bonney
Barmera
Monash
Glossop
Berri
Kuru
Taldra
STURT HWY
Taparoo
Eudunda
Waikerie
Lowbank
Cobdogla
Loveday
Winkie
Pyap
Loxton
Noora
Nangari
Taplan
Kapunda
Blanchetown
Lock 1
New Well
Boolgun
Myrla
Wunkar
Tookayerta
Pata
Nadda
Nuriootpa
Angaston
Tanunda
Sedan
Swan Reach
Netherleigh
Mercunda
Mantung
Caliph
Veitch
Malpas
Paruna
Meribah
Williamstown
Lyndoch
Cambrai
Eden Valley
Wongulla
Nildottie
Bakara
Galga
Kunlara
Copeville
Mindarie
Cobera
Alawoona
IZABETH
Mt. Pleasant
Walker Flat
Claypans
Goondooloo
Wanbi
Bernook
Peebinga
Birdwood
Tungkillo
Palmer
Purnong Landing
Bow Hill
Kalyan
Halidon
Sandalwood
Billiatt Conservation Park
Kringin
Karte
Lobethal
Mannum
Teal Flat
Coolcha
Perponda
Kilpalie
Borrika
Pilcherra Bore
Karte Con. Pk.
Woodside
Balhannah
Nairne
Mypolonga
Tepko
Mindiyarra
Lowaldie
Gurrai
Wirha
Barker
Monarto Sth
Wynarka
Karoonda
Wingamin
Nunkeri
Kulkami
Mulpata
Pinnaroo
Panitya
Callington
Murray Bridge
Kulde
Yurgo
Marama
Smithville
Carinya
Ngallo
Macclesfield
Woodchester
Tailem Bend
Naturi
Moorlands
Lameroo
Parilla
Chandos
Green Hills
Strathalbyn
Jervois
Elwomple
Sherlock
Buccleuch
Peake
Bews
Wilkawatt
Langhorne Creek
Wellington
Cooke Plains
Jabuk
Geranium
Parrakie
Belvidere
Finniss
Milang
Lake Alexandrina
Pomanda Pt.
Coomandook
Netherton
Mt. Elephant
Scorpion Springs Con. Park
Pt. Sturt
Narrung
Malinong
Ashville
Two Sisters
Yumali
Ki Ki
Mt. Timothy
Ngarkat Conservation Park
Encounter Bay
Murray Mouth
Lake Albert
Waltowa
Binnie Lookout 170m
Carcuma
Carcum Con. Pk
Mt. Rescue
Younghusband
Meningie
Coonalpyn
Coonalpyn Downs
Mt. Shaugh
Mt. Shaugh Con. Park
Culburra
Mt. Boothby Con. Park
Tintinara
Mt. Rescue Conservation Park
Gosse Hill
PRINCES
Magrath Flat
Mt. Boothby 130m
Kumorna
Coombe
COORONG NATIONAL PARK
PENINSULA
Woods Well
Messent Con. Park
Mt. Charles
DUKES
Banealla
Wirrega North
Inglewood
Telopea Downs
Policemans Point
Tauna Downs
Keith
Brimbago
Lowan Vale
Salt Creek
Bunbury
Monster Mt.
Brecon
HWY
Wirrega
Cannawigara
HWY
Kongal
Bordertown
WESTERN HWY
Willalooka
Gum Lagoon Con. Park
Wampoony
Buckingham
Mundalla
Wolseley
Serviceton
Dinyarrak

SOUTH AUSTRALIA
VICTORIA

60
56

J K L M N O P Q R

A B C D 84 E F G H I

1 Yalymboo · Charlinga · Bookaloo · Lake Torrens · Kalioota · Neuroodla · Yeppala · Mt. Plantagenet 949m · Hawker · Willow Waters

Lake MacFarlane · Warrakimbo · Partacoona · Wilson · Yourambulla Peak Caves · Cradock · Yednalue

2 Yudnapinna · Hesso · Uro Bluff · Yadlamalka · Wilkatana · Mt Arden 839m · Wilkatana Warren Gorge · Willochra · Buckaringa Gorge · Gordon · 98 · Watts + Sugarloaf 633m · Price Hill 756m · Belte

3 The Rocks · Seven Mile Outstation · Gairdners House · South Tent Hill + 319m · Mt. Arden · Depot Creek · Quorn · The Devils Peak · Richi Richi Pass · Kingswood · Bruce · Moockra Tower + 777m · 108 · Carrieton · Joh

Old Siam · Cariewerloo · Corraberra · Pt. Augusta West · -14 · Mt Brown + 965m · Oladdie Ck. · Price Hill

4 Nonning · Miccollo Hill 362m + · Lord Kitchener Dam · Wartaka · Illeroo · Myall Creek · Corraberra Hill + 310m · Port Augusta · Stirling North · Horrocks Pass · Hammond · Wilmington · 82 · Coomooroo Hill + · Walloway · Eurelia · Orroroo · 83

5 water 402m · Uno · Harris Bluff + 393m · Lake Gilles · Corunna · HWY · 42 · Iron Knob · Katunga · Roopena · Katunga 298m · Mt Whyalla + 232m · Lincoln Gap · Winninowie · Simmens Hill 247m · Old Point Lowly · 74 · Blanche Harbour · Nectar Brook · Hancocks Lookout · Terka · ALLIGATOR GORGE NATL. PK. · MAMBRAY CREEK NATL. PK. · 84 · Mt Remarkable 959m + · Mt Remarkable Con. Park · Melrose · Wepowie · Perroomba · Maurice Hill + · Pekina + Hill 732m · 40 · Pekina · Bla

6 Wilcherry · Lake Gilles Conservation Park · EYRE · 153 · 87 · Gilles Downs · Iron Baron · Middleback · Myola · 21 · Tregolana 278m · Tregalana · Cultana · Monument Hill 198m · Backy Pt. Fitzgerald Bay · False Bay · Port Lowly Pt. · Barootà · Germein Bay · Port Bonython · Ward Ck. · Baroota Resr. · Bengor · Telowie Gorge C/Pk. · Murray Town · Yandiah · Wirrabara · Appila · 26 · Hornsdale · Mt Lock 743m + · 19 · Mannanarie · Yongal

WHYALLA · Port Germein · Broad Ck. + The Bluff · Stone Hut · Booleroo Centre · Yatina · Tarcowie · Belal

7 Nammuldi · Hills View · Kimba · 1 · RANGE · MIDDLEBACK · HWY · Mt Young + 136m · 26 · PORT PIRIE · Germein Bay · Nelshaby · Napperby · Mt Zion + · Beetaloo Resr. · Laura · 29 · Caltowie · Brown Hill + · Jamestow · 83

Belmonie · Broadacres · 93 · Ash Hill · Mt Middleback · Warnertown · 37 · 27 · Beetaloo Valley · 21 · Huddleston · Gladstone · New + Campbell Hill 702m + · Georgetown · 34 · 19

8 EYRE PENINSULA · Yalana · 76 · Pine Hill · 108 · 64 · Moonabie · Midgee · Plank Pt. · Port Davis · Jarrold Pt. · River · Nurom · Merriton · 43 · Crystal Brook · Narridy · 84 · Bundaleer Resr. · Spalding · Boo · Andrew

9 Mt.Desperate · Mangalo · Mittalie · Mt Olinthus · Pinelodge · Minbrie · Mt Ghearthy + · Pondooma · Single Pine · Warrayappa · Mitchellville · Wandearah East · Wandearah West · Wood Pt. · Fisherman Bay · Port Broughton · Webling Pt. · Mundoora · Clements Gap · Barn Hill · Redhill · Koolunga · Yacka · Mt + Gregory 486m · 63 · Hilltop

Coolanie · 16 · 18 · Nurrondi · Sharps Well · 43 · Collinsfield · Lake View · Brinkworth · 5 · Rochester · Came Hur

10 Cleve · 23 · Boothby · Carpa · 18 · Elbow Hill · Franklin Harbour · Cowell · Victoria Pt. · Germein Pt. · Shoalwater Pt. · Tickera Bay · Tickera · 47 · Brucefield · Lincolnfields · 74 · Bute · Barunga Gap · Snowtown · 101 · Illawarra Hill + · Wokurna · Lake View · 1 · Condowie · Hart · Blyth · Clare · Seven

Mt Priscilla · Arno Bay · Pt. Gibbon · Port Gibbon · 47 · Myponie Pt. · Alford · Mona · L. Bumbunga · Kybunga · Boowilla · SPRING GULLY NATL. PK. · Penw · 26

11 LINCOLN · 34 · Arno Bay · Cape Driver · Wallaroo · Pt.Hughes · Kadina · 10 · Pt. Riley · Wallaroo Bay · Willamulka · Thomas Plains · Ninnes · Myphree · Lochiel · Bumbunga · Everard Cent. · Nantawarra · Stow · Hoyleton · Watervale · Lessingham · Mu

12 Port Neill · Cape Burr · Dutton Bay · SPENCER · Warburto Pt · Tiparra Bay · Moonta · Moonta Bay · Port Hughes · Yelta · Boors Plain · Paskeville · 50 · Kulpara · Beaufort · Melton · Kainton · Sunnyvale · Agery · 53 · 67 · Port Arthur · Port Wakefield · Port Clinton · Clinton Centre · Bowmans · 26 · Whitwarta · Saints · Balaklava · 31 · 31 · Undalya · Halbury · Rhynie · Salters Springs · Gile · Alma

13 GULF · YORKE PENINSULA · Balgowan · Maitland · Kilkerran · Petersville · Weetulta · Winulta · Arthurton · Dowlingville · 47 · Inkerman · Avon · Sandy Pt. · Mangrove · Mary Burts Corner · Wild Horse Plains · 52 · 56 · Windsor · Dublin · Hamley Bridge · 69 · Mallala · Wasleys

Reef Pt · Pt. Pearce Mission · South Kilkerran · Cunningham · Yorke Valley · Cape Elizabeth · Ardrossan · Long Plains · Stockyard Ck. · Pinery

84 · 78

0   20   40   60   80   100 km

J   K   L   M   N   83   O   P   Q   R

1

Holowilena
Mattawarrangala
Bibliando
Baratta
River
Killawarra
Glenorchy
Old Telechie
Kalabity
Mundi Mundi

Siccus
Milang
Dry
Nillinghoo
Mt. Victor 464m
Koonamore
Plumbago
Bimbowrie
Ck
Whey Whey
Binbowie Ck
Binberrie Hill 501m
Wompinie
Cockburn
32

Witchitie
Oopina
Mt. Victor
Outalpa
Boolcoomata
Old Lake Dismal

Marchant Hill +799m
Gum
Ck
Melton
Mt. Misery
Waukaringa
Teetulpa Gold Field
Bonnie Brae
Morialpa
Weekeroo
Karolta
Kings Bluff +428m
Bulloo Creek
HWY 27
Mingary
26
Aroona
Pine Creek
Oa

nburra
Wabricoola
34
Winnininnie
43
267
37
Olary
15
29
Radium Hill
Ballara
Burta 16

Meadow Downs
Weddington Bluff
Waroonee Hill
Yunta
BARRIER
Oulnina Park
Oulnina
Benda
Wadnaminga
Devonborough Downs
Mutooroo

Bundara
McCoys Well
Whyngoon
Chewing Knob +23
Yunta
Dare Hill 452m
Benda RA
Dlorah Downs
Gairloch Dam
Kimberley

Rock Rock 839m
Dawson
Nackara + Hill 661m
Paratoo + Station Hill
16
Nackare
19
Tiverton
Ocalia Ck
Manunda
Netley Gap

Morowie Hill
Oodla Wirra
Nantabibbie
11
32
Oak Park
Loch Lilly

Ucolta
Pitcairn
588m
Pualco + West
Lilydale
Oakvale
22

Peterborough
56 14
Waite Hill +735m
Pualco
Oakbank
SOUTH AUSTRALIA
NEW SOUTH WALES

24
23
Franklyn
The Oaks Pine Creek
Loch Winnoch
Faraway Hill
Quandong Vale
Dangali Conservation Park

Terowie 23
Hiles Lagoon
Pandappa
Wngoone +Hill
48
Braemar
Bendigo
Sturt Vale
Morgan Vale

Whyte Yarcowie
Mt. Scrub
Mt. Pullen
Ketchowla
Willara
Pine Valley
Lords Well Outstation

88
Mallett
Collinsville
Kia Ora
Hypurna

Witto
Hog Back
Fords Lagoon
Canopus

Hallett
Mt. Bryan East
Caroona
Caroona Ck
Woolgang
Glenora

Mt. Bryan 932m
Newikie
Murkaby
Koomooloo
Old Koomooloo
Pine Camp

Hallett Hill +756m
Sugarloaf Hill
Mongalata
Chalk Cliffs
Canegrass
Parcoola

Mt. Bryan
Mt. Cone 793m
Thistle Beds
Sugarloaf
Ck
New Paradise Dam
Narweena

64
15
Baldina
Redbanks
Grassville
Redcliffs
Balah
Gluepot

Burra
14
Stein Hill
Sampsons Well
Baldina
Bunyung

32
Hanson
Porter Lagoon
Burra Hill
Worlds End Creek
10
The Gums
Florieton
37 82
Bungunnia

Black Springs
Emu Downs
19
Church Land
Whites Dam Con. Park
31
Murray
Chowilla Ck
Kulkurna

53
Lagoon +Hill
26
Brady Ck
Geranium Plains
Robertstown
29
Morgan
11
Westons Flat
Lock 2
Pooginook Con. Park
Hawks Nest Dam
Cooltong
Murtho Park

Appinga
Waterloo
Mandora
Ngapala
Point Pass
Australia Plains
Bower
58
Eba
Fk
10
Cadell
23
Taylorville
Overland Corner
Lock 3
Renmark
Renmark West
Paringa

Saddleworth
Julia
Tarnma
Peep Hill
13
Sutherlands
Mt. Mary
Quelco
Ramco
13
River
37
34
Kingston O.M.
Lake Bonney
47
Lock 5
Wonuarra

Marrabel
Eudunda
Hampden
Neales Flat
Brownlow
39
Murbko
Waikerie
Lowbank
Cobdogla
Monash
Berri
45
Yamba

Verton 34 23
Hansborough
Frankton
Kanni
Holder
Kurlana
Moorook
Moorook Sth
Loveday
Winkie
Glossop
Lyrup
29
Taldra

Tarlee
Allendale
15
Mt. Rufus +547m
Bagot Well
HWY 42
20
Kurla
Yinkanie
Gerard Mission
New Residence
40
Loxton Nth.
Noora

Kapunda 16
Dutton
Truro
Stonefield
Blanchetown
Lock 1
New Well
Boggun
Maggea
Pyap
Loxton
Nangari

Nuriootpa Angaston
35
29
Greenock
20
STURT 103
Murray
16
Notts Well
13
16
Myrla
Wunkar
Tookayerta
19
Taparoo
STURT HWY
20

J   K   L   M   N   79   O   P   Q   R

A B C D 104 E F G H I

1
MANN RANGES
Mulga Park
NORTHERN TERRITORY
SOUTH AUSTRALIA
Amata
Kulgera
Mt Cavenagh
74
Tieyon
Abminga Ruin
Eringa Ruin

Ernabella
MUSGRAVE
RANGES
Agnes Creek
One Tree
Marryat
Mt Irwin
Hamilton

2
60
Fregon
Granite Downs
Lambina
Everard Park
Chandler
Toomorden
240
Albe

3
PITJANTJATJARA
LAND
Entry Permit Required
EVERARD
RANGES
Wallatinna
Marla
411
83
Welbourn Hill
Wintinna
Copper Hill
Arckaringa

4
Cadney Park
Mt Willoughby
STUART
Evelyn Down

5
GREAT VICTORIA DESERT
CONSERVATION PARK
Lake Meramangye
STUART HIGHWAY
132
N
Coo Pe

6
Serpentine Lakes
WESTERN AUSTRALIA
SOUTH AUSTRALIA

7
Wyola Lake
Lake Dey - Dey
Lake Maurice
Wilkinson Lakes
Ingomar
McDouall Peak
91

8
Lake Anthony
Half Moon Lake
Commonwealth Hill
Goode
Bulgunnia
Maralinga
Muckanippie
Carnes
Durkin
Mulgathing
Gilbraltar Rocks
Warrior
Jok

9
NULLARBOR
Yarle Lakes
O'Malley
Watson
Ooldea
Immarna
Barton
Fisher
Wynbring
Carnding Road House
Cook
Lyons
Harcoola
Hughes
Malbooma
Wilgena

10
PLAIN
Ifould Lake

WARNING: Although an indication of road surface types is shown on this map, it is imperative that visitors obtain full information as to road conditions ahead before proceeding on their journey. During the period October to May "wet" season conditions may cause severe flooding, making many roads impassable.
The majority of water features shown on this map do not contain permanent water.
Entry to Aboriginal Reserves is strictly prohibited unless a permit is obtained.

11
Roadhouse
Nullarbor
YALATA ABORIGINAL
30
Roadhouse
NULLARBOR
Koonalda
NATIONAL
EYRE
LAND
HIGHWAY
Yalata Mission
469
Colona
185
Head of Bight
Roadhouse
YUMBARRA
CONSERVATION PARK
Eucla
Travellers Village
Nundroo
45
Bookabie
Satellite Communication Station
Koonibba Mission
1
See 'Crossing the Nullabor' between pages 216-217
Shredde
35
Cundilippy
Penong
74
Wookata
Point Fowler
Maltee
Mudamukla
35
40
50

12
GREAT AUSTRALIAN BIGHT
Points Bell
St Peter Island
Goat Island
Lake Macdonnel
Point Peter
Smoky Bay
Eyre Island
Ceduna
Smoky Bay
Nunjikompita
Wirrulla
Yanta

13
St Francis Isles
Point Brown
Streaky Bay
Cu
Pool
FLINDERS
74
46
64
Cape Bauer
Streaky Bay
Calca
CALPATANNA WATER HOLE CON PARK

A B C D 84 E F G H I

0 30 60 90 120 150 180 210 240 270 300 330 360 km

J K L M N 122 O P Q R

NORTHERN TERRITORY

SOUTH AUSTRALIA

SIMPSON DESERT
CONSERVATION PARK

QUEENSLAND

Mt Dare
Bloods Creek Bore
Purni Bore
Roseberth
Birdsville
Pandie Pandie
Haddon Corner

Dalhousie Thermal Ponds
Lake Etamunbanie
STURTS

Pedirka Ruin
Hamilton
Mt Sarah
SIMPSON
Alton Downs
STONY

Macumba
DESERT
Clifton Hills
Lake Uloowaranie
DESERT
Cordillo Downs
Arrabury

Macumba
EPHEMERAL LAKES
Coongie (abandoned)
Congie Lakes

River
Kudriemitchie (abandoned)

Oodnadatta
Nappa Merrie
Warburton
Lake Howitt
Covanie
New Kalamurina
Lake Koodnanie

Mt Dutton Ruin
Neales Ck
520
Gidgealpa
Innamincka
QUEENSLAND
122

Warrina Ruin
River
Mungcranie
Lake Kittakittaooloo
Moomba Oil Field

Edwards Creek Ruin
Ruin Ooroowilanie
Lake Warrakalanna
Lake Walpayapeninna

Nilpinna
LAKE EYRE (NORTH)
Mulka
SOUTH AUSTRALIA

Box Creek Ruin
Cooper Creek
Etadunna
Lake Killamperpunna
Lake Kopperekoppinna
Merti Merti
STRZELECKI TRACK

William Creek Ruin
403
Lake Florence
Lake Gregory
Bollards Lagoon
Cameron

Strangways Bore
ELLIOT PRICE CONSERVATION PARK
Dulkaninna
Lake Blanche

RANGE
Beresford Bore
LAKE EYRE SOUTH
Clayton
Clayton

Coward Springs Bore
Curdimurka Bore
Frome River
Marnpeowie
Lake Callabonna
Winnaree

Stuart Creek
Bopeechie Bore
Wangianna Ruin
Marree
Callabonna
Hacker Gate Creek

Finniss Springs
Callanna
Mundowdna
Yandama

Billa Kalina
Witchelina
Witchelina
Wilpoorinna
Mt Freeling
Moolawatana

332
The Twins
Millers Creek
Farina
Mt Fitton
Smithville House

Mt Eba
Bamboo Swamp
Avondale
Mt Lyndhurst Freeling Heights

Curdlawidny Lagoon
Mulgaria
Lyndhurst
Yankaninna
Umberatana
North Mulga
Moorab

Bon Bon
Orwell Well
Parakylia
Andamooka Opal Fields
Myrtle Springs
Copley
Mt Painter
Arkaroola

Mt Vivian
South Vivian
Leigh Creek South
Leigh Creek
Wootana
GAMMON RANGES NATIONAL PARK

Locks Well
Roxby Downs
Aroona Valley
Angepena
Balcanoona

North Well
Younghusband Knoll
Andamooka
Purple Downs
Warraweena
Old Arrowie
LAKE FROME

Kingoonya
Glendambo
Beltana
Old Warraweena
Broughams Gate

Coondambo
Lake Hanson
Bosworth
Beltana Narrina
Eurinilla
Avenel

Kokatha
East Well
Arcoona
Blinman
Great Wall
Wirealpa
Frome Downs

Woomera
Wirraminna
Old Motpena
Motpena
Parachilna
Kanyaka

LAKE EVERARD
Island Lagoon
Pimba
Parachilna
FLINDERS RANGES
Oraparinna
Martins Well
Benagerie

Blue Dam
LAKE GAIRDNER
Lake Windabout
Commodore
156
NATIONAL PARK
Wilpena Pound
Erudina
Mulyungarie

Mahanewo
Wirrappa
Birthday
McGinson Lagoon
Moralana
Wilpena Ck
Curnamona
Mooleulooloo

Kumburta
Moolaree
Lake Finniss
South Gap
Lake Torrens
Holowilena
Bibliando
Old Telechie

Lake Acraman
Charlinga
Bookaloo
Kallioota
Baratta
Koonamore
Killawarra

170
Woocalla
Hawker
Warrakimbo
Cradock
Bagalowie
Itumbago
Old Lake Dismal
Cockburn

Hesso
Willetana
Willand
66
Belton
Melton
Mt Victor
Morialpa
Mingary
Aroona

Minnipa
Iron Knob
Quorn
Arden Vale
East Bootcunda
Wirra Downs
Waukaringa
BARRIER
Cutana
Ballara

Port Augusta
46
108
Carrieton
Ivy Glen
Meadow Downs
HIGHWAY
Olary
Bringa
Coultra Hut

31
Wilmington
Willowie
Yalpara
Teetulpa
Yunta
Outhina
Wadnaminga Downs
Burta

HIGHWAY
42
74
51
Orroroo
Black Rock
267
Mannahill
Devonborough Downs
Moorroo

EYRE
Iron Baron
Melrose
Pekina
Dawson
Paratoo
Tiverton
Netley Gap
Mazar

Lodge
PRINCES
Spencer Gulf
Murray Town
Booleroo Centre
Oak Park
Oodla
Manunda

Buckleboo
LINCOLN HWY
Tent Hill
14
Pitcairn
Lilydale

293 PINKAWILLINIE CON PARK
WHYALLA CON PARK
LAKE GILLES CON PARK
Whyalla
Port Germein
Peterborough

J K L M N 80 O P Q R

30 60 90 120 160 km

A B C D E F G H I

1
Muckanippie
Mulgathing
Carnes
Bulgunnia
Mount Eba
Durkin
Warrior
Gibraltar Rocks
Curdlawidny Lagoon
Mulgaria
Andamooka
Opal Fields

2
Wynbring
Lyons
Malbooma
Tarcoola
Wilgena
Wymlet
Lake Labyrinth
Bon Bon
Mt Vivian
Locks Well
Parakylia
Roxby Downs
Andamooka
Purple Downs
Bosworth
PARTRIDGE RANGE
120
34
STUART HIGHWAY
Lake Younghusband

3
+ Mt Finke 361m
Kingoonya
55
Yerda
Glendambo
Coondambo
Lake Ross
East Well
Lake Hanson
Wirraminna
Lake Hart
Knoll
34
Arcoona
Woomera
Pimba
RANGES
Lake Eyre tracks

4
EVERARD
Blue Dam
LAKE GAIRDNER
Mahanew
Lake Finniss
58
318
Oakden Hills
91
STUART HWY
Lake Windabout
Pernatty
South Gap

5
Satellite Communication Station
Yarlbrinda Hill 348m
Lake Everard
Yarna
Lake Acraman
Moonaree
Yalymboo
Lake Dutton
Bookaloo
29
87
Hesso

6
EYRE
Ceduna
The Venant
Whidbee Con Park
Mudamuckla
Nunjikompita
St Peter Island
Laura Bay Con Park
Smoky Bay
Smoky Bay
Eyre Island
Nuyts Arch Con Park
Wirrulla
HWY 93
110
GAWLER RANGES
Mt Kolendo + 487m
51
Port Augusta
24

7
Point Dillon
Franklin Islands
Point Collinson
Streaky Bay
Olives Islands
Cape Bauer
Corvisart Bay
Chandada
Streaky Bay
63
Yantanabie
225
Cungena
Poochera
EYRE
Mt Nett 431m
LAKE GILLES
Iron Knob
42
153
Whyalla Con Park
Port Bonython
1 HWY
34
60
82

8
Point Westall
Scale Bay
Calpatanna Waterhole Con Park
Dalca
127
Port Kenny
FLINDERS
Mount Cooper
Minnipa
85
Yaninee
Lake Yaninee
Pygery
Wudinna
Kyancutta
Samphire Flats
HWY 40
Warramboo
Waddikee Rocks
Pinkawillinie Con Park
50
Buckleboo
Caralue Bluff 484m
Iron Baron
87
Mt Middleback 446m
Kimba
82
26
HWY
WHYALLA
Searcy Bay
Cape Labatt
Pt Labatt Con Park
Cape Radstock
90

9
GREAT
AUSTRALIAN
Talia
409
Colton
Venus Bay
55
Kopi
42
Lock
Caralue
Hambidge Con Park
Darke Peak 448m +
Darke Peak
Sheaoak Hill Con Park
Carappie Con Park
Middle Camp Hills Con Park
Rudall Con Park
108
Munyaroo Con Park
Plank Point
Jarrold Point
LINCOLN
153
117

10
BIGHT
Anxious Bay
Waldegrave Islands
Cape Finnis
Elliston
Flinders Island
Ward Islands
INVESTIGATOR GROUP
Pearson Islands
74
HWY
EYRE
Sheringa
09
Bascombe Well Con Park
Kielpa
Rudall
Cleve
43
47
Elbow Hill
Franklin Harbour Con Park
Cowell
Shoalwater Point
34
Arno Bay
PENINSULA
172
Verran
Wharminda
Hincks Con Park
146
SPENCER
Tickera
Wallaroo
Moonta Bay
Moonta
Port Hughes
78

11
Mount Hope
Drummond Point
Round Lake
Kapinnie
09
Yeelanna
Karkoo
Ungarra
Cockaleechie
26
42
Lipson
Cape Hardy
Port Neill
Warrow
Coulta
Edillilie
37
Yallunda Flat
Cummins
149
Cape Elizabeth
GULF
Weetulta
Arthurton
Balgowan
Maitland
53
46
145

12
Point Sir Isaac
Coffin Bay
Coffin Bay Peninsula
Mount Dutton Bay
Point Whidbey
Avoid Bay
Killdie Bay
Wanilla
Greenly Island
WHIDBEY ISLES
Perforated Island
Coffin Bay
Goomunga
Wangary
North Shields
Boston Point
Boston Island
Cape Donington
Reevesby Island
Sir Joseph Banks Group Con Park
Roxby Island
Splisby Island
Tumby Bay
Port Victoria
Wardang Island
Urania
Sandilands
Minlaton
Brentwood
Point Vincent
32
YORKE
PENINSULA

13
Rocky Island
N
Cape Carnot
Sleaford Mere Con Park
Sleaford Mere
Taylor Island
Lincoln National Park
Thistle Island
West Point
Williams Island
Waterhouse Point
North Island
GAMBIER ISLANDS
Wedge Island
West Cape
Innes National Park
Inneston
North Neptunes
Marion Bay
Stenhouse Bay
Corny Point
Hardwicke Bay
Warooka
Oaklands
Stansbury
Wool Bay
Yorketown
Point Davenport
Edithburgh
49

Port Lincoln

A B C D E F G H I

BAROSSA VALLEY

0 1 2 3 4 5km

N

79

20

Bilyara

HIGHWAY

Greenock
PASS

Daveyston
STURT
BYE
20

Plush Corner

Nuriootpa
Light Pass

Tolley, Scott & Tolley
Penfolds
Penrice

Seppelts
Patersons Hill +300m
Lutheran Church
Seppelts Tomb
Marananga
Kaiser Stuhl
River
Saltram

Seppeltsfield

Woodley Wines
Dorrien
Angaston

Greenock Ck
Pedare Wines
Cement Works
Quarry

Seppelts
Drive-In Theatre
Hardy

Hoffmanns North Para
Para
Vine Vale
Angas Park

Bernkastel
Veritas
Leo Buring
Yalumba

Basedows
Marble Quarry

Tanunda
Northern
+Mengler Hill

Chateau Tanunda

Bethany
Scenic
Drive

High Wycombe
Tanunda Ck

Gomersal
Bethany Wines

St. Halletts
Rifle Range

Kabininge

SOUTHERN VALES

0 1 2 3km
Caravan Park
Darlington
Sturt Gorge Rec Park
River

N

Marino
Coromandel Valley

MORPHETT
MAJORS RD
BLACK
Flagstaff Hill

North Para River
Chatterton
BOULEVARD
RD
RD
Torresans

ST VINCENT
O'Halloran Hill
LANDER RD
Marienberg

Chateau Yaldara
OCEAN
Happy Valley Res
Aberfoyle Park

Karlsburg
Field
River
St Francis
SOUTH
Happy Valley
Horndale
Chandlers Hill

Wilsford
Reynella
Coolawin Estate

Rowland Flat
SHERRIFFS RD
Shopping Centre
PIMPALA RD
Reynell

Das Alte Weinhaus
Altond
Orlando
O'Sullivan Beach
BAINS
RD
Trennert

Liebichs Rovalley
O'SULLIVAN BEACH RD
Morphett Vale

Lyndoch
GULLY
Pioneer Village
HILL

Barossa Settlers
Pewsey Vale
Christies
FLAXMILL
RD
COX
RD

Christies Beach
Drive In Theatre
Hardy's Morphett Vale Cellars
BEACH
RD

Port Noarlunga
DYSON
BRODIE
Hackham

HONEYPOT RD

GULF
RD
River

Onkaparinga
Chapel Vale
CHAPEL
HILL
RD
Elysium

Seaford
Coriole
Seaview
CHAFERS RD
ELLIOTS RD
Blewitt Springs

Oliverhill
Kay Bros

SEAVIEW RD
KAYS RD
Maglieri
Woodstock

Caravan Park
Moana
d'Arenberg
Berenyi
Ingoldby

COMMERCIAL
Pedler Creek
SOUTH
Taranga
Settlement
Merrivale
Tinlins
Ryecroft
Fern Hill

Palladio
CHALK HILL RD
Chalk Hill
Scarpantoni Winery
McLaren Flat

Hardys Tintara
Southern Vales
Genders
James Haselgrove Wines
Middlebrook Estate

Maslin Beach
Piramimma
TATACHILLA RD
Daringa Cellars
Wirra Wirra

BAYLISS RD
MAIN RD
McLaren Vale
McMURTRIE RD

Noons

78

Richard Hamilton

Many visitors to South Australia will enjoy a trip to some of the most accessible vineyards in Australia.

There are over 40 wineries in the Southern Vales area just south of Adelaide. Most are centred around McLaren Vale, often tucked away in the countryside, but well signposted so they are easy to find. Don't miss the Bushing Festival, held for a week each October, which includes tastings, tours and an Elizabethan feast.

The Barossa Valley 50 kilometres from Adelaide is also well worth a visit. Scores of beautiful vineyards cover the gently rolling hills and the delightful Germanic-style towns are readily accessible over excellent roads. The Vintage Festival held every second year in April is the highlight of the area.

Maps of
Western Australia

Location Map

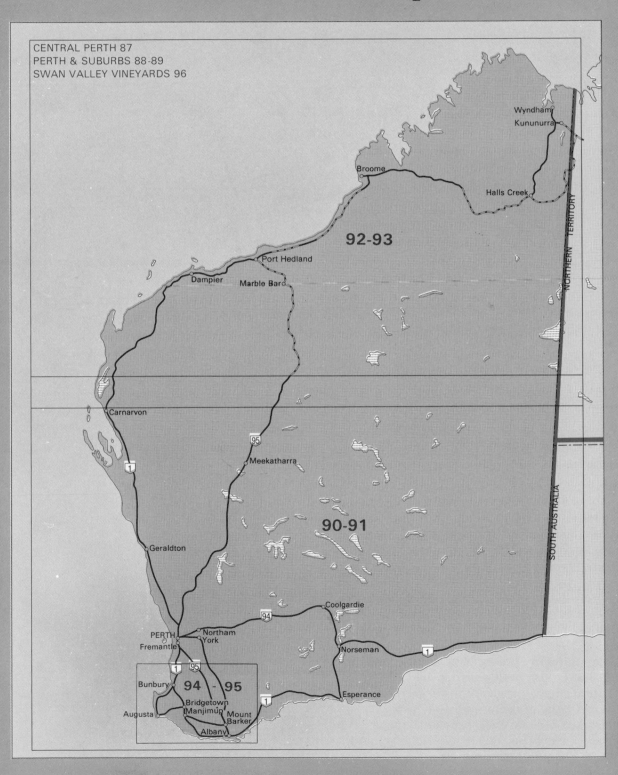

CENTRAL PERTH 87
PERTH & SUBURBS 88-89
SWAN VALLEY VINEYARDS 96

Wyndham
Kununurra

Broome

Halls Creek

92-93

Port Hedland

Dampier

Marble Bar

NORTHERN TERRITORY

Carnarvon

95

Meekatharra

90-91

SOUTH AUSTRALIA

Geraldton

Coolgardie

94

PERTH
Northam
York
Fremantle

Norseman

1

94 - 95

Bunbury

Bridgetown
Manjimup
Mount
Barker

Augusta

Albany

Esperance

1

95

1

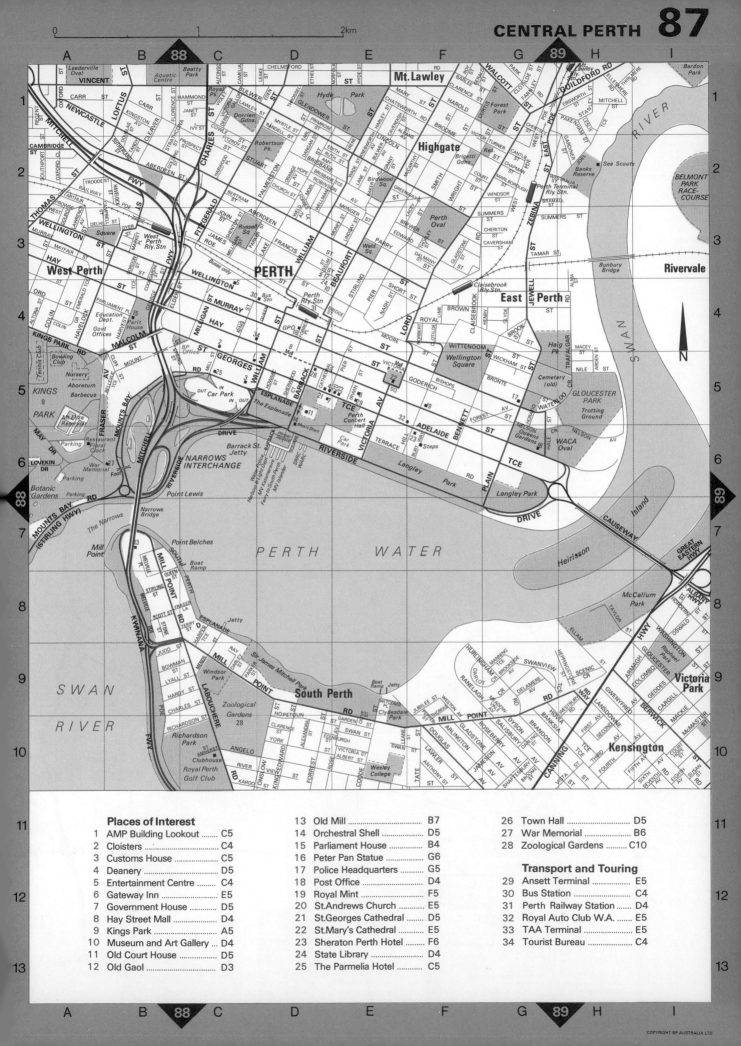

Places of Interest

1 AMP Building Lookout C5
2 Cloisters C4
3 Customs House C5
4 Deanery D5
5 Entertainment Centre C4
6 Gateway Inn E5
7 Government House D5
8 Hay Street Mall D4
9 Kings Park A5
10 Museum and Art Gallery .. D4
11 Old Court House D5
12 Old Gaol D3

13 Old Mill B7
14 Orchestral Shell D5
15 Parliament House B4
16 Peter Pan Statue G6
17 Police Headquarters G5
18 Post Office D4
19 Royal Mint F5
20 St.Andrews Church E5
21 St.Georges Cathedral D5
22 St.Mary's Cathedral E5
23 Sheraton Perth Hotel F6
24 State Library D4
25 The Parmelia Hotel C5

26 Town Hall D5
27 War Memorial B6
28 Zoological Gardens C10

Transport and Touring

29 Ansett Terminal E5
30 Bus Station C4
31 Perth Railway Station D4
32 Royal Auto Club W.A. E5
33 TAA Terminal E5
34 Tourist Bureau C4

90

Grid columns: A B C D E F G H I
Grid rows: 1 2 3 4 5 6 7 8 9 10 11 12 13

OCEAN

INDIAN OCEAN

Wembley Downs
Woodlands
Churchlands
City Beach
Herdsman
Glendalough
Mt. Hawthorn
Joondanna
Coolbinia
Menora
North Perth
Lake Monger
Leederville
Floreat
Wembley
Cambridge
West Leederville
Jolimont
Daglish
Subiaco
West Perth
PERTH
Shenton Park
Swanbourne
Graylands
Karrakatta
Kings Park
Crawley
Univ of WA
Matilda Bay
South Perth
Nedlands
Claremont
Peppermint Grove
Cottesloe
North Cottesloe Beach
Cottesloe Beach
Dalkeith
Freshwater Bay
Melville Water
Como Beach
Como
Mosman Park
Mosman Bay
SWAN RIVER
Pt. Resolution
Applecross
Nth Fremantle
Bicton
Attadale
Alfred Cove
Ardross
Mt. Pleasant
Melville
Myaree
Booragoon
Brentwood
Palmyra
East Fremantle
FREMANTLE
Royal Fremantle Golf Club
Fremantle Cemetery
Willagee
O'Connor
Bateman
White Gum Valley
Beaconsfield
South Fremantle
Hilton
Kardinya
Bull Creek
Murdoch University

COPYRIGHT BP AUSTRALIA LTD

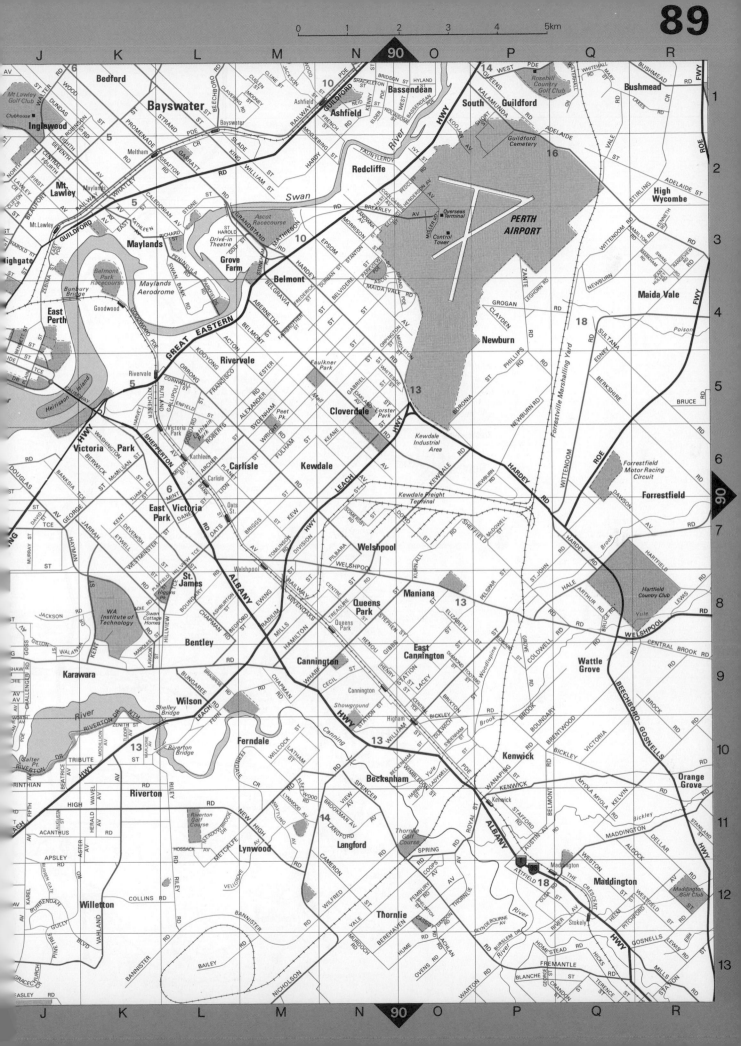

A B C D E F G H I

92

1
Cape Cuvier
Quobba
Hill Springs
Manberry
Moogoonie
Minnie Creek
Gifford Creek
Cobra
Dooley Downs
Mt Vernon
Tangadee
COLLIER RANGE NAT. PARK
NORTHERN HIGHWAY
Lake Macleod
Cooralya
Mardathuna
KENNEDY RANGE NAT. PARK
Eudamullah
Lyons River
Mt Augustus
Mt Phillip
Yinnatharra
Waldberg
Woodlands
Mulgul
Kumarina Motel
225
Beyondie

2
Bernier Island
Carnarvon
Doorawarrah
Tracking Station
Binthalya
Mooka
Jimba Jimbu
Gascoyne Junction
Bidgemia
Dalgety Downs
Moolon Downs
Mt James
Landor
Mt Clere
Milgun
Mingah Springs
35
Neds Creek
Marymia
Dorre Island
Callagiddy
Ella Valla
Edagee
Winderie
Yalbalgo
Towrana
Dairy Creek
Glenburn
Yalbra
Errabiddy
Erong Springs
Yarlarweelor
Mt Padbury
Bryah
Lake Nab
Shark Bay
Cape Peron North
Marron
Pimbee
Wahroonga
Carey Downs
Innouendy
Three Rivers

3
Dirk Hartog Island
Dirk Hartog
Useless Loop
Freycinet Reach
Peron
Denham
Nanga
Carbla
Hamelin
Meedo
Gilroyd
Wooramel
Yaringa
Woodleigh
Yalardy
Byro
Milly Milly
Beringarra
Mt Hale
Koonmarra
Mileura
Belele
Karalundi Mission
Munarra
Paroo
Diamond Well
Cunya
Yanbil
423
Meekatharra
Wiluna Mission
Wilu

4
Carrarang
Coburn
Tamala
Meadow
Billabong Roadhouse
486
Nerren Nerren
PIA ABORIGINAL RESERVE
New Forest
239
Yallalong
Muggon
Meeberrie
Mt Narryer
Twin Peaks
Murgoo
Meka
NICHOLSON RA
Boolardy
Cue
Coodarby
Killi
Glen Beebyn
Tuckanarra Roadhouse
Karbar
Nallan
Taincrow
Cogla Downs
118
Polelle
Youno Downs
Yarrabubba
Gidgee
Nannine
Murchison Downs
Hillview
No-Ibla
Yeelirrie
Albion Downs
Lake Way

5
KALBARRI NATIONAL PARK
Murchison House
Kalbarri
Ross Graham Lookout
Bluff Point
Eurardy
Coolcalalaya
Lake Nerrunyne
Pinegrove
Narloo
Tardie
Noongal
Yuin
Gabyon
Carlaminda
Yowergabbie
Mount Magnet
Lakeside
Lake Austin
Melangata
Jingemara
Challa
Hy Brazil
Atlex
Dandaraga
Black Hill
Pinnacle
Yarraquin
Barrambie
Wondinong
Wynyangoo
Windsor
Sandstone
Booylgoo Springs
Kaluwa
Lake Mason
80
Balline
Mt View
Bullardoo

6
Port Gregory
Yuna
Northhampton
Nabawa
52
Geraldton
Cape Burney
Greenough
Easter Group
Pelsaert Group
Tallering
Yalgoo
Wagga Wagga
Mullewa
335
Barnong
Mellenbye
Badja
Burnbumm
239
Nalbarra
Mongers Lake
Iona
Mteline
Kirkalocka
Narndee
Oudabunna
Paynes Find
144
Boodanoo
Windimurra
Youangarra
Cashmere Downs
Lake Barlee
Perrinva
96

7
Port Denison
Dongara
Three Springs
216
Carnamah
Latham
Perenjori
Morawa
Karara
Lochada
Kadji Kadji
Thundalarra
Warriedar
Pullagaroo
Pindabunna
Maranalgo
Lake Barlee
Mt Elvire
Walling Rock
125
Whitewells
Mt Gibson
Bimbijy
Mouroubra
546
Lake Moore
Diemals
153
GREAT NORTHERN HWY
Knobby Head

8
Leeman
Jurien Bay
Jurien
Ronsard Bay
Cervantes
BRAND HWY
Eneabba
Badgingarra
Coorow
Wubin
Dalwallinu
Watheroo
Miling
Bindi Bindi
Cadoux
Remlap
Kalannie
Beacon
Wialki
Bonnie Rock
Bencubbin
Mukinbudin
Lake Deborah
Elmvin
Koolyanobbing
Jaure
Jau
Moora

9
MOORE RIVER NATIONAL PARK
398
146
Dandaragan
New Norcia
Lancelin
213
Wongan Hills
Koorda
Trayning
Calingiri
Dowerin
Wyalkatchem
Nungarin
Burracoppin
109
Southern Cross
84
EASTERN
18
Gin Gin
95
Toodyay
Goomalling
Meckering
Kellerberrin
Bodallin
Marvel Loch
507
Merredin

10
PERTH
FREMANTLE
Rottnest Island
Kalamunda
Kwinana
Rockingham
Mandurah
32
Armadale
Bullsbrook East
Mundaring
Wundowie
York
Northam
163
Tammin
GT
Bruce Rock
GREAT
112 1135
Beverley
Brookton
140
Quairading
Narembeen
Corrigin
60
Hyden
518
Karlgarin
138
FRANK HANN NAT. PAR

11
Pinjarra
159
Preston Beach
Dwellingup
Waroona
Williams
Boddington
Pingelly
Wandering
Wickepin
Narrogin
Highbury
Kukerin
Lake Grace
Newdegate
68
425
Yealering
Kondinin
66
95
SOUTHERN HWY
Wagin
Dumbleyung
Lake Magenta
Pingrup
Ravensthorpe

12
Bunbury
Collie
Boyanup
Geographe Bay
Busselton
Yallingup
Capel
Donnybrook
Darkan
Woodanilling
Nyabing
110
390
Katanning
Broomehill
Kojonup
Gnowangerup
Ongerup
Jerramungup
289
Hopeto
FITZGERALD R NATIONAL PA
146
Jarrahwood
Greenbushes
Boyup Brook
Bridgetown
83
67
Tambellup
Borden
60
Bremer Bay
Margaret River
Nannup

13
Augusta
Cape Leeuwin
Pemberton
Manjimup
Nyamup
Frankland
96
185
Northcliffe
Point D'Entrecasteaux
367
65
Rocky Gully
Mt Barker
Cranbrook
Boxwood Hill
STIRLING RA NAT P
54
Kendenup
119
Denham
King River
Albany
King George Sound
Cheyne Bay
Cape Knob
Dillon Bay
SOU
Walpole
Cliffy Head

INDIAN OCEAN

N

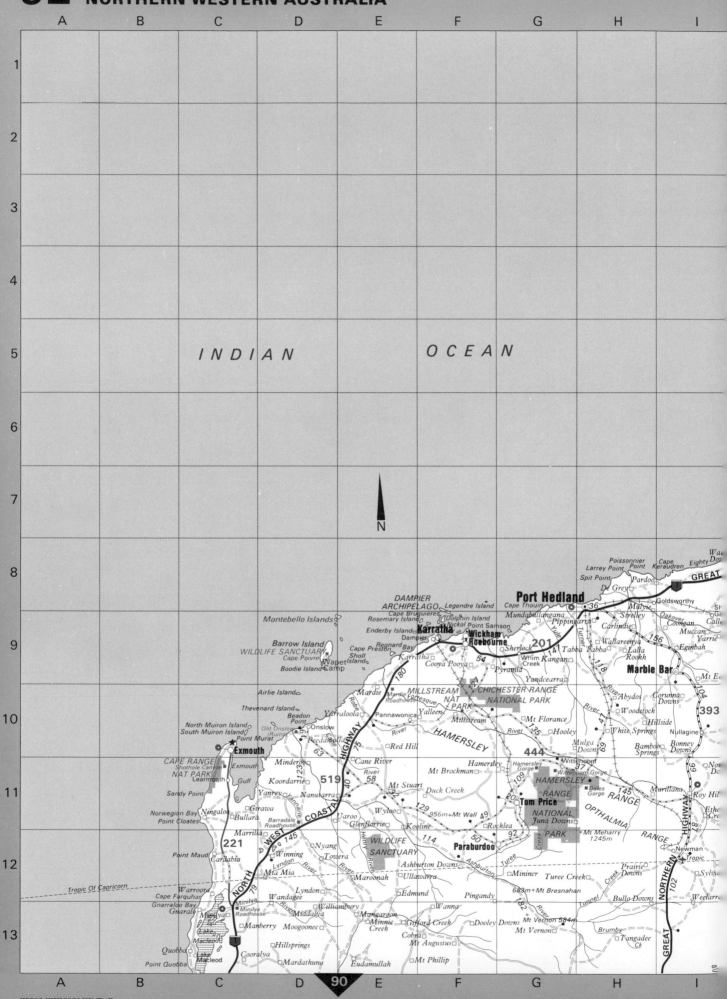

INDIAN   OCEAN

N

DAMPIER
ARCHIPELAGO
Cape Bruguieres
Rosemary Island
Montebello Islands
Enderby Island
Legendre Island
Dolphin Island
Nickol Point Samson
Cape Thouin
Port Hedland
De Grey
Pardoo
Spit Point
Larrey Point
Poissonnier Point
Cape Keraudren
Eighty
Wa
Doo
Wa
GREAT
Goldsworthy
St
Ga
Calle

Karratha
Wickham
Roebourne
Mundabullangana
Pippingarra
Yule
36
Mulyie
Strelley
Carlindie
201
Wallareenya
Lalla
Rookh
Muccan
Yarrie
Eginbah
Coongan
156

Barrow Island
WILDLIFE SANCTUARY
Cape Poivre
Boodie Island
Cape Preston
Regnard Bay
Dampier
Sholl
Island
Karratha
Cooya Pooya
54
Pyramid
Yandeurra
Sherlock
Whim Kangan
Creek
Tabba Tabba
Marble Bar
Mt E
Wapet
Camp

Airlie Island
Mardie
Mardie
Roadhouse
Fortescue
MILLSTREAM
NAT
PARK
CHICHESTER RANGE
NATIONAL PARK
River
Abydos
Woodstock
Gorunna
Downs
104
393

Thevenard Island
Beadon
Point
Yarraloola
Pannawonica
Yalleen
Millstream
Mt Florance
River
135
Hooley
White Springs
Hillside
Nullagine

North Muiron Island
South Muiron Island
Point Murat
Old Onslow
(Ruins)
Onslow
HIGHWAY
75
Red Hill
HAMERSLEY
River
Mulga
Downs
99
Bamboo
Springs
Bonney
Downs

Exmouth
CAPE RANGE
Shothole Canyon
NAT PARK
Learmonth
Minderoo
Exmouth
Gulf
Koordarrie
Cane River
River 58
Mt Stuart
Duck Creek
Mt Brockman
Hamersley
109
Hamersley
Gorge
Wittenoom
37
Wittenoom Gorge
519
Dales
Gorge
HAMERSLEY
RANGE
444
145
Marillana
Roy Hill
Ethe
Cre
Nor
Do

Sandy Point
Yanrey
Nanutarra
129
956m+Mt Wall
49
Tom Price
NATIONAL
Juna Downs
PARK
OPTHALMIA
RANGE

Norwegian Bay
Point Cloates
Ningaloo
Bullara
Girawa
Barradale
Roadhouse
Uaroo
Glenflorrie
Wyloo
Kooline
Rocklea
92
Mt Meharry
1245m
Newman
102
Tropic
Sylb

Marrilla
221
WEST
145
Henry
Nyang
Towera
114
50
Paraburdoo
Ashburton
Turee
NORTHERN
HIGHWAY

Point Maud
Cardabia
Winning
Lyndon
Mia Mia
River
Maroonah
Ashburton Downs
Ullawarra
Mininer
Turee Creek
Prairie
Downs
Bullo Downs
Weelarr

Tropic Of Capricorn
Warroora
Cape Farquhar
Gnarraloo Bay
Gnarale
Minilya
Minilya
Roadhouse
Wandagee
Lyndon
River
Williambury
Wanna
Pingandy
683m+Mt Bresnahan
182
River
Tunnel
Brumby

Quobba
Point Quobba
Lake
Macleod
Cooralya
Mardathunu
Hillsprings
Middalya
Manberry
Moogooree
Minnie
Creek
Mangaroon
Gifford Creek
Eudamullah
Dooley Downs
Cobra
Mt Augustus
Mt Phillip
Mt Vernon 584m
Mt Vernon
GREAT
Tangadee
Ck

COASTAL
180
Robe
River
63
Fortescue
River
Feedamulla
River
1123
Tamerlane
40
79
Beasley
River
Henry
River
Minilya
River

0 50 100 150 200 250 300 350 400km

J K L M N O P Q R

TIMOR SEA

Cape Talbot Cape Londonderry
Cape Bougainville Vansittart
Gibson Point Napier Broome Bay Cape Rulhieres
Bay Cape Bernier
Admiralty Pago Mission Joseph Bonaparte
Gulf (Aband)
Montague Sound ADMIRALTY Kalumburu Cape St Lambert Gulf
ABORIGINAL Mission Buckle Head
Bigge Island RESERVE Carson FORREST RIVER
Cape Pond River Theda (WYNDHAM)
York Sound Mitchell DRYSDALE ABORIGINAL
Coronation Island River RIVER RESERVE
Brunswick Doongan NAT Oombulgurrio Cambridge
Heywood Bay Mitchell PARK Forest River Gulf
Island River Mission (Aband)
Champagny Isc. GARDNER PLATEAU
Camden Sound Moran Wyndham
KUNMUNYA River Drysdale River Ivanhoe Kimberley
Hall Point Ellenbrae El Questro Research Stn
(CAMDEN SOUND) Kwinalie Home Kununurra
ABORIGINAL RESERVE Mission George Valley
Cockatoo Is (Aband) Water Prince Regent River Pentecost 56 Lake
Doubtful Bay Downs Dunham Argyle
Koolan Is Calder River Tourist
One Arm Point Collier Mt Elizabeth Gibb River Chapman River 68 Village
Thomas Bay Bay 482m+Tabletop Mt Wood Dunham Argyle
Cygnet Walcott Inlet Beverley Durack River CARR BOYD RA Cockewood
Bay Secure Bay Springs 93 375 Glen Hill HWY
Pender Bay Lombadina Isdell Bow River Lissadell Spring
BEAGLE BAY (BROOME) Mission Mt Hart 374 Mt House Tableland Creek
Beagle Bay King Mt House 539m+ Bedford Mabel Texas
ABORIGINAL RESERVE Sound 936m+Mt Ord VIOLET VALLEY Downs Downs
Beagle Bay Disaster Bay Napier Mt Broome 935m ABORIGINAL Osmond Valley
Cape Baskerville Stokes Bay Downs Glenroy RESERVE 158 Mabel
Carnot Bay Mt Jowaenga Barker River KIMBERLEY Downs Alice Downs Old Flora
Cape Bertholet Fraser River Kimberley Fairfield KING Springvale Regeneration
Coulomb Point Mt Jowaenga Downs LEOPOLD Mornington HIGHWAY Depot
James Price Point Derby WINDJANA RANGES Lansdowne Saunders Nicholson
Cape Boileau Kilto 145 43 GORGE Mt Broome Creek Flora Valley
Broome Waterbank NAT PARK Leeda TUNNEL CREEK GEIKIE GORGE Watery Springvale Sophie 174
229 42 NAT PARK NAT PARK Moola Downs
Gantheaume Point Roebuck Plains Blina Ellendale 323m+Mt Winifred Bulla Halls Downs Gordon Downs
Roebuck Bay Mt Anderson 259 Leopold Fossil Downs Creek NORTHERN Koongie
Thangoo Luluigua Calwynyardah Downs O'Donnell Park DENISON PLAINS
Cape Villaret Dampier Downs Myroodah Fitzroy Crossing Mt Amhurst Ruby Plains
Cape Latouche Treville Nerrima Quanbun Jubilee Margaret River Louisa
False Cape Bossut Kalyeeda Downs Downs Downs
Lagrange Bay Noonkanbah 291 Bohemia Downs Carranyu
Cape Bossut Cherrabun Christmas GREAT WOLF CREEK CRATER
Admiral Bay Lagrange Mission Creek Christmas Ck NAT PARK Sturt Creek
Cape Frezier Frazier Downs Gordon Downs
Cape Jaubert Nita Downs Lake Jones Sturt Billiluna
Anna Plains Lake Betty Lake McLernon Balgo
NORTHERN Mission
624 GREAT SANDY DESERT BALWINA (BALGO)
HIGHWAY Sandfire ABORIGINAL RESERVE
Flat Roadhouse

BUCCANEER ARCHIPELAGO
BONAPARTE ARCHIPELAGO

Yurrawagine

Lake Waukarlycarly Lake Willis
Lake White
Telfer Mining Centre Lake Hazlett
Percival Lakes
Tobin Lake
Lake Dora
Oakover River RUNDALL RIVER Lake Auld
ROBERTSON RANGE NATIONAL PARK Lake Mackay
Rudall GIBSON DESERT CENTRAL
algunya ROUTE
Jiggalong Mission Lake Disappointment Tropic Of Capricorn ABORIGINAL
Capricorn
Robertson Range STOCK Lake Cobb
White Lake Lake Hopkins
RESERVE

100

101

WARNING: Although an indication of road surface types is shown on this map, it is imperative that visitors obtain full information as to road conditions ahead before proceeding on their journey. During the period October to May "wet" season conditions may cause severe flooding, making many roads impassable.

The majority of water features shown on this map do not contain permanent water.

Entry to Aboriginal Reserves is strictly prohibited unless a permit is obtained.

WESTERN AUSTRALIA / NORTHERN TERRITORY

CANNING STOCK ROUTE

1 2 3 4 5 6 7 8 9 10 11 12 13

90

N

OCEAN

INDIAN

Lake Clifton
YALGORUP NATIONAL PARK
Preston Beach
Lake Preston
Waroona
Hamel
Wagerup
Yarloop
Cookernup
Myalup
Binningup
Harvey
Wokalup
Benger
Brunswick Junction
Leschenault Inlet
Australind
Koombana Bay
BUNBURY
Picton Junction
Dardanup
Stratham
Boyanup
Gwindinup
Elgin
Capel
Argyle
Donnybrook
Cape Naturaliste
Bunker Bay
Eagle Bay
Meelup
Dunsborough
Sugarloaf Rock
Ngilgi Cave
Yallingup Caves
Quindalup
Carbunup
Canal Rocks
Wyadup
Cape Clairault
Vasse
Jindong
Busselton
Wonnerup Inlet
Ludlow
Wonnerup
Tutunup
LEEUWIN-
Moses Rock
Woodlands
Yelverton
Metricup
NATURALISTE
Willyabrup
Cowaramup Bay
Gracetown
Cowaramup
Treeton
Margaret River
NATIONAL
Prevelly Park
Calgardup Beach
Calgarup
Mowen
Rosa Glen
Witchcliffe
Mammoth Cave
Lake Cave
Forest Grove
Warner Glen
Cape Freycinet
PARK
BROCKMAN
Alexandra Bridge
Hamelin Is.
Hamelin Bay
Karridale
Moondyne & Jewel Caves
SCOTT NAT. PARK
Scott
Hardy Inlet
Augusta
Flinders Bay
Cape Leeuwin
St. Alouarn Is.
Cape Beaufort
L. Gingilup
L. Quilaijup
L. Jasper
D'ENTRECASTEAUX NAT. PARK
Claymore
Maryvale
Quilergup
Cundinup
Jarrahwood
Cambray
Sussex Mill
Bibilup
Nannup
Carlotta
WARREN NATL. PK.
BEEDELUP NAT. PARK
Willow Spring
Donnelly Mill
Yanmah
Glenoran
Dean Mill
Jardee
Pemberton
The Cascades
Brockman
Kingdom of the Karri
Yeagerup
Warren
Donbakup
Calicup Hill 229m
Northcliffe
Meerup R.
Mt. Chudalup 229m
Windy Harbour
L. Maringup
Point D'Entrecasteaux
Sandy Is.
West Cliff Point
Cliffy Head
Chatham Is.
Broke Reefs
Pt. Nuyts
WALPOLE NORNALUP NATIONAL PARK
Geographe Bay
WHICHER RANGE

Murray
Nanga
68
Waroona Dam
Samson Bk. Dam
Marradong
Boddington
64
Dwarda
Crossman
Logue Bk. Dam
Hoffmans Mill
Stirling Dam
Harvey Weir
Quindanning
60
Treesville
Beela
Roelands
Worsley
Brekepan
Waterloo
Atherson
Collie
Griffin
Wellington Dam
Shotts
Buckingham
Bingham
Darkan
Gibbs Crossing
Boolading
Bowelling
93
Bennelacking
Collieburn
Collie Cardiff
Muja OpenCut
Centaur Colliery
Lyalls Mill
Mumballup
Cordering
Wellington Mills
Lowden
L. Ngartiminny
Cape
Brookhampton
Newlands
Noggerup
McAlinden
Trigwell Bridge
Kirup
Grimwade
Wilga
Mullalyup
Benjinup
Balingup
Greenbushes
Lewana Park
Asplin
Maltrup
Kulikup
Boyup Brook
Dinninup
15
Catterick
Hester
Bridgetown
Blackwood
Cardup
Mayanup
Chowerup
Yornup
Wilgarup
Palgarup
Balbarrup
Dingup
Manjimup
Nyamup
Deeside
MUIRS
Tone River Mill
98
Lake Muir
Diamond Tree
Eastbrook
Collins
Barronhurst
Gloucester Tree
Quininup
Shannon River
Mt. Burnside Tower
61
Deep River
Walpole
69
Gladstone Falls
Broke Inlet
Beach Ridge
Weld
Shannon
East Branch
SOUTH WESTERN
Tone
WESTERN

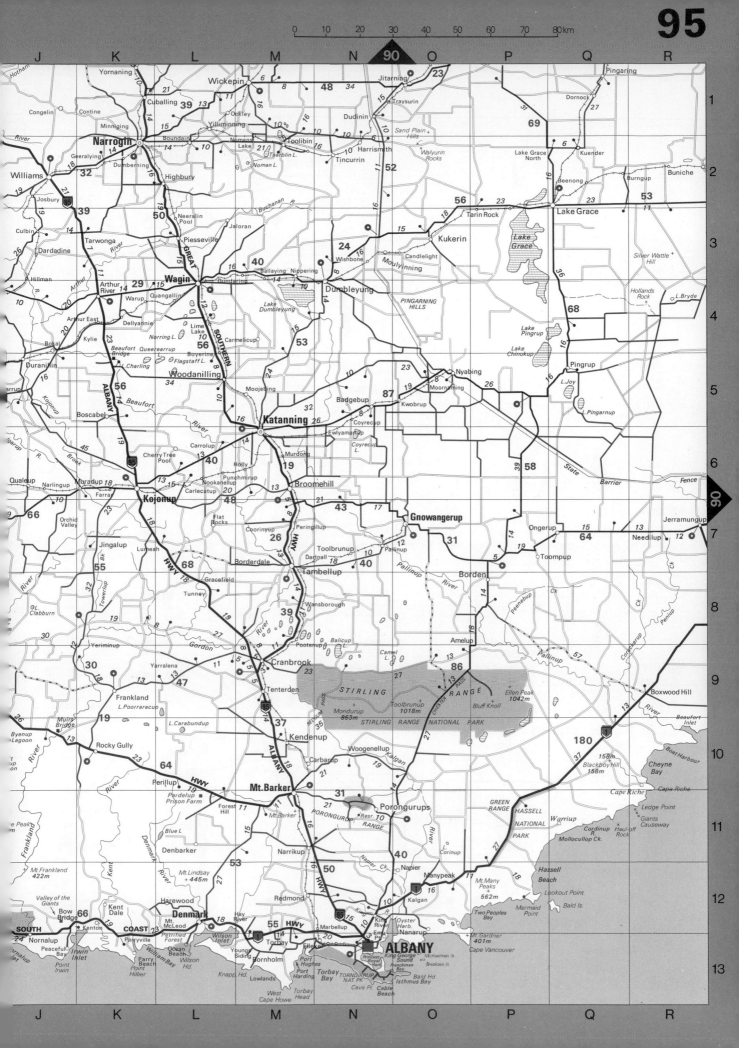

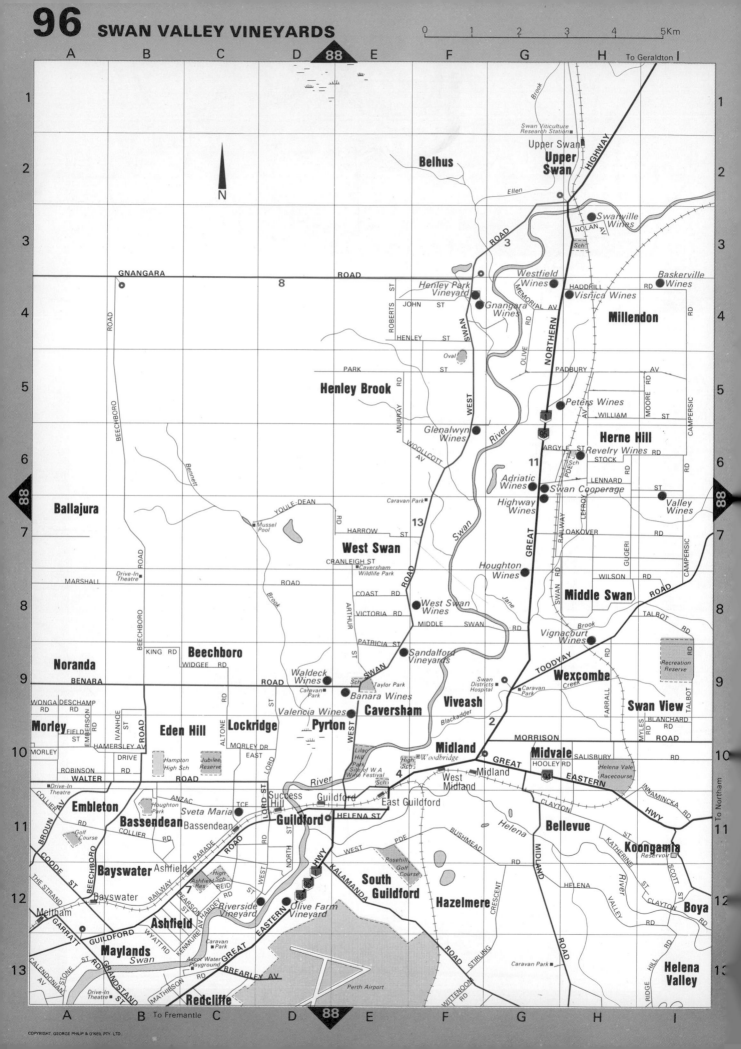

Maps of
Northern Territory

Location Map

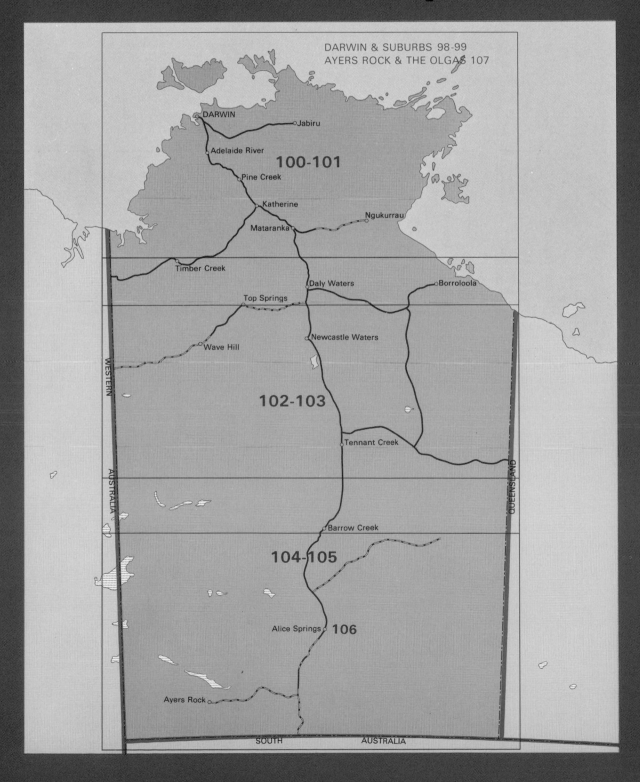

DARWIN & SUBURBS 98-99
AYERS ROCK & THE OLGAS 107

DARWIN
Jabiru

Adelaide River

100-101

Pine Creek

Katherine

Ngukurrau
Mataranka

Timber Creek

Daly Waters
Borroloola
Top Springs

Newcastle Waters
Wave Hill

102-103

Tennant Creek

WESTERN

AUSTRALIA

QUEENSLAND

Barrow Creek

104-105

Alice Springs **106**

Ayers Rock

SOUTH   AUSTRALIA

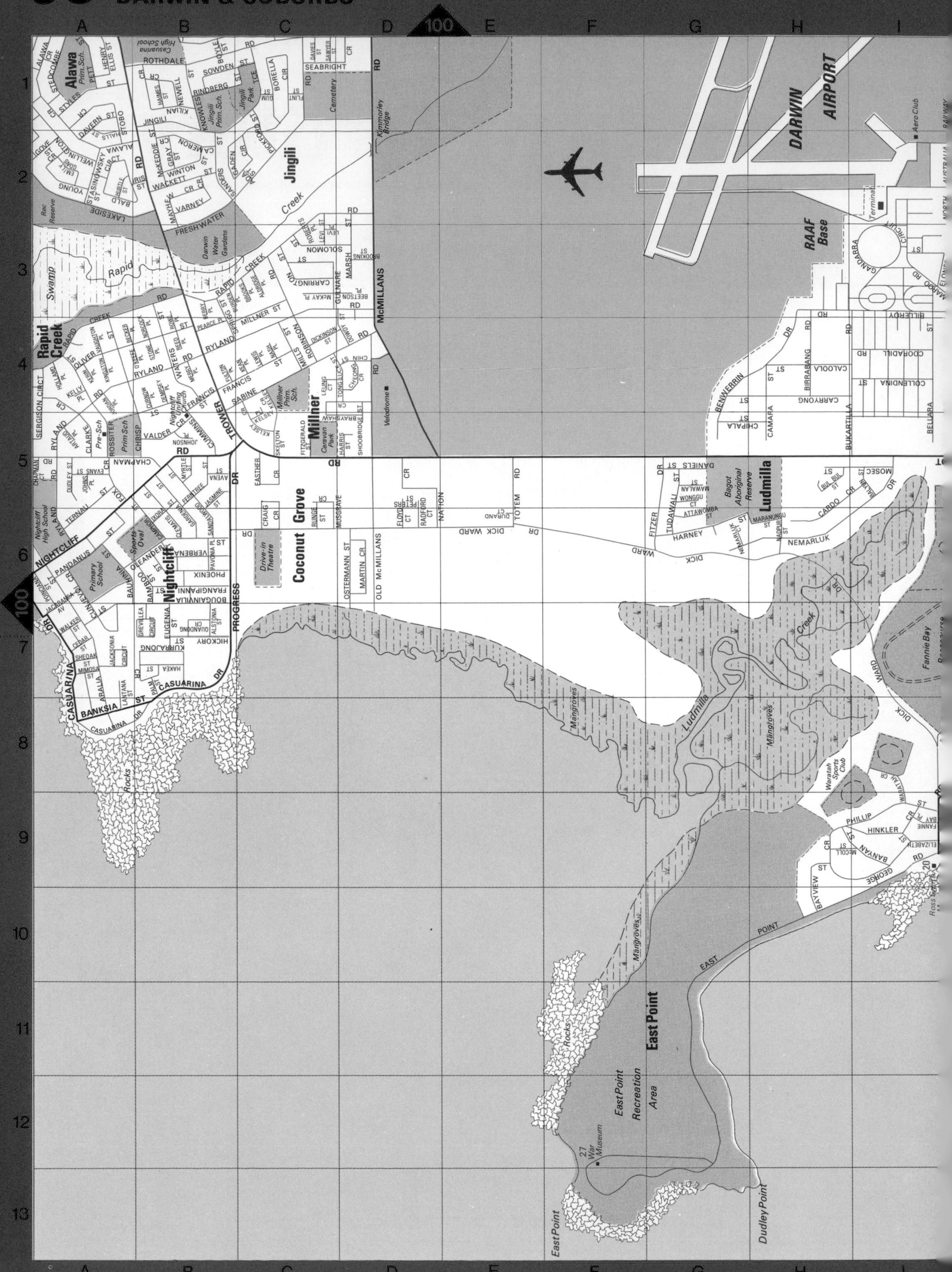

DARWIN AIRPORT

RAAF Base

Jingili

Alawa Prim. Sch.

Casuarina High School

Rapid Creek

Millner Prim. Sch.

Coconut Grove

Nightcliff

Nightcliff High School

Primary School

Casuarina

Banksia

Ludmilla

Bagot Aboriginal Reserve

East Point

East Point Recreation Area

War Museum

East Point

Dudley Point

Fannie Bay

Waratah Sports Club

Aero Club

Drive-in Theatre

Sports Oval

Darwin Water Gardens

Kinmorley Bridge

Cemetery

Rapid Creek

McMillans RD

Old McMillans RD

Totem RD

East Point RD

Rocks

Mangroves

Ludmilla Creek

Swamp

Places of Interest

1 Administration Offices	Q8
14 Amphitheatre	N9
2 Botanical Gardens	M9
3 Casino	N10
4 Catholic Cathedral	P9
5 Chinese Cemetery	M6
6 Chinese Temple	Q7
7 Christchurch Cathedral	Q7
8 Civic Centre	Q7
23 Darwin Cultural Centre	P9
9 Don Motel Hotel	Q7
10 Government Residency	R7
11 Historical Cemetery	L8
12 Leichhardt Memorial	P9
28 Municipal Golf Course	N9
13 Museum & Art Gallery	L9
15 Olympic Pool	J8
16 Police Headquarters	Q8

17 Port Authority	Q7
18 Post Office	Q8
19 Public Library	Q8
20 Ross Smith Memorial	J9
21 Smith Street Mall	Q8
22 Telford Intl. Hotel	O9
24 Travelodge Hotel	P9
25 War Memorial	Q7

Transport and Touring

26 Office/Terminal for Ansett, Airlines of Northern Aust. & Airlines of Western Australia	Q8
27 Bus Terminal	Q7
29 Qantas	Q8
30 TAA Terminal	Q7
31 Tourist Bureau	Q8

A B C D E F G H I

1
2
3
4
5
6
7
8
9
10
11
12
13

TIMOR

SEA

Joseph
Bonaparte
Gulf

Cape Van Dieman
St Asaph Bay
Deception Pt
Rocky Pt
Shark Bay
Radford Pt
Pulanumbi
Milikapiti
Snake Bay
Lethbridge Bay
Cape Fleeming
Cape Croker
McCluer Is
Grant Is
Minjilang
CROKER ISLAND
Cape Cockburn
Vashon Head
Smith Pt
Danger Pt
Palm Bay
Blue Mud Bay
Lingi Pt
Ponham Pt
Boradil Bay
Tinganoo Bay
Cape Don
COBOURG PENINSULA
Napier Bay
Cape Keith
Greenhill Is
Morsell Is
Murgenella
Brogden Pt
Goulburn Islands
Aurart Bay
Warruvi

BATHURST ISLAND
Gordan Bay
Bathurst Is Aboriginal Land
Cape Helvetius
Port Hurd
Mitchell Pt
Nguiu
Pickertaramoor
MELVILLE ISLAND
Melville Island Aboriginal Land
Cobham Pt
Conder Pt
Cape Gambier
Clarence Strait
Nth Vernon Islands
Sth East
Cape Hotham
Van Dieman Gulf
Field Is
Barron Is
MURGENELLA WILDLIFE SANCTUARY
Mt Borradaile
Mt Permain
Cooper
King

Beagle Gulf
Gunn Pt
Shoal Bay
Lee Pt Hope Inlet
Chambers Bay
Pt Stuart
Finke Bay

DARWIN
Charles Pt
Radio Aust. Transmitting Stn.
Wagait
Mandorah
Cox Peninsula
Belyuen
Nootamah
Berry Springs
Darwin River Dam
Port Darwin
Berrimah
Howard Springs
McMinns
Humpty Doo
Beatrice Hill Exp. Farm
Fogg Dam
Woolner
Point Stuart ruins
Ft Stuart Abattoirs
KAKADU NATIONAL PARK
'Kapalga' ruins
'Munmarlary'
Obiri Rock
Cahills Crossing Store
Gunbalanya
Mt Howship
Mudginberri
Jabiru
Uranium
Mt Brockman
Nourlangie
Woolwonga Abor.Lnd
Woolwonga Wildlife Sanc.
South Alligator Inn
Cooinda
Jim Jim
Nourlangie Rock
Nangaloar Caves
Mt Cahill
Mt Basedow
Table Top
Kub-O-Wer Hill
Patonga
Deaf Adder Ck
Mt Gilruth
Jim Jim Falls
Baramundi Lagoon
UDP Falls
Mundogie Hill
El Sherana
Christmas Creek
Gimbat
Mt Evelyn
Birdie Ck

ARNHEM HWY

Koolpinyah
Coastal Plain Research Stn
Wildman River
Mt Bundey Mine
Marrakai
Wildman River
STUART HWY
McKinley River
Annaburroo
Mary River
Black Jungle Spring
Spring Peak

Nookamah
Berry Springs
Southport
Tumbling Waters
Acacia Gap
Adelaide River
Manton Dam
Batchelor
'Mt Bundey'
Mt Ringwood
Woolnough
'Mt Bundey Outstation'
Mt Bundey Abattoirs
Mary River
Mt Harris
Tin Mine
Mt Douglas
Mt Mosson
'Goodparla'
Mt Partridge

'Welltree'
'Woolaning'
'Wangi'
Stapleton
Adelaide River
War Cemetery
Goodilla
Mt Paqualin
Ban Ban Springs
Howley
Mt George
Fountain Head
Grove Hill
Mt Wells Battery
Frances Ck
Moline Mine (closed)
Mt Davis
Coronet Hill

Peron Is Nth
Peron Is Sth
Anson Bay
Cape Ford
Litchfield
Robin Falls
Reynolds
'Blyths'
Mt Ringwood
Reynolds
Skews
Mt Raymond
'Douglas'
Mt Smit
Hayes Ck
Korkscrew
Boomleera
Umoo Ruins
Mt Gardiner
McCarthy
'Bonrook'

DALY RIVER WILDLIFE SANCTUARY
'Elizabeth Downs'
'Woolianna'
Mt Haywood
Daly River Police Stn
'Tipperary'
Douglas-Daly Exp.Stn
Douglas
Pine Creek
Umbrawarra Gorge
Cullen
Mt Ebsworth
Mt Stow
Mt Lambell
Mt Harvey

Mt Greenwood
Mt Thomas
Mt Boulder
Mt Muriel
Mt Briggs
'Oolloo'
Jindare
Fergusson River
Horseshoe Ck
Mt Todd
Edith River
Edith Falls
KATHERINE GORGE NAT PK
'Eva Valley'
Mt Felix

DALY RIVER ABORIGINAL LAND
Wadeye
Peppimenarti
'Fish River'
Oolloo Crossing
Bamboo
Daly
Helling
Katherine Gorge
Kintore Caves
Mt Shepherd
Beswick Aboriginal Land
Bamyili
'Beswick'

Pearce Pt
Treachery Bay
Cape Dombey
Hyland Bay
Port Keats
Cape Hay
Swamp Pt
Turtle Pt
Daly River Aboriginal Land
MOUNTAINS
'Wombungi'
Claravale
'Florina'
Hornet Hill
Katherine
'Manbullco'
Maranboy Police Stn
Maranboy
'Goondoolot'
'Goondoo'

Pearce Pt
Mt Greenwood
WINGATE
'Dorisvale'
Mt Pearce
'Mullens Ridge'
Mt Armstrong
Flott
Copper Hill
King River
Hot Springs
'Mataranka'
Mt Solitary
Elsey

NORTHERN TERRITORY
WESTERN AUSTRALIA
'Legune'
River Peak
River
Transit Hill
Fitzmaurice River
Mt Hogarth
Butchers Hill
126
Mataranka
We of the Never Never Graves
Warlock Ponds
82

Queens Channel
'Victoria'
Bradshaw
Ikymbon
YAMBARRAN RANGE
Mt Kukpalli
'Angalarri'
MrChia Gola
Mt Thyrnanan
Mt Leonard
Mt Gertrude
Mt+ Needham
'Willeroo'
VICTORIA
49
'Dry River'
'Gorrie'
'Western Creek'
Larrimah
172

'Newry'
Bullo R
'Bullo River'
Auvergne
66
Baines
Fitzroy
'Fitzroy'
'Coolibah'
163
Nari Hill
McGoose
MtGregory
Delamere
93
'Innesvale'
Mt+Arnold
'Delamere'
DELAMERE
164
Mt Peake
Romula Knob
105
Gallery Hill
Mt Compton
'Killarney'
'Kalala'
Daly Waters

25
'Newry'
17
VICTORIA
56
Baines
63
'Jasper Gorge'
Jasper
'Bullita'
115
Battle Ck
Price Hill
Frayne Knob
Mt Sullivan
'Hidden Valley'

Timber Creek
Police Stn & Store
HWY
174
40
East
27
43
Gregory
Victoria River Crossing
Victoria River
248
'Amanbidji'
'Humbert River'
47
Victoria River Downs'
MtMervh
River
Top Springs
Roadhouse
BUCHANAN
HWY
185
Dunmarra

Lake Argyle
Rosewood
Mt Duncan
79
Mt Mary+
West
Flour Hill
Tree Dee Hill
Mt+ Flour Hill

93

102

WARNING: Although an indication of road surface types is shown on this map, it is imperative that visitors obtain full information as to road conditions ahead before proceeding on their journey. During the period October to May "wet" season conditions may cause severe flooding, making many roads impassable.

The majority of water features shown on this map do not contain permanent water.

Entry to Aboriginal Reserves is strictly prohibited unless a permit is obtained.

0   50   100   150   200   250 km

J   K   L   M   N   O   P   Q   R

ARAFURA   SEA

1

WESSEL ISLANDS

Cape Wessel

Marchinbar Island

2

Cumberland Strait

Drysdale Is

Strait

Guluwuru Island

Cuthbert Pt
Braithwaite Pt
Junction Bay
Rolling Bay
Hawkesbury Pt
Nth East Pt
Boucaut Bay

North West Crocodile Island

ELCHO ISLAND

Brown

Cunningham Islands

Alger Is

The English Company's Islands

Wigram Island

Cape Wilberforce

3

Cape Stewart

Mooroongga Is

Galiwinku

Pt. Napier

Ingis Is

Maly Road

Bremer Is

Maningrida

Milingimbi

HOWARD ISLAND

Flinders Is

Buckingham Bay

Mallison Is

Melville Bay

Nhulunbuy

Yirrkala

GOVE PENINSULA

4

Castlereagh Bay

Nangalala

Ramingining

Woolen

Buckingham

Arnhem Bay

Cape Arnhem

Blyth

River

Goyder

Ck

Gapuwiyak
Lake Evella

Port Bradshaw

Liverpool

Mann

River

Cadell

Mann

Imimbar

Suyuyu

Blyth

R

Goyder

R

Ck

FREDERICK HILLS

Mitdunga

Camburinga

5

ARNHEM   LAND

Arnhem   Land
Aboriginal   Land

MITCHELL RA

Koolatong

Durabudboi

BATH RA

Mt Caledon +

Pt Alexander

Caledon Bay

Cape Grey

Trial Bay
Bald Pt

6

PARSONS

RANGE

Anne

Mt Flemming

Mt Ranken +

Jalma Bay

Strelley Bay

Myaoola

Isle Woodah

Nicolls

Cape Shield

GULF OF

'Weemal'
'Bullman' + Mt Marumba
+ Mt Weir
Mt Stretton +
Mt Bridges +

Waterhouse

Morgan

Blue Mud Bay

Burney Is

7

Mt Gap
Black Mtn

R

Mt Bray

Rhello

Rose

Cape Barrow

Bennet Bay

Bickerton Is

Winchelsea Is

Port Langdon

GROOTE EYLANDT

Lowrie Channel

Warwick Channel

Alyangula

GROOTE EYLANDT Aboriginal Land

Umbakumba

8

'Mountain Valley'
10
43
+ Mt Throsby
+ Three Graces
Mt Furner
Mt Bagster

Mainoru

+ Whatnelk Bluff

Mt Karmain

River

COLLIERS MTNS

BOWNERS RA

River

187

Angurugu

Tasman Pt

South Pt

Cape Beatrice

Numbulwar

9

'Moroak'
Mt Chapman +
Roper
Mt Warrington
31
Ngukurr

Uburunga

Mt Philla +
Mt Faveno +

Roper Bar Police Stn

St Vidgeon

Port Roper

CARPENTARIA

Mt Price
'Roper'
ROPER
+Mt. Harriet
HWY
66
213
Mt Eclipse
+ Mt St Vidgeon
Hodgson
82

Roper Valley

Maria Is

Limmen Bight

10

Hodgson Downs

Mt Forrest +
51
Mt Davidson +
+ Mt Hughes
+ Mt Kelly

Towns

River

Limmen Bight Aboriginal Land

'Mayfield Ck'
95
122

Arnold

Cox

R

'Nathan River'

The Four Archers

Rosie

SIR EDWARD PELLEW GROUP

North Is

West Is

11

'Rosie Creek'

Bing Bong

Vanderlin Is

'Nutwood Downs'

Hodgson

R

Limmen

Bight

Pine

80

Battern Ck

Port McArthur

SW White Centre

12

103

Cox River

Ck

Bauhinia

Borroloola Aboriginal Land

Borroloola PO

River

Mt Easterntop

74

24

'Manangoora'

'Greenbank'

31

'Seven Emu'

CARPENTARIA

171

HWY

Williams

R

Lagoon

Tanumbirini

October

Ck

Limmen

Bauhinia

Barney Ck

Battern Ck

'Bauhinia'

'Tawallah'

CARPENTARIA

McArthur

HWY

The Fletcher

Wearyan

R

Foelsche

R

Robinson

Calvert

Sandy

13

'Tanumbirini'

21

'Broadmere'

'OT Downs'

'McArthur River'

J   K   L   M   N   O   P   Q   R

A B C D 100 E F G H I

Timber Creek Police Stn & Store

'Cooliban'
Mt Gregory
'Delamere'

Larrimah

STUART

'Auvergne'

HWY

174

PINKERTON

'Newry'

VICTORIA

25

AMH

Lake Argyle

'Rosewood'

Mt Duncan

'Amanbidji'

'Humbert River'

248

Victoria River Crossing

Gregory

Mt Peake

'Delamere' Ck

Romula Knob

'Killarney'

Mt Compton
Price Hill

DELAMERE ROAD

Western Ck

Sunday Ck

'Kalala'

Daly Waters

Mt Sullivan

Gallen Hill
Frayne Knob
Coolibah
115

Birrimba

'Hidden Valley'

'Dungowan'
Stoney Knob

BUCHANAN HWY 185

54 Dunmarra Roadhouse

Victoria River Downs'

Top Springs Roadhouse

'Montejinni'

'Muranji'

PMG Memorial

DUNCAN

263

'Mistake Creek'
Mt Wickham
Warriki Hill

Mt Elder

Nagri R

46

Mt Kimon

'Mt Sanford'

142

Mt Hoggson
Gregory's Remarkable Pillar

Mt Stevens

'Pigeon Hole'

Armstrong
Townshend Ck

Cusack Rock
Mt Northcote

127

'Camfield'
Mt Williams

59

35

HWY

'Limbunya'

Stirling

Depot

82

Blackgin Hill

31

Wave Hill Red Hill

29

'Wave Hill'

Victoria River

Cattle Ck

Newcastle Waters

Mt Copley

48

108

Mt Rose

97

Gum Ck

238

50

Mt Seale
Toms Rock
Mt Gordon
Gap Hill

16

Mt Barton

105

Camfield

Camfield Ck

'Cattle Creek OS'

Lake Woods

SEMI

DESERT

'Kirkimbie'

Mt Maivo

Inverway

Mt Fargharson

'Riveren'

DUNCAN HWY

178

BUCHANAN

80

Stuart Ck

Mt Archie

70

Nongra Lake

Cattle Ck

'Nicholson'

(Abandoned) Wallamunga

124

'Birrindudu'

Hooker Ck

Lajamanu

Winnecke Ck

Ck

WARNING: Although an indication of road surface types is shown on this map, it is imperative that visitors obtain full information as to road conditions ahead before proceeding on their journey. During the period October to May "wet" season conditions may cause severe flooding, making many roads impassable.

The majority of water features shown on this map do not contain permanent water.

Entry to Aboriginal Land is strictly prohibited unless a permit is obtained.

NORTHERN TERRITORY WESTERN AUSTRALIA

238

Wheel Drive Only

'Suplejack'

Wilson Ck

'Lothari Hill'

BUCHANAN HILLS

Aboriginal Land

N

210

Mallee Hill

Mt Frederick

Lake Buck

82

Mt Tanami

Tanami

40

Rabbit Flat Roadhouse

Lake Surprise

SEMI DESERT

Lander

Locked Gate

60

Mt Davidson

Mt Solitaire

'Mongrel Downs'

The Granites

Hordern Hills

TANAMI

124

65

Aboriginal Land

Mt Bennett

River

Mt Windajong

Lake Lucas

Lake White

McDiarmid Hill

Mt Theo

Mt Patricia

Sowden Hill

Willowra

Mt Rennie

Ingallan Ck

1 2 3 4 5 6 93 7 8 9 10 11 12 13

A B C D 104 E F G H I

0   50   100   150   200   250 km

▼ 101 ▼

J   K   L   M   N   O   P   Q   R

CARPENTARIA

'Nutwood Downs'
Hodgson R
'103'
171
'Tanumbirini'
'Amungee Mungee'
October Ck
272
21
'OT Downs'
101
'Broadmere'
Rosie Ck
Rosie
'Bing Bong'
West Is
North Is
St Vidgeon
Vanderlin Is
Port McArthur
Borroloola Aboriginal Land
Borroloola PO
18
Mt Feathertop
'Manangoora'
'Greenbank'
74
24
31
'Seven Emu'
73
'Tawallah' Ck
101
106
88
HWY
Barney
McArthur River
Battern
Pine
Bauhinia
Bauhinia Ck
Limmen Bight R
Wearyan River
Foelsche River
'Spring Creek'
'McArthur River'
Glyde River
(59)
Calvert
Sandy Ck
Running Ck
'Pungalina'
'Robinson River'
14
6
Surprise Ck
84
'Balbirini' R
33
'Mallapunyah'
13
Kilgour Ck
Spellcreek Ck
Lancewood River
Robinson River
Calvert River
196
'Calvert Hills'
Little Calvert R
76
'Wollogorang'
Gold Ck
Settlement Ck
Branch
Newcastle Ck
145
Newcastle Ck
'Kiana'
Bluey Ck
Buddycurrawa Ck
Puzzle Ck
93
CHINA WALL
Nicholson R
'Benmara'
Cleanskin Ck
South Nicholson R
'Highland Plains'
'Elliott'
19
STUART
74
339
63
'Ucharonidge'
'Mungabroom'
79
74
'Eva Downs'
'Walhallow'
100
10
Anthony Lagoon PS
34
'Cresswell Downs'
Cresswell Ck
404
100
93
Fish Hole Ck
Benmara Ck
Carrara
58
Mt Willieray
51
19
'Renner Springs PO'
'Helen Springs'
'Muckaty'
Tomkinson Ck
42
'Banka Banka'
Morphett Ck
29
45
Churchills Head
'Brunchilly'
70
Brunchilly Ck
BARKLY
119
'Rockhampton Downs'
40
100
108
12
'Brunette Downs'
'Mittiebah'
'Alexandria'
58
134
'Gallipoli'
26
TABLELANDS
90
Aboriginal Land
Stuart Memorial
47
HWY
'Phillip Creek'
Phillip
BARKLY
185
John Flynn Memorial
97
35
79
Playford
Buchanan Ck
66
80
Cigarette Hole
54
'Herbertvale'
Herbert R
61
'Orlando'
24
Warramunga Aboriginal Land
53
Prentice Lake
56
'Alroy Downs'
19
TABLELAND
'Ranken Store'
Rego Mine
Devils Pebbles
31
24
Tennant Ck
'Dalmore Downs'
Roadhouse
63
HWY
54
54
'Rocklands'
Tennant Creek
Peko Mine
Nobles Nob
Gosse R
Copper & Gold Mines
El Dorado Mine
Wonarah Repeater Stn
35
35
'Soudan'
275
24
BARKLY
37
Camooweal
HWY
97
10
Barry Caves
10
37
Avon Downs Police Stn
34
70
'McLaren Creek'
248
51
'Kurundi'
'Epenarra'
13
'Burramurra' (Abandoned)
13
42
'Austral Downs'
'Singleton'
18
Devils Marbles Conservation Reserve
Mt Cairns
74
13
48
64
61
Georgina R
19
Devils Marbles
Wauchope
Hotel
Frew R
Murray R
NORTHERN TERRITORY
QUEENSLAND
48
Buckley R
Mt Michael
'Arcadia'
'umagalong'
37
Warrabri Aboriginal Land
58
HWY
22
Ali-Curung
21
'Murray Downs'
51
34
'Elkedra'
SANDOVER
32
29
51
76
Elkedra River
88
'Annitowa'
58
'Georgina'
43
Mt Nelson
Scar Hill
'row Creek'
'Neutral Junction'

▼ 105 ▼

J   K   L   M   N   O   P   Q   R

1
2
3
4
5
6
7
8
9
10
11
12
13

102

Locked Gate
'Mongrel Downs'
The Granites
+ Mt Davidson
+ Mt Solitaire
Lake Lucas
Hordern Hills +
124
65
TANAMI
+ Mt Bennett
Aboriginal Land
+ McDiarmid Hill
+ Mt Windajong
'Willowra'
Lake White
+ Mt Theo
136
+ Mt Patricia
ROAD
+ Mt Barkly
+ Mt Bennie
+ Mt Peake
69
Lake Hazlett
Sowden Hill +
Chilla Well
+ Mt Campbell
+ Mt Leichhardt
Central Mt Stua
'Anningie'
43
Aboriginal Land
+ Mt Singleton
+ Mt Stafford
Nancy Hill +
'Ti-Tree'
+ Mt Farewell
64
+ Mt Nardy
59
Yuendumu Aboriginal Land
'Mt Denison'
+ Mt Treachery
Quartz Hill +
'Coniston'
+ Mt Gardiner
58
+ Mt Finniss
'Pine Hill'
59
28
Ethel Ck
'Vaughan Springs'
Yuendumu
+ Mt Allan
Ck
'Napperby'
48
Prow Gap
Ailer
Mt Nicker +
+ Mt Davenport
58
TANAMI
22
29
Mt Bootby +
70
PO
'Aileron'
8
Mt Stanley +
Mt Gurner +
22
'Newhaven'
'Mt Wedge'
35
+ West Bluff
+ Mt Hammond
32
+ Mt Cockburn
106
+ Central Mt Wedge
Lake Bennett
77
+ Mt Harris
CSIRO Experime Plots
63
296
93
4 Wheel Drive Only
188
'Derwent'
'Narwietooma'
29
Mt Strickland +
85
18
Papunya
62
+ Mt Chapple
'Amburla OS
Mt Leisler +
+ Mt Liebig
Haasts Bluff +
19
'Glen Helen'
+ Mt Ziel
'Milton Park'
TROPIC OF CAPRICORN
87
32
+ Mt Hay
111
Mt Udor
Haasts Bluff
'Hamilton Downs'
RO
Lake Macdonald
Mt Mein +
NAMATJIRA
+ Mt Sonder
48
Jay Ck Aborigin Land
Haasts Bluff
+ Mt Forbes
Mt Solitary +
Undendita
Glen Helen
26
MACDONNELL RANGES
129
DR
Aboriginal Land
Hermannsburg Aboriginal Land
56
LARAPINTA
125
Gosse Bluff
Pile Hill
78
Sor
+ Mt Winter
Camels Hump +
Hermannsburg Mission
+ Laycocks Hill
Areyonga
Palm Valley
FINKE GORGE NAT PARK
+ Mt Olifent
Lake Hopkins
+ Mt Murray
Mt Tucker +
+ Carmichael Crag
+ Mt Keartland
Kings Ck
Kings Canyon
Mt Lewis +
Tent Hill +
'Orange Creek
Lake Neale
Petermann
Ck
'Tempe Downs'
34
202
+ Mt Cowle
Mt Levi +
Hanbu
Mt Harris +
+ Mt Carruthers
Yowa Bluff +
Henbury Meteorite Craters
97
Palme Valley
Docker Ck
Lake Amadeus
Wallara Ranch Tourist Chalet
The Twins
River
20
+ Mt Skene
70
+ Desert Oak Hill
Petermann Ranges
'Angas Downs'
STUART
70
Docker River
Aboriginal Land
Mt Curdie +
Aboriginal Land
122
+ Mt Ebenezer
Ippia Hill +
'Erldunda'
Mt Deering +
Mt Miller +
206
Mt Currie +
'Mt Ebenezer'
59
PETERMANN RANGES
Mt Bowley +
242
38
56
ROAD
+ Mt Phillips
+ Mt McCulloch
Mt Olga
19
ULURU NATIONAL PARK
Yulara
Curtin Springs
12
Karinga
Ck
Giles
Armstrong
31
Ayers Rock
PETERMANN
77
74
+ Katamala Cone
Mt Connor
94
Stevenson + Peak
68
'Kulgera'
+ Butler Dome
Benda Hill +
Mt Robert +
Mt Reynolds +
Mt Sir Henry +
19
Ku
Cavena
Mt Daisy Bates +
324
141
26
Mt Gosse +
Surveyor General's Corner
Mt Le Hunte +
Mt Cockburn +
Mt Mann +
Mt Charles +
Victory Downs
'Sundown'
MANN RANGES
Mt Aloysius +
Mt Edwin +
Mt Whinham +
Mt Woodward +
Mt Cuthbert +
+ Sentinel Hill
Bell Rock +
Mt Hardy +
255
North West Aboriginal Land
Mt Morris +
Musgrave Park Aboriginal Community
80
+ Mt Davies
+ Mt Davenport
Mt Everard +
Ernabella
'Kenmore Park'
Mt Woodroffe +

82

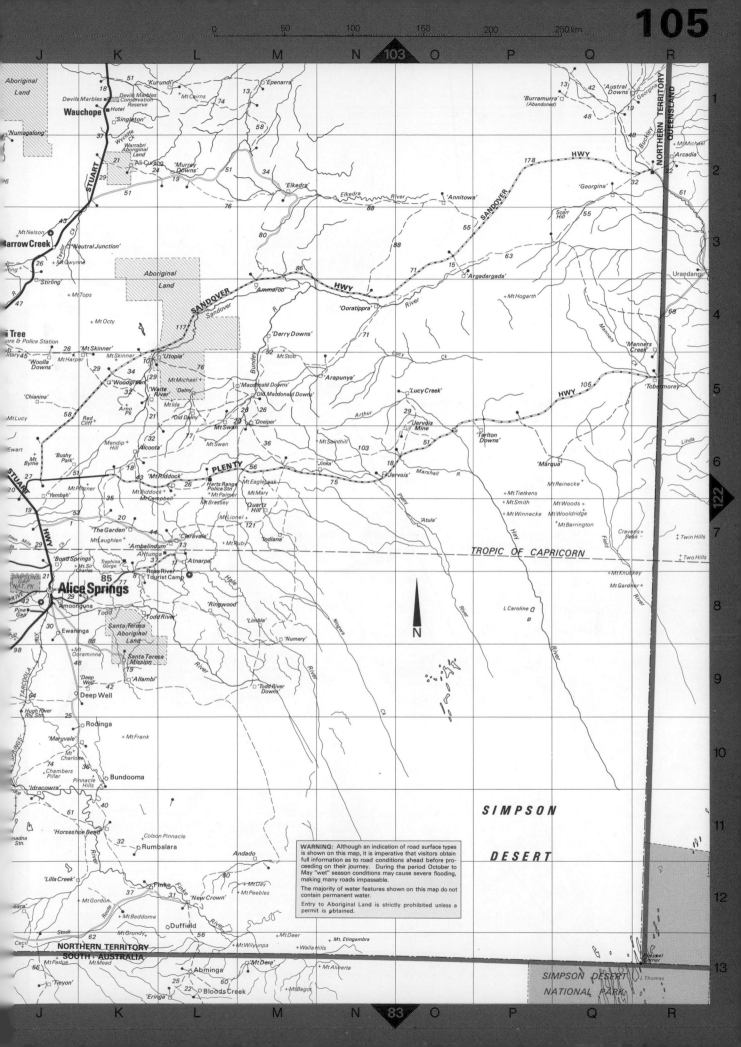

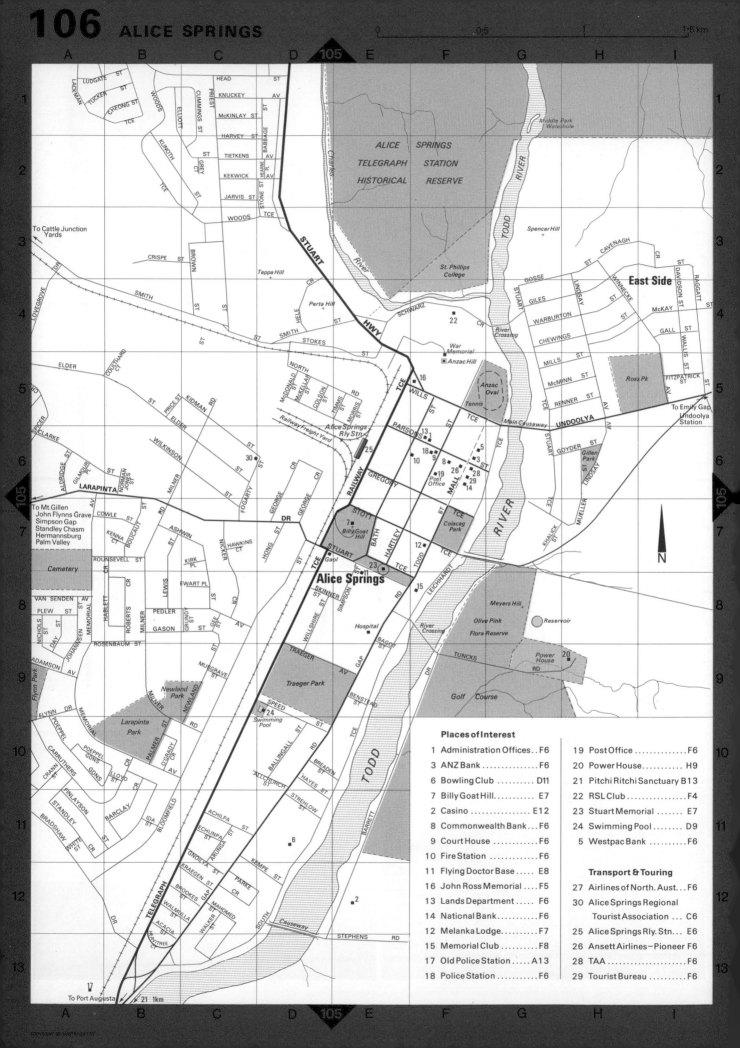

0   0·5   1   1·5 km

Places of Interest

1 Administration Offices . . F6
3 ANZ Bank F6
6 Bowling Club D11
7 Billy Goat Hill E7
2 Casino E12
8 Commonwealth Bank . . . F6
9 Court House F6
10 Fire Station F6
11 Flying Doctor Base E8
16 John Ross Memorial F5
13 Lands Department F6
14 National Bank F6
12 Melanka Lodge F7
15 Memorial Club F8
17 Old Police Station A13
18 Police Station F6

19 Post Office F6
20 Power House H9
21 Pitchi Ritchi Sanctuary B13
22 RSL Club F4
23 Stuart Memorial E7
24 Swimming Pool D9
5 Westpac Bank F6

Transport & Touring

27 Airlines of North. Aust . . . F6
30 Alice Springs Regional
     Tourist Association . . . C6
25 Alice Springs Rly. Stn . . . E6
26 Ansett Airlines–Pioneer F6
28 TAA F6
29 Tourist Bureau F6

A   B   C   D   E   F   G   H   I

104

0   20   40   60km

1
HAASTS BLUFF ABORIGINAL RESERVE
+ Camels Hump
Undandita
Glen Helen
MACDONNEL
48
34
NAMATJIRA
RANGES
59
JAY CK
ABOR RES
42
Alice Springs
Amoonguna
Simpsons Gap
DRIVE
Jay Creek   Pine Gap
Owen Springs
HIGHWAY 92
Todd
30
River

2
+ Mt Olifent
Pile Hill
+
Areyonga
Hermannsburg Mission
Palm Valley
Larapinta Waters
FINKE
GORGE
+ Mt Keartland
74
Ewaninga
48
+ Mt Tucker
NAT PARK
Mt Caldwell
STUART

104
3
PETERMANN RANGES
ABORIGINAL RESERVE
+ Carmichael Crag
■ Kings Canyon
+ Tent Hill
Mt Lewis +
□ Tempe Downs
Finke
+ Orange Creek
54
Deep Well
202
34
Henbury Meteorite Craters
□ Henbury
Rodinga
25
105

4
90
Petermann
+ Mt Levi
Ck
Palmer
Yowa Bluff
Wallara Ranch Tourist Chalet
97
River
The Twins
+
□ Palmer Valley
+ Desert Oak Hill
70
Margvale
Mt Charlotte +
74

5
Lake Amadeus
53
Angas Downs
+ Mt Ebenezer
Ippia Hill +
River
Chambers Pillar
Idracowra
122
18
ROAD
39
Mt Ebenezer
Erldunda
70

6
19
Mt Olga   31
Ayers Rock
92
PETERMANN
66
246
Curtin Springs
59
Karinga
Ck
NATIONAL PARK
+ Mt Connor

Note: This section not suitable for conventional vehicles (very rocky terrain)

MOUNT OLGA

Mt Bubia
Valley of the Winds
Mt Ghee
Olga Gorge
Mt Wulpa
Katatjuta Lookout
Picnic Ground
Liru Mountain
Mt Olga
Twin Rockhole
Walpa Rockhole
Valley of the Kangaroo

0   1   2   3   4km

AYERS ROCK

Aborigine Area (Closed to Public)
Kangaroo Tail
Cave of the Women
Organ Cave
Kandju Gorge
Owityera Tree
Djugaba Rockhole
Sound Shell
Paintings
Climbing Slope to Summit
Cairn
Kuna Stone
Loongardi Stone
Leru Stone
Kudjuk Kundunda Cave
Mutitjulu Maggie Springs (Paintings)
Ininti Waterhole
Airstrip

0   1   2km

The Olgas

Ayers Rock

Maps of
Queensland

Location Map

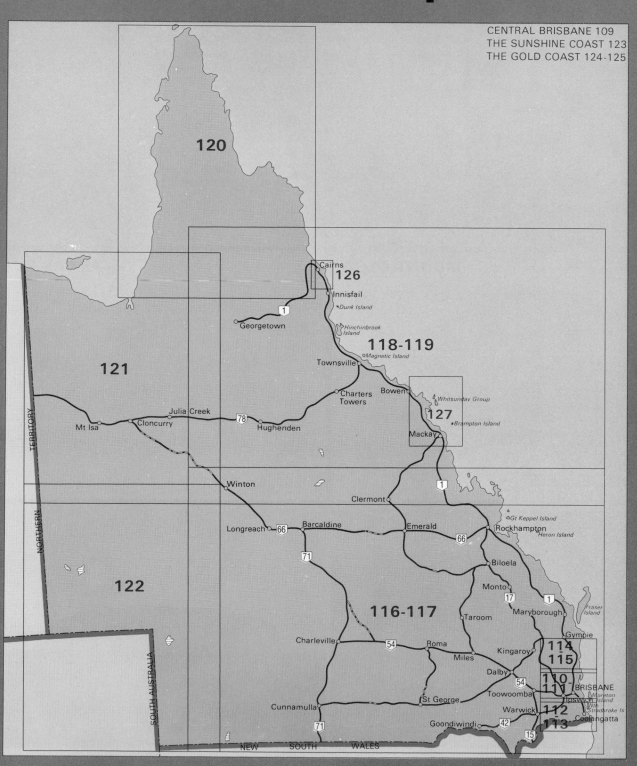

CENTRAL BRISBANE 109
THE SUNSHINE COAST 123
THE GOLD COAST 124-125

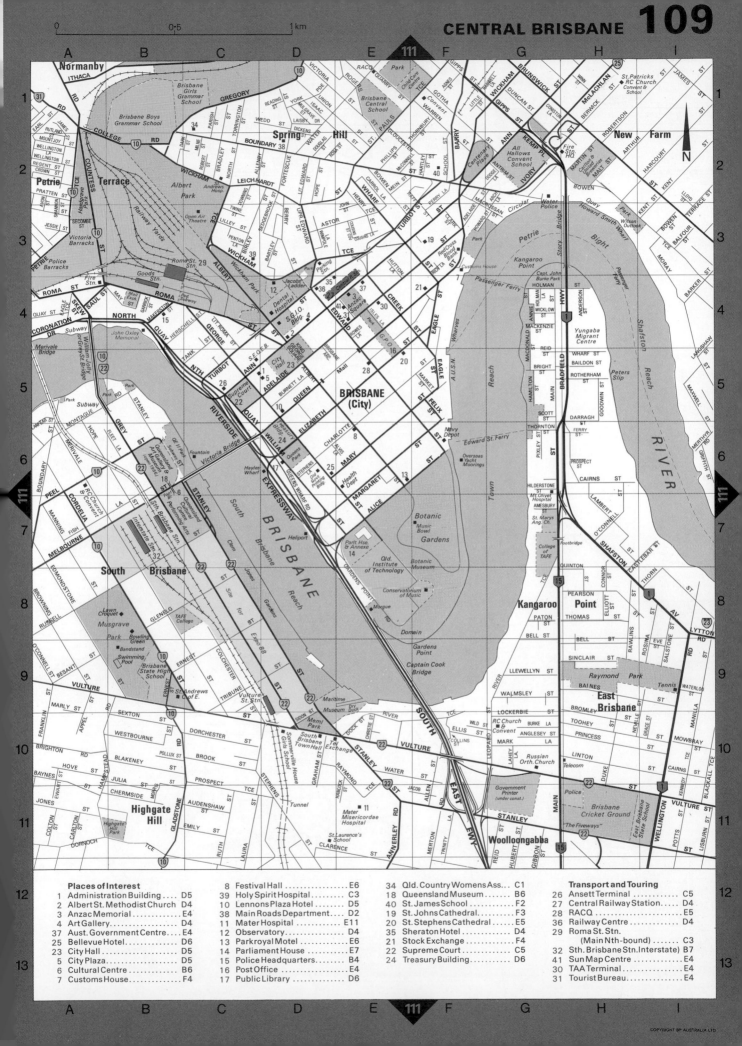

Places of Interest				**Transport and Touring**
1 Administration Building D5	8 Festival Hall E6	34 Qld. Country Womens Ass... C1		26 Ansett Terminal C5
2 Albert St. Methodist Church D4	39 Holy Spirit Hospital C3	18 Queensland Museum B6		27 Central Railway Station..... D4
3 Anzac Memorial E4	10 Lennons Plaza Hotel D5	40 St. James School F2		28 RACQ E5
4 Art Gallery D4	38 Main Roads Department D2	19 St. Johns Cathedral F3		36 Railway Centre D4
37 Aust. Government Centre....E4	11 Mater Hospital E11	20 St. Stephens Cathedral E5		29 Roma St. Stn.
25 Bellevue Hotel............. D6	12 Observatory.............. D4	35 Sheraton Hotel D4		(Main Nth-bound) C3
23 City Hall D5	9 Parkroyal Motel E6	21 Stock Exchange F4		32 Sth. Brisbane Stn.Interstate) B7
5 City Plaza................. D5	14 Parliament House E7	22 Supreme Court C5		41 Sun Map Centre........... E4
6 Cultural Centre B6	15 Police Headquarters B4	24 Treasury Building D6		30 TAA Terminal E4
7 Customs House............. F4	16 Post Office E4			31 Tourist Bureau............. E4
	17 Public Library D6			

COPYRIGHT BP AUSTRALIA LTD

A B C D 114 E F G H I

1
BALFOUR RANGE · D'AGUILAR · Lookout · The Round Mtn. · Gwendolen Hill + · Mt. Lionell + · Mt. Moore · Mt. Kilcoy · Station · Mt. Marysmokes 657m + · Picnic Area · Mt. McLean + 465m · River · Commissioners Flat · Numerous timber tracks · Moore · Colinton · Brisbane HWY · Nurinda · Limestone Hill · Oaky · Spring Ck · Mt. Kilcoy 351m + · Sandy · Kalangara · 11 · Stanmore · Rest Area

2
Opossum Ck · Emu Ck · Picnic Areas · Lookout · Mt. Glen Howden + · Picnic Area · Harlin · Subject to Flooding · D'AGUILAR · 22 · HWY · 24 · Gregors Ck · 11 · Mt. McConnel 489m + · 2 Kilcoy · Rest Area Subject to Flooding · Winya · Glenfern · Villeneuve · Neurum · Subject to Flooding · 18 · 17 · Durundur · 25 · Stanley · Woodford · Rest Area

3
Mt. Calabash + 430m · Glenmaurie · Marronghi Ck · Biarra Range Mtn. · BRISBANE · BIARRA RANGE · Yimbun · Ivory Ck · Scrub Ck · Cressbrook Nature Reserve · Cressbrook Lower · Hazeldene · Lake Somerset · Lookout · Camping Area & Skiing · 22 · Oaky · Delaneys Ck · Mt. Delaney + 373m · D'AGUILAR · Durundur · D'Aguilar · Delaneys Ck · 10 · Bracalb · Wamuran · Wamuran Basin · Ringbarked Hill · Milford Rocks · +Sugarloaf

4
Eskdale · Eskdale West · Toogoolawah · Picnic Area · 12 · Eskvale · VALLEY · 32 · Mt. Beppo · Caboonbah · Fulham Vale · Mt. Brisbane + 678m · Picnic Area · Cooeeinbardi · Mt. Somerset + Mt. Booran + · Somerset Dam Picnic Area · Water Sports · 9 · Mt. Byron 617m + · 13 · Mt. Mee + 495m · Mt. Mee · Campbells Pocket · Rocksberg · 40

5
Ivory Ck · Eskvale · Biarra · Mt. Tin Tin 390m + · Round Mtn. 454m · Mt. Deongwar + 548m · Ottaba · + Mt. Beppo · Coal Ck · Murrumba · Crossdale · 9 · Reedy Ck · Dianas Bath · D'AGUILAR RANGE · Mt. Pleasant · 21 · Ocean View · Mt. Pleasant 524m +

6
Mt. Sevastopol · Perkins Knob · Cressbrook Ck · Kipper · Gallanani · Gallanani · Redbank Ck · 3 · Esk · +Burrundoon Mtn. · Glen Esk · Sandy · Mt. Sim Jue + 608m · The Bulls Knob · Leacys Ck · Upper Laceys Ck · 10 · Nth Pine · Dayboro Rest Area · Armstrong Ck · Kobble · Mt. Kobble · Samsonvale · 18 · 117

7
Mt. Jockey + · 33 · 9 · Paddy Gully · Moombra · Wivenhoe Reservoir · Dundas · Northbrook · BRISBANE · NATIONAL · Mt. D'Aguilar + 745m · Love Ck Falls · The Summit · MAIALA NATIONAL PARK · Mt. Samson + 689m · Mt. Samson · Mt. Lawson 473m · Closeburn · Yuga

8
Ravensbourne · RAVENSBOURNE NATIONAL PARK · Picnic Areas · Buraba · Buaraba · Mt. Mulgowie · Mt. Hallen · Mt. Hallen 388m · Coorragook · Logans Ck · Running Ck · 39 · BRISBANE · Coominya · Pine Hill + · Split Yard Creek Dam · Catarh Ck · Englands Ck · Northbrook · FOREST · Picnic Area · Mt. Glorious · Greenes Falls · MANORINA NAT. PK. · Mt. O'Reilly + · Highvale

9
Mt. Perseverance + 804m · Mt. Cross + 625m · Yellow Gully + 410m · Yellow Gully · Buaraba Ck · Picnic Area · Atkinsons Lagoon · 6 · Clarendon · Patrick Estate · Wivenhoe Dam · Ardmory · Subject to Flooding · Picnic Mtn. · + Mt. England 305m · Horse Mtn. · CABBAGE TREE RANGE · Dwyers Lookout · Jollys Lookout · Mt. Nebo · Picnic Area · Camp Mtn. · D'AGUILAR PARK · Upper Brookfield

10
Balaam Hill · + Vinegar Hill · Redbank · Lake Clarendon · Kentville · 5 · 10 · Lockrose · Brightview · Mt. Tarampa · 45 · 13 · Lowood · Tarampa · 11 · Glamorgan Vale · Fairney View · Wanora · 18 · 16 · Borallon · VALLEY · 31 · Mt. Crosby · Picnic Area · Lake Manchester · Holts Hill · Mt. Crosby · Picnic Area · Ugly Hill

11
Gatton · 54 · 5 · Lockyer Ck · Agricultural College · 13 · 11 · Glenore Grove · 3 · WARREGO · HWY · 18 · Minden · 64 · 6 · Marburg · Haigslea · WARREGO · 10 · Mt. Crosby · 54 · Colleges Crossing · HWY

12
Rest Area · Grantham · Tenthill · Lawes · Forest Hill · Plainland · Hatton Vale · 5 · 8 · Summerholm · 11 · Malabar · Tallegalla · Birru · Kunkala · Cabanda · Walloon · Thagoona · Brassall · IPSWICH · Bundamba · 10 · Churchill · Redbank Plains · Amberley RAAF Base

13
Ma Ma Creek · Winwill · Upper Tenthill · Mt. Whitestone · Caffey · Woodlands · Ropeley · Blenheim · Laidley · Coopers Hill · Mt. Bines 451m + · Grandchester · Calvert · Lanefield · Rosewood · Ebenezer · Bremer River · Jeebropilly · 15 · CUNNINGHAM HWY · 42 · 31 · Loamside · Purga · Ripley · Swanbank Lagoon · Bypass · Lower Mt. Walker · Hidden Vale · Paradise Falls · Mt. Berryman

A B C D 112 E F G H I

0   5   10   15   20   25km

J K L M N O P Q R

Coochin Ck **Beerwah**
Mt. Coochin
Subject to Flooding
Coochin

Mt. Beerwah 556m Coonowrin 375m Ngungun 236m
NAT. PK. NAT. PK. NAT. PK.

Glasshouse Mountains

Tibrogargan 282m

Tibberoowuccum

Rest Area 276m Beerburrum

Beerburrum
Subject to Flooding

Bribie

Donnybrook

Long Is.

Goat Is.

Island

Toorbul

Ningi

Bellara

Bongaree **Woorim**

Skirmish Pt.

Pt. Sandstone

South Pt.

Caboolture

Morayfield

Upper Caboolture

Burpengary

Oaky Flats

Narangba

Lakeside Racing Circuit

Lake Kurwongbah

Dakabin

Kallangur

Petrie

Deception Bay

Beachmere

Deception Bay

Oyster Point

Reef Point

Scarborough
Osbourne Pt.
Queens Beach

Redcliffe

Margate
Scotts Point
Woody Point

Hayes Inlet

Pearl

MORETON BAY Ideal fishing, noted for crabs, launch cruises

Moreton

MOUNT TEMPEST NATIONAL

Mt. Campbell +216m

Highest sandhill in Australia

PARK Mt. Tempest 279m

MORETON ISLAND NATL. PARK

Island

Tangalooma Tourist Resort

Tangalooma Point

Cowan Cowan Pt. Lighthouse

Bulwer

Comboyuro Point

North Point Lighthouse

Cape Moreton Lighthouse

Marietta Dal Wreck

Smith Rock

Flinders Reef

Shark Spit

Campbell Pt. Kooringal

Reeders Pt.

'Rufus King' Wreck

NATIONAL PARK

MORETON

BAY

Mud Is

Juno Pt.

Bishop Is

Fisherman Islands

ST HELENA ISLAND NAT. PARK

St.Helena Is.

South Pt.

Green Is

Convict Settlement Ruins

Roue

South Passage

Channel

Amity Point

Amity Banks

Rocky Pt.
Capt.Cook Memorial
Whale Rock

Point Lookout
Blowhole

WILDFLOWER RESERVE

SANDGATE

SHORNCLIFFE

Bramble Bay

Nudgee Beach

Boondall

NUDGEE

CRIBB ISLAND

Brighton

Bald Hills

Albany Creek

ASPLEY

ZILLMERE

Geebung

BANYO

MYRTLETON

International Airport (under const.)

BRISBANE AIRPORT

LOWER NUDGEE

PINKENBA

Whyte Is

LYTTON

WYNNUM

Dunwich

Historical Cemetery

Myora

Brown Lake

219m + Mt.Hardgrave

Sand Mining

North

Peel Is

Bird Is Goat Is.

Stradbroke

Mt. Vane

Blue Lake

Swamp

BLUE LAKE NATIONAL PARK

Mt.Corrie + 196m

Island

Herring Lagoon

CHERMSIDE

STAFFORD KEDRON

WAVELL HEIGHTS

WOOLOOWIN

CLAYFIELD

ASCOT

HAMILTON

EAGLE FARM

MEEANDAH

HEMMANT

Gateway Bridge (under const.)

MURARRIE

MANLY

LOTA

Waterloo Bay

Wellington Point

Wellington Point

Picnic Area

THORNESIDE

BIRKDALE

Ormiston House

Whepstead Raby Bay

Ormiston

Lighthouse

Cleveland

Old Court House

Raby Bay

Redlands Museum

Thornlands

Oyster Pt.

NEWMARKET WINDSOR

THE GAP

ASHGROVE

HERSTON

BRISBANE

MOUNT COOT-THA PARK

PADDINGTON

MILTON

TOOWONG

WEST END

ST. LUCIA

Ironside

NORMAN PK

SEVEN HILLS

CARINA

CAPALABA

Mt. Petrie

Leslie Harrison Dam

Ibis Lagoon

Macleay Is.

Coochiemudlo Is.

Halloran

Boat Ramp

Enoggera Reservoir

Gold Creek Reservoir

CHAPEL HILL

BROOKFIELD

INDOOROOPILLY

KENMORE

CHELMER

Long Pocket

FAIRFIELD

GRACEVILLE

SHERWOOD

ANNERLEY

MOORVALE

Moorooka

ROCKLEA

OXLEY

MORNINGSIDE

HOLLAND PK

MT GRAVATT

MANSFIELD

WISHART

BELMONT

35

ROCHEDALE

Burbank

Pine Lodge Equestrian Park

Big Strawberry

Mt. Cotton

Stoneleigh Gemstone Display

Redland Bay

Mt.Carmel Orchards

Garden

Lamb Is.

Karragarra

Mt. Wies + 134m

Mt. Hutton + 124m

PULLENVALE

MOGGILL

BRISBANE

DARRA

WACOL

GOODNA

15

CUNNINGHAM

30

INALA

Archerfield Aerodrome

SALISBURY

ROBERTSON

SUNNYBANK

ACACIA RIDGE

RUNCORN

EIGHT MILE PLAINS

Kuraby

32

SPRINGWOOD

WOODRIDGE

Calamvale

Woodridge

Slacks Ck

Victoria Pt.

10

Venman Bushland Res

10

Panhikin Is.

Green Dragon Museum

Russell

Ibis Lagoon

Native Companion Lagoon

Mt.Scott 158m

Mt. Hutton

Lagoon Is.

Long Is.

Kingston

Browns Plains

Loganlea

Wild Waters Waterslide

Bethania Junction

Loganholme

18

Carbrook

Aquatic Gardens

Eagleby

Rest Area

Waterford

PACIFIC HWY

J K L M N O P Q R

A B C D 110 E F G 31 H I

1

Caffey — Mt. Sylvia — Ingoldsby — Mt. Berryman — Ladidey — Mulgowie — Hidden Vale — Mt. Walker Lower — Purga — Ripley — GRAMPIAN HILLS — Wogarba

2

Woodbine — Mt. Cooper — Porlock — Mt. Haldon 930m — Junction View — Mt. Zahel 871m — Mt. Beau Brummel 700m — Mt. Mort — Mt. Forbes — Mt. Walker — Mutdapilly — Flinders — Peak Crossing — Mt. Goolman 454m — Ivorys Rock — Mt. Perry — Mt. Blaine 457m — Bundamba or Dalys Lagoon — Subject to Flooding — Rest Area

3

Haldon East — Dry — Mt. William — Mt. Lowe — Thornton — Coleyville — Coleyville Gap — Warrill View — Harrisville — 13 — Limestone Ridge — Flinders Peak 679m — Mt. Elliott 436m — Mt. Welcome 332m — Mt. Wilbraham — Subject to Flooding — Adams Bridge — Rosevale

MISTAKE NATIONAL PARK — MISTAKE MOUNTAINS

4

Mt. Philip 910m — Mt. Edgar — Mt. Mistake — Mt. Machar — Point Pure — Falls — Mt. Hennessey — Townson — Grass Tree Knob 805m — Kangaroo Mtn 770m — Moorang — Bald Hills 251m — Warroolaba — Silverdale — 16 — Roadvale — Kulgun — Millbong — 27 — Ivorys Knob — Wollaman — Rock Knob — Mt. Joyce 469m — Subject to Flooding

5

Inverramsay — Dairymple — Warrill — Tarome — Mt. Castle 914m — Mt. Fraser — Frazerview — Kangaroo Mtn 267m — Aratula — Fassifern Valley — Kalbar — Templin — 13 — Coulson — Dugandan — Boonah — Goans Hill — Maddoxs Hill — Mt. Moy 357m — Mt. Crumpet — Mt. Jeberra — Rest Area — NAT. PK — Picnic Area — Mt. French — TEVIOT RANGE — DUGANDAN — Allan

6

Branch — Maryvale — 11 HWY — Tregony — 68 — Mt. Cordeaux 113m — Cunninghams Gap — Mt. Mitchell 1167m — CUNNINGHAM — Clumber — Mt. Edwards 390 — Water Sports — Lake Moogerah — Charlwood — Bunjurgen Sch. — Mt. Alford — Bunburra — Milford — Sugarloaf 408m — Cannonvale School — Mt. Tilley — Gladfield — Glengallen — 10 Ck — CUNNINGHAMS GAP NATIONAL PARK — Picnic Areas

7

Mt. Dumaresq — Lookout 244m — Spicers Gap — Lookout — Spicers Peak 1219m — Mt. Doubletop — Mt. Greville — Scenic Area — Moogerah — Mt. Moon — Scenic Area — Coochin Coochin — Wild Horse Mtns — Quarry — Moodys Valley — Knapps Peak 649m — Knapps — Kooralbyn — FIVE MILE MTNS. — Prouts Hill — GREAT

8

Freestone — Upper Freestone — Mt. Sturt — Swan — Swanfels — SWANFELS NAT. PARK — Mt. Guymer — The Steamers — Mt. Huntley 1265m — Mt. Asplenium 1280m — Panorama Pt. — MT. ROBERTS–JIRRAMUN NATIONAL PARK — Carneys Ck — Mt. Toowoonan — Maroon Dam — Picnic Area — Boat Ramp — Maroon — 47 — 14 — Teviot School — Tamrookum

9

Yangan — Mt. Sturt — Rockbrae — Emu Vale — 45 — Danderoo — Jingarry — Wiyarra — Hoffmans Peak — MERIVALE NAT. PARK — Mt. Roberts 1329m — Bald Mtn 365m — Mt. Superbus 1379m — NAT. PK — Mt. Ballow — Mt. May 823m — MT. MAY NAT. PARK — Mt. Maroon 963m — Barney View — Rathdowney — Palen Ck — DIVIDING — Burnett — MT. MAROON — Rest Area

10

Mt. Colliery — Tannymorel — The Head — River — Wilsons Peak 1230m — MT. BARNEY NATL. PARK — Mt. Barney 1356m — Mt. Ernest — Mt. Gillies — Campbells Folly — Tylerville — 39 — Tylerville School — Pine — Yellow Pinch Res. — RANGE

11

Loch Lomond School — Killarney — Killarney Sth — The Falls — The Falls — Mt. Leslie — Acacia Plateau — 50 — HWY 10 — Dalman — Mt. Cluff 1135m — Lindsay Ck — Mt. Lindsay — Mt. Glennie — Glennies Chair — Dairy Flat — MT. LINDSAY — McPHERSON RANGE — Sawpit — Lindsay View — DIVIDING

12

Acacia Ck — Acacia Ck Lwr — Legume — MT LINDSAY — Central Koreelah School — Old Koreelah — Woodenbong — Aboriginal Settlement — Lindsay Ck Butter Factory — 11 — Castille — The Dome 915m — (Imensons) Unumbar — Budgeam — Mt. Grevillia 569m — Grevillia — 50 — RICHMOND RANGE — Terrace

13

New Koreela — Toloom Lookout — 45 — 18 — Toloom — Toloom Falls — Urbenville — Nth. Obelisk 729m — TOOLOOM RANGE — Roseberry — Maryland River — Koreelah — Beaury — Edinburgh Castle 894m — Boomi — Tooloom

A B C D 29 E F G H I

GYMPIE

Kilkivan, Kandanga, Imbil, Kenilworth, Jimna, Monsildale, Linville, Gobongo, Manumbar, Gallangowan, Elgin Vale, Avoca Vale, Conondale, Booloumba, Bellthorpe, Cedarton, Stanmore, Woolooga, Mouingba, Nondiga, Bular, Oakview, Rossmore, Cinnabar, Wonga Lower, Wonga Upper, Bells Bridge, Curra, Downsfield, North Deep Ck, Mt South Goomboorian, Goomboorian, Rossmount, Wilsons Pocket, Enterprise, Corella, Mt Corella 336m, Chatsworth, Tamaree, Harveys Siding, Fishermans Pocket, Highbury Hill, Greendale, Scrubby Ck, Glastonbury, Stratigos, Mary Ck, Nashville, Monkland, Cedar Pocket, Beenam Range, Mt Mothar 427m, Mothar Mtn, Woondum, Mt Boulder 495m, Dawn, Long Flats, Lagoon Pocket, Kybong, Tandur, Gildora, Calico Ck, Dagun, Mooloo, Langshaw, Greenridge, Mt Cooroora, Cooran, Traveston, Mt Cooroora 439m, Federal, Goomong, Nobby Glen, Melawondi, Yabba Vale, Mt Tuchekoi 292m, Bergins Pocket, Black Mtn, Kandanga Ck, Kandanga Upper, Heigh Ridge, Carters Ridge, Ridgewood, Bella, Derriers Flat, Brooloo, Belli Park, Picnic Area, Lake Borumba 623m, Borumba Mtn, Water Sports, Kenilworth Bluff 529m, Moys Pocket, Gheerulla, Brooloo Gap, Coomon Gibber, Mt Gibbarnee 396m, Yabba, Yabba Falls, Diaper Mtn, Mt Stanley 536m, Mt Stanley, Mt Monsildale, Summer Mtn 789m, Little Yabba Camping Area & Picnic Res, Mt Walli, Kidaman Ck, Obi Obi, Coolabine, Maplet Fa., MAPLETON FALLS NAT PK, Booloumba, Mt Cabinet 732m, Mt Langley 867m, Mt Gerald, Mt Ramsden 792m, Donovans Knob 662m, Witta, Conondale, Reesville, Woothakata, Booroobin, Avoca Vale, Hellhole, Mt Pascoe, Monsildale, Jinker Hill, Mt Denmark 732m, Mt Adelaide 739m, Yednia, Sheep Station, North West Mt 599m, Cooyar, Taromeo, Brisbane Range, Mt Spencer 489m, Linville, Marion Hill, Lawler, Gwendolen Hill, Mt Lionell, Mt Miner, Mt Moore, Limestone Hill, Spring, Oaky, Mt Kilcoy 351m, Mt Kilcoy, Mt Marysmokes 657m, Bellthorpe, Mt McLean 465m, Cedarton, Commission Flat, Stanmore, Round Mtn, Moore, Blackbutt Range, BALFOUR, D'AGUILAR HWY

Mt Clara 488m, Mt Coora 594m, The Breezer 457m, Kinbombi, Kinbombi Falls Picnic Area, Mt Mia 610m, Gobongo North, Toomcul, Manumbar Mill, Mt Tavinghi 685m, Widgee Upper, Widgee Mtn 688m, Mt Chucki, Mt Misery, Station, Mt Ghrooman + Bille, Gibraltar Rock, Woonga, Serpentine, Hookey, Mt Glastonbury 575m, Warrawee, Mt Moorooreerai 610m, Mt Warrawee 549m, Mt Mittatula, Mt Gentle + Annie, Cherry Tree Ck, Mt Teewoo 625m, Mt Wilwarrel, Amamoor, Amamoor Lookout, The Pocket, Mt Amamoor Forest Station, Mt Kandanga 576m, Eel Creek

COAST RANGE, WIDE BAY HWY, BRUCE HWY, RANGE, AMAMOOR RANGE, KANDANGA RANGE, YABBA RANGE, BRISBANE RANGE, JIMNA RANGE, CONONDALE RANGE, NAT PARK, KONDALI NAT PA, BEENAAM, TAGGAN, TAGGIGAN RANGE

Mary River, Mary, Eel, Yabba, Belli, Cedar, Little Yabba, Sunday Creek, Six Mile, Sheep Station, East, West, Middle, Monsildale, Mortimer, Nth Amamoor, Sth Amamoor, Coppermine, Kabunga, Stony, Gobongo, Barambah, Sawpit, Serpentine, Widgee, Fat Hen, Wide Bay

0 5 10 15 20 25km

1

2

Coondoo

COOLOOLA

Kings Bore

Round Mtn. 152m

Coondoo

Mt. Coondoo 282m

Sanctuary (Prohibited Entry)

WOLVI LO

16

RANGE

NATIONAL

COOLOOLA

3

Moran Group

Kin

Eulama

Lake Como

Lake Cooloola

N

Wahpunga School

Kimba Information Centre

Ck

PARK

COAST

Elanda Pt.

4

Kin Kin Juntion

Lake Cootharaba

Seawah Hill

Cootharaba

Boreen Pt.

Teewah Coloured Sands

RANGE

Cooloothin

Noosa

5

inbarren

NOOSA RIVER NAT. PARK

Subject to Flooding

Ringtail

Rocky Pt.

Lake Cooroibah

omona

Lake Mc Donald

House of Bottles & Big Shell

Laguna Bay

North Hd.

Granite Bay

6

Yurol

Mt. Tinbeerwah 265m

Tewantin

Noosa Heads

Noosa Head

NOOSA NATIONAL PARK

Tinbeerwah

16

Cooroy

22

Noosaville

Lookout

Black Mtn.

Nandroya

Mt.Cooroy 427m

Lake Weyba

Sunshine Beach

SOUTH

6

Cooroy West 10

Doonan

7

Eerwah Vale

Mt.Eerwah 419m

Eumundi

Peregian Beach

THE

PACIFIC

18

18

BLACKALL

North Arm

13

Valdora

Yandina Ck

Coolum Beach Point Perry

SUNSHINE

8

ottle ss

Cooloolabin Dam

Cooloolabin

21

Ninderry 306m

Yandina

19

Coolum

Pt. Arkwright

Mt.Coolum

OCEAN

Yandina

Weppa Dam

Dunethin Rock

Mt.Coolum 208m

Yaroomba

Kiamba

Big Cow

Maroochy River

Yandina

11

Marcoola Beach

Kulangoor

18

Image Flat

Poona Dam

NAT. PKS

Fairytale Castle

Maroochy Airport

9

reelpa

NAMBOUR

BRUCE

10

Bli Bli

Mudjimba

Mudjimba Is.

COAST

apleton

13

Burnside

Maroochy

Pioneer Village

ulong

Perwillowen

18

River

Ninderry

Keils Mtn.

Subject to Flooding

Flexton

Petrie

Big Pineapple

Didillibah

Maroochydore

10

Woombye

HWY

3

Mt. Buderim

3

Alexandra Headland

Hunchy

4

Buderim

Mooloolaba

Palmwoods

3

Mons

Ginger Factory

Pt Cartwright

ville

Lookout

Buddina

aroon ocket

11

Eudlo

Forest Glen

Subject to Flooding

Koala Park & Zoo

Mountain

Dinesaurs

Warana Beach

Landers Shoot

Eudlo

31

MOOLOOLAH RIVER NAT. PK.

Bokarina Beach

11

MOOLOOLAH

6

Mt.Sippy 180m

1

Kawana Waters

13

RANGE

River

Wurtulla Beach

Diamond Valley

Mooloolah

Subject to Flooding

NICKLIN

WAY

Bald Mooloolah Knob 465m

6

HWY

Currimundi

Bald Knob

3

10

Dickie Beach

13

NAT. PK.

Moffatt Beach

mhurst

BRUCE

12

Mt.Mellum 404m

Landsborough

Golden Beach

Caloundra

Mt. Mellum

Ballcock Beach

Deep Water Point

Subject to Flooding

10

Channel

Beerwah

Coochin Ck

13

chester

Mt. Coochin

Subject to Flooding

Coochin

Pumicestone

rwah

NAT. PK

Coonowrin

A B C D 118 E F G H I

1
SWORDS RA.
Woodstock
CARTERS RA.
KENNEDY DEVELOPMENTAL RD.
Subject to Flooding
Dondooroo
Opal Fields 1st Flying Surgeon Service 1958
Bonnie Downs
Tower Hill
Inverness
Marie Downs
Corinda
Carmichael
Moray Downs
Elgin Downs
Diamond Downs
EPPING FOREST NAT. PARK
MAZEPPA NAT. PK
Kilcumm
Middleton Ck.
Western
72
Apsley
Kywong
Beryl
Kensington
Cornish 65 Ck.
Reedy
Fleetwood
Lake Galilee
Shuttleworth
Lou Lou Park
Mistake
68
Winton
Drumlion Downs
Muttaburra
Bowen Downs
L.Barcoorah
Eastmore
Laglan
Beresford

2
Tulmur
Kalkadoon CORYS RA.
ALLENS RA.
Clyde
Charregon
Bude
Darr River Downs
124
66
Ambo
Highbury
Stainburn Downs
151
L.Dunn
L. Widgeman
L. Mueller
Ravenswood
Dunrobin
Albro
Degulla
Lennox
Forrester
Belyando
Narrien
NARRIEN RA.
Surbiton
Red Mtn.
Banchory
Peak Vale
Annmore
Clermont
179

Old Cork
Diamantina
240
Cork
Wamambool Downs
FORSYTH RA.
Weonaworri
Evesham
Motella
Darr
114
Fairfield
Aramac
Rodney Downs
GREAT DIVIDING RA.
Hobartville
Mt. Donnybrook
Craven
Ruby

3
Brighton Downs
KANGAROO MTS.
Rosebrook
Mayneside
Gemstones
Opalton
180
Wammadoo
Maneroo
Bimbah
Darr
Longreach
Dartmouth 108
Barcaldine
Jericho 55
CAPRICORN HWY
Beta
Alpha
66
HWY
Bogantungan
Gemst
169
Mt. Tabletop
Mt. Leura
Withersfield

Ilfracombe HWY 80
Brixton
88
Lochnagan
143
738m
Mt. Beaufort +
63
Subject to Flooding
Pine Hill
61

4
Eden
Opals
Tonkoro
Vergemont
Thornson
Westland
Cecil Park
Nerrena
Wellshot
106
Alice
Greycroft
Yalleroi
169
Durrandie
Alpha
Lockington
SNAKE RA.

Connemara RA.
Onoto
Westerton
35
Noonbah
Wakefield
105
Isisford
39
Isis Downs
Tarves
Barcoo
Blackall
101
Mt. Solitary
106
Castlevale
241
Mantaun Downs
Tane
Buck Table
KA KA M NAT. PARK

5
Warbreccan
309
Stonehenge
34
58
Bimerah
97
Thornleigh
Benlidi
Malvern Hills
Northampton Downs
Birkhead
WARREGO RA.
DEVELOPMENTAL
Flodden Hills
Lochiel
Trewalla
Glenariff
80
Swan Vale
Arno
Needle Ck.
Smith Lagoon
Albilbah
Emmet
67
Lorne
GOWAN RANGE
Tambo
Carwell
DAWSON R.
Salvator Rosa Natl. Park
Murphy Tableland

6
Berrimpa
Opals
90
Galway Downs
Barcoo
340
Glenara
Highlands
Wakes Lagoon
Minnie Downs
119
Caldervale
Babbiloora
Bogarella

Waverney
57
52
Humond Downs
55
Retreat
Oakham
CHEVIOT RANGE
RANGE
Gilmore
Listowel Downs
216
Langlo Downs
Nive Downs
Killarney
Warrenville

7
Cuddapan
32
South Galway
24
DIAMANTINA
29
Clifton
38
Lynwood
37
Opal Field
Bulgroo
134
97
Milo
Blackwater
Mt. Morris
Oakwood
Augathella
CHESTERTON RA.
Forest

Tanbar
Creek
Kyabra
Keeroongooloo
Raymore
33
GREY
Adavale
Arawee
Ambathala
113
185
Box Creek
82
Barduthulla
Clara Creek
92
Mt. Londsdale

8
47
Gilpeppie
Area Subject to Inundation
Malagarga
Opal Field
Mt. Howitt
COLEMAN RA.
RANGE
Thylungra
138
Ray
Cornwall
Earlstoun
Opal Field
Pinkilla
Kyabra
45
DEVELOPMENTAL ROAD
Quilpie
100
Comongin
Pingine
Boothulla
Cheepie
Cooladdi
Charleville
Royal Flying Doctor Base & School of the Air
Sommariva 54
92
Morven
WARREGO
92
Mung
Wom.

9
Eromanga
35
68
Mt. Margaret
Congie
Moble
Sth. Comongin
76
Cowley
Bierbank
Yarranvale
Allambie
Rosevale
MITCHELL HWY 104
Woodside
Ularunda
Bonus Downs
Leinster
Tomoo
Abbiege
280
204
Lus

10
Karmona
Cooper
145
Jackson Oil Field
Pipeline to Moonie under const.
Durham Downs
Nockatunga
GREY RANGE
Dewalla Ck.
114
Archerch
Opal Field
Dundoo
Humeburn
Boobara
Claverton
Yarmouth
Elmina
Wyandra
212
108
232
Grassmere
Homebои
Bindeban

11
Wilson
Prairie
186
Thargomindah
BULLOO
Lake Bindegolly
Dynevor Downs
Black Gate Opal Field
Yowah Opal Field
Yowah
Tilbooroo
Clover L.
Coongoola
Balbuna
135
BALONNE
Bendena
183
Yunnerman
Binda
Bollon
48
Mona

Orientos
Nooyeah Downs
Area Subject to Inundation
727
130
DEVEL.
Bingara
Cunnamulla
64 RD.
Eulo
Aboriginal Community
Charlotte Plains
Bonna Vonna
Murra Murra
Fernlee
Woolerin

12
164
GREY RANGE
Bulloo Downs
119
Bulloo Lake
Yakara
145
Boorara
122
Lake Wyara
L. Numalla
Tuen
122
Sports Centre Nuorama
Bundaleer
Mulga Downs
Mungallala
Widgeegoara
Tambingey
Naryilco
34
Currawinya
Tinnenburra
MITCHELL HWY
Barringun
Hebe
Goodo

13
Warri House
Woompah
Adelaide Gate House
SILVER CITY HWY
53
48
Tibooburra
Connulpie
Hamilton Gate
Berawinna Downs
Thurloo Downs
Glenhope
Yantabulla
Waverley Gate
Hungerford
Vermin
Warroo
Proof
Fence
NEW SOUTH WALES
Weilmoringle
Enngonia
Culgoa R.
Birrie R.
Bokhara R.

A B C D 28 E F G H I

Aboriginal Reserve
Mitchell & Alice Rivers Nat. Park
The Desert
GT. DIVIDING RA
Koolburra
Laura Field Nat. Pk
26
18
Laura
Fairview
Subject to Flooding
77
Fairlight
Aboriginal Paintings 15000 years old
Springvale
55
ENDEAVOUR R. NAT. PARK
Hope Vale Aboriginal Community
Cooktown
Capt. Cook repaired Endeavour here June 1770.
82
Helenvale
Rossville
Mt. Finnigan
CEDAR BAY NAT. PARK
Ayton
Weary Bay
Alice Mitchell Nat. Park
Koolatah
Strathleven
Palmer
Drumduff
Dunbar
Clerk
52
108
110
84
Highbury
Back
Palmerville
Maytown ruins from Palmer River gold rush days of 1873.
Area of alluvial & reef gold workings
Mitchell
St. George R.
124
China Camp
DAINTREE RIVER GORGE NAT. PK
Daintree
Miallo
266 Mossman
Port Douglas
Cape Tribulation
THORNTON PK NAT. PARK
GREAT
Vanrook
Echo
Red
Staaten
STAATEN RIVER NATIONAL PARK
Gamboola
Subject to Flooding
63
45
43
Walsh
Wrotham Park
Blackdown
50
Walsh
Mungana
26
Chillagoe
Mt. Carbine
Mt. Molloy
Cassowary
Mt. Mulligan
Kuranda
Mareeba
CAIRNS
Yarrabah Aboriginal Community
Gordonvale
Trinity Bay
GREAT
Miranda Downs
Minnies O.S.
Einasleigh
Abingdon Downs
Eden Vale
NEWCASTLE
Dagworth
O'Briens Ck Gemfields (Topaz)
Byrimine
Lyndbrook
Fossilbrook
Sundown
Bullock Creek
Nymbool
Mt. Garnet
Dimbulah
CHILLAGOE-MUNGANA LIMESTONE CAVES NAT. PARK
34
Tate
Bulwarra
Almaden
Petford
Watsonville
Irvinebank
Herberton
Atherton
155
92
BELLENDEN KER NAT. PARK
Mt. Bartle Frere
Babinda
Innisfail
97
Ravenshoe
155
Highest peak in Qld 1612 m
PALMERSTON NAT. PK.
Wallabadah
Strathmore
Etheridge
55
Gilbert
Chadshunt
Gilbert River
Ironhurst
Hot Springs
Talaroo
151
Mt. Surprise
St. Ronans
FORTY MILE SCRUB N.PK.
114
Innot Hot Springs
Koombooloomba Reservoir
Tully Falls
Tully
166
Mission Beach
Dunk I.
Bedarra I. Resort
GREAT BARRIER REEF MARINE PARK CAIRNS SECTION
Croydon
GULF
74
79 DEVELOPMENTAL
Forest Home
Georgetown Gemstones Agate Onyx
100
Green Hills Gold
Einasleigh
194
Kidston
Carpentaria Downs
93
Wairuna
Meadowbank
Most recent volcanic activity in Australia
Cashmere
HERBERT R. FALLS NAT. PK
Murray Falls
Bilyana
Kennedy
Herbert Vale
Cape Sandwich
Hinchinbrook Island
HINCHINBROOK NAT. PK
Idalia
Blackfellow
Forsayth
72
North Head
Robertson
Agate Creek Gemfields
The Lynd
Conjuboy
Camel Ck.
Lake Lucy
Michael Creek
Lannercost
Trebonne
Lucinda
Halifax
Orpheus I. Resort
Palm Islands
Palm Island Aboriginal Community
Great Palm I.
Yappar
52
Esmeralda
Glenora
Nara
Gilberton
Oak Park
Lyndhurst
Pandanus
Clarke River
59
Greenvale
Nickel Mine
Kangaroo Hills
CRYSTAL CK MT SPEC N.P.
JOURAMA FALLS N.P.
+Mt. Fox Extinct volcano
Highest single drop in Aust. 278m
Bambaroo
Mutarnee
Rollingstone
116
Ingham
BRUCE HWY
GREAT BARRIER REEF MARINE PARK CENTRAL SECTION
Prospect
40
Crooked Ck
Savannah Downs
Pelham
GREGORY
RANGE
Woodstock
Cheviot Hills
Chudleigh Park
256
Gregory Springs
Wando Vale
Clarke
Cuba
270
Maryvale
Hill Grove
Dotswood
Burdekin
Paluma Lookouts
Star
TOWNSVILLE
Queensland's largest provincial city
Magnetic I.
CLEVELAND N.PK
Alligator Creek
Ross River Dam
Woodstock
Fanning River
Reid River
Mingela
Clare
Giru
90
Ayr
Brandon
Home H
Inkerm
Gumlu
Guthal
Dalbeg
Bowling Green Bay
Cape Bowling Green
135
Cooradine Ck
Saxby Downs
Elmore
Somerville
Coalbrook
Stawell
GRAMPIAN HILLS
Dutton
Burleigh
Rainscourt
Dalkeith
Mt. Sturgeon
Boonderoo
150
Mt. Emu Plains
Lake Cargoon
Lolworth
Mt. Pleasant
Glencoe
Cargoon
LOLWORTH
Oak Vale
Gold
Mt. Stewart 914m
Campaspe R. Rest Area
Homestead
Museum Town of goldfield era
Macrossan
Sellheim
Ravenswood
Charters Towers
246
108
Brittania
Burdekin
Burdekin Downs
76
Burdekin Irrigation Area
Scottsv
Lorneleigh
Harvest Home
Corea Plains
Victoria Downs
204
Mt. Elsie
Proposed Burdekin Falls Dam
27
Bunda Bunda
72
Kilterry
Clutha
Runnymede
Yan Yeun
Compton Downs
Blantyre
Torrens Ck
Prairie
Redcliff
45
Lascelles
Longton
Egera
Julia Creek
Neva
Nonda
FLINDERS
Richmond
Resort
116
HWY
Hughenden
FLINDERS
GREAT DIVIDING RANGE
Longreach
116
Natal Downs
Mirtna
103
Mt. Hope
Yacamunda
Mt. Coolon
56
Mt. Douglas
Old Pasha
Eaglefie
84
50
150
50
Maxwelton
Talmoi
50
Marathon
43
Prairie
Arrara
53
Launceston
Oakley
Lammermoor
Webb Lake
Yarrowmere
Nunkumbil
Thirlstone
Lake Buchanan
Mt. Tutah
Bulliwallah
Avon Downs
116
Tarbrax
Dimora
Coleraine
Dundee
Albion Downs
Stamford
Whitewood
Kiriwina
Katandra
216
Woolfield
Tangorin
217
Barenya
Glenariff
33
42
Uanda
Aberfoyle
Prairie Vale
Bowie
Carmichael
Moray Downs
Mistake
Elgin Downs
Diamond Downs
MAZAPPA RANGE
169
LANDSBOROUGH
Kynuna
Under Construction
Opals
Dagworth
SWORDS RA
Woodstock
161
Olio
Corfield
Malboona
Bonnie Downs
Tower Hill
Inverness
Marie Downs
Corinda
RANGE
Carmichael
Fleetwood
Lou Lou Park
EPPING FOREST NAT. PARK
Shuttleworth
CARTERS RA
Western
Winton
Opal Fields
HWY
Oondooroo
Kywong
Beryl
Apsley
Fairymead
Drumlion Downs
Kensington
Cornish
Muttaburra
Highbury
Rest Area
24
Ambo
Marie
Stainburn Downs
Lake Baroorah
L. Dunn
+Mt. Donnybrook
Dunrobin
Albro
Degulla
Beresford
Eastmere
Laglan
Blair Athol
Clermont

0   100   200   300 km

1

2

S O U T H

3

P A C I F I C

4

O C E A N

5

GREAT BARRIER REEF
MARINE PARK
CENTRAL SECTION

6

GREAT

7

BARRIER

REEF

8

CAPE UPSTART
NAT PARK

119   Abbot Pt.   Bowen
Merinda   GLOUCESTER IS.
NAT.PK.

Longford   Hayman I.
Ck   Hook I.
N. PK.
Airlie
Binbee   Cannon   Beach   Whitsunday I.
vale   N. PK.
Proserpine   N.PK.   Shute
Harbour   Lindeman I.
Conway   Shaw I.
Collinsville   Beach
Cape Conway

Noorlah
Bloomsbury   Midgeton   Cumberland
77   196   Islands
Emu   Elaroo   Brampton I.
Plains   Yalbaroo   CAPE HILLSBOROUGH
NAT.PK.
BROKEN   Caleri   Mt.Ossa
RIVER RA   EUNGELLA
Tiverton   Mt Charlton   56   Kattabul
wlands   82   Farleigh
Suttor   Eungella   MACKAY   Sugar Mills
Ck   156   Eungella   Mirani   Hay Point   Coal Shipping Terminal
Resr   Finch   Eton
Lenton   Mt.   Hatton   Homevale   Sarina Beach
Downs   Hillalong   Hail Ck   Sarina
ENHAM   Lake   114   Koumola   CAPE PALMERSTON NAT PARK   Middle I.
Elphinstone   RA   CONNORS   Ilbilbie
Oponyella   Nebo   Ra   South I.
Coal Mine   WEST HILL IS   NAT PARK
Broadmeadow   142   29   NAT.PK   Carmila   Northumberland
DOWNS   55   Bee Cr   DIPPERU   Islands
ranbah   286   NAT.PARK   Collaroy   Broad Sound Channel
Subject to   Sultbush Park   240   Broad
Flooding   Bombandy   Subject to   Sound
Peak Downs   Flooding   Flood   St Lawrence
Coal Mine   Saraji   gate   Flood gate   Pearl Bay
Logan   Coal Mine   Subject to   Port Clinton
Downs   Flooding   Croydon
Mt. Phillips   Dysart   Ogmore   Banksia   MILITARY
tley   May   Marlborough   TRAINING
Downs   HWY   AREA   Prohibited
Area

9

BARRIER

REEF

GREAT BARRIER REEF
MARINE PARK –
CAPRICORN SECTION

10

11

12

13

REGION   BOUNDARY

MILITARY TRAINING AREA–
SEAWARD BDY

CAPRICORNIA
SECTION

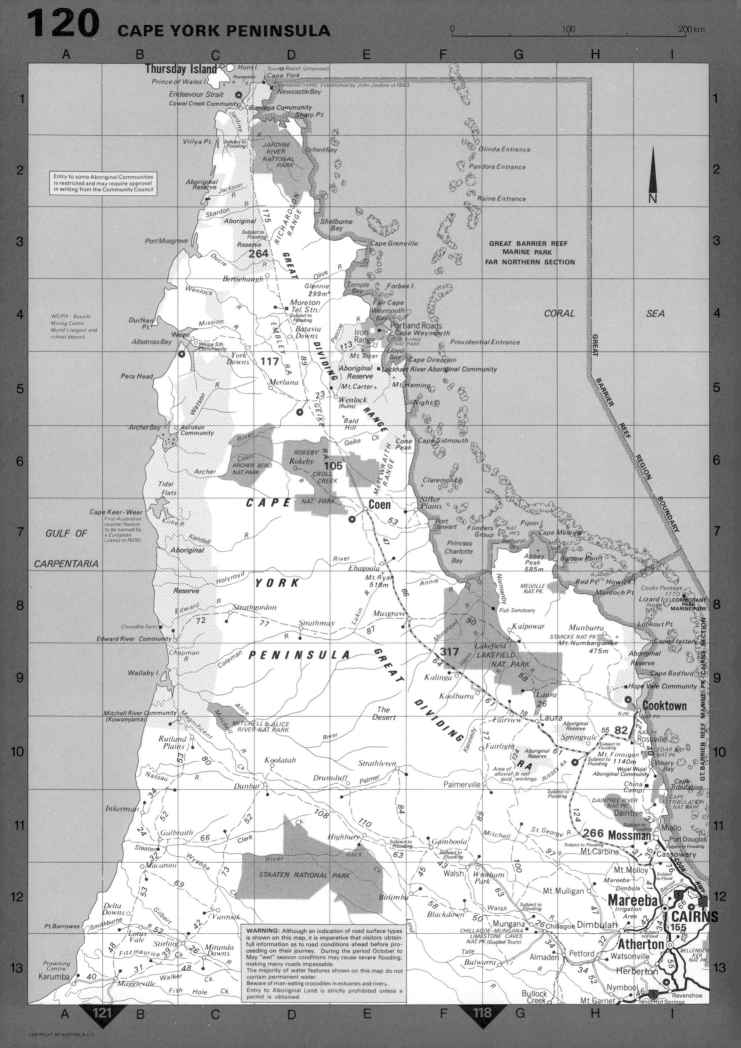

0   100   200 km

A B C D E ◆120◆ F G H I

CAUTION: Tropical estuaries are a crocodiles habitat.

GULF OF CARPENTARIA

WARNING: Although an indication of road surface types is shown on this map, it is imperative that visitors obtain full information as to road conditions ahead before pro-ceeding on their journey. During the period October to May "wet" season conditions may cause severe flooding, making many roads impassable.

The majority of water features shown on this map do not contain permanent water.

Entry to Aboriginal Reserves is strictly prohibited unless a permit is obtained.

Mornington Island
Mornington Peninsula Aboriginal Local Government Area
Denham I.
Forsyth I.
C. Van Diemen
Sydney I.
Bountiful I.
Wellesley Islands
Bentinck I.
Sweers I.
Allen I.
Parker Pt.

Tully Inlet
Massacre Inlet
8 mile Ck.
Lagoon
Cliffdale
Padmore
James Ck.
Moonlight
Tarrant Pt.
Westmoreland
Wild Horse Ck.
Gore Pt.
Pt. Burrowes
Smithburne
Staaten River
Macaroni
53
69

Corinda Ruins
Doomadgee Aboriginal Reserve
Doomadgee Community
Burketown
Barramundi fishing & wildlife observation safaris
Aboriginal Reserve
Morning Inlet
Karumba
Prawning Centre
Alligator Pt.
Delta Downs
Lotus Vale
52
Stirling
26
Fitzmaurice Ck.
Miranda Downs
Walker
48
Echo Ck.
Vanrook
42
Gilbert River
Minnies O.S.
Abingdon Downs
106

Accident Ck.
Nicholson
Albert
Leichhardt
Armraynald
Inverleigh
Wernadinga
Normanton
Magowra
Glenore
May Vale
Black Bull
Wallabadah
63
Old gold mining town Croydon
74
Subject to Flooding
Gilbert River ROAD
Chadshunt
55
Eden Vale
Strathmore
Forest Home
Einasleigh

Musselbrook
Lawn Hill RA
Punjaub
Almora
Floraville
Leichhardt Falls
Alexandra
Neumayer Downs
Milgarra
Belmore Ck.
79
Idalia
61
Blackfellow

Herbert Vale
Lawn Hill
Hotel Gregory Downs
Augustus Downs
182
Talawanta
68
Bang Bang
Wondoola
Vena Park
Claraville
Clara
71
40
Esmeralda
Glenora
Nara

Gallipoli
Riversleigh
SMITHS RA
113
Sandy Ck.
Nardoo
Lorraine
Cloncurry
Dismal Ck.
Burke & Wills Roadhouse
Kamilleroi
76 NORMANTON
Wurung
Saxby
Iffley
Munduro
Norman
Prospect
Taldora
Savannah Downs
89
Arizona
Crooked Ck.
Cooradine Ck.
Woodstock
Pelham

Morstone
Shannassy
Thornton
Chidna
Mt. Oxide Mine
Gunpowder
Thorntonia
Mammoth Mines
Gunpowder
Waggaboonya Lake
Dobbyn
Alsace
Boomarra
Alcala
Coolullah
Dugald
Brinard
285
Millungera
Numil
Saxby Downs
Mt. Norman
Elmore

BARKLY TABLELAND
103
109
Undilla
Camooweal
60
Nowranie
Crater of Caves
188
Yelvertoft
88
Julius Lake
Calton Hills
Leichhardt
114
Quamby
243
Granada
Clonagh
Sedan Dip.
Dalgonally
64
Manfred Downs
Kilterry
72
Clutha
Runnymede
Ranmoor
Yan Yean
Somerville
Burleigh

Buckley PILPAH RANGE
Barkly Downs
Hilton Mine
40
Lake Moondarra
Glenroy
Parkside
Corella Park
Corella
Fort Constantine
Williams
Fullarton
71
Julia ROAD Ck.
64
53
Nonda HWY
Nelia
Richmond
Talmoi 50

MT. ISA
Royal Flying Doctor Service Base
Mary Kathleen former uranium mining town now demolished
Lake Corella
Burke & Wills Mem!
64
124 Cloncurry
Oorindi
115
146
Gilliat
Subject to Flooding
FLINDERS
31
Julia Creek
78
50
150
Maxwelton
50

Mingera
Arcadia
Templeton
Yaringa
92
Malbon
Devoncourt
Kuridala
McKinlay
74
116
Tarbrax
Dimora
Yorkshire Downs
Lucindale
Coleraine
80

Lake Nash
Headingly
187
155
Bushy Park
Subject to Flooding Ck.
Duchess
52 RAS
Ardmore
SELWYN RANGE
69
Selwyn
64
Beaudesert
182
Subject to Flooding
Kynuna
LANDSBOROUGH
Albion Downs
Workingham
Kirwina
Dundee

Urandangi
Walgra
Carandotta
Linda Downs
MANGANESE RIDGE
N
Dajarra
STANDISH RA
66
68
The Monument
Phosphate Hill Mine
Digby Peaks
19
Chatsworth
142
108
Burke
Diamantina Ranges Valley
Dagworth
Banjo Paterson composed "Waltzing Matilda" at Combo Waterhole in 1895
Bendemeer
161
Oondooroo
72
Winton

NORTHERN TERRITORY
Roxborough Downs
Alderley
Strathelbiss
77
Warenda
Hamilton Hotel
Lucknow
Toolebuc
Mackunda Downs
Middleton
Denbigh Downs
Woodstock
356
121
Chiltern Hills
Tulmur
158
Kalkadoon
Western RANGE
Warnambool Downs

PLENTY HWY
TOKO RANGE
Glenormiston
Georgina
Herbert Downs
Marion Downs
Boulia
Major Airport
KENNEDY
Hamilton
DEVELOPMENTAL
MACARTNEY RA
Diamantina
Cambeela
Middleton ROAD
Old Cork
TULLY RANGE
Cork
Brighton Downs
Rosebrook
KANGAROO MTNS
Gemstones Opalton
Mayneside
Weonawarri
FORSYTH RA

TOOMBA RA

A B C D E ◆122◆ F G H I

COPYRIGHT BP AUSTRALIA LTD

0   100   200 km

121

A B C D E F G H I

1
Kelly Ck
Roxborough Downs
Ck
Cottonbush
Alderley
Warenda
R
Lucknow
KENNEDY DEVELOPMENTAL
Chiltern Hills
Tulmur
Kalkadoon
RA
FORSYTH RA
Hamilton Hotel
Strathbliss
Cambeela
Warnamboot Downs
240

2
Glenormiston
TOKO RANGE
Georgina
Herbert Downs
Boulia
Major Airport
77
Hamilton R
MACARTNEY RANGES
Diamantina
Old Cork
Cork
240
Weonaworri
Gemstones
Opalton
TOOMBA RANGE
Mulligan
Carlo
Brighton Downs
KANGAROO MTS.
Rosebrook
McKenzie
Mayneside
Vergmont

3
QUEENSLAND
NORTHERN TERRITORY
Marion Downs
Tropic of Capricorn
Springvale
Mt. Windsor
Mayne
R
Diamantina Lakes
HARDINGS
Eden Ck
Opals
Tonkoro
35
Wantagong
Westerton
39
206
Pigeongah Ck
Coorabulka
CHANNEL
Davenport Downs
RANGES
Onoto
Breadalbane
Mama Ck

4
SIMPSON
Sandringham
King Ck
Davenport R
Connemara
Warbreccan
Lake Phillippi
Bedourie
Flood Bypass
Cluny
DIAMANTINA
Farrars Ck
Flodden Hills
Lochiel
Trewalla
80
Jundah

5
DESERT
Eyre Ck
Glengyle
Lake Machattie
Lake Koolivoo
Flood Bypass
Monkira
253
DEVELOPMENTAL
COUNTRY
Palparara
Berrimpa
90
Galway Downs
CK

6
DESERT
217
Diamantina R
Mooraberree
Morney
Currawilla
47
Waverney
Whitula
ROAD
52
156
57
100
Hammond Downs
24
29
Windorah
Major Airport
N
105
116

7
Simpson Desert National Park
Roseberth
179
BIRDSVILLE DEVELOPMENTAL RD
Moonda Lake
Betoota
113
270
Planet Downs
Cuddapan
South Galway
Tanbar
COLEMAN RA.
Opal Fields
Keeroongooloo
Raymore
Poeppels Corner
Birdsville
QUEENSLAND

8
SOUTH AUSTRALIA
Alton Downs
Eyre Ck
Miranda (Ruins)
Pandie Pandie
Cadelga Outstation (Uninhabited)
L.Etamunbanie
Haddon Corner
Curalle
Gilpeppee
Nullah
Area subject to Inundation
Lake Yamma Yamma
Full only twice this century
Malagarga
Mt. Howitt
Pleyna Downs
McGREGOR RANGE
Numerous Opal Fields

WARNING: Although an indication of road surface types is shown on this map, it is imperative that visitors obtain full information as to road conditions ahead before pro-ceeding on their journey. During the period October to May "wet" season conditions may cause severe flooding, making many roads impassable.

The majority of water features shown on this map do not contain permanent water.

Entry to Aboriginal Reserves is strictly prohibited unless a permit is obtained.

9
Perra Perra Poolanna Lake
Diamantina R
Uloowarane
Track 148
Cordillo Downs
Sturts Stony Desert
Arrabury
Lake Pure
L.Pure
DurhamDowns

10
Warburton
Birdsville Track 127
Clifton Hills
Coongie
"THE DIG TREE" Burke & Wills Monument
Innamincka
Nappa Merrie
Cooper Ck
Karmona
Jackson Oil Field
Oil pipeline Jackson to Moonie under const
Nockatunga
Wilson R

11
The
Lake Koodnanie
Cowarie
Mungeranie
40
Cooper
Creek
Aboriginal Rock Carvings
Gidgealpa
Moomba
SOUTH AUSTRALIA
QUEENSLAND
Orientos
GREY RANGE

12
Lake Eyre
Mulka
Etadunna
84
Strzelecki Creek
STOKES RANGE
Naryilco
119
Bulloo Lake
Bulloo Downs

13
Dulkaninna
Lake Gregory
Lake Blanche
Cameron Corner
Bollards Lagoon
Fort Grey
Vermin Proof Fence
Woompah
48
Adelaide Gate House
Connulpie
STURT NATIONAL PARK
Warri House
SILVER CITY HWY
Tibooburra
N.S.W.

A B C D E F G H I

26

0 2 4 6 8 10 12 14km

A B C D 117 E F G H I

1
Mt Cooroora +439m
Skyring
Federal Creek
BRUCE
18
Middle
Creek
State Forest
Six Mile Dam
State Forest
HIGHWAY
Yuroi
Lake McDonald
Mt Tinbeerwah +65m
Timbeerwah
COOROY
House of Bottles
Big Shell
Ferry
Laguna Bay Granite
North Head
Camping Area
Noosa Head
Nangaroo Lookout
Noosa Heads
Noosaville
Noosa Hill
NOOSA
Tewantin
ROAD
Devils Kitchen Paradise Caves
Cooks Monument
NATIONAL PARK
Sunshine Beach

2
Black Mountain
Black Mountain +
Cooroy
Nandroya
8
427m + Mt Cooroy
25
Lookout
State Forest
Scenic Drive
Doonan
NOOSA
Noosa Information Centre
Noosa Airstrip
Lake Weyba
Timber Reserve
Marcus Beach

3
Ridgewood
Cooroy West
16
17
Rest Area
Eumundi
Mt Cooroy
Best Area
State Forest
Maroochy River
Yandina Creek
19
COAST
ROAD
Peregian Beach

4
Belli
Creek
5
State Forest
Rest Area
+Mt Eerwah
North
Creek
State Forest
Yandina Creek
Mt Peregian (Emu Mt)
N
Reserve

5
Belli Park
State Forest
RANGE
York Creek
Forest Creek
Coolooloobin
+Mt Bottle & Glass
Wappa Falls
Picnic Area
10
Bridges
State Forest
Yandina Creek
Mt Ninderry
Sugar Cane
18
Lows Lookout
Coolum
ROAD
Coolum Beach
Point Perry
Pt Arkwright

6
State Forest
BLACKALL
Cedar Creek
East Cedar Creek
Coolooloobin Dam
Wappa Dam
Kiamba
+Mt Wappa
Farmland & The Big Cow
Mt Combe
Kiamba Falls
Image Flat
Yandina
Maroochy River
YANDINA
Dunethin Rock
Maroochy River
Coolum Creek
Yaroomba
Mt Coolum +208m
Yaroomba Beach
18
PACIFIC

7
Mapleton Falls
State Forest
Poona Dam
NP
NP
Rest Area
10
10
Bli Bli
Fairyland Castle
Historic Locomotive
Pioneer Village
Maroochy Airport
Marcoola Beach
Mudjimba
Old Woman Island (Mudjimba Island)
Mudjimba Beach

8
Connors Knob
Mapleton
Kureelpa
11
Burnside
Moreton Sugar Mill
Lookout
NAMBOUR
Dulong
Perwillowent
Keils Mountain
Didilliban
Maroochy River
Chambers Channel Island
Goat Island
Ninderry
Rec Res
Pincushion Island

9
Obi Obi
Picnic Area Lookout
Baxter Creek
Model English Village
Flaxton Gardens & Pottery
Flaxton
Flaxton Barn
9
KONDALILLA NATIONAL PARK
State Forest
Kondalilla Falls
Hunchy
CSR Macadamia Nut Factory
The Big Pineapple
Rest Area
8
Keils Mountain +152m
Waterslide
Drive-In Theatre
12
Buderim
Mons
Deer Sanctuary
Ginger Factory
Museums Lookout
Tourist Information Centre
Mooloolaba
Maroochydore
Alexandra Headland
Point Cartwright
Buddina
Buddina Beach
Night Club

10
State Forest
Obi Obi Forest
The Train Dome
Museum
Montville
Pottery
De'Lisle Gallery
Crawfords Lookout
9
Picnic Area
NATIONAL PARK
Eudlo
Forest Glen
Dino's Funpark
Creek
Buderim Zoo & Koala Park
Super Bee
15
Mountain
MOOLOOLAH RIVER NATIONAL PARK
Kawana Waters
20
Warana Beach
Bokarina Beach
SOUTH

11
Witta
Baroon Pocket
Landers Shoot
10
BLACKALL RANGE
Reeseville
Howells Knob Lookout
Malenny
Butter Factory
Picnic Area
Eudlo
MOOLOOLAH
RANGE
180m +Mt Sippy
Rest Area
Palm View
Sippy Creek
World of Matchcraft
Currimundi
Reserve
Wurtulla Beach

12
Elaman Creek
Wootha
Mary Cairncross Park
Diamond Valley (Opal)
Bald Knob
Rainforest Tourist Park
Mountain Scenery Forest
State Forest
Mooloolah
DULARCHA NATIONAL PARK
Ewen Maddock Dam
MOOLOOLAH
River
Palm View
HIGHWAY
CALOUNDRA ROAD
12
Hospital
Caloundra Airport
Drive-In Theatre
Endeavour Replica
Dickey Beach
Moffatt Beach
Shelly Beach
Caloundra
Caloundra Head
Kings Beach
Golden Beach

13
+Mt Peachester
Cedarton
Stanley Picnic Areas
Peachester
Ewan
16
Historical Museum
Landsborough
Mount Mellum
BRUCE
HIGHWAY
10
Mellum Creek
State Forest
Bell Creek
Bribie Island
Deep Water Point
Pumicestone Channel
OCEAN

A B C D E F G H I

1 2 3 4 5 6 7 8 9 10 11 12 13

113

S O U T H

P A C I F I C

O C E A N

MAIN BEACH

SURFERS PARADISE

BROADBEACH

MERMAID BEACH

Museum of Australiana
Narrow Neck
Macintosh Island Park
Cronin Island
Surfers Paradise Beach
Chevron Island
Paradise Waters
Andalucia Park
Shark Expo
Sea World
Sea Park
Bar Park
The Bar
Boat Ramp
Yacht Club
Tuesleys Jetty
Wall
Boat Ramp
The Broadwater
The Rip
Landers End
Sundarewa Head
Chirang Head
Southport Point

Runaway Bay
MORALA
MARINE PDE
Labrador
SOUTHPORT
CENTRAL AV
MUSGRAVE AV
KUMBARI
Botanical Gardens
Lawn Cemetery
Biggera Waters State School
Drive-In Theatre
South Coast Dairy Co-op
COOMBABAH RD
RIDGE ROAD
GOLD COAST HIGHWAY
PINE
OLSEN AV
NERANG ST
Southport State High School
South Southport
Broadwater Trotway
Stephens Southport
SOUTHPORT ROAD
HINDE ST
CURRUMBURRA ROAD
COTEEW ST
NERANG ST
ROSS ST
Timber Top
Ashmore
NERANG
Florida Gardens
Bundall
Benowa
Benowa Waters
Raceourse
Sewage Works
SLATYER AV
FERRY RD
ROAD
ISLE OF CAPRI
SALERNO
BUNDALL
Racecourse
Pindarra Park
BENOWA ROAD
ASHMORE ROAD
International Motor
Jump Racing
Nerang River
Gaelach
COAST ROAD
NERANG
Carrara
Trail Rides
NIELSEN AV
SPRINGBROOK ROAD
CLEAR ISLAND ROAD
GOLD COAST ROAD
Merrimac
Kelgry
Boobagan
drains
Mermaid Waters
BERMUDA ST
Hooker BLVD
GOLD COAST
Mermaid School
Sunshine
Pacific Fair
Surfers Paradise Golf Club
Pacific
MARKERI
HOOKER
NINDEE
DRIVE
Aquatic
MERRIMAC

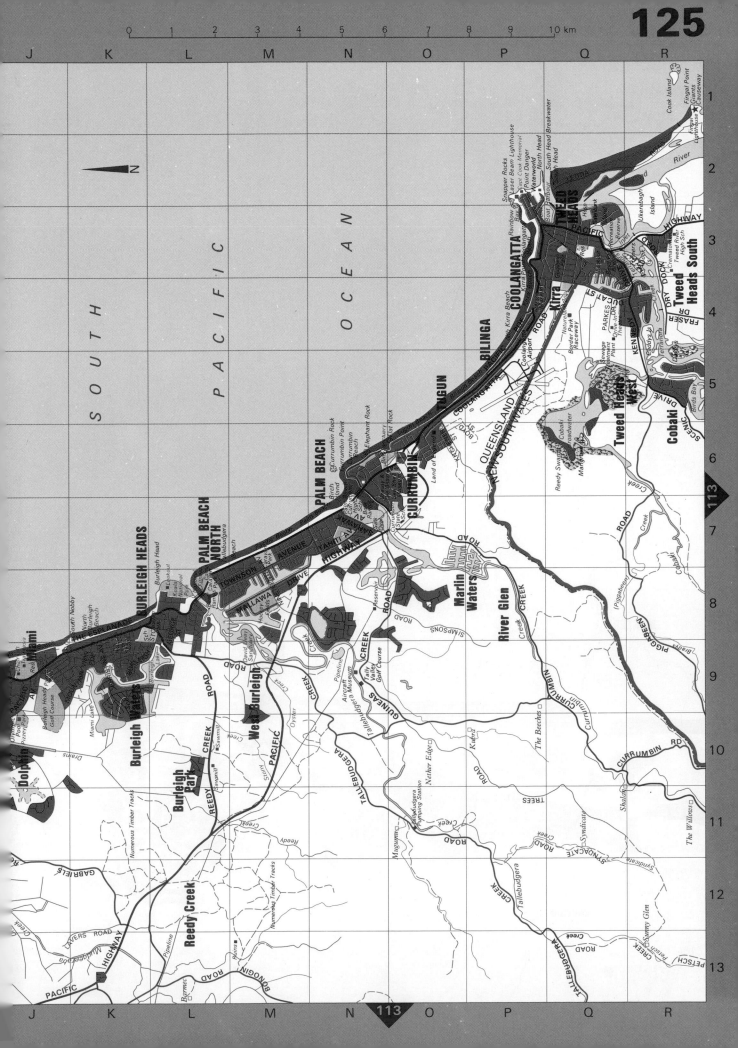

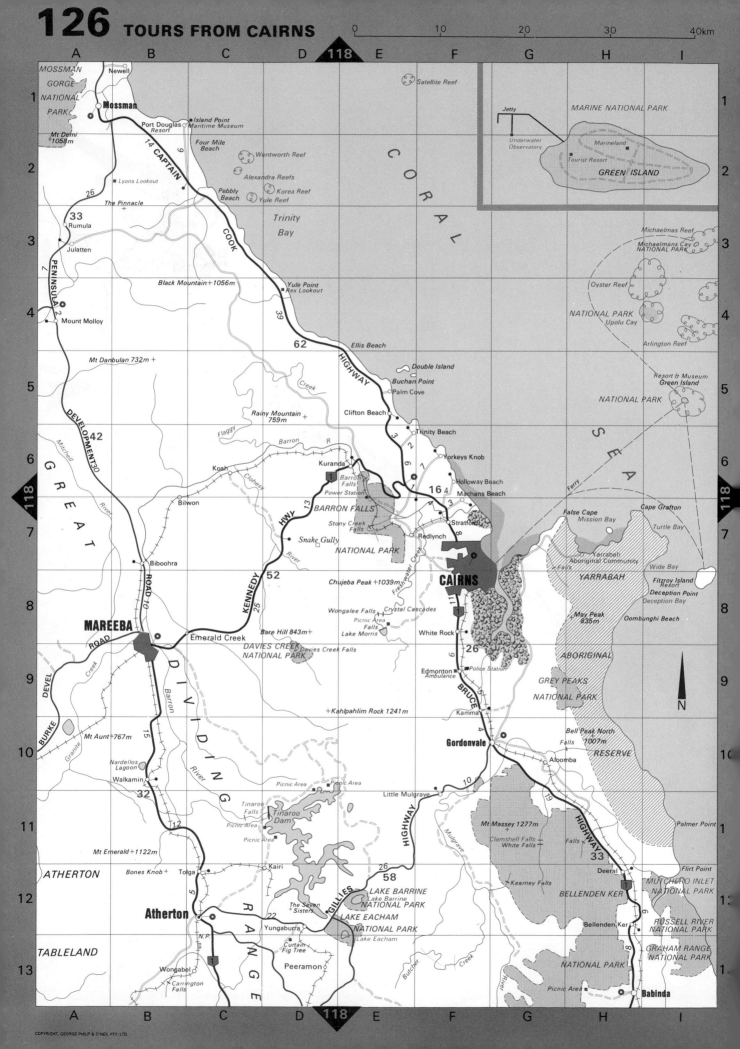

0   10   20   30   40km

MOSSMAN GORGE NATIONAL PARK

Newell

Mossman

Mt Demi +1058m

Port Douglas Resort

Island Point Maritime Museum

Four Mile Beach

Satellite Reef

MARINE NATIONAL PARK

Jetty

Underwater Observatory

Marineland

Tourist Resort

GREEN ISLAND

14 CAPTAIN

9

Lyons Lookout

26

The Pinnacle

33 Rumula

Julatten

PENINSULA

COOK

Black Mountain +1056m

Wentworth Reef

Alexandra Reefs

Pebbly Beach

Korea Reef

Yule Reef

Trinity Bay

Yule Point Rex Lookout

39

62

Ellis Beach

HIGHWAY

Double Island

Buchan Point

Palm Cove

CORAL

Michaelmas Reef

Michaelmans Cay NATIONAL PARK

Oyster Reef

NATIONAL PARK Upolu Cay

Arlington Reef

Mount Molloy

Mt Danbulan 732m +

DEVELOPMENT 30

42

Mitchell

Flaggy

Barron

Creek

Rainy Mountain + 759m

Clifton Beach

Trinity Beach

3

2

Yorkeys Knob

Resort & Museum Green Island

NATIONAL PARK

GREAT

River

Koah

Clohesy

Kuranda

Barron Falls Power Station

6

7

Holloway Beach

16 4

Machans Beach

SEA

Ferry

False Cape

Mission Bay

Cape Grafton

Turtle Bay

ROAD 10

Bilwon

HWY

13

BARRON FALLS

Stony Creek Falls

Snake Gully

NATIONAL PARK

8

Stratford

Redlynch

3

Yarrabah Aboriginal Community

Falls

Wide Bay

Fitzroy Island Resort

Deception Point

Deception Bay

118

Biboohra

KENNEDY

52

25

River

Chujeba Peak +1039m

Freshwater Creek

CAIRNS

11

YARRABAH

MAREEBA

ROAD

DIVIDING

Emerald Creek

DAVIES CREEK NATIONAL PARK

Davies Creek Falls

Wongalee Falls

Picnic Area Falls

Crystal Cascades

Lake Morris

White Rock

1

26

6

May Peak 835m

Oombunghi Beach

ABORIGINAL

DEVEL

BURKE

Creek

Granite

Mt Aunt +767m

Bare Hill 843m +

Kahlpahlim Rock 1241m

Edmonton Ambulance

Police Station

Kamma

GREY PEAKS NATIONAL PARK

RESERVE

N

Barron

15

Nardellos Lagoon

Walkamin

RANGE

Tinaroo Falls

Picnic Area

Picnic Area

Tinaroo Dam

Picnic Area

Little Mulgrave

Gordonvale

Aloomba

10

BRUCE

4

26

Bell Peak North 1007m

Falls

Palmer Point

32

12

Mt Emerald +1122m

HIGHWAY

Mulgrave

Mt Massey 1277m

Clamshell Falls

White Falls

19

Falls

HIGHWAY

33

ATHERTON

Bones Knob +

Tolga

Kairi

GILLIES

26

58

Lake Barrine NATIONAL PARK

Lake Eacham NATIONAL PARK

Kearney Falls

Deeral

MUTCHERO INLET NATIONAL PARK

BELLENDEN KER

Flirt Point

1

Atherton

5

22

Yungaburra

The Seven Sisters

Curtain Fig Tree

Lake Eacham

Bellenden Ker

RUSSELL RIVER NATIONAL PARK

TABLELAND

N.P.

Wongabel

1

Carrington Falls

Peeramon

Butcher

Creek

River

Picnic Area

8

GRAHAM RANGE NATIONAL PARK

Babinda

118

0   10   20   30   40   50km

A B C D E 119 F G H I

CORAL SEA

Scale / grid numbers: 1 2 3 4 5 6 7 8 9 0 1 2 3 (left and right edges)

119

N

Queen's Beach
Cape Edgecumbe Middle Island
BOWEN
NATIONAL PARK
Rattray Island
Gloucester Island
Eshelby Island
Hayman Island Resort
WHITSUNDAY GROUP
Stone Island
Saddleback Island
George Point
Langford Island
Hook Peak
Hook Island
Edgecumbe Bay
Dingo Beach
Armit Island
Double Cone Island
NATIONAL PARK
Mookarra Intaburra
Olden Island
Border Island
Deloraine Island
Port of Bowen
Grassy Island
To Hook, Hardy & Black Reefs
Longford Creek
Ben Lamond
Double Bay
Underwater Observatory
Harold Island
Edward Island
BRUCE
Earlando
North Molle Island
Cid Island
Whitsunday
Haslewood Island
Debella
Mt Dryander 820m
Island Cruise Departure Point
Airlie
Daydream Island Resort
South Molle Island
Whitsunday Island
To Tideway & Square Reefs
Mt McGuire 738m
Bubialo
Cannonvale
Island Cruise Departure Point
Shute Harbour
Coral Art
HIGHWAY
Koolachu
Mt Hayward 441m
Henning Island
Resort
Happy Bay
Dent Island
Perseverance Island
CUMBERLAND
Crystal Brook
Foxdale
Mount Julian
CONWAY
Pine Island
Long Island
Hamilton Island Resort
Proserpine
Cedar Creek Falls
MOUNT
Pentecost Island
Shaw Peak
Kelsey Creek
Mt Proserpine 439m
CONWAY
Lindeman Island Resort
NATIONAL
Wilsons Beach
Conway Beach
PARK
Mansell Island
Proserpine Aerodrome
Repulse Bay
RANGE
Round Head
Shaw Island
NATIONAL PARK
LINDEMAN GROUP
Gunyarra
Thomas Island
ISLANDS
Andromache
Thoopara
Lethebrook
Cape Conway
Silversmith Island
Mt Flat Top 680m
Mt Hector 890m
River
Repulse Islands
Blacksmith Island
SIR JAMES SMITH GROUP
Caping
Midgeton
NATIONAL PARK
Linne Island
Mowp
Bloomsbury
Midge Island
Goldsmith Island
Tinsmith Island
Mt Bullock 332m
CLARKE
O'Connell
Cave Island
Carlisle Island
Mt Crompton 792m
Elaroo 130
Pigeon Island
NATIONAL PARK
RANGE
River
Yalboroo
Wagoora
Rabbit Island
Outer Newry Island Resort
Brampton Island Resort
Broken
NATIONAL PARK
Pindi Pindi
St Helens
NATIONAL PARK
Hillsborough Channel
River
PARK
Calen
Halliday Bay
Ball Bay
HIBISCUS
Seaforth Ball Bay
Cape Hillsborough
Mount Pelion
NATIONAL PARK
Andrews Point
BROKEN RIVER RANGE
DICKS TABLELAND
Mount Ossa
Cape Hillsborough
COAST
EUNGELLA NATIONAL PARK
BRUCE
Buthurra
Sand Bay
NATIONAL PARK
Mt Dalrymple 1259m
NATIONAL PARK
Green Island
Pease's Lookout
HIGHWAY
Shoal Point
Mt Dingo 719m
Kuttabul
Mt Blackwood 590m
Habana
Bucasia
Eungella Dam
CLARKE
Aminungo
Emeo
Eungella
Finch Hatton Trueman
Pinnacle
The Leap
Farleigh
Blacks Beach
Slade Point
Netherdale
RANGE
Benholme
Pioneer Marian
Pleystowe
Port of Mackay
Bevans Lookout & Kiosk
Gargett
River
MACKAY
Mirani
Nabilla
Walkerston
Mt Bruce
74
Mackay Aerodrome
Round Top Island
DENHAM RANGE
PISGAH RANGE
PEAK
Eton
DOWNS
Bakers Creek
Sandringham Bay
Blacks Creek
Oakenden
Marwood
Homebush
Dudgeon Pt
HWY
Munbura
Balberra
Hay Point
Pipeline
BRUCE HWY
Dawlish
Alligator Creek

119

Index

A

A.I. Mine Settlement Vic. 53 N3
Abbeyard Vic. 59 P10
Abbotsford NSW 10 I3
Abbotsford Vic. 38 I8
Abbotsham Tas. 72 H6
Abercorn Qld 117 N6
Abercrombie NSW 24 F7, 30 E2
Aberdeen NSW 29 J13, 25 J1
Aberfeldy Vic. 53 N4
Aberglasslyn NSW 18 E2
Abermain NSW 18 D4, 25 L3
Abernethy NSW 18 D5
Abminga SA 82 I1, 105 L13
Acacia Creek NSW 112 C11
Acacia Creek Lower NSW 112 B12
Acacia Gap NT 100 E5
Acacia Plateau NSW 112 C11
Acheron Vic. 48 F5, 53 K1, 59 K13
Acton ACT 34 C8
Adaminaby NSW 30 D8, 31 H3
Adamsfield Tas. 70 I6
Adamstown NSW 18 H5
Adavale Qld 116 E7
Addington Vic. 51 P2
Adelaide SA 75, 76, 78 I6
Adelaide Airport SA 76 B9
Adelaide Lead Vic. 57 P12
Adelaide River NT 100 E6
Adelong NSW 23 R11, 24 C11, 30 B6
Adjungbilly NSW 24 D10, 30 C5
Admiralty Gulf Aboriginal Res. WA 93 O1
Advancetown Qld 113 N7
Adventure Bay Tas. 71 M10
Agery SA 78 F3, 80 F12
Agnes Vic. 53 O11
Agnes Banks NSW 15 J5
Agnes Creek SA 82 G2
Aileron NT 104 I5
Ailsa Vic. 56 I6
Ainslie ACT 34 G5
Aireys Inlet Vic. 44 C12, 52 C10
Airlie Beach Qld 127 E4
Airly Vic. 53 R7, 54 B9
Airport West Vic. 38 D3
Alanwick NSW 18 H3
Alawa NT 98 A1
Alawoona SA 79 P5
Albacutya Vic. 56 G3
Albany WA 90 G13, 95 N13
Albert NSW 23 Q2, 24 B2, 27 Q13
Albert Park Vic. 37 B13
Alberton Qld 111 N13, 113 N1
Alberton Tas. 73 O10
Alberton Vic. 53 P11
Albion Vic. 52 F5
Albion Park NSW 17 N7
Albury NSW 23 P13, 59 R4, 62 B4
Alco WA 94 G8
Alcomie Tas. 72 C4
Alderley Qld 122 D1
Aldgate SA 79 J7
Aldinga SA 78 I8
Alectown NSW 24 D4
Alexandra Vic. 48 F4, 53 K1, 59 K12
Alexandra Bridge WA 94 C8
Alexandra Headland Qld 115 M10, 123 H9
Alexandria NSW 11 M6
Alford SA 78 F1, 80 F10
Alfred National Park Vic. 30 E13, 55 M6
Alice NSW 29 O3
Alice Springs NT 105 J8, 106
Allambee Vic. 53 M8
Allambie Heights NSW 13 N8
Allanby Vic. 56 F5
Allandale NSW 18 D3
Allandale Vic. 46 A7
Allans Flat Vic. 59 I6, 62 B6

Allansford Vic. 51 K9
Allanson WA 94 G4
Allawah NSW 10 I12, 23 L6
Alleena NSW 23 P7, 24 A7
Allendale East SA 77 H12
Allendale North SA 79 J3, 81 J12
Allies Creek Qld 117 N8
Alligator Creek Qld 118 H4, 127 I13
Alligator Gorge National Park SA 80 G5
Allora Qld 117 O11
Alma Vic. 57 P11
Alma SA 78 I3, 80 I12
Almaden Qld 118 E4, 120 G13
Almonds Vic. 59 M5
Alonnah Tas. 71 M10
Aloomba Qld 119 G10
Alpha Qld 116 H3
Alpine NSW 17 K5
Alstonville NSW 29 Q3
Alton Qld 117 K11
Altona SA 85 C9
Altona Vic. 38 B12, 52 F6
Alton Downs SA 122 C8
Alvie Vic. 51 P8
Alyangula NT 101 O7
Amamoor Qld 114 G5
American River SA 78 F11
Ambrose Qld 117 N4
Amby Qld 117 J8
Ambyne Vic. 55 J2
Amelup WA 95 P9
Amherst Vic. 57 P12
Aminungo Qld 127 G11
Amity Point Qld 111 Q9
Amoonguna NT 105 J8
Amosfield NSW 29 N2, 117 O12
Amphitheatre Vic. 51 O1, 57 O12
Anakie Vic. 44 D4, 52 C6
Anakie Qld 116 I3
Anakie Gorge Vic. 44 E3, 46 E13
Anarel NSW 14 A6
Ancona Vic. 48 G1, 59 L11
Andamooka SA 84 H1
Anderson Vic. 53 J10
Ando NSW 30 E10
Andover Tas. 71 N3, 73 N13
Andrews SA 80 I9
Angaston SA 79 K4, 81 K13, 85 H4
Angip Vic. 56 H5
Angledool NSW 117 J13
Anglers Paradise Qld 113 P5
Anglers Reach NSW 31 G3
Anglers Rest Vic. 54 D2, 62 E11
Anglesea Vic. 44 D11, 52 C9
Angurugu NT 101 O8
Angus Place NSW 14 B2
Angustown Vic. 58 H9
Anna Creek SA 83 K6
Annandale NSW 11 K5
Annangrove NSW 15 M6
Annuello Vic. 22 F10, 61 K7
Antechamber Bay SA 78 G11
Antill Ponds Tas. 71 N2, 73 N12
Antwerp Vic. 56 G6
Anzac Village NSW 15 M10
Apoinga SA 79 J2, 81 J11
Apollo Bay Vic. 51 Q12
Appila SA 80 H6
Appin Vic. 57 Q3, 58 A3
Appin NSW 17 N2, 25 J8, 30 I3
Apple Tree Creek Qld 117 P6
Apple Tree Flat NSW 24 G3
Apslawn Tas. 71 Q1, 73 Q11
Apsley Tas. 71 L4
Apsley Vic. 56 B11, 77 I7
Araluen NSW 30 F7
Aramac Qld 116 F2
Aramara Qld 117 P7
Arapiles Vic. 56 F9
Ararat Vic. 51 M1, 57 L13
Aratula Qld 112 E5
Arcadia NSW 15 N4
Arcadia Vic. 58 I8
Arcadia Vale NSW 18 G8
Archdale Vic. 57 O10
Ardeer Vic. 38 A7
Ardlethan NSW 23 P8
Ardmona Vic. 58 I6

Ardmory Qld 110 F9
Ardno Vic. 50 C5
Ardrossan SA 78 G4, 80 F13
Areegra Vic. 57 J6
Areyonga Aboriginal Reserve NT 104 G9
Argalong NSW 24 D11, 30 C6
Argyle Vic. 58 F11
Argyle WA 94 F5
Ariah Park NSW 23 P8, 24 B8
Aringa Vic. 50 I9
Arkaroola SA 83 P9
Arkona Vic. 56 G7
Armadale Vic. 39 J11, 40 A12
Armatree NSW 28 E10
Armidale NSW 29 L8
Armstrong Vic. 51 L1, 57 L13
Armstrong Creek Qld 110 I6
Armstrong Heights NSW 18 H6
Armytage Vic. 51 R9, 52 B9
Arncliffe NSW 11 K9
Arnhem Land NT 101 J6
Arnhem Land Aboriginal Reserve NT 101 J6
Arno Bay SA 78 A2, 80 A11, 84 G10
Arnold Vic. 57 Q9, 58 A9
Arrabury Qld 122 F9
Arrilalah Qld 116 D3
Artarmon NSW 13 L11
Arthur East WA 95 K4
Arthur River WA 95 K4
Arthurs Creek Vic. 47 O9, 48 A9, 52 H3
Arthurs Lake Tas. 73 K11
Arthurs Seat Vic. 42 H7
Arthurton SA 78 F3, 80 F12, 84 I11
Arumvale WA 94 C8
Arwakurra SA 80 H6
Ascot Vic. 51 Q2, 52 A2
Ascot Vale Vic. 38 F7
Ashbourne SA 79 J8
Ashbourne Vic. 46 G7
Ashburton Vic. 39 M12, 40 B8
Ashbury NSW 10 I7
Ashens Vic. 57 J10
Ashfield NSW 11 J6
Ashfield WA 96 B12
Ashford NSW 29 K4, 117 N13
Ashley NSW 28 H4, 117 L13
Ashville SA 79 L9
Aspendale Vic. 41 J8
Asplin WA 94 H6
Asquith NSW 12 G4
Atherton Qld 118 F4, 120 I13, 126 C12
Athlone Vic. 53 K8
Attunga NSW 29 J9
Aubrey Vic. 56 H6
Auburn NSW 10 C4
Auburn SA 78 I2, 80 I11
Auburn Tas. 71 M1, 73 M11
Audley NSW 15 O12
Augathella Qld 116 H7
Augusta WA 90 E12, 94 C9
Aurukun Mission Qld 120 B6
Austinmer NSW 17 P3
Austral NSW 15 L10
Australia Plains SA 79 K2, 81 K11
Australind WA 94 E3
Avalon NSW 21 M3
Avenel Vic. 58 I10
Avenue SA 77 F7
Avoca NSW 17 K8
Avoca Tas. 73 O10
Avoca Vic. 57 O12
Avoca Beach NSW 15 R2
Avoca Vale Qld 114 B11
Avon SA 78 H3, 80 H12
Avondale NSW 17 N6, 18 E8
Avondale Heights Vic. 38 C6
Avonmore Vic. 58 E8
Avon Plains Vic. 57 L8
Awaba NSW 18 F7
Awonga Vic. 56 D11
Axe Creek Vic. 58 D10
Axedale Vic. 58 E9
Ayers Rock NT 104 E11, 107
Ayers Rock Mt Olga Nat. Park NT 104 E11
Aylmerton NSW 17 K5
Ayr Qld 118 I8
Ayrford Vic. 51 L10
Ayton Qld 118 F2, 120 I10

B

Baan Baa NSW 28 H8
Baarmutha Vic. 59 P7
Babinda Qld 118 G4, 126 H13
Bacchus Marsh Vic. 46 G11, 52 D4
Back Creek NSW 23 R6, 24 C6
Back Creek Vic. 59 Q6, 62 A6
Backwater NSW 29 M6
Baddaginnie Vic. 59 L8
Baden Tas. 71 N4
Badgerys Creek NSW 15 K9
Badgingarra WA 90 E8
Bael Bael Vic. 57 P1, 61 P13
Baerami NSW 24 I2, 28 I13
Bagdad Tas. 68 H3, 71 M5
Bagnoo NSW 29 O11
Bago NSW 62 H1
Bagot Well SA 79 J3
Bagshot Vic. 58 D9
Bahrs Scrub Qld 113 M2
Bailieston Vic. 58 G9
Bairnsdale Vic. 54 E8
Bajool Qld 117 N4
Bakara SA 79 M5
Baker Vic. 56 E5
Bakers Creek Qld 127 H12
Bakers Swamp NSW 24 F3
Balaam Hill Qld 110 C9
Balaklava SA 78 H3, 80 H12
Balbarrup WA 94 G8
Balberra Qld 127 H13
Balcolyn NSW 18 F8
Balcombe Vic. 43 J5, 52 H8
Bald Hills Vic. 46 A8
Bald Knob NSW 29 M5
Bald Knob Qld 123 J12, 115 C12
Bald Rock Vic. 58 C4
Baldry NSW 24 E3
Balfour Tas. 72 B6
Balgowan SA 78 E4, 80 E13, 84 I11
Balgowlah NSW 13 O9
Balgowlah Heights NSW 13 P10
Balgownie NSW 17 O4
Balhannah SA 79 J7
Balingup WA 94 G6
Balladonia WA 91 L10
Balladoran NSW 28 E12
Ballajura WA 96 A7
Ballalaba NSW 30 F6
Ballan Vic. 46 E10, 52 C4
Ballandean Qld 29 M2
Ballangeich Vic. 51 K8
Ballapur Vic. 57 K4
Ballarat Vic. 46 A9, 51 Q3, 52 A3
Ballarat Vic. 63
Ballarat North Vic. 63 E9
Ballarat East Vic. 63 F11
Ballarat South Vic. 63 C13
Ballark Vic. 44 C1, 46 D12, 52 C5
Ballaying WA 95 M3
Ballbank NSW 22 I11
Ball Bay Qld 127 G9
Balldale NSW 23 O12, 59 O3
Ballendella Vic. 58 E6
Balliang Vic. 44 E3, 46 F13, 52 D5
Ballimore NSW 28 F13
Ballina NSW 29 R3, 117 Q13
Ballyrogan Vic. 51 N2
Balmain NSW 11 L3
Balmattum Vic. 59 K9
Balmoral NSW 13 O11, 17 K4, 18 G7
Balmoral Vic. 50 G1, 56 F13
Balnarring Vic. 43 L8, 52 H9
Balook Vic. 53 O10
Balranald NSW 22 H9, 61 O6
Balrootan North Vic. 56 F6
Balumbah SA 84 F8
Balwina Aboriginal Reserve WA 93 Q9
Balwyn North Vic. 39 M7
Bamaga Qld 120 C1
Bamarang NSW 17 L12
Bamawm Vic. 58 E6
Bambaroo Qld 118 G7
Bambill Vic. 60 D4
Bambra Vic. 44 A10, 51 R9, 52 B9
Bamganie Vic. 44 A4
Baminboola Vic. 62 E8

Bamyili NT 100 H9
Banana Qld 117 M5
Bancroft Qld 117 N6
Bandiana Vic. 59 R5, 62 B5
Bandon Grove NSW 25 L2, 29 L13
Banealla SA 77 F3, 79 O12
Bangalow NSW 29 Q2, 117 Q12
Bang Bang Qld 121 E4
Bangerang Vic. 57 J5
Bangham SA 56 A8, 77 I5
Bangholme Vic. 41 K4
Bangor SA 80 G6
Bangor Tas. 73 L6
Banksia NSW 11 K10
Banksmeadow NSW 11 M10
Bankstown NSW 10 D9
Bannaby NSW 30 G3
Bannerton Vic. 22 F9, 61 K6
Bannister NSW 24 G9, 30 E4
Bannockburn Vic. 44 C6, 52 C7
Bantry Bay NSW 13 N9
Banyan Vic. 57 K1, 61 K13
Banyena Vic. 57 K8
Banyenong Vic. 57 M6
Baradine NSW 28 F9
Barakula Qld 117 M8
Baralaba Qld 117 L4
Baranduda Vic. 59 R5, 62 B5
Barcaldine Qld 116 F3
Bardwell Park NSW 11 J9
Barellan NSW 23 O8
Barfold Vic. 46 H2, 58 E12
Bargara Qld 117 P6
Bargo NSW 17 L3, 24 I8, 100 H3
Barham NSW 22 I12, 61 R13
Barham Vic. 57 R1, 58 C1
Baring Vic. 60 G11
Baringhup Vic. 46 B1
Baringhup East Vic. 57 R11, 58 B11
Barjarg Vic. 59 M11
Barkers Creek Reservoir Vic. 46 E1
Barkly Vic. 57 N11
Barkstead Vic. 46 C8, 52 C3
Barmah Vic. 58 G4
Barmedman NSW 23 Q7, 24 B7
Barmera SA 79 P3, 81 P12
Barmundu Qld 117 N4
Barnadown Vic. 58 E8
Barnawartha Vic. 59 P5, 64 I5
Barnes NSW 23 K13, 58 F4
Barnes Bay Tas. 69 J11, 71 M8
Barney View Qld 112 H9
Barngeong Reservoir Vic. 45 B3
Barnsley NSW 18 F6
Barongarook Vic. 51 P10
Barooga NSW 23 M13, 59 K3
Baroon Pocket Qld 115 J11, 123 B10
Baroota SA 80 F6
Barossa Valley SA 85 D9
Barpinba Vic. 51 P7
Barraba NSW 29 J7
Barrabool Vic. 44 D7
Barrakee Vic. 57 O6
Barramunga Vic. 51 Q11, 52 A11
Barraport Vic. 57 P4
Barrengarry NSW 17 L9
Barrington NSW 25 M1, 29 M12
Barrington Tas. 72 I7
Barrington Lower Tas. 72 H6
Barrington Tops National Park NSW 25 L1,
29 L12
Barringun NSW 27 M3, 116 F13
Barrogan NSW 24 E5
Barron Falls National Park Qld 126 E7
Barronhurst WA 94 G9
Barrow Creek NT 103 J13, 105 A3
Barrow Island WA 92 D9
Barry NSW 24 F6, 30 E1
Barry Caves NT 103 O10
Barrys Reef Vic. 46 E8, 52 D3
Barton ACT 34 E12
Barton SA 82 F9
Barton Vic. 51 K2, 57 J13
Barunga Gap SA 78 G1, 80 G10
Barwidgee Creek Vic. 59 Q8, 62 A8
Barwite Vic. 59 N11
Barwo Vic. 58 H4
Barwon Downs Vic. 51 Q10, 52 A10

Barwon Heads Vic. 44 G9, 52 E9
Baryulgil NSW 29 O4, 117 P13
Bass Vic. 53 J10
Bassendean WA 96 B11
Bass Hill NSW 10 C8
Batchelor NT 100 E6
Batchica Vic. 56 I5
Bateau Bay NSW 18 F13
Batehaven NSW 30 G7
Batemans Bay NSW 30 G7
Batesford Vic. 44 E6, 52 D7
Bathumi Vic. 59 M4
Bathurst NSW 24 G5
Bathurst Island NT 100 D3
Batlow NSW 23 R11, 24 D11, 30 B6
Battery Point Tas. 67 F10
Battle Creek Qld 117 O5
Baulkham Hills NSW 12 B9
Bauple Qld 117 P7
Baw Baw National Park Vic. 53 N6
Bawley Point NSW 30 H6
Baxter Vic. 43 M2
Bayindeen Vic. 51 N2, 57 N13
Bayles Vic. 53 J8
Baynton Vic. 46 I3, 58 F12
Bayswater Vic. 45 A6, 48 A13
Bayswater WA 96 B12
Bayview NSW 15 Q5
Beachmere Qld 111 L5
Beachport SA 77 E10
Beachport National Park SA 77 E9
Beacon WA 90 G8
Beacon Hill NSW 13 O7
Beaconsfield NSW 11 M7
Beaconsfield Tas. 73 K6
Beaconsfield Vic. 52 I7
Beagle Bay Aboriginal Reserve WA 93 L4
Bealiba Vic. 57 O10
Bearbung NSW 28 E11
Beardmore Vic. 53 O5
Beargamil NSW 24 D4
Bearii Vic. 58 I3
Bears Lagoon Vic. 57 R6, 58 B6
Beauchamp Vic. 57 O1, 61 O13
Beaudesert Qld 113 K5, 117 Q11
Beaufort SA 78 H2, 80 G11
Beaufort Vic. 51 O3
Beaumont NSW 17 L11
Beaumaris Tas. 73 R7
Beaumaris Vic. 40 H10
Beauty Point NSW 13 O11
Beauty Point Tas. 73 K5
Beazleys Bridge Vic. 57 M9
Bebeah NSW 18 C9
Beckom NSW 23 P8
Bedarra Island Qld 118 G5
Bedgerebong NSW 24 C5
Bedourie Qld 122 D4
Beeac Vic. 51 P8
Beebo Qld 117 N12
Beechboro WA 96 C9
Beechford Tas. 73 L5
Beech Forest Vic. 51 P11
Beechmont Qld 113 M7
Beechworth Vic. 59 P6
Beechworth Park Vic. 59 Q6
Beecroft NSW 12 E8
Beedelup National Park WA 94 F9
Beela WA 94 F3
Beenak Vic. 53 K6
Beenam Range Qld 114 I3
Beenleigh Qld 113 N1, 117 Q11
Beenong WA 95 Q2
Beerburrum Qld 111 K2
Beerwah Qld 111 K1, 115 K13, 117 Q9
Beetaloo Valley SA 80 G7
Bega NSW 30 F10
Beggan Beggan NSW 24 D9, 30 B4
Belair National Park SA 76 F11
Belalie SA 80 I7
Belanglo NSW 16 H8
Belaringar NSW 27 Q11, 28 B11
Belbora NSW 25 N1, 29 N12
Belfield NSW 10 H7
Belford NSW 18 B2
Belgrave Vic. 45 E10, 52 I6
Belhus WA 96 F2
Bell NSW 14 E4, 24 I5

Bell Qld   117 O9
Bellambi NSW   17 O4
Bellara Qld   111 M4
Bellarine Vic.   44 H7, 52 E8
Bellarwi NSW   24 A7
Bellata NSW   28 H6
Bellawongarah NSW   17 M10
Bell Bay Tas.   73 K5
Bellbird NSW   18 C5, 25 K4
Bellbird Creek Vic.   30 D13, 55 K7
Bellbrae Vic.   44 D10, 55 C9
Bellellen Vic.   57 K12
Bellerive Tas.   67 I7
Bellevue WA   96 G11
Bellevue Hill NSW   11 P4
Bellingen NSW   29 P8
Bellingham Tas.   73 M4
Belli Park Qld   114 I8, 123 A4
Bellmere Qld   111 J4
Bellmount Forest NSW   24 F10, 30 E5
Bells Beach Vic.   44 E10, 52 D9
Bells Bridge Qld   114 F2
Bellthorpe Qld   114 G13
Belltrees NSW   25 K1, 29 K12
Belmont NSW   18 H7, 25 L4
Belmont Vic.   63 D7
Belmore NSW   10 H8
Beloka NSW   30 C9, 31 H10
Belrose NSW   13 M5
Beltana SA   83 N10
Belton SA   80 I2
Belvidere SA   79 J8
Bemboka NSW   30 E10
Bembridge Vic.   43 O4
Bemm River Vic.   30 D13, 55 L7
Bena NSW   23 P5, 24 A5
Bena Vic.   53 K9
Benalla Vic.   59 M8
Benambra Vic.   54 F2, 62 F11
Benandarah NSW   30 G7
Benaraby Qld   117 N4
Ben Boyd National Park NSW   30 F11, 55 Q3
Ben Bullen NSW   14 A1
Bencubbin WA   90 G8
Bendalong NSW   30 H6
Bendemeer NSW   29 K9
Bendick Murrell NSW   24 D7, 30 C2
Bendigo Vic.   58 C9
Bendoc Vic.   30 D11, 55 L3
Bendolba NSW   25 L2, 29 L13
Benetook Vic.   60 G4
Benger WA   94 F3
Bengworden Vic.   54 D9
Benholme Qld   127 E12
Beni NSW   28 E13
Benjeroop Vic.   61 Q12
Benjinup WA   94 H6
Benlidi Qld   116 E5
Ben Lomond NSW   29 L6
Ben Lomond National Park Tas.   73 O8
Bennelacking WA   94 I4
Ben Nevis Vic.   51 M1, 57 M12
Benobble Qld   113 M5
Benowa Qld   113 P6, 124 F12
Benowa Waters Qld   124 G11
Bensville NSW   15 Q2
Bentleigh Vic.   40 D11
Bentley NSW   29 P2
Benwerrin Vic.   44 A12, 51 R10, 52 B10
Berala NSW   10 E5
Berambing NSW   14 G4, 30 H1
Beremboke Vic.   44 D2, 46 E12, 52 C5
Berendebba NSW   24 C7, 30 A1
Beresfield NSW   18 G4
Bergalia NSW   30 G8
Bergins Pocket Qld   114 H6
Berkeley NSW   17 O5
Berkeley Vale NSW   18 E12
Bermagui NSW   30 G9
Bernook Vic.   60 B8, 79 R6
Berowra NSW   15 O5, 21 M13
Berowra Heights NSW   21 L13
Berri SA   22 A8, 79 P3, 81 P12
Berridale NSW   30 D9, 31 I8
Berriedale Tas.   68 H6
Berrigan NSW   23 M12, 59 L1
Berrima NSW   16 I7, 24 I8, 30 G3

Berrimah NT   100 D4
Berrimal Vic.   57 O7
Berrimpa Qld   122 H5
Berringa Vic.   51 Q5, 52 A5
Berringama Vic.   62 F6
Berriwillock Vic.   57 L1, 61 L13
Berry NSW   17 N10, 25 J9, 100 H4
Berrybank Vic.   51 P6
Berry Springs NT   100 E5
Berwick Vic.   52 I7
Bessiebelle Vic.   50 H8
Beswick Aboriginal Reserve NT   100 I8
Beta Qld   116 G3
Bet Bet Vic.   57 P10, 58 A10
Bete Bolong Vic.   54 I7
Bethanga Vic.   62 C5
Bethania Junction Qld   111 M13, 113 M1
Bethany SA   85 E6
Bethungra NSW   24 C9, 30 A4
Betley Vic.   57 Q10, 58 A10
Betoota Qld   122 F7
Beulah Tas.   72 I7
Beulah Vic.   22 E13, 56 I3
Beulah Lower Tas.   72 I7
Bevendale NSW   24 F8, 30 D3
Beverford Vic.   61 O10
Beveridge Vic.   47 M8, 52 G3
Beverley WA   90 F10
Beverley Hills NSW   10 H10
Beverley Park NSW   11 K12
Bews SA   79 P8
Bexhill NSW   29 Q2
Bexley NSW   11 J10
Bexley North NSW   10 I9
Beyal Vic.   57 K5
Biala NSW   24 F9, 30 E4
Biarra Qld   110 C5
Bibbenluke NSW   30 E10, 55 N1
Bibilup WA   94 E7
Biboohra Qld   126 B7
Bicheno Tas.   73 R10
Biddaddaba Qld   113 L5
Biddon NSW   28 E11
Big Desert Wilderness Vic.   56 B2, 60 B12
Bigga NSW   24 F7, 30 E2
Biggara Vic.   62 H6
Biggenden Qld   117 O7
Big Heath National Park SA   77 G8
Big Hill NSW   16 F8
Big Pats Creek Vic.   48 G12
Big River Camp Vic.   48 I9
Bilambil NSW   113 Q9
Bilinga Qld   113 Q8, 125 P5
Billabong Vic.   60 H3
Billiatt National Park SA   79 P6
Billinudgel NSW   29 Q2, 113 Q13
Billys Creek NSW   29 O7
Billys Lookout NSW   24 A6
Biloela Qld   117 M5
Bilpin NSW   14 G4, 24 I5
Bilyana Qld   118 G5
Bimbi NSW   23 R7, 24 C7, 30 B2
Binalong NSW   24 E9, 30 C4
Binalong Bay Tas.   73 R6
Binbee Qld   119 J9
Binda NSW   24 F8, 30 E3
Bindi Vic   54 F3, 62 F12
Bindi Bindi WA   90 F8
Bindle Qld   117 K10
Bingara NSW   29 J5
Bingera Qld   117 P6
Binginwarri Vic.   53 O11
Biniguy NSW   28 I4
Binjour Qld   117 O7
Binnaway NSW   28 G11
Binningup WA   94 E3
Binnum SA   56 B10, 77 I6
Binya NSW   23 N7
Birchip Vic.   22 F13, 57 L4
Birchs Bay Tas.   68 H12
Birdsville Qld   83 P1, 122 D7
Birdsville Track Qld   122 D7
Birdsville Track SA   83 N7-P1
Birdwood NSW   29 N10
Birdwood SA   79 J6
Birdwoodton Vic.   60 G3
Birralee Tas.   73 K7
Birrego NSW   23 O10

Birregurra Vic.   51 Q9, 52 A9
Birriwa NSW   28 G12
Birrong NSW   10 D7
Birru Qld   110 F12
Birthday SA   83 L11, 84 H4
Bishopsbourne Tas.   73 L8
Bishops Bridge NSW   18 E3
Bittern Vic.   43 M7, 52 H9
Black Vic.   63 G9
Blackall Qld   116 F5
Blackalls Park NSW   18 G7
Blackburn Vic.   39 P9
Blackbutt Qld   121 G3
Blackfellows Caves SA   77 G12
Blackheath NSW   14 E6, 24 I6, 30 G1
Blackheath Vic.   56 I7
Black Hill NSW   18 G4
Black Hills Tas.   68 F4
Blackmans Bay Tas.   68 I9, 71 M8
Black Mountain NSW   29 L7
Black Mountain Qld   114 I6, 123 B2
Black River Tas.   72 D3
Black Rock SA   80 I5, 83 O13
Black Rock Vic.   40 G11, 52 G6
Blacks Beach Qld   127 H11
Blacksmiths NSW   18 H8
Black Springs NSW   24 G6, 30 F1
Black Springs SA   81 J10, 79 J1
Black Swamp NSW   29 N3
Blackville NSW   28 I11
Blackwall NSW   15 Q2, 20 F3
Blackwarry Vic.   53 P10
Blackwater Qld   117 K3
Blackwood SA   76 E12
Blackwood Vic.   46 F8, 52 D3
Blackwood Creek Tas.   73 K9
Blackwood Ranges Vic.   46 F9
Blair Athol Qld   116 I2, 118 I13
Blairgowrie Vic.   42 D8, 52 F9
Blakehurst NSW   10 I13
Blakeville Vic.   46 E8, 52 C3
Blampied Vic.   46 C7, 52 B2
Blanche Town SA   79 M3, 81 M13
Bland NSW   23 Q7, 24 B7, 30 A2
Blanket Flat NSW   24 F7, 30 E2
Blaxland NSW   14 I7
Blaxlands Ridge NSW   15 J3
Blayney NSW   24 F5
Bleak House Vic.   56 D6
Blenheim Qld   110 C12
Blessington Tas.   73 N8
Blewitt Springs SA   85 I12
Bli Bli Qld   115 L9, 123 F7
Blighty NSW   23 L12
Blinman SA   83 O10
Bloods Creek SA   105 L13
Bloomsbury Qld   119 K10, 127 D8
Blow Clear NSW   24 C4
Blue Gum Forest NSW   17 P1
Blue Mountains NSW   14
Blue Mountains National Park NSW   14 F5, 24 I6, 30 H1
Bluff SA   78 E6
Bluff Rock NSW   29 M4
Blyth SA   78 I1, 80 I10
Boambee NSW   29 P7
Boara NSW   24 D8, 30 B3
Boat Harbour NSW   113 O10
Boat Harbour Tas.   72 E4
Boatswain SA   77 D8
Bobadah NSW   23 O1, 27 O13
Bobbin Head NSW   13 J1, 21 O12
Bobin NSW   29 N11
Bobinawarrah Vic.   59 O8
Bobs Creek Vic.   59 N11
Bochara Vic.   50 G5
Bodalla NSW   30 G8
Bodallin WA   90 H9
Boddington WA   90 F11, 94 H1
Bogan Gate NSW   23 R4, 24 C4
Bogantungan Qld   116 I3
Boggabilla NSW   28 I2, 117 M12
Boggabri NSW   28 H8
Bogolong NSW   23 R6, 24 C6, 30 B1
Bogong Vic.   62 C10
Boho Vic.   59 L9
Boigbeat Vic.   57 L1, 61 L12
Boinka Vic.   60 E10

Boisdale Vic. 53 R6, 54 B8
Bokal WA 95 J4
Bolangum Vic. 57 L9
Bolganup WA 95 N11
Bolinda Vic. 47 J7, 52 F2
Bolivia NSW 29 M4
Bollon Qld 116 I11
Bolong NSW 17 N11
Bolton Vic. 61 L8
Bolwarra NSW 18 F2
Bolwarra Vic. 50 F9
Bolwarrah Vic. 46 C9
Bomaderry NSW 17 M12, 24 I9, 30 H4
Bombala NSW 30 E11, 55 N2
Bombo NSW 17 O8, 25 J9, 30 I4
Bomera NSW 28 H11
Bonalbo NSW 29 O2
Bonang Vic. 30 C11, 55 K3
Bonaparte Archipelago WA 93 M2
Bonbeach Vic. 41 L7
Bondi NSW 11 Q5
Bonegilla Vic. 59 R5, 62 B5
Boneo Vic. 42 F9, 52 G10
Bongaree Qld 111 M4, 117 Q10
Bonnells Bay NSW 18 F8
Bonnie Doon Vic. 48 H1, 59 L11
Bonnie Rock WA 90 G8
Bonnyrigg NSW 15 M9
Bonshaw NSW 29 L3, 117 N13
Bonville NSW 29 P7
Booborowie SA 81 J9
Boobyalla Tas. 73 P4
Bookabie SA 82 F11
Bookaloo SA 80 D1, 83 M11, 84 I5
Bookar Vic. 51 M7
Booker Bay NSW 15 Q2, 20 F2
Bookham NSW 24 E9, 30 C4
Boolading WA 94 I4
Boolaroo NSW 18 G6
Boolarra Vic. 53 N9
Boolba Qld 117 J11
Booligal NSW 23 K6
Boolboonda Qld 117 O6
Booleroo SA 80 H5
Boolgun SA 79 N4, 81 N13
Boolite Vic. 57 K6
Bool Lagoon SA 77 H8
Booloumba Qld 114 G10
Boomahnoomoonah Vic. 59 M5
Boomi NSW 28 G2, 117 L12
Boomleera NT 100 F7
Boonah Qld 112 G5, 117 P11
Boonah Vic. 44 A11, 51 R10, 52 B10
Boonangar Qld 117 L12
Boonoo Boonoo NSW 29 N3
Boonoonar Vic. 60 H5
Booral NSW 25 M2
Boorcan Vic. 51 M8
Boorhaman Vic. 59 N5
Boorindal NSW 27 N7
Boorolite Vic. 59 N12
Boorongie Vic. 60 I9
Booroobin Qld 114 H12
Booroopki Vic. 56 C10
Booroorban NSW 23 K10
Boorowa NSW 24 E8, 30 C3
Boors Plain SA 78 F2, 80 F11
Boort Vic. 57 P5, 58 A4
Boosey Vic. 59 L4
Boolthby SA 78 A1, 80 A10
Boowillia SA 78 H2, 80 H11
Booyal Qld 117 O6
Bopeechee SA 83 M7
Boppy Mount NSW 27 N11
Borallon Qld 110 G11
Boralma Vic. 59 O5
Borambil NSW 28 H12
Boraning WA 94 I2
Borden WA 90 H12, 95 P8
Borderdale WA 95 M7
Bordertown SA 77 H4, 79 Q13
Boree NSW 24 E4
Boree Creek NSW 23 O10
Bornholm WA 95 M13
Boro NSW 24 G10, 30 F5
Boronia Vic. 45 A8, 48 A13
Boronia Park NSW 11 J1, 13 J12
Bororen Qld 117 O5

Borrika SA 79 N7
Borroloola NT 101 O12, 103 O2
Borung Vic. 57 P6, 58 A6
Boscabel WA 95 K5
Bostobrick NSW 29 O7
Bostock Creek Vic. 51 N9
Boston Island SA 84 F12
Botany NSW 11 N9
Bothwell Tas. 71 L3
Bouddi State Park NSW 20 H2
Boulia Qld 121 D13, 122 D2
Boulka Vic. 60 I9
Boundain WA 95 L2
Boundary Bend Vic. 22 G9, 61 M6
Bourke NSW 27 M6
Bow NSW 28 I13
Bow Bridge WA 95 J12
Bowden SA 75 B3
Bowelling WA 94 I4
Bowen Qld 119 J9, 127 A1
Bowenfels NSW 14 C4
Bowen Mountain NSW 14 I5
Bowenvale Vic. 57 P11
Bowenville Qld 117 O10
Bower SA 79 L2, 81 L12
Boweya Vic. 59 M6
Bow Hill SA 79 M6
Bowling Alley Point NSW 29 K10
Bowman NSW 25 M1
Bowman Vic. 59 P7
Bowmans SA 78 H3, 80 H12
Bowna NSW 23 P13, 62 C4
Bowning NSW 24 E9, 30 D4
Bowral NSW 17 J6, 24 I8, 30 H3
Bowraville NSW 29 P8
Bowser Vic. 59 O6
Box Creek Qld 116 G8
Box Creek SA 83 K6
Box Hill Vic. 39 N9, 52 H5
Box Tank NSW 22 D2, 26 D13
Boxwood Vic. 59 L6
Boxwood Hill WA 90 H12, 95 R9
Boya WA 96 I12
Boyacup WA 95 L8
Boyankil Qld 113 P4
Boyanup WA 90 E12, 94 F4
Boydtown NSW 30 F11, 55 P3
Boyeo Vic. 56 E6
Boyer Tas. 68 G5, 71 L6
Boyerine WA 95 L4
Boyland Qld 113 M5
Boys Town Qld 113 K5
Boyup Brook WA 90 F12, 94 H6
Bracalba Qld 110 I3
Brackendale NSW 29 L10
Bracknell Tas. 73 K9
Braddon ACT 34 E6
Bradford Vic. 57 R10, 58 B10
Bradvale Vic. 51 O5
Brady Creek SA 79 K2
Braefield NSW 29 J11
Braemar NSW 17 K6
Braeside Vic. 40 H7
Braidwood NSW 24 G11, 30 F6
Bramfield SA 84 D9
Brampton Island Qld 119 L10, 127 I9
Brandon Qld 118 I8
Bransby Qld 122 H11
Branxholm Tas. 73 O6
Branxholme Vic. 50 G6
Branxton NSW 18 C2, 25 K3
Brawlin NSW 24 C9, 30 B4
Braybrook Vic. 38 C8
Bray Junction SA 77 E9
Bray Park NSW 113 P11
Brays Creek NSW 113 M11
Brayton NSW 16 E10
Breadalbane NSW 24 G9, 30 E4
Breadalbane Qld 122 D3
Breadalbane Tas. 73 M8
Breakfast Creek NSW 24 E7, 30 D2
Breakfast Creek NSW 24 H3
Break O'Day Vic. 47 P6, 48 B6
Breakwater Vic. 63 H6
Bream Creek Tas. 69 O6
Breamlea Vic. 44 F9, 52 D9
Bredbo NSW 30 D3

Breelong NSW 28 E11
Breeza NSW 28 I10
Bremer Bay WA 90 H12
Brentwood SA 78 E6, 84 I12
Brentwood Vic. 56 H4
Breona Tas. 73 J10
Bretti NSW 29 M12
Brewarrina NSW 27 O6, 28 A6
Brewster Vic. 51 P3
Briagalong Vic. 53 R6, 54 B8
Bribbaree NSW 23 R7, 24 C7, 30 A2
Bribie Island Qld 111 M2, 123 F13
Bridge Creek Vic. 59 M11
Bridgenorth Tas. 73 L7
Bridges Qld 115 K8, 123 D5
Bridgetown WA 90 F12, 94 G7
Bridgewater Tas. 68 H5
Bridgewater Vic. 57 Q8, 58 B8
Bridport Tas. 73 N4
Brigalow Qld 117 N9
Bright Vic. 59 R9, 62 B9
Brighton Qld 111 L7
Brighton SA 76 B12, 85 G8
Brighton Tas. 68 I4, 71 M6
Brighton Vic. 40 D13
Brighton Downs Qld 122 G2
Brighton-le-Sands NSW 11 L11
Brightview Qld 110 E10
Brightwaters NSW 18 F9
Brim Vic. 56 I4
Brimbago SA 77 G3, 79 P12
Brimboal Vic. 50 D2
Brimin Vic. 59 N4
Brimpaen Vic. 56 H11
Brimpaen Vic. 56 H11
Brindabella NSW 24 E11, 30 D6
Brinerville NSW 29 O8
Bringagee NSW 23 M8
Bringalbert Vic. 56 C10
Bringelly NSW 15 K10
Brinkworth SA 80 H10
Brisbane Qld 109-15, 117 Q10
Brisbane Ranges National Park Vic. 44 D3, 46 E13, 52 D5
Brisbane Water National Park NSW 15 P2, 20, 25 K5
Brit Brit Vic. 50 F3
Brittons Swamp Tas. 72 B4
Brixton Qld 116 E3
Broad Arrow WA 91 J8
Broadbeach Qld 113 P6, 124 H9
Broad Creek SA 80 G7
Broadford Vic. 47 M4, 52 H1, 58 G12
Broadmarsh Tas. 68 G3, 71 L5
Broadmeadows Vic. 38 E1
Broadwater NSW 29 Q3
Broadwater Vic. 50 H8
Brocklehurst NSW 28 E13
Brocklesby NSW 23 O12, 59 P2
Brocks Creek NT 100 E7
Brockman WA 94 G10
Brodies Plains NSW 29 K5
Brodribb River Vic. 55 J7
Brogo NSW 30 F10
Broke NSW 25 K3
Broken Bay NSW 15 Q3
Broken Hill NSW 22 B1, 26 B12
Bromelton Qld 113 J5
Brompton SA 75 A2
Bronte NSW 11 Q5
Bronte Tas. 70 I2, 72 I12
Bronte Park Tas. 70 I2, 72 I12
Bronzewing Vic. 60 I10
Brookhampton WA 94 F5
Brooklyn NSW 15 P3, 20 I9
Brooklyn Vic. 38 B9
Brookside Vic. 59 Q9, 62 A9
Brookton WA 90 F10
Brookvale NSW 13 P7
Brookville Vic. 54 E4
Brooloo Qld 114 G7
Broome WA 93 K5
Broomehill WA 90 G12, 95 M6
Broomfield Vic. 46 A7
Brooms Head NSW 29 Q5
Broughton Vic. 56 D5
Broughton Vale NSW 17 N10
Broughton Village NSW 17 O10
Broula NSW 24 E6, 30 C1

131

Broulee NSW 30 G7
Brown Hill Vic. 46 A9
Brownlow Hill NSW 15 J12
Brownlow SA 79 L3, 81 L12
Brown Range Vic. 47 N4
Browns Plains Qld 111 L13
Browns Plains Vic. 59 P4
Brownsville NSW 17 O6
Bruarong Vic. 59 Q7, 62 A7
Bruce SA 80 G4
Brucefield SA 78 F1, 80 F10
Bruce Rock WA 90 G10
Brucknell Vic. 51 M10
Brundee NSW 17 N12
Brungle NSW 24 D10, 30 B5
Brunkerville NSW 18 E6
Brunswick Vic. 38 G6
Brunswick Heads NSW 29 R2, 117 Q12
Brunswick Junction WA 94 F3
Bruny Island Tas. 71 M9
Brush Creek NSW 18 C10
Bruthen Vic. 54 F7
Bryden Qld 110 F7
Buangor Vic. 51 N2
Buaraba Qld 110 C8
Buaraba Creek Qld 110 D9
Bubialo Qld 127 C4
Bucasia Qld 127 H11
Buccan Qld 113 M2
Buccaneer Archipelago WA 93 L3
Buccarumbi NSW 29 O6
Buccleuch SA 79 N8
Buchan Vic. 54 H6
Buchanan NSW 18 F4
Bucheen Creek Vic. 62 E7
Buckaroo NSW 24 G2
Buckenderra NSW 30 C8, 31 H5
Buckety NSW 18 A9, 25 K4
Buckety Place Vic. 54 D1, 62 D11
Buckingham SA 77 G4, 79 P13
Buckingham WA 94 H4
Buckland Tas. 69 M3, 71 O5
Buckland Vic. 59 Q10, 62 A10
Buckleboo SA 83 K13, 84 F8
Buckley Vic. 44 C8, 52 C8
Buckleys Swamp Vic. 50 H6
Buckrabanyule Vic. 57 O6
Bucks Lake National Park SA 77 G12
Buddabuddah NSW 27 P12, 28 A12
Buddina Qld 115 M10, 123 I9
Buderim Qld 115 L10
Budgeam NSW 112 I12
Budgee Budgee NSW 24 G2
Budgeree Vic. 53 N10
Budgerum Vic. 57 P2
Budgewoi NSW 18 G10, 25 L5
Buffalo Vic. 53 M11
Buffalo River Vic. 59 P9
Buff Point NSW 18 F10
Bugaldie NSW 28 F9
Bugilbone NSW 28 E6
Bugong Gap NSW 17 K11
Builyan Qld 117 O5
Bukalong NSW 30 E10
Bukkulla NSW 29 K4
Bulahdelah NSW 25 N2
Bular Qld 114 C1
Bulart Vic. 50 G4
Buldah Vic. 55 L4
Bulga NSW 25 K3, 29 N11
Bulga National Park Vic. 53 P10
Bulgandramine NSW 24 D2
Bulgandry NSW 23 O12
Bulgobac Tas. 72 E8
Bulla Vic. 47 K10, 52 F4
Bullaburra NSW 14 G7
Bullarah NSW 28 F4, 117 K13
Bullarook Vic. 46 B9, 51 R3, 52 B3
Bullarto Vic. 46 E7,52 C2
Bulleen Vic. 39 M6
Bullengarook Vic. 46 G9
Bullfinch WA 90 H9
Bullhead Creek Vic. 62 D7
Bulli NSW 17 P3, 25 J8, 30 I3
Bullio NSW 16 G5, 30 G3
Bullioh Vic. 62 D5
Bull Island SA 77 F7
Bullock Creek Qld 118 E5, 120 G13

Bulloo Downs Qld 122 I12
Buln Buln Vic. 53 L7
Buloke Vic. 57 L6
Bulumwaal Vic. 54 D6
Bumbaldry NSW 24 D7, 30 C1
Bumberry NSW 24 E4
Bumbunga SA 78 H2, 80 H11
Bunburra Qld 112 G6
Bunbury WA 90 E11, 94 E4
Bundaberg Qld 117 P6
Bundalaguah Vic. 53 R7, 54 B9
Bundaleer Qld 27 O2
Bundall Qld 124 F11
Bundalong Vic. 59 N4
Bundanoon NSW 16 I9, 24 I9, 30 G4
Bundarra NSW 29 K6
Bundeena NSW 15 P11
Bundella NSW 28 H11
Bunding Vic. 46 D9, 52 C3
Bundook NSW 25 M1, 29 M12
Bundooma NT 105 K10
Bundoora Vic. 39 K2, 52 H4
Bundure NSW 23 N10
Bunga NSW 30 G9
Bungador Vic. 51 O9
Bungal Vic. 44 C1, 46 C11, 52 C4
Bungarby NSW 30 D10
Bungaree Vic. 46 B9, 51 R3, 52 B3
Bung Bong Vic. 57 O12
Bungeet Vic. 59 M6
Bungendore NSW 24 G11, 30 E6
Bungil NSW 62 D4
Bungonia NSW 16 E13, 24 H9, 30 G4
Bungulla NSW 29 M3
Bunguluke Vic. 57 N4
Bungunya Qld 117 L12
Buniche WA 95 R2
Buninyong Vic. 46 A11, 51 Q4, 52 A4
Bunker Bay WA 94 C5
Bunnaby NSW 16 E7
Bunnaloo NSW 23 J12, 58 E2
Bunnan NSW 25 J1, 29 J12
Bunya NSW 25 N2, 29 N13
Bunyan NSW 30 D8
Bunyip Vic. 53 K7
Burcher NSW 23 P5, 24 B5
Burekup WA 94 F4
Burgooney NSW 23 O5
Burkes Flat Vic. 57 O8
Burketown Qld 121 C3
Burleigh Vic. 45 G8
Burleigh Heads Qld 113 Q7, 125 K8
Burleigh Park Qld 125 L11
Burleigh Waters Qld 125 K10
Burnbank Vic. 51 P1, 57 P13
Burnie Tas. 72 G5
Burns NSW 26 A13, 22 A1
Burns Creek Tas. 73 N6
Burnsfield SA 80 H10
Burnside Qld 115 J9, 123 D7
Burnside SA 76 F9
Buronga NSW 22 D8, 60 H2
Burpengary Qld 111 K5
Burra SA 81 J9
Burra Bee Dee NSW 28 G10
Burraboi NSW 23 J11
Burracoppin WA 90 H9
Burradoo NSW 17 J7
Burraga NSW 24 G7, 30 F2
Burragate NSW 30 F11, 55 O2
Burramine Vic. 59 L4
Burrawang NSW 17 K8
Burraway NSW 28 D12
Burrell Creek NSW 25 N1
Burrendong Dam NSW 24 F3
Burren Junction NSW 28 F6
Burrereo Vic. 57 K8
Burrier NSW 17 K12
Burrill Lake NSW 24 I11, 30 H6
Burringbar NSW 29 Q1, 113 Q12
Burrinjuck NSW 24 E10, 30 C5
Burroin NSW 56 I1, 60 I13
Burrowapine National Park Vic. 62 F5
Burrowye Vic. 30 A8, 62 E4
Burrum Vic. 57 K8
Burrumbeet Vic. 51 P3
Burrumboot Vic. 58 F8

Burrumbuttock NSW 23 O12, 59 Q3, 62 A3
Burrum Heads Qld 117 P6
Burrungule SA 77 G11
Burtundy NSW 22 D7
Burwood NSW 10 H5
Burwood Vic. 39 M11, 40 A8, 52 H5
Bushfield Vic. 51 J9
Bushy Park Tas. 68 E4, 71 K6
Bushy Park Vic. 53 R6, 54 B8
Busselton WA 90 E12, 94 D5
Butchers Ridge Vic. 54 H4, 62 I13
Bute SA 78 G1, 80 G10
Buthurra Qld 127 F10
Butler Sa 84 F11
Buttercup Vic. 59 N12
Buxton NSW 17 K3
Buxton Vic. 48 F7, 53 K2
Byaduck Vic. 50 G6
Byangum NSW 113 O11
Byawatha Vic. 59 O6
Bylands Vic. 47 L6, 52 G2
Bylong NSW 24 H2, 28 H13
Bymount Qld 117 J8
Byrne Vic. 59 O8
Byrneside Vic. 58 H7
Byrnestown Qld 117 O7
Byrneville Vic. 56 I8
Byrock NSW 27 N8
Byron Bay NSW 29 R2, 117 Q12
Bywong NSW 24 F10, 30 E5

C

Cabanda Qld 110 F12
Cabarita NSW 113 R11
Cabawin Qld 117 M10
Cabbage Tree Creek Vic. 55 K7
Cabbage Tree Point Qld 113 O2
Caboolture Qld 111 K4, 117 Q10
Caboonbah Qld 110 E5
Cabramurra NSW 30 C8, 31 D2
Caddapan Qld 122 G6
Caddens Flat Vic. 50 G2
Cadelga Outstation SA 122 E7
Cadell SA 79 M2, 81 M11
Cadney Park SA 82 H4
Cadoux WA 90 F8
Caffey Qld 110 A13, 112 A1
Cahills Crossing NT 100 H4
Caiguna WA 91 N10
Cairnbank SA 77 F7
Cairn Curran Reservoir Vic. 46 B1, 57 R11, 58 B11
Cairns Qld 118 G3, 126 F8
Cairns Bay Tas. 68 E12, 71 K9
Calamuale Qld 111 L12
Calca SA 84 C8, 82 I13
Calder Tas. 72 E5
Calderwood NSW 17 N7
Caldwell NSW 23 J12, 58 E1
Calectasia National Park SA 77 G9
Calen Qld 119 K10, 127 E9
Calga NSW 15 P1, 25 K5
Calgardup WA 94 C7
Calico Creek Qld 114 G4
Calingiri WA 90 F9
Caliph SA 79 O5
Calivil Vic. 57 R6, 58 B6
Cal Lal NSW 22 B7, 60 B2
Callawadda Vic. 57 K10
Calleen NSW 23 P6, 24 A7
Callen Range Vic. 47 P1
Callide Qld 117 M5
Callignee Vic. 53 P9
Callington SA 79 K7
Calliope Qld 117 N4
Caloona NSW 28 G2
Caloundra Qld 115 M12, 117 Q9, 123 I12
Calpatanna Water Hole Conservation Park SA 82 I13
Calperum SA 79 Q3, 81 Q12
Caltowie SA 80 H7
Calvert Qld 110 E13
Calvert Vic. 51 L3
Cambarville Vic. 48 H9
Cambeela Qld 122 G1
Camberwell Vic. 39 L10
Cambewarra NSW 17 L11

Cambrai SA 79 L5
Cambray WA 94 E7
Cambrian Hill Vic. 46 A10, 51 Q4, 52 A4
Cambridge Tas. 69 J6, 71 N7
Camburinga NT 101 P5
Camden NSW 15 K12, 25 J7, 30 H2
Camellia NSW 10 D2, 12 D13
Camena Tas. 72 G5
Camira Creek NSW 29 P4
Cammeray NSW 9 C1
Cammeray NSW 11 N1, 13 M12
Camooweal Qld 103 R10, 121 A7
Campania Tas. 69 J4, 71 N5
Campbell ACT 34 G9
Campbells Bridge Vic. 57 K10
Campbells Creek Vic. 46 D3, 58 C12
Campbells Forest Vic. 58 C8
Campbells Pocket Qld 110 I4
Campbelltown NSW 15 L12, 25 J7, 30 I2
Campbelltown SA 76 G7
Campbell Town Tas. 71 N1, 73 N11
Campbelltown Vic. 46 B4, 51 R1, 52 B1, 57 R12, 166 B12
Camperdown NSW 11 L6
Camperdown Vic. 51 N8
Camp Mountain Qld 110 I9
Campsie NSW 10 I8
Campup WA 95 K8
Camurra NSW 28 H4
Canadian Vic. 46 A10
Canary Island Vic. 57 Q4, 58 A4
Canbelego NSW 27 N11
Canberra ACT 24 F11, 30 D6, 33-35
Candlelight WA 95 O3
Candelo NSW 30 F10, 55 P1
Cangai NSW 29 O5
Caniambo Vic. 59 K7
Canimbla NSW 24 E6, 30 C1
Cannawigara SA 77 H4, 79 Q13
Cannie Vic. 57 O2
Cannons Creek Vic. 43 Q3
Cannonvale Qld 119 K9, 127 E4
Cann River Vic. 30 D13, 55 L6
Cannum Vic. 56 H6
Canoelands NSW 15 N3
Canonba NSW 27 Q10, 28 B10
Canowie SA 80 I8
Canowie Belt SA 80 I7
Canowindra NSW 24 E6
Canterbury NSW 10 I8, 11 J8
Canterbury Vic. 39 L10, 42 D8
Canunda National Park SA 77 F11
Canungra Qld 113 M6
Canyon Leigh NSW 16 G9
Caoura NSW 16 H12
Capacabana NSW 15 R2
Cape Arid National Park WA 91 L12
Cape Barren Island Tas. 70 A6, 73 Q1
Cape Borda SA 78 B11
Cape Bridgewater Vic. 50 E10
Cape Clear Vic. 51 P5
Cape Hillsborough Qld 127 G10
Cape Howe NSW 30 F12
Cape Jaffa SA 77 D7
Cape Jervis SA 78 G10
Capel WA 94 E5
Cape Labatt Recreation Park SA 84 B8
Cape Leeuwin-Naturaliste National Park WA 94 C9
Cape Le Grand National Park WA 91 K12
Capella Qld 117 J3
Capels Crossing Vic. 57 R1, 58 B1, 61 Q3
Cape Nelson State Park Vic. 50 F10
Cape Patterson Vic. 53 K11
Cape Range National Park WA 92 C11
Capercup WA 95 J5
Capertree NSW 24 H4
Cape Schanck Vic. 52 F10
Cape York Peninsula Qld 120
Caping Qld 127 D7
Capricorn Coast Qld 117 N3
Capricornia Qld 117
Captains Flat NSW 30 E7
Carabost NSW 23 Q12, 30 A7, 62 F1
Caragabal NSW 23 R6, 24 C6, 30 A1
Caralue SA 84 F9
Caramut Vic. 51 J6
Carapooee Vic. 57 N9

Carapook Vic. 50 E4
Carbarup WA 95 M10
Carboor Vic. 59 P8
Carbrook Qld 111 N13, 113 N1
Carbunup WA 94 C5
Carcoar NSW 24 F6, 30 E1
Carcuma SA 77 E1, 79 N10
Cardiff NSW 18 G5
Cardigan Vic. 51 Q3
Cardinia Vic. 53 J8
Cardinia Creek Reservoir Vic. 45 F13
Cardross Vic. 60 G3
Cardup WA 94 H7
Cardwell Qld 118 G6
Cargerie Vic. 44 A2, 46 B13, 51 R5, 52 B5
Carina Vic. 60 B10
Carinda NSW 27 Q7, 28 C7
Caringbah NSW 15 P11
Carinya Vic. 79 R8
Carisbrook Vic. 57 Q11, 58 A11
Cargo NSW 24 E5
Carlecatup WA 95 L6
Carlingford NSW 12 D10
Carlisle River Vic. 51 O11
Carlo Qld 122 B3
Carlotta WA 94 F8
Carlsruhe Vic. 46 H5, 52 E1, 58 E13
Carlton NSW 11 J11
Carlton Tas. 69 M7, 71 O7
Carlton Vic. 37 D2
Carmelicup WA 95 M4
Carmila Qld 119 L12
Carnamah WA 90 E7
Carnarvon WA 90 C2
Carnarvon Range National Park Qld 117 J5
Carnegie Vic. 39 K13, 40 C10
Carneys Creek Qld 112 F9
Carngham Vic. 51 P4
Caroda NSW 28 I6
Caroline SA 50 B6, 77 I12
Carool NSW 113 P9
Caroona NSW 28 I10
Carpendeit Vic. 51 N9
Carpenter Rocks SA 77 G12
Carpa SA 78 B1, 80 B10
Carrajung Vic. 53 P9
Carranballac Vic. 51 N4
Carrara Qld 124 G13
Carrathool NSW 23 L8
Carrick NSW 16 D11
Carrick Tas. 73 L8
Carrieton SA 80 I3, 83 N12
Carrington NSW 19 G4
Carroll NSW 28 I9
Carroll Gap NSW 29 J9
Carrolup WA 95 L6
Carron Vic. 57 K6
Carrow Brook NSW 25 K2, 29 K13
Carrowidgin NSW 30 D11
Carrum Vic. 41 M7, 52 H7
Carrum Downs Vic. 41 M3
Carters Ridge Qld 114 H7
Carwarp Vic. 60 H4
Cary Bay NSW 18 G7
Cashmore Vic. 50 E9
Casino NSW 29 P3, 117 Q13
Cascades Tas. 67 B10
Cassilis NSW 28 H12
Cassilis Vic. 54 E3, 62 E13
Cassowary Qld 118 F3, 120 I11
Castella Vic. 47 Q8, 48 C9, 53 J3
Casterton Vic. 50 D4
Castille NSW 112 F11
Castle Cove NSW 13 N9
Castlecrag NSW 13 N10
Castle Forbes Tas. 71 K8
Castle Forbes Bay Tas. 68 E11
Castle Hill NSW 12 B7
Castlemaine Vic. 46 E2, 58 C11
Castlereagh NSW 15 J6
Castra Upper Tas. 72 H6
Casula NSW 15 M10
Catagunya Tas. 71 J4
Catamaran Tas. 71 K11
Catani Vic. 53 K8
Cathcart NSW 30 E10, 55 N1
Cathcart Vic. 51 L2, 57 L13

Cathedral Range National Park Vic. 48 F7, 53 K2
Cathedral Rock Vic. 57 J13
Catherine Field NSW 15 K11
Catherine Hill Bay NSW 18 G9
Cathkin Vic. 48 E3, 59 J12
Cathundral NSW 27 R12, 28 C12
Cattai NSW 15 L4
Catterick WA 94 G6
Catumnal Vic. 57 P4
Caulfield Vic. 39 K13, 40 B11
Cavan NSW 24 E10, 30 D5
Caveat Vic. 47 R2, 48 D2, 59 J12
Cavendish Vic. 50 H3
Cave of Fishes Vic. 50 I1
Cave of Hands Vic. 50 I2
Caversham WA 96 E9
Caves Beach NSW 18 H8
Caveside Tas. 72 I8
Cawdor NSW 15 J12
Cawongla NSW 29 P2
Cecil Park NSW 15 L9
Cecil Plains Qld 117 N10
Cedar Brush NSW 18 C10
Cedar Glen Qld 113 L9
Cedar Grove Qld 113 K3
Cedar Pocket Qld 114 H3
Cedarton Qld 123 A13
Ceduna SA 82 H12, 84 A6
Ceduna Satellite Communication Station SA 84 A5
Cement Creek Vic. 48 F11, 53 K4
Central Aboriginal Res. WA 91 Q2, 93 Q10
Central Castra Tas. 72 H6
Central Mangrove NSW 18 C12
Central Tilba NSW 30 G9
Ceratodus Qld 117 N6
Ceres NSW 28 D13
Ceres Vic. 52 D8
Cessnock NSW 18 C5, 25 K3, 32 H12
Cethana Tas. 72 H7
Chadoora WA 94 G1
Chain Valley NSW 18 G9
Chakola NSW 30 E8
Challambra Vic. 57 J6
Chambigne NSW 29 O5
Chandada SA 84 C7
Chandler SA 82 G3
Chandlers Creek Vic. 30 E12, 55 M4
Chandos SA 79 Q8
Channel Country Qld 116, 121, 122
Chapple Vale Vic. 51 O11
Charam Vic. 56 E11
Charbon NSW 24 H3
Charleroi Vic. 62 C6
Charlestown NSW 18 H6
Charleville Qld 116 G8
Charley Creek Vic. 51 P11
Charleyong NSW 24 H11, 30 F6
Charlton NSW 27 O6
Charlton Vic. 57 N6
Charmhaven NSW 18 F10
Charlwood Qld 112 F6
Charters Towers Qld 118 G9
Chatsbury NSW 24 H9, 30 F3
Chatswood NSW 13 L11
Chatsworth Qld 114 F2
Chatsworth Vic. 51 K6
Cheeple Qld 116 E9
Cheesemans Creek NSW 24 E4
Cheethams Flats NSW 14 B5
Chelsea Vic. 41 L7, 52 H7
Cheltenham NSW 12 F8
Cheltenham SA 76 C6
Cheltenham Vic. 40 G10
Chepstowe Vic. 51 O4
Cherokee Vic. 46 I7
Cherrypool Vic. 56 H12
Cherry Tree Pool WA 95 L6
Cheshunt Vic. 59 O10
Chesney Vale Vic. 59 M7
Chester Hill NSW 10 C7
Chetwynd Vic. 50 D2, 56 D13
Cheviot Vic. 47 R4, 48 D4, 53 J1, 59 J13
Chevron Island Qld 124 F10
Chewton Vic. 46 E2, 58 C11
Chichester Range National Park WA 92 F10
Chifley NSW 11 P10

Chifley WA 91 L8
Childers Qld 117 P6
Childers Vic. 53 M9
Chillagoe Qld 118 E4, 120 G12
Chillingham NSW 29 Q1, 113 N10
Chillingollah Vic. 61 M10
Chiltern Vic. 59 P5, 64 G7
Chiltern Hills Qld 122 G1
Chiltern Park Vic. 59 P5
Chiltern Valley Vic. 64 E6
Chilwell Vic. 63 E4
Chinamans Wells SA 77 E9
Chinchilla Qld 117 M9
Chinderah NSW 29 R1, 113 R9
Chinkapook Vic. 22 F11, 61 L10
Chinocup WA 95 P5
Chintin Vic. 47 K7, 52 F2
Chippendale NSW 8 B13
Chipping Norton NSW 10 A10
Chirnside Park Vic. 45 C1
Chirrup Vic. 57 M5
Chiswick NSW 11 J3
Chittaway Point NSW 18 F12
Chorkerup WA 95 M12
Chorregon Qld 116 C2, 118 C13
Chowerup WA 94 I8
Chowilla SA 22 A7
Christmas Creek Qld 113 K8
Christmas Hills Tas. 72 C4
Christmas Hills Vic. 47 P10, 48 B10, 52 I4
Chudleigh Tas. 72 I8
Chullora NSW 10 E7
Church Land SA 79 L1, 81 L10
Church Point NSW 15 Q5, 21 N5
Churchill Qld 110 H12
Churchill Vic. 53 O9
Churchill National Park Vic. 40 F1, 52 I6
Chute Vic. 51 O2, 57 O13
Cinnabar Qld 114 A2
Clandulla NSW 24 H4
Clara Creek Qld 116 H8
Clare Qld 118 I8
Clare SA 78 I1, 80 I10
Claremont Tas. 68 H5, 71 M6
Clarence NSW 14 D4
Clarence Town NSW 25 L3
Clarendon NSW 15 K5
Clarendon SA 78 I7
Clarendon Qld 110 E9
Clarendon Vic. 44 A1, 46 B11, 51 R4, 52 B4
Claretown Vic. 46 C9
Clare Valley SA 80 I10
Clareville Beach NSW 15 Q4
Clarkefield Vic. 47 J8, 52 F3
Clarke Island Tas. 73 Q1
Clarks Hill Vic. 46 B8
Claude Road Tas. 72 H7
Claymore WA 94 E6
Claypans SA 79 M6
Clayton Qld 117 P6
Clayton Vic. 40 E6
Clay Wells SA 77 F9
Clear Lake Vic. 56 F11
Clear Ridge NSW 24 B6
Cleland National Park SA 76 G10
Clematis Vic. 45 G12
Clements Gap SA 80 G9
Clempton Park NSW 10 I8
Clermont Qld 116 I2, 118 I13
Cleve SA 80 A10, 84 G10
Cleveland Qld 111 O11
Cleveland Tas. 73 N10
Clifton NSW 17 P2
Clifton Qld 117 O11
Clifton Tas. 69 K9
Clifton Beach Qld 126 E5
Clifton Beach Tas. 71 N8
Clifton Gardens NSW 11 O1, 13 O13
Clifton Springs Vic. 44 H7, 52 E8
Clinton Centre SA 79 G3, 80 F12
Clintonvale Qld 117 O11
Clonbinane Vic. 47 N6, 52 H2, 58 H13
Cloncurry Qld 121 E8
Clontarf NSW 13 P11
Closeburn Qld 110 I8
Clothiers Creek NSW 113 Q11
Clouds Creek NSW 29 O6
Clovelly NSW 11 Q6

Cluan Tas. 73 K8
Club Terrace Vic. 30 D12, 55 L6
Clumber Qld 112 E6
Clunes NSW 29 Q2
Clunes Vic. 51 Q1, 52 A1, 57 Q13, 58 A13
Clwydd NSW 14 D5
Clybucca NSW 29 P9
Clyburn NSW 10 D3
Clyde NSW 10 C3
Clyde Vic. 52 I8
Clydebank Vic. 54 C9
Clydesdale Vic. 46 C4, 52 C1, 57 R12, 58 B12
Coal Point NSW 18 G7
Coalcliff NSW 17 P2
Coal Creek Qld 110 D5
Coaldale NSW 29 O4
Coalstoun Lakes Qld 117 O7
Coalville Vic. 53 N8
Cobains Vic. 53 R7, 54 B10
Cobaki NSW 113 Q9, 125 R6
Cobar NSW 27 M11
Cobargo Vic. 30 F9
Cobark NSW 25 L1, 29 L12
Cobaw Vic. 46 I5, 52 E1, 58 E13
Cobbadah NSW 29 J7
Cobbannah Vic. 54 C6
Cobbitty NSW 15 J11
Cobbora NSW 28 F12
Cobden Vic. 51 M9
Cobdogla SA 79 P3, 81 P12
Cobera SA 79 P5
Cobourg Peninsula NT 100 G2
Cobram Vic. 23 M13, 59 K3
Cobrico Vic. 51 M9
Cobungra Vic. 54 D3, 62 D12
Coburg Vic. 38 G5, 52 G5
Cocamba Vic. 61 L9
Cochranes Creek Vic. 57 P9
Cockaleechie SA 84 F11
Cockatoo Vic. 53 J6
Cockburn SA 26 A13, 22 A1, 81 R2, 83 R12
Cocklebiddy WA 91 O10
Coconut Grove NT 98 C6
Cocoparra National Park NSW 23 N7
Cocoroc Vic. 52 E6
Codrington Vic. 50 H9
Coen Qld 120 E7
Coffin Bay SA 84 E12
Coffs Harbour NSW 29 P7
Coghills Creek Vic. 51 Q2, 52 A2
Cohuna Vic. 22 I12, 58 C2
Colac Vic. 51 P9
Colac Colac Vic. 62 G5
Colbinabbin Vic. 58 F8
Coldstream Vic. 47 Q11, 48 C11, 52 I5
Coleambally NSW 23 M9
Colebrook Tas. 69 J1, 71 M5
Coledale NSW 17 P3, 25 J8, 30 I3
Coleraine Vic. 50 F4
Coles Bay Tas. 71 R2, 73 R12
Coleyville Qld 112 F3
Colignan Vic. 60 I5
Colinroobie NSW 23 O8
Colinton NSW 30 D7
Colinton Qld 110 C1
Collarenebri NSW 28 E4
Collaroy NSW 13 Q6, 28 H12
Collector NSW 24 G10, 30 E5
College Park SA 75 H4
Collerina NSW 27 O5
Collie NSW 28 D11
Collie WA 90 F11, 94 G4
Collieburn WA 94 G4
Collie Cardiff WA 94 G4
Collingullie NSW 23 P10, 24 A10
Collins WA 94 G9
Collins Cap Tas. 68 G6, 71 L7
Collinsfield SA 80 H9
Collinsvale Tas. 68 H6, 71 M7
Collinsville Qld 119 J10
Collombatti Rail NSW 29 O9
Colly Blue NSW 28 I10
Colo NSW 15 K2
Colo Heights NSW 15 J1, 25 J5
Colo Vale NSW 17 K5
Colquhoun Vic. 54 G7
Colton SA 84 D9
Comara NSW 29 N9

Comaum SA 56 B13, 50 A2, 77 I8
Combara NSW 28 D9
Combienbar Vic. 55 L5
Comboyne NSW 29 N11
Come-by-Chance NSW 28 E7
Comet Qld 117 J3
Comleroy Road NSW 14 I4
Commissioners Flat Qld 110 I1, 114 I13
Como NSW 15 O10
Compton SA 77 H11
Compton Downs NSW 27 O7
Conara Junction Tas. 73 N10
Conargo NSW 23 L11
Concord NSW 10 H4
Condah Vic. 50 F7
Condamine Qld 117 M9
Condell Park NSW 10 D9
Condingup WA 91 K12
Condobolin NSW 23 P4, 24 A4
Condong NSW 113 P10
Condoulpe NSW 61 O6
Condowie SA 78 H1, 80 H10
Conewarre Vic. 44 F9
Congelin WA 95 J1
Congewai NSW 18 C7
Congo Park NSW 30 G8
Congupna Road Vic. 59 J6
Coningham Tas. 68 I10
Coniston NSW 17 P5, 19 C13
Conjola NSW 24 I11, 30 H6
Conmurra SA 77 F8
Connangorach Vic. 56 G11
Connells Point NSW 10 I13
Connels Peak Vic. 62 D7
Connemara Qld 122 H4
Connemarra NSW 28 H11
Connewirricoo Vic. 50 E1, 56 D13
Connulpie NSW 122 I13
Conondale Qld 114 H11
Contine WA 95 K1
Conway Qld 127 E6
Conway Range National Park Qld 127 E5
Coober Pedy SA 82 I6
Coobowie SA 78 F7, 84 I13
Coochin Coochin Qld 112 G7
Coochin Creek Qld 111 J1, 115 J13
Cooee Tas. 72 G5
Cooeeinbardi Qld 110 E4
Coogee NSW 11 Q7
Cooinda NT 100 H5
Coojar Vic. 50 F2
Cook SA 82 C9
Cookamidgera NSW 24 D4
Cookardinia NSW 23 P12, 24 A11, 62 C1
Cooke Plains SA 79 M9
Cooks Gap NSW 24 G2, 28 G13
Cookville Tas. 71 M10
Cookernup WA 94 F2
Cooktown Qld 118 F1, 120 I9
Coolabah NSW 27 O9
Coolabine Qld 114 H9
Coolac NSW 24 D10, 30 B5
Cooladdi Qld 116 F9
Coolah NSW 28 H12
Coolamatong NSW 31 H8
Coolamon NSW 23 P9, 24 A9
Coolana Qld 110 E11
Coolangatta NSW 17 N12
Coolangatta Qld 29 R1, 113 R8, 117 Q12, 125 P4
Coolanie SA 80 B9, 84 G9
Coolatai NSW 29 J4, 117 M13
Coolcha SA 79 M6
Coolgardie WA 91 J8
Coolongolook NSW 25 N2, 29 N13
Cooloola National Park Qld 115 L3
Cooloolabin Qld 115 J8, 123 C5
Cooltong SA 24 A8, 79 Q2, 81 Q11
Coolum Qld 115 L8, 123 G5
Coolum Beach Qld 115 L8, 123 H5
Coolup WA 94 F1
Cooma NSW 30 D8
Cooma Vic. 58 H7
Coomalbidgup WA 91 J12
Coomandook SA 79 M9
Coombabah Lakes Qld 113 P4
Coombe SA 77 F2, 79 O11
Coombell NSW 29 P3

Coombogolong NSW 28 D7
Coomera Qld 113 O4
Coominglah Qld 117 N6
Coominya Qld 110 E8
Coomoora Vic. 46 D6
Coomunga SA 84 E12
Coonabarabran NSW 28 G10
Coonalpyn SA 77 E1, 79 N10
Coonamble NSW 28 D9
Coonawarra SA 50 A2, 77 H9
Coondambo SA 83 K10, 84 E3
Coondoo Qld 115 J3
Coongoola Qld 116 G10
Coongulmerang Vic. 54 D8
Coonong NSW 23 N10
Coonooer Bridge Vic. 57 N7
Cooper Creek SA 83 P5
Coopernook NSW 29 O12
Coopers Creek Vic. 53 O7
Coopers Hill Qld 110 C12
Cooplacurripa NSW 29 M11
Coorabulka Qld 122 E3
Cooragook Qld 110 D8
Cooran Qld 114 I5
Cooranbong NSW 18 E8, 25 L4
Coorong National Park SA 77 C2, 79 L11
Cootamundra NSW 23 R9, 24 C9, 30 B4
Cooyar Qld 117 O9
Cope Cope Vic. 57 M7
Copeville SA 79 N6
Corella Qld 114 G2
Corfield Qld 118 C12
Cork Qld 122 H2
Corny Point SA 78 C7, 84 H13
Corrigin WA 90 G10
Cortlinye SA 84 G8
Coorinyup WA 95 M7·
Coorow WA 90 E7
Cooroy Qld 115 J6, 123 C2
Cooyal NSW 24 H2
Copmanhurst NSW 29 O5
Copping Tas. 69 N6, 71 O7
Corack Vic. 57 M5
Coradgery NSW 24 C3
Coragulac Vic. 51 P8
Coraki NSW 29 Q3, 117 Q13
Coral Bay WA 92 C12
Coral Bank Vic. 59 R8, 62 B8
Coral Ville NSW 29 O12
Cora Lynn Vic. 53 K8
Coramba NSW 29 P7
Cordering WA 94 I5
Coree South NSW 23 L11
Coreen NSW 23 N12, 59 O2
Corindhap Vic. 51 Q6, 52 A6
Corindi NSW 29 P6
Corinella Vic. 52 I10
Corinna Tas. 72 C9
Corio Vic. 44 F6
Cornella Vic. 58 F9
Corobimilla NSW 23 O9
Corowa NSW 23 N13, 59 O4, 64 A2
Cornwall Tas. 73 Q8
Cornwallis NSW 15 K5
Coromby Vic. 57 J8
Coronation Beach Qld 115 L8
Corop Vic. 58 F7
Cororooke Vic. 51 P9
Corrimal NSW 17 P4, 25 J8, 30 I3
Corringle Vic. 54 I8
Corryong Vic. 23 Q13, 30 A8, 62 G5
Cosgrove Vic. 59 K6
Cosmo Newberry Aboriginal Res. 91 M5
Costerfield Vic. 58 F10
Cotabena SA 83 N11
Cottles Bridge Vic. 47 O10, 48 A10
Couangalt Vic. 46 I9
Cougal NSW 29 P1, 113 J11
Coulson Qld 112 H5
Coulta SA 84 E11
Countegany NSW 30 E8
Courabyra NSW 30 B7, 62 H2
Courada NSW 28 I6
Couran Qld 113 P3
Couridjah NSW 17 K2
Coutts Crossing NSW 29 P6
Cowabbie West NSW 23 P8
Cowal Creek Mission Qld 120 C1

Cowan NSW 15 O4, 21 K12
Cowangie Vic. 60 D10
Cowaramup WA 94 C6
Coward Springs SA 83 L7
Cowell SA 80 C10, 84 H9
Cowes Vic. 43 O11, 52 I10
Cowleys Creek Vic. 51 M10
Cowper NSW 29 P5
Cowra NSW 24 E6, 30 C1
Cowwarr Vic. 53 P7
Coyrecup WA 95 N5
Crabbes Creek NSW 29 Q2, 113 Q13
Crabtree Tas. 68 G8
Cracow Qld 117 M6
Cradle Mountain Lake St Clair National Park
  Tas. 70 G1, 72 G10
Cradoc Tas. 68 F10, 71 L8
Cradock SA 80 H2, 83 N12
Craigie NSW 30 D11
Craigieburn Vic. 47 L10, 52 G4
Crament Vic. 60 I7
Cranbourne Vic. 52 I7
Cranbrook Tas. 71 Q1, 73 Q11
Cranbrook WA 90 G12, 95 M9
Cranebrook NSW 15 J7
Craven NSW 25 M1, 29 M13
Cravensville Vic. 62 E7
Crawfordville NSW 18 B6
Creek Junction Vic. 59 L10
Creek View Vic. 58 E8
Creighton Vic. 59 J9
Creightons Creek Vic. 59 J10
Cremorne NSW 11 N1, 13 N13
Cremorne Tas. 69 K8, 71 N7
Cremorne Point NSW 11 O2, 13 O13
Crescent Head NSW 29 P10
Cressbrook Lower Qld 110 D3
Cressy Tas. 73 L9
Cressy Vic. 51 P7
Creswick Vic. 46 A7, 51 R2, 52 B2
Crib Point Vic. 43 N8, 52 H9
Croajingalong Nat. Park Vic. 30 E13, 55 M7
Croftby Qld 112 F8
Crohamhurst Qld 115 J12
Croker Island NT 100 H2
Cromer NSW 13 P6
Cronulla NSW 15 P11
Crooble NSW 28 I3
Crooked River Vic. 53 R2, 54 B5
Crookhaven Heads NSW 17 O12, 25 J10,
  30 H5
Crookwell NSW 24 F8, 30 E3
Croom NSW 17 O7
Croppa Creek NSW 28 I3, 117 M13
Crossdale Qld 110 F5
Crossman WA 94 I1
Crotty Tas. 70 E2
Crowlands Vic. 57 M12
Crow Mountain NSW 29 J7
Crows Nest NSW 9 A3, 11 M1, 13 M12
Crows Nest Qld 117 O10
Crowther NSW 24 D7, 30 C2
Croxton East Vic. 50 I5
Croydon NSW 10 I5
Croydon Qld 118 A6, 121 H4
Croydon Vic. 45 A3, 48 B13, 52 I5
Croydon Park NSW 10 I6
Crymillan Vic. 56 I5
Cryon NSW 28 E6
Crystal Brook SA 80 G8
Crystal Brook Qld 127 C4
Crystal Creek NSW 113 O10
Cuballing WA 95 K1
Cubbaroo NSW 28 F6
Cubbie Qld 116 I12
Cudal NSW 24 E5
Cuddell NSW 23 N9
Cudgee Vic. 51 K9
Cudgegong NSW 24 H3
Cudgen NSW 29 R1, 113 R10
Cudgera Creek NSW 29 Q1, 113 Q11
Cudgewa Vic. 30 A8, 62 F5
Cudmirrah NSW 30 H6
Cue WA 90 G4
Culbin WA 95 J3
Culburra NSW 17 O13, 25 J10
Culburra SA 77 E2, 79 N11

Culcairn NSW 23 P12, 59 R1, 62 B1
Culfearne Vic. 57 R1, 58 B1, 61 R13
Culgoa Vic. 22 G13, 57 M2, 61 M13
Culla Vic. 50 F1, 56 E13
Cullen NT 100 F8
Cullen Bullen NSW 14 A2
Cullerin NSW 24 G9, 30 E4
Cullulleraine Vic. 22 C8, 60 D3
Cumborah NSW 27 R5, 28 C5
Cummins SA 84 E11
Cumnock NSW 24 E3
Cundare Vic. 51 P7
Cundeelee Aboriginal Reserve WA 91 L8
Cunderdin WA 90 G9
Cundinup WA 94 F6
Cungena SA 82 I13, 84 C7
Cunliffe SA 78 F2, 80 F12, 84 I11
Cunnamulla Qld 116 F11
Cunningar NSW 24 D8, 30 C3
Cunningham SA 78 F4, 80 F13
Cunninghams Gap National Park Qld
  112 C6, 117 P11
Cuprona Tas. 72 G5
Curalle Qld 122 G7
Curban NSW 28 E11
Curdie Vale Vic. 51 L10
Curdimurka SA 83 M7
Curl Curl NSW 13 P8
Curlewis NSW 28 I9
Curlewis Vic. 44 G8
Curlwaa NSW 22 D7, 60 F2
Curra Qld 114 F1
Curramulka SA 78 F5, 84 I12
Currabubula NSW 29 J10
Currans Hill NSW 15 K12
Currarong NSW 25 J10, 30 I5
Currawang NSW 24 G10, 30 E5
Currawarna NSW 24 A10
Curraweela NSW 16 B4
Currawilla Qld 122 G5
Currigee Qld 113 P4
Currimundi Qld 115 M12, 123 I11
Currowan Corner Upper NSW 30 G7
Currumbin Qld 113 Q8, 125 O7
Curtis Island Qld 117 N3
Curyo Vic. 57 K3
Custon SA 56 A7, 77 I5
Cuttabri NSW 28 F7
Cygnet River SA 78 E10
Cygnet Tas. 68 G11, 71 L9
Cynthia Qld 117 N6
Cypress Gardens Qld 124 H11

D

Daceville NSW 11 O8
Dadswells Bridge Vic. 57 J11
D'Aguilar Qld 110 I2
Dagun Qld 114 G5
Dahlen Vic. 56 H9
Daintree Qld 118 F2, 120 I11
Dairy Flat NSW 112 G11
Daisey Dell Tas. 72 G8
Daisy Hill Vic. 57 P12, 58 A12
Dajarra Qld 121 D10
Dakabin Qld 111 K6
Dalbeg Qld 118 I9
Dalby Qld 117 N10
Dalgety NSW 30 D9, 31 I10
Dallarnil Qld 117 O7
Dalma Qld 117 M3
Dalmallee Vic. 56 H4
Dalman NSW 112 E11
Dalmeny NSW 30 G8
Dalmorton NSW 29 N6
Dalton NSW 24 G9, 30 E4
Dalveen Qld 29 M1
Dalwallinu WA 90 F8
Dalwood NSW 18 D2
Daly River NT 100 D7
Daly River Aboriginal Reserve NT 100 B8
Daly River Wildlife Sanctuary NT 100 C7
Dalyston Vic. 53 J11
Daly Waters NT 100 I12, 102 I2
Dampier WA 92 F9
Danby Siding Tas. 69 J2
Dandaloo NSW 23 Q2, 24 B1, 27 Q13, 28 B13
Dandaragan WA 90 E8

135

Dandenong Vic. 40 H3, 52 H6
Dandenong Ranges Vic. 45
Danderoo Qld 112 A9
Dandongadale Vic. 59 P10
Dangarfield NSW 25 K1
Dangarsleigh NSW 29 M8
Danyo Vic. 60 C10
Dapto NSW 17 N6, 25 J8, 30 I3
Darbys Falls NSW 24 E7, 30 D2
Darbyshire Vic. 62 D5
Dardadine WA 95 J3
Dardanup WA 94 F4
Dareton NSW 22 D7, 60 G2
Dargo Vic. 54 C5
Darkan WA 90 F11, 94 I4, 95 J4
Dark Corner NSW 24 H5
Darke Park SA 84 F9
Darkes Forest NSW 17 O2
Darkwood NSW 29 O8
Darley Vic. 46 G11, 52 D4
Darling Downs Qld 117 N10-11
Darlinghurst NSW 8 G9
Darling Point NSW 11 O3
Darlington NSW 11 L5
Darlington Tas. 69 Q2, 71 Q5
Darlington Vic. 51 M7
Darlington Point NSW 23 M9
Darnick NSW 22 H3
Darnum Vic. 53 M8
Daroobalgie NSW 24 C5
Darr Qld 116 D3
Darradup WA 94 E8
Darraweit Guim Vic. 47 L7, 52 G2
Darriman Vic. 53 Q10, 54 A12
Dart Dart Vic. 56 H7
Dartmoor Vic. 50 D6
Dartmouth Qld 116 E3
Dartmouth Dam Vic. 62 E8
Dartnall WA 95 M7
Darwin NT 98, 99, 100 D4
Dattuck Vic. 56 I1, 60 I12
Davenport Downs Qld 122 F4
Daveyston SA 85 A2
Davidson NSW 13 L6
Davies Creek National Park Qld 126 D9
Davis Creek NSW 25 K1
Daviston NSW 15 Q2, 20 D2
Dawes Qld 117 N5
Dawlish Qld 127 H13
Dawn Qld 114 G4
Dawson SA 81 J5
Dawson Vic. 53 P7
Dawsons Hill NSW 25 K2
Dayboro Qld 110 I6, 117 P10
Daydream Island Qld 127 E4
Daylesford Vic. 46 D6, 52 C2, 58 C13
Daymar Qld 28 F1, 117 K12
Daysdale NSW 23 N12, 59 N1
Day Trap Vic. 61 K10
Dead Horse Gap NSW 30 B9
Deakin WA 91 Q8
Dean Vic. 46 B8, 51 R3, 52 B3
Deanmill WA 94 G8
Deans Marsh Vic. 51 R9, 52 B9
Debella Qld 127 B3
Deception Bay Qld 111 L5
Deddick Vic. 55 J3
Deddington Tas. 73 N8
Dederang Vic. 59 R7, 62 B7
Dee Tas. 73 J13
Deep Creek Vic. 54 F1, 62 F10
Deepdene WA 94 C9
Deep Lead Vic. 57 K11
Deep River WA 94 I12
Deepwater NSW 29 M4
Deep Well NT 105 J9
Deer Park Vic. 52 F5
Deeside WA 94 H9
Dee Why NSW 13 P7
Delaneys Creek Qld 110 I3
Delatite Vic. 59 M12
Delburn Vic. 53 N9
Delegate NSW 30 D11, 55 L3
Delegate River Vic. 30 D11, 55 K3
Delissaville NT 100 D5
Dellicknora Vic. 55 K3
Dellyannie WA 95 K4
Delmont Tas. 73 L9

Deloraine Tas. 73 J8
Delungra NSW 29 J5
Delvine Vic. 54 D8
Denbarker WA 95 L11
Denham WA 90 C3
Denial Bay SA 84 A6
Denicull Creek Vic. 51 L2
Deniliquin NSW 23 K12
Denistone NSW 12 G11
Denman NSW 29 J13, 25 J2
Denmark WA 90 G13, 95 L12
Dennes Point Tas. 68 I10, 71 M8
Dennington Vic. 51 J9
Denver Vic. 46 E5, 52 D1, 58 D13
Depot Creek SA 80 F2
Deptford Vic. 54 E6
Derby Tas. 73 P5
Derby Vic. 57 R8, 58 B8
Derby WA 93 M5
Dereel Vic. 51 Q5, 52 A5
Dergholm Vic. 50 C2
Dering Vic. 60 H11
Deringulla NSW 28 G10
Derriers Flat Qld 114 G7
Derrinal Vic. 58 E10
Derrinallum Vic. 51 N6
Derriwong NSW 23 Q4, 24 B4
Derwent Bridge Tas. 70 H2, 72 H12
Derwent Park Tas. 67 B3
Desert Camp National Park SA 77 F5
Detpa Vic. 56 F5
Devenish Vic. 59 L6
Devils Marbles Nat. Park NT 103 K11, 105 K1
Devils Peak SA 80 G3
Devoit Tas. 73 K6
Devon Vic. 53 P10
Devondale Vic. 51 N11
Devonport Tas. 72 I5
Dharug National Park NSW 15 M1, 18 A13, 25 K5
Dhurringle Vic. 58 I8
Diamantina Lakes Qld 122 F3
Diamond Creek Vic. 39 P1
Diamond Tree WA 94 G9
Diamond Valley Qld 115 J11, 123 C11
Dianas Bath Qld 110 G5
Diapur Vic. 56 D6
Dickie Beach Qld 115 M12, 123 I12
Dickson ACT 34 F4
Dicks Tableland Eungella National Park Qld 127 C10
Didillibah Qld 115 L10, 123 F8
Didleum Plains Tas. 73 N6
Digby Vic. 50 E5
Diggers Rest Vic. 47 J10, 52 F4
Diggora Vic. 58 E6
Dilkoon NSW 29 P5
Dilpura NSW 61 P9
Dimboola Vic. 56 G7
Dimbulah Qld 118 E4, 120 H12
Dingee Vic. 58 C6
Dingo Qld 117 L3
Dingup WA 94 G8
Dingwall Vic. 57 O2, 58 A2
Dinninup WA 94 I6
Dinoga NSW 29 J6
Dinyarrak Vic. 56 B6, 77 I4, 79 R13
Dirranbandi Qld 28 D1, 117 J12
Discovery Bay Coastal Park Vic. 50 C8
Dixie Vic. 51 M9
Dixons Creek Vic. 47 Q10, 48 C10, 53 J4
Djerriwarrah Reservoir Vic. 46 H9, 52 E4
Dobbyn Qld 121 D7
Doble Vic. 51 M2, 57 M13
Dobroyd Point NSW 11 J4
Docker Vic. 59 O7
Docker River NT 104 A10
Doctors Flat Vic. 54 F4, 62 F13
Dodges Ferry Tas. 69 L7, 71 O7
Dolls Point NSW 11 K13
Dolphin Qld 125 D12
Donald Vic. 57 L7
Donbakup WA 94 G10
Doncaster Vic. 39 O7
Dongara WA 90 D7
Dongolocking WA 95 N3
Donnelly River Mill WA 94 F8
Donnybrook Vic. 47 M9, 52 G3

Donnybrook WA 90 E12, 94 F5
Donors Hill Qld 121 E5
Donovans Landing SA 77 I12
Donvale Vic. 39 Q7
Dooboobetic Vic. 57 M7
Dooen Vic. 56 I9
Dookie Vic. 59 K6
Doomadgee Mission Qld 121 B3
Doonan Qld 115 K7, 123 F3
Doondoon NSW 113 O13
Doonside NSW 15 L7
Dooralong NSW 18 D10
Dopewarra Vic. 56 D10
Dora Creek NSW 18 F8
Doreen NSW 28 G6
Doreen Vic. 47 N10
Dornock WA 95 Q1
Dorodong Vic. 50 C2
Dorrien SA 85 F4
Dorrigo NSW 29 O7
Double Bay NSW 11 O4
Douglas Vic. 56 F12
Douglas Park NSW 17 L1
Douglas River Tas. 73 R10
Dover Tas. 71 L10
Dover Heights NSW 11 R3
Doveton Vic. 40 H2
Dowerin WA 90 F9
Dowlingville SA 78 G4, 80 F13
Downer ACT 34 G3
Downsfield Qld 114 G1
Downside NSW 24 B10
Doyalson NSW 18 F10, 25 L5
Drake NSW 29 N3
Dreeite Vic. 51 P8
Drik Drik Vic. 50 D7
Drillham Qld 117 L9
Dripstone NSW 24 F3
Dromana Vic. 42 H7, 52 G9
Dromedary Tas. 68 H5, 71 L6
Dropmore Vic. 47 R1, 48 C1, 59 J11
Drouin Vic. 53 L8
Drumborg Vic. 50 F7
Drummartin Vic. 58 D7
Drummond Vic. 46 F5, 52 D1, 58 D13
Drummoyne NSW 11 J3
Drung Drung Vic. 56 I9
Dry Creek Vic. 59 L11
Drysdale Vic. 44 H7, 52 E8
Drysdale River National Park WA 93 P2
Duaringa Qld 117 L4
Dubbo NSW 24 E1, 28 E13
Dublin SA 78 H4, 80 H13
Duchess Qld 121 D10
Duckenfield NSW 18 G3
Duckmaloi NSW 14 A8
Duddo Vic. 60 C10
Dudinin WA 95 N1
Dudley NSW 18 H6
Dudley Vic. 53 J11
Duff Creek SA 83 K5
Duffholme Vic. 56 F9
Duffield NT 105 L12
Duffys Forest NSW 13 K2
Dugandan Qld 112 G6
Duggan WA 95 O3
Dulacca Qld 117 L9
Dulbolla Qld 113 J9
Dullah NSW 23 P9, 24 A9
Dulong Qld 115 J10, 123 C8
Dululu Qld 117 M4
Dulwich Hill NSW 11 J7
Dumbalk Vic. 53 M10
Dumberning WA 95 K2
Dumbleyung WA 90 G11, 95 N4
Dum Dum NSW 113 O11
Dumosa Vic. 22 G13, 57 N3
Dunach Vic. 51 Q1, 52 A1, 57 P13, 58 A13
Dunalley Tas. 69 N7, 71 O7
Dunbible NSW 113 P11
Dundas Tas. 72 D10
Dundas NSW 10 D1, 12 D12
Dundas Qld 110 F7
Dundas Valley NSW 12 E11
Dundee NSW 29 M5
Dundonnell Vic. 51 M6
Dundurrabin NSW 29 O7
Dunedoo NSW 28 G12

Dungay NSW   113 O10
Dungog NSW   25 L2
Dungowan NSW   29 K10
Dunheved NSW   15 K7
Dunkeld NSW   24 G5
Dunkeld Vic.   50 I4
Dunk Island Qld   118 G5
Dunluce Vic.   57 P10
Dunmarra NT   100 I13, 102 I3
Dunmore NSW   17 O8, 23 R3, 24 C3
Dunmore Vic.   50 H8
Dunneworthy Vic.   51 M1, 57 M12
Dunns Creek NSW   18 G1
Dunnstown Vic.   46 B10, 51 R4, 52 B4
Dunolly Vic.   57 P10, 58 A10
Dunrobin Tas.   68 C1
Dunrobin Vic.   50 D4
Dunsborough WA   94 C5
Duntroon ACT   34 H11
Dunwich Qld   111 P10
Dural NSW   12 B4
Duranbah NSW   113 Q10
Duranillin WA   95 J5
Durdidwarrah Vic.   44 D2, 46 D13, 52 C5
Durham Downs Qld   122 H9
Durham Lead Vic.   46 A11, 51 Q4, 52 A4
Durham Ox Vic.   57 Q5, 58 B5
Durong Qld   117 N8
Durran Durra NSW   24 H11, 30 F6
Durras NSW   30 G7
Durren Durren NSW   18 E10
Durrie Qld   122 E6
Durrumbul NSW   113 P13
Durundur Qld   110 H2
Dutson Vic.   54 C10
Dutton SA   79 K4, 81 K13
Duverney Vic.   51 P7
Dwarda WA   94 I1
Dwellingup WA   90 F11
Dwyers NSW   27 N7
Dyliabing WA   95 N5
Dynnyrne Tas.   67 D12
Dysart Qld   117 J3, 119 J12
Dysart Tas.   68 H2, 71 M5

E

Eagle Bay WA   94 C5
Eagleby Qld   111 N13, 113 N1
Eaglehawk Vic.   58 C9
Eaglehawk Neck Tas.   67 H2, 69 P9, 71 P8
Eagle Heights Qld   113 N4
Eagle Point Vic.   54 E8
Earlston Vic.   59 K8
Earlwood NSW   11 J9
Eastbrook WA   94 G9
Eastern Creek NSW   15 L7
Eastern View Vic.   44 B12, 51 R10, 52 B10
East Hills NSW   10 C12
Eastlakes NSW   11 N8
East Melbourne Vic.   37 H6
East Perth WA   87 G4
East Point NT   98 G11
East Sydney NSW   8 F8
Eastwood NSW   12 G10
Eastwood SA   75 H10
Eaton WA   94 E4
Eatonsville NSW   29 P5
Eba SA   79 M2, 81 M11
Ebden Vic.   59 R5, 62 B5
Ebenezer NSW   15 L4
Ebenezer Qld   110 F13
Eberys Vic.   46 B4
Ebor NSW   29 N7
Eccleston NSW   25 L2, 29 L13
Echuca Vic.   23 K13, 58 F5
Ecklin Vic.   51 M9
Eddington Vic.   57 Q10, 58 A10
Eden NSW   30 F11, 55 P3
Eden Hill WA   96 B10
Edenhope Vic.   56 C12
Eden Park Vic.   47 N8
Eden Valley SA   79 K5
Edgecliff NSW   11 O4
Edgecombe Vic.   46 G4, 52 E1, 58 E12
Edgeroi NSW   28 H6
Edgeworth NSW   18 G5
Edi Vic.   59 O8

Edillilie SA   84 E11
Edith NSW   14 A9, 24 H6, 30 G1
Edithburgh SA   78 F7, 84 I13
Edith Creek Tas.   72 C4
Edith River NT   100 G8
Edithvale Vic.   41 K7, 52 H7
Edlands NSW   29 N11
Edward River Mission Qld   120 B8
Edwards Creek SA   83 K5
Eerwah Vale Qld   115 J7
Eganstown Vic.   46 C6
Egelabra NSW   27 R11, 28 C11
Eglinford NSW   18 C6
Eidsvold Qld   117 N7
Eildon Vic.   48 H4, 53 L1, 59 L13
Eildon State Park Vic.   59 M13
Eimeo Qld   127 H11
Einasleigh Qld   118 D6
Elaine Vic.   44 B2, 46 C12, 51 R5, 52 B5
Elanora NSW   13 O3
Elanora Heights NSW   21 R6
Elaroo Qld   119 K10, 127 D8
Elbow Hill SA   78 B1, 80 B10, 84 G10
Elcho Island NT   101 N3
Elcombe NSW   28 I5
Elderslie NSW   18 B1
Elderslie Tas.   68 G3, 71 L5
Eldon Tas.   69 J1, 71 N4
Eldorado Vic.   59 O6
Eleebana NSW   18 G6
Elgin WA   94 E5
Elgin Vale Qld   114 A6
Elimbah Qld   111 J3
Elingamite Vic.   51 M9
Elizabeth SA   76 G1, 78 I5
Elizabeth Bay NSW   11 O4, 18 G10
Elizabeth Town Tas.   73 J7
Ellalong NSW   18 C6
Ellam Vic.   56 G4
Elleker WA   95 N13
Ellenborough NSW   29 N11
Ellendale Tas.   68 C3, 71 J5
Ellingerrin Vic.   44 A7
Ellerslie Vic.   51 K8
Ellerston NSW   29 K12
Elliminyt Vic.   51 P9
Ellinbank Vic.   53 L8
Elliott NT   103 J5
Elliott Tas.   72 F5
Elliot Price Conservation Park SA   83 M6
Elliston SA   84 D9
Elmhurst Vic.   51 N1, 57 N12
Elmore Vic.   58 E7
Elong Elong NSW   28 F12
Elphinstone Vic.   46 F3, 58 D12
Elsinore NSW   27 K11
Elsmore NSW   29 L5
Elsternwick Vic.   40 C12
Eltham NSW   29 Q2
Eltham Vic.   39 P3, 52 H5
Elwomple SA   79 M8
Embleton WA   96 A11
Emerald Qld   117 J3
Emerald Vic.   45 H12
Emerald Hill NSW   28 I9
Emerald Lake Vic.   45 I12
Emmaville NSW   29 L4
Emmet Qld   116 E5
Empire Bay NSW   15 Q2, 20 E1
Empire Vale NSW   29 Q3
Emu Vic.   57 O9
Emu Bay SA   78 E10
Emu Downs SA   79 J1, 81 J10
Emu Flat Vic.   47 J3, 58 F12
Emu Park Qld   117 N3
Emu Plains NSW   15 J7
Emu Point WA   95 N13
Emu Vale Qld   112 B9
Eneabba WA   90 E7
Enfield NSW   10 H6
Enfield SA   76 E6
Enfield Vic.   51 Q5, 52 A5
Engadine NSW   15 N11
Englefield Vic.   50 G2
Enmore NSW   11 L6, 29 M8
Enngonia NSW   27 M4, 116 G13
Enoch Point Vic.   53 M2
Ensay Vic.   54 F5

Enterprise Qld   114 H2
Eppalock Vic.   58 E10
Epping NSW   12 F9
Epping Vic.   47 M10, 52 G4
Epping Forest Tas.   73 M9
Epsom Vic.   58 D9
Eraring NSW   18 F8
Eribung NSW   24 C3
Erica Vic.   53 O6
Erigolia NSW   23 N6
Erina NSW   15 R1
Erith SA   78 H3, 80 H12
Ermington NSW   10 E1, 12 E13
Ernabella SA   104 G13
Eromanga Qld   116 C9
Erriba Tas.   72 H7
Errinundra Vic.   55 L5
Erskine Park NSW   15 K8
Erskineville NSW   11 M6
Esk Qld   110 D6, 117 P10
Eskdale Vic.   62 C7
Esk Upper Tas.   73 O7
Esmond NSW   59 N4
Esperance WA   91 K12
Essendon Vic.   38 E5
Eton Qld   119 K11, 127 G13
Ettalong NSW   15 Q2, 20 F3
Ettamogah NSW   59 R4, 62 B4
Ettrick NSW   29 P2
Euabalong NSW   23 O4
Euchareena NSW   24 F4
Eucla WA   82 A11, 91 Q9
Eucumbene NSW   30 C8, 31 G5
Eudlo Qld   115 K11, 123 D10
Eudunda SA   79 K3, 81 K12
Eugowra NSW   24 D5
Eulama Qld   115 J3
Eulin WA   95 J6
Eulo Qld   116 F11
Eumundi Qld   115 K7, 123 D3
Eumungerie NSW   28 E12
Eungai Creek NSW   29 P9
Eungella NSW   113 O11, 119 K11, 127 C11
Eurack Vic.   51 Q8, 52 A8
Eurambeen Vic.   51 N2
Eureka Vic.   63 I12
Eureka Stockade Vic.   46 A9
Eurella SA   80 I4
Euroa Vic.   59 J9
Eurobin Vic.   59 Q9, 62 A9
Eurobodalla NSW   30 F8
Euroll NSW   23 L9
Eurongilly NSW   23 R10, 24 C10, 30 A5
Euston NSW   22 F9, 61 K5
Evandale Tas.   73 M8
Evansford Vic.   51 P1, 57 P13
Evans Head NSW   29 Q4
Everard Central SA   78 H2, 80 H11
Eversley Vic.   51 N1, 57 M12
Everton Vic.   59 P7, 64 I11
Ewaninga NT   105 J8
Ewans Ponds SA   50 A7, 77 H12
Ewlyamartup WA   95 N6
Exeter NSW   16 I9, 30 G4
Exeter Tas.   73 L6
Exford Vic.   44 H1, 46 H12, 52 E5
Exmouth WA   92 C10
Exton Tas.   73 J8
Eyre Peninsula SA   84

F

Fairfield Vic.   39 J7
Fairhaven Vic.   52 C10
Fairholme NSW   23 Q4, 24 A4
Fairley Vic.   57 Q2, 58 A1, 61 Q13
Fairlight NSW   13 P10
Fairney View Qld   110 G10
Fairview Vic.   57 N5
Fairview National Park SA   77 G6
Fairy Dell Vic.   58 F6
Fairy Hill NSW   29 P2
Fairy Meadow NSW   17 P4
Falls Creek NSW   25 I10, 30 H5
Falls Creek Vic.   54 C1, 62 C10
Falmouth Tas.   73 R8
Fannie Bay NT   99 K9
Faraday Vic.   46 E2, 58 D11

Farina SA 83 N8
Farleigh Qld 119 L10, 127 H11
Farley NSW 18 E3
Farmeadow NSW 17 N11
Farnborough Qld 117 N3
Farnham NSW 24 G3
Farrar WA 95 K6
Farrell Flat SA 79 J1, 81 J10
Fassifern NSW 18 G6
Fassifern Valley Qld 112 F5
Fassifern Valley National Park Qld 112 F5
Faulconbridge NSW 14 H7
Fawcett Vic. 48 F3, 59 K12
Fawkner Vic. 38 H3
Federal Qld 114 I6, 123 A1
Feilton Tas. 68 E6
Fennell Bay NSW 18 G7
Fentonbury Tas. 68 C3, 71 K5
Fentons Creek Vic. 57 O8
Fenwick Vic. 44 G8
Ferguson Vic. 51 P11
Fergusson River NT 100 G8
Fernbank Vic. 54 C8
Ferndale NSW 23 O12
Fern Hill Vic. 46 F6
Fernihurst Vic. 57 Q5, 58 A5
Fernshaw Vic. 48 E10, 53 K4
Ferntree Tas. 68 H8, 71 M7
Ferntree Gully Vic. 45 A9
Ferntree Gully Nat. Park Vic. 45 C9, 52 I6
Fernvale Qld 110 G10, 113 P11
Ferny Creek Vic. 45 C9
Ferny Glen Qld 113 M7
Fiery Flat Vic. 57 Q7, 58 A7
Fifield NSW 23 Q3, 24 B3
Fig Tree NSW 11 J2, 13 J13, 17 O5, 19 A12
Finch Hatton Qld 119 K11, 127 D11
Fine Flower Creek NSW 29 O4
Fingal Tas. 73 P9
Fingal Head NSW 113 R9
Finke NT 105 K12
Finley NSW 23 M12, 59 J1
Finniss SA 79 J9
Fish Creek Vic. 53 M12
Fisher SA 82 D9
Fishermans Bend Vic. 38 E10
Fishermans Pocket Qld 114 F2
Fish Point Vic. 61 P11
Fiskville Vic. 46 E11
Fitzgerald Tas. 68 B5, 71 J6
Fitzgerald River National Park WA 90 I12
Fitzroy SA 75 D1
Fitzroy Vic. 38 H7
Fitzroy Crossing WA 93 O6
Fitzroy Falls NSW 17 K9, 25 I9, 30 H4
Five Dock NSW 10 I4
Five Ways Vic. 43 Q1
Flagpole Hill Vic. 48 B6
Flat Rocks WA 95 L7
Flaxton Qld 115 J10, 123 C8
Flemington NSW 10 F5
Flemington Vic. 38 E7
Fleurieu Peninsula SA 78 H9
Flinders Qld 112 H2
Flinders Vic. 42 I12, 52 G10
Flinders Bay WA 94 C9
Flinders Chase National Park SA 78 B11
Flinders Island Tas. 70 A4
Flinders Peak Vic. 44 F4
Flinders Ranges National Park SA 83 O10
Flinton Qld 117 L11
Flodden Hills Qld 122 H5
Florida NSW 27 N11
Florida Gardens Qld 124 G10
Florieton SA 79 L1, 81 L10
Flowerdale Tas. 72 F4
Flowerdale Vic. 47 P6, 48 B6, 58 I13
Flowery Gully Tas. 73 K6
Flying Fox Qld 113 M7
Flynn Vic. 53 P8
Flynns Creek Vic. 53 P8
Footscray Vic. 38 E8
Forbes NSW 23 R5, 24 C5
Forcett Tas. 69 L6, 71 O6
Fords Bridge NSW 27 L5
Forest Tas. 72 D3
Forester Tas. 73 O5
Forest Glen Qld 115 K10, 123 E9

Forest Grove WA 94 C8
Forest Hill Qld 110 C12
Forest Hill Vic. 39 Q10
Forest Hill WA 95 L11
Forestier Peninsula Tas. 69 P8, 71 P7
Forestville NSW 13 M8
Forge Creek Vic. 54 E8
Forrest ACT 34 C13
Forrest Vic. 51 Q10, 52 A10
Forrest WA 91 P8
Forresters Beach NSW 18 F13
Forrest River Aboriginal Reserve WA 93 Q2
Forsayth Qld 118 C6
Forster NSW 25 N2, 29 N13
Forster SA 79 M5
Fort Grey NSW 122 G13
Forth Tas. 72 H6
Fortitude Valley Qld 109 C1
Foster Vic. 53 N11
Fosterville Vic. 58 D9
Fountain Head NT 100 F6
Foxdale Qld 127 C5
Fox Ground NSW 17 O9
Foxhow Vic. 51 O7
Fox Valley NSW 12 G6
Framingham Vic. 51 K8
Frampton NSW 24 C10, 30 B4
Frances SA 56 B9, 77 I6
Frankford Tas. 73 K7
Frankland WA 90 G13, 95 K9
Franklin Tas. 68 F10, 71 L8
Franklinford Vic. 46 C5, 52 C1, 57 R13, 58 B13
Frankston Vic. 41 P7, 43 L1, 52 H8
Frankton SA 79 K3, 81 K12
Fraser Island Qld 117 Q6
Fraser National Park Vic. 48 G3, 59 L12
Frazerview Qld 112 E5
Frederickton NSW 29 P9
Freeburgh Vic. 59 R9, 62 B9
Freeling SA 79 J4, 81 J13
Fremantle WA 90 E10
French Island Vic. 43 Q7, 52 I9
Frenchmans Cap National Park Tas. 70 F3, 72 F13
Freemans Reach NSW 15 K4
Freemans Waterholes NSW 18 E7
Freestone Upper Qld 112 A7
Frenchmans Vic. 57 N11
Frenchs Forest NSW 13 M7
Freshwater Creek Vic. 44 E9, 52 D8
Freycinet National Park Tas. 71 R2, 73 R13
Freycinet Peninsula Tas. 73 R13
Frogmore NSW 24 F8, 30 D3
Fryerstown Vic. 46 E3
Fulham Vic. 53 R7, 54 B10
Fulham Vale Qld 110 D4
Fullerton NSW 24 H8, 30 F2
Fumina Vic. 53 M6
Furner SA 77 F9
Furracabad NSW 29 L5
Fyans Creek Vic. 57 J12
Fyansford Vic. 44 E7, 63 A1

G

Gabo Island Vic. 55 P6
Gadara NSW 24 D11, 30 B6
Gaffneys Creek Vic. 53 N3
Galah Vic. 60 H9
Galaquil Vic. 56 I4
Galga SA 79 N5
Galiwinku NT 101 N3
Gallanan Qld 110 D6
Gallangowan Qld 114 C6
Galong NSW 24 E9, 30 C4
Galore NSW 23 P10
Galston NSW 12 C2
Galway Downs Qld 122 I5
Gama Vic. 61 J12
Gammon Ranges National Park SA 83 O9
Gannawarra Vic. 58 C2
Gap NSW 29 J10
Gapsted Vic. 59 P8
Garah NSW 28 G3, 117 L13
Garden Island Creek Tas. 68 G13, 71 L9
Gardner Plateau WA 93 O3
Gardners Bay Tas. 68 G12, 71 L9
Garema NSW 24 C5

Garfield Vic. 53 K7
Gargett Qld 127 E12
Garibaldi Vic. 46 A12, 51 R4, 52 B5
Garie NSW 15 O13, 17 Q1, 25 K8, 30 I2
Garland NSW 24 F6, 30 D1
Garra NSW 24 E4
Garrawilla NSW 28 G9
Garvoc Vic. 51 L9
Gascoyne Junction WA 90 D2
Gateshead NSW 18 H6
Gatton Qld 110 B11, 117 P10
Gatum Vic. 50 G2
Gawler SA 79 J5
Gayndah Qld 117 O7
Gazette Vic. 50 I6
Geehi NSW 30 B9, 31 B9, 62 H7
Geelong Vic. 44 E7, 52 D8, 63
Geelong East Vic. 63 H3
Geelong South Vic. 63 F4
Geelong West Vic. 63 D1
Geeralying WA 95 K2
Geeveston Tas. 68 E11, 71 K9
Geikie Gorge National Park WA 93 O6
Geilston Bay Tas. 67 G4
Gelantipy Vic. 62 I13, 54 H3
Gellibrand Vic. 51 P10
Gelliondale Vic. 53 P11
Gembrook Vic. 173 J6
Gemstones Qld 122 I2
Genoa Vic. 30 E12, 55 N5
Georges Creek Vic. 62 C5
Georges Hall NSW 10 B9
Georges Heights NSW 11 P1, 13 P12
Georges Plains NSW 24 G5
Georgetown Qld 118 C6
Georgetown SA 80 H8
George Town Tas. 73 K5
Georgica NSW 29 Q2
Geraldton WA 90 D6
Gerangamete Vic. 51 Q10, 52 A10
Gerang Gerung Vic. 56 F7
Geranium SA 79 O9
Geranium Plains SA 79 K2, 81 K11
Gerogery NSW 23 P12, 59 R3, 62 B3
Gerringong NSW 17 O10, 25 J9, 30 I4
Gerroa NSW 17 O10
Geurie NSW 24 E2, 28 E13
Gheerulla Qld 114 H8
Gheringhap Vic. 44 D6, 52 C7
Ghin Ghin Vic. 47 Q3, 48 B3, 58 I12
Gibraltar Range National Park NSW 29 N4
Gibson WA 91 K11
Gibson Desert WA 91 O1, 93 L11
Gidginbung NSW 23 Q8, 24 B8, 30 A3
Giffard Vic. 53 R10, 54 B12
Gilberton Vic. 75 G2
Gilbert River Qld 118 B5, 121 I4
Gilderoy Vic. 48 F13, 53 K6
Gildora Qld 114 G4
Giles Corner SA 78 I3, 80 I12
Gilgai NSW 29 K5
Gilgandra NSW 28 E11
Gilgooma NSW 28 E8
Gilgunnia NSW 23 M2, 27 M13
Gilliat Qld 121 G8
Gillieston Vic. 58 H6
Gillingal Vic. 54 H4
Gilmore NSW 24 D11, 30 B6
Gilpeppee Qld 122 G7
Gilston Qld 113 O6
Gindie Qld 117 J4
Gin Gin NSW 27 R12, 28 D12
Gin Gin Qld 117 O6
Gingin WA 90 E9
Gingkin NSW 14 A11, 24 H7, 30 G1
Ginquam Vic. 60 G4
Gippsland Lakes Park Vic. 54 E10
Gipsy Point Vic. 30 F12, 55 O5
Girgarre Vic. 58 G7
Girilambone NSW 27 P10, 28 A9
Girral NSW 23 P6
Giru Qld 118 I8
Gisborne Vic. 46 I8, 52 E3
Gladesville NSW 10 I12, 11 J2, 12 I13, 13 J13
Gladfield Qld 112 A6
Gladfield Vic. 57 Q4, 58 B4
Gladstone Qld 117 N4
Gladstone SA 80 H7

Gladstone Tas. 73 Q4
Gladysdale Vic. 48 F13, 53 K5
Glamis NSW 29 M11
Glamorgan Vale Qld 110 F10
Glasshouse Mountains Qld 111 K1
Glastonbury Qld 114 E3
Glaziers Bay Tas. 68 F11
Glebe NSW 11 L5
Glebe Tas. 67 E8
Glenaire Vic. 51 O12
Glenaladale Vic. 54 C7
Glenaladale National Park Vic. 54 D7
Glenalbyn Vic. 57 P7, 58 A7
Glen Alice NSW 24 I4
Glen Aplin Qld 29 M2
Glenapp Qld 113 J10
Glenariff NSW 27 O8
Glenaroua Vic. 47 L3, 58 G12
Glenbrae Vic. 51 P2
Glenbrook NSW 14 I8
Glenburn Vic. 47 Q7, 48 C7, 53 J2
Glenburnie SA 50 B6, 77 H11
Glencairn Vic. 53 P3
Glencoe NSW 29 M6
Glencoe SA 77 G11
Glen Creek Vic. 59 R7, 62 B7
Glen Davis NSW 24 I4
Glendevie Tas. 68 F13, 71 L9
Glendinning Vic. 50 G2
Glendon NSW 18 B1
Glendon Brook NSW 25 K2
Gleneagle Qld 113 K4
Glenelg SA 76 B11, 85 G7
Glen Elgin NSW 29 N5
Glenelg National Park Vic. 50 D8
Glen Esk Qld 110 E6
Glenfern Qld 110 F2
Glen Fern Tas. 68 F6, 71 L6
Glenfield NSW 15 M10
Glenfyne Vic. 51 M10
Glengarrie NSW 113 P9
Glengarry Tas. 73 K7
Glengarry Vic. 53 P8
Glen Geddes Qld 117 M2
Glengower Vic. 46 A5, 51 Q1, 52 A1, 57 Q13, 58 A13
Glengyle Qld 122 D5
Glenhaven NSW 12 A5, 15 M6
Glen Helen NT 104 H8
Glenhope Vic. 58 E12
Glenhuntly Vic. 39 L13, 40 C11
Glen Huon Tas. 68 E9, 71 K8
Glen Innes NSW 29 M5
Glen Iris Vic. 39 L11, 40 A9
Glenisla Vic. 50 I1, 56 H13
Glenlee Vic. 56 F6
Glenlofty Vic. 57 N12
Glenloth Vic. 57 N5
Glenluce Vic. 46 E4, 52 C1, 58 C12
Glenlusk Tas. 68 H6, 71 M6
Glenlyon Qld 29 L2
Glenlyon Vic. 46 E5, 52 C1, 58 C13
Glenmaggie Vic. 53 Q6
Glenmaggie Reservoir Vic. 53 Q6, 54 A8
Glenmore NSW 14 I12
Glenmore Vic. 44 E1, 46 F11
Glenmorgan Qld 117 L10
Glen Oak NSW 18 G1
Glenora Tas. 68 E4, 71 K6
Glenoran WA 94 G8
Glenorchy Tas. 68 I6, 71 M7
Glenorchy Vic. 57 K10
Glenore Grove Qld 110 D11
Glenorie NSW 15 M4
Glenormiston Qld 122 B2
Glen Osmond SA 76 F10
Glen Park Vic. 39 O2, 46 B9
Glenpatrick Vic. 57 N12
Glenquarry NSW 17 K7
Glenreagh NSW 29 P6
Glenrowan Vic. 59 N7, 64 C13
Glenroy SA 56 A13, 50 A1, 77 H8
Glenroy Vic. 38 E3
Glenshee Vic. 57 N12
Glenthompson Vic. 51 K4
Glenvale Vic. 47 N8
Glen Valley Vic. 54 D1, 62 E10
Glenwarning NSW 113 N12

Glen Waverley Vic. 39 P13, 40 B4
Glen Wills Vic. 54 E1, 62 E10
Glenworth Valley NSW 15 O2
Glossodia NSW 15 K4
Glossop SA 79 P3, 81 P12
Gloucester NSW 25 M1, 29 M12
Gloucester Park WA 87 H5
Gnar-Purt Vic. 51 O7
Gnarraloo WA 92 C13
Gnarraloo Bay WA 92 C13
Gnarwarre Vic. 44 C7
Gnotuk Vic. 51 N8
Gnowangerup WA 90 G12, 95 O7
Goangra NSW 98 D6
Gobarralong NSW 24 D10, 30 B5
Gobongo Qld 114 A5
Gobur Vic. 48 E1, 59 K11
Gocup NSW 24 D10, 30 B5
Godfreys Creek NSW 24 E7, 30 C2
Gogango Qld 117 M4
Golconda Tas. 73 M5
Gold Coast Qld 124-5
Golden Beach Qld 115 M12, 123 H12
Golden Beach Vic. 54 D11
Golden Point Vic. 46 E2
Golden Valley Tas. 73 J9
Goldsborough Vic. 57 P10
Goldsmith Tas. 71 M1, 73 M11
Goldsworthy WA 92 H8
Golf Hill Vic. 44 C5
Gol Gol NSW 22 E8, 60 H2
Gollan NSW 24 F2, 28 F13
Golspie NSW 16 A5, 24 G8, 30 F3
Gomersal SA 85 B6
Gongolgon NSW 27 P7, 28 A7
Gonn Crossing Vic. 61 Q12
Good Hope NSW 24 E10, 30 D4
Goodilla NT 100 E6
Goodings Corner Qld 113 P6
Goodnight NSW 61 N8
Goodooga NSW 27 Q3, 28 B3, 116 I13
Goodwood Tas. 67 B2
Goolgowi NSW 23 M7
Goolma NSW 24 F2, 28 F13
Goolmangar NSW 29 Q2
Gooloogong NSW 24 D6, 30 C1
Goolwa SA 79 J9
Goomalibee Vic. 59 L7
Goomalling WA 90 F9
Goomboorian Qld 114 I1
Goomeri Qld 117 O8
Goomong Qld 114 H5
Goondah NSW 24 E9, 30 D4
Goondiwindi Qld 28 I1, 117 M12
Goondooloo SA 79 N6
Goonellabah NSW 29 Q3
Goongerah Vic. 55 K4
Goon Nure Vic. 54 D9
Goonumbla NSW 23 R4, 24 D4
Gooram Vic. 59 K10
Goorambat Vic. 59 L7
Goornong Vic. 58 E8
Gooroc Vic. 57 M7
Gooulgen Qld 117 M4
Goowarra Qld 117 L3
Gorae Vic. 50 E9
Gordon NSW 13 J8
Gordon SA 80 G1
Gordon Tas. 68 H13, 71 M9
Gordon Vic. 46 C10, 52 C4
Gordon River Tas. 70 F5
Gordonvale Qld 118 G4, 126 G10
Gore Hill NSW 13 L12
Gormandale Vic. 53 P9
Gormanston Tas. 70 E1, 72 E11
Gorokan NSW 18 F11
Goroke Vic. 56 D9
Goschen Vic. 61 O12
Gosford NSW 15 Q1, 18 E13, 20 A2, 25 K5
Gosforth NSW 18 D2
Goshen Tas. 73 Q6
Gough Bay Vic. 53 M1, 59 M12
Goulburn NSW 16 C12, 24 G9, 30 F4
Goulburn Island NT 100 I3
Goulburn Weir Vic. 58 H9
Goulds Country Tas. 73 Q6
Gove Peninsula NT 101 P4
Gowanford Vic. 61 M11

Gowangardie Vic. 59 K7
Gowar Vic. 57 R11, 58 C11
Gowrie Park Tas. 72 H7
Goyura Vic. 56 I2
Grabben Gullen NSW 24 G8, 30 E3
Gracefield WA 95 L8
Gracetown WA 94 B6
Gradgery NSW 27 R10, 28 C9
Gradule Qld 28 G1, 117 K12
Grafton NSW 29 P5
Graham NSW 24 E7, 30 D2
Graham Range National Park Qld 126 I13
Grahamstown NSW 24 C11, 30 B6
Grahamvale Vic. 59 J6
Graman NSW 29 K4
Grampians Mountains Vic. 57 J13
Grandchester Qld 110 D13
Grange SA 76 A8
Granite Vic. 47 O3, 48 A3, 58 H12
Granite Flat Vic. 62 D8
Grantham Qld 110 A11
Granton Tas. 68 H5, 71 M6
Grantville Vic. 53 J10
Granville NSW 10 C3
Granville Harbour Tas. 72 C10
Granya Vic. 62 D5
Grassdale Vic. 50 F5
Grass Flat Vic. 56 F9
Grassmere Vic. 51 K9
Gravesend NSW 28 I5
Grawin NSW 27 Q5, 28 C4
Gray Tas. 73 Q9
Grays Point NSW 15 O11
Graytown Vic. 58 G10
Great Australian Bight SA 82 B12
Great Keppel Island Qld 117 N3
Great Lake Tas. 73 J10
Great Northern Vic. 59 O4
Great Ocean Road Vic. 51 L11, 52 A12
Great Palm Island Qld 118 H6
Great Sandy Desert WA 93 L8
Great Victoria Desert WA 91 N6
Great Western Vic. 57 L12
Gredgwin Vic. 57 P4
Greenacre NSW 10 F7
Greenbank Qld 113 K1
Greenbushes WA 90 E12, 94 G6
Greendale NSW 15 J10
Greendale Qld 114 E2
Greendale Vic. 46 F9, 52 D3
Greenethorpe NSW 24 D7, 30 C2
Greengrove NSW 15 O1, 18 B13
Green Gully Vic. 46 C3
Green Hill Vic. 46 G4
Green Island Qld 126 H2
Green Lake Vic. 56 I10, 57 L1, 61 L13
Greenmount Vic. 53 P11
Greenock SA 79 J4, 81 J13, 85 C2
Green Pigeon NSW 113 L13
Green Point NSW 15 Q2, 20 C1
Greenridge Qld 114 H5
Greens Beach Tas. 73 K5
Greensborough Vic. 39 M2
Greens Creek Vic. 57 L11
Greenvale Vic. 47 L10
Green Valley WA 95 N12
Greenwald Vic. 50 D7
Greenways SA 77 F8
Greenwell Point NSW 17 O12, 25 J10, 30 H5
Greenwich NSW 11 L2, 13 L13
Greenwich Park NSW 16 E9
Greg Greg NSW 30 B8
Gregors Creek Qld 110 D2
Gregory Downs Qld 121 C5
Gre Gre Vic. 57 M9
Greigs Flat NSW 30 F11
Grenfell NSW 24 D6, 30 B1
Grenville Vic. 46 A12, 51 R5, 52 B5
Gresford NSW 25 L2
Greta NSW 18 D2
Greta Vic. 59 N8
Gretna Tas. 68 E4, 71 K5
Grevillia NSW 29 O1, 112 I12
Grey Peaks National Park Qld 126 G9
Griffin WA 94 G4
Griffith NSW 23 N8
Grimwade WA 94 G6
Gringegalgona Vic. 50 G3

139

Gritjurk Vic.   50 F4
Grogan NSW   23 R8, 24 C8, 30 A3
Grong Grong NSW   23 O9
Groote Eylandt NT   101 P8
Grose Vale NSW   14 I5
Grose Wold NSW   14 I5
Grosvenor Qld   117 N7
Grove Tas.   68 G9, 71 L8
Grovedale Vic.   44 E8, 52 D8
Grove Hill NT   100 F6
Gruyere Vic.   47 R12, 48 C12, 53 J5
Gubbata NSW   23 O6
Guichen Bay National Park SA   77 D8
Guildford NSW   10 B5
Guildford Tas.   72 F7
Guildford Vic.   46 D3, 58 C12
Guildford WA   96 D11
Gular Rail NSW   28 E10
Gulargambone NSW   28 E10
Gulf Country Qld   121
Gulf Creek NSW   29 J6
Gulgong NSW   24 G2, 28 G13
Gulnare SA   80 H8
Gulpa NSW   23 K12
Gumble NSW   24 E4
Gumbowie SA   81 J6
Gum Creek SA   81 J9
Gumeracha SA   79 J6
Gum Lake NSW   22 G3
Gumlu Qld   118 I8
Gumly Gumly NSW   24 B10
Gunbar South NSW   23 L7
Gunbower Vic.   23 J13, 58 D3
Gundagai NSW   23 R10, 24 C10, 30 B5
Gundaring WA   95 L3
Gundaroo NSW   24 F10, 30 E5
Gunderman NSW   15 N2
Gundowring Vic.   59 R7, 62 B7
Gundurimba South NSW   29 Q3
Gundy NSW   25 K1, 29 K12
Gunebang NSW   23 O4
Gungal NSW   24 I2, 28 I13
Gunnary NSW   24 E8, 30 D3
Gunnedah NSW   28 I9
Gunner Vic.   60 F10
Gunnewin Qld   117 J7
Gunning NSW   24 F9, 30 E4
Gunningbland NSW   24 C4
Gunning Grach NSW   30 D10
Gunns Plains Tas.   72 G6
Gunpowder Creek Qld   121 C7
Gunyah Vic.   53 N10
Gunyarra Qld   127 D6
Gurley NSW   28 H5
Gurrai SA   79 P7
Gurrundah NSW   24 G9, 30 E4
Guthalungra Qld   119 J8
Guthega NSW   31 D8
Guy Fawkes National Park NSW   29 N6
Guyra NSW   29 M7
Guys Forest Vic.   62 F4
Gwabegar NSW   28 F8
Gwandalan NSW   18 G9
Gwandalan Tas.   67 D2, 69 M9, 71 O8
Gwongorella National Park Qld   113 O8
Gwynneville NSW   19 D9
Gymbowen Vic.   56 E9
Gymea NSW   15 O11
Gympie Qld   114 G3, 117 P8
Gypsum Vic.   60 I10

H

Haasts Bluff NT   104 G7
Haasts Bluff Aboriginal Reserve NT   104 C8
Habana Qld   127 H11
Haberfield NSW   11 J5
Hackett ACT   34 I4
Hackham SA   85 G11
Hackney SA   75 H5
Haddon Vic.   51 Q4
Haden Qld   117 O10
Hadspen Tas.   73 L8
Hagley Tas.   73 K8
Hahndorf SA   79 J7
Haig WA   91 N9
Haigslea Qld   110 F11

Hakea WA   94 H1
Halbury SA   78 I2, 80 I11
Haldon East Qld   112 A3
Hale Village Qld   113 K6
Halfway Creek NSW   29 P6
Halidon SA   79 O6
Halifax Qld   118 G6
Hall ACT   24 F10, 30 D5
Hallett SA   81 J8
Hallidays Point NSW   25 N1, 29 N13
Halls Creek WA   93 Q6
Halls Gap Vic.   51 J1, 57 J12
Hallston Vic.   53 M9
Halton NSW   25 L2, 29 L13
Hamel WA   94 F1
Hamelin Bay WA   94 C8
Hamelin Pool WA   90 C3
Hamersley Range WA   92 F10
Hamersley Range National Park WA   92 G11
Hamilton NSW   19 E7, 18 H5
Hamilton SA   79 J3, 81 J12
Hamilton Tas.   68 D2, 71 K5
Hamilton Vic.   50 H5
Hamilton Gate NSW   26 G3
Hamilton Hotel Qld   122 E1
Hamley Bridge SA   78 I4, 80 I13
Hammond SA   80 H4
Hammond Downs Qld   122 I6
Hammondville NSW   10 A11
Hampden SA   79 K3, 81 K12
Hampshire Tas.   72 F6
Hampton NSW   14 B7, 30 G1
Hampton Qld   117 O10
Hampton Vic.   40 E12
Hanging Rock Vic.   46 I6
Hannahs Bridge NSW   28 G12
Hansborough SA   79 K3, 81 K12
Hanson SA   79 J1, 81 J10
Hansonville Vic.   59 N8
Hanwood NSW   23 N8
Happy Valley SA   85 I9
Happy Valley Vic.   51 P5, 53 R2, 59 Q8, 61 K6
Harbord NSW   13 Q8
Harcourt Vic.   46 E1, 58 C11
Harden NSW   24 D8, 30 C3
Hardwicke Bay SA   84 I13
Hardys Beach NSW   15 Q3
Harefield NSW   24 B10, 30 A5
Harewood WA   95 L12
Harford Tas.   73 J6
Hargraves NSW   24 G3
Harkaway Vic.   52 I7
Harlin Qld   110 C2
Harrietville Vic.   54 B1, 59 R10, 62 B10
Harrington NSW   25 O1, 29 O12
Harris Park NSW   10 C2
Harrismith WA   95 N2
Harrisville Qld   112 G3
Harrow Vic.   50 E1, 56 E13
Harrys Creek Vic.   59 K9
Harston Vic.   58 H7
Hart SA   78 H1, 80 H10
Hartley NSW   14 D5, 24 H6, 30 G1
Hartley Vale NSW   14 D5
Hartz Mountains National Park Tas.   68 A13, 71 J9
Harvey WA   94 F2
Harveys Siding Qld   114 G1
Harwood Island NSW   29 Q4
Haslam SA   84 B7
Hastings Tas.   71 K10
Hastings Vic.   43 N6, 52 H9
Hastings Point NSW   29 R1, 113 R11
Hatfield NSW   22 H7
Hatherleigh SA   77 F10
Hattah Vic.   60 H7
Hattah Kulkyne National Park Vic.   60 H6
Hatton Vale Qld   110 D11
Havelock Vic.   57 Q11, 58 A11
Haven Vic.   56 H9
Havilah Vic.   59 R8, 62 A8
Hawker SA   80 H1, 83 N11
Hawkesbury River NSW   20 H8
Hawkesdale West Vic.   50 I7
Hawks Nest NSW   25 M3
Hawthorn Vic.   39 J9
Hay NSW   23 K8
Haydens Bog Vic.   55 K3

Hayes Tas.   68 F5, 71 L6
Hayes Creek NT   100 E7
Hayman Island Qld   119 K9, 127 F2
Haymarket NSW   8 C10
Hay River WA   95 L12
Haysdale Vic.   61 N7
Hazel Park Vic.   53 N11
Hazelbrook NSW   14 G7
Hazeldene Qld   110 F3
Hazeldene Vic.   47 P6, 48 B6, 52 I2, 58 I13
Hazelmere WA   96 F12
Hazelwood Vic.   53 N9
Healesville Vic.   47 R10, 48 D10, 53 J4
Healesville Sanctuary Vic.   48 D11
Heartlea WA   94 I8
Heathcote Vic.   58 F10
Heathcote Junction Vic.   47 M6
Heatherton Vic.   40 F8
Heathfield Vic.   50 C4
Heath Hill Vic.   53 K8
Heathmere Vic.   50 F8
Hebel Qld   27 R2, 28 C2, 116 I13
Hebden NSW   25 K2, 29 K13
Heddon Greta NSW   18 E4
Hedley Vic.   53 O11
Heidelberg Vic.   39 L6
Heigh Ridge Qld   114 H6
Heiling NT   100 G8
Heka Tas.   72 G6
Helena Valley WA   96 I13
Helensburgh NSW   15 N3, 17 P1
Henbury Meteorite Craters NT   104 I10
Henley NSW   11 J3
Henley Beach SA   76 A8
Henley Brook WA   96 E5
Henrietta Tas.   72 F5
Hensley Park Vic.   50 H4
Henty NSW   23 P11
Henty Vic.   50 E4
Hepburn Lagoon Vic.   46 B7
Hepburn Springs Vic.   46 D6, 52 C2, 58 C13
Herbert Downs Qld   122 C2
Herberton Qld   118 F4, 120 I13
Herbert Vale Qld   118 G6
Hermannsburg Mission NT   104 H8
Hermidale NSW   27 O11
Hermitage Tas.   71 K3, 73 K13
Hernani NSW   29 N7
Herne Hill Vic.   63 C1
Herne Hill WA   96 H6
Heron Island Qld   117 P2
Herons Creek NSW   29 O11
Herrick Tas.   73 P5
Herring Lagoon Qld   111 Q12
Hervey Bay Qld   117 Q6
Hesketh Vic.   46 I6
Hesso SA   80 D2, 83 M12, 84 I6
Hester WA   94 G7
Hewetsons Mill NSW   29 O1
Hexham NSW   18 G4
Hexham Vic.   51 K7
Heybridge Tas.   72 G5
Heyfield Vic.   53 Q6, 54 A9
Heytesbury Lower Vic.   51 M11
Heywood Vic.   50 F8
Hiamdale Vic.   53 P9
Hiawatha Vic.   53 O10
Hibiscus Coast Qld   117 N3, 119 L11, 127 H11
Hidden Vale Qld   110 D13, 112 D1
Higginsville WA   91 J9
Highbury WA   90 G11, 95 L2
High Camp Vic.   47 L4, 52 G1, 58 G12
Highclere Tas.   72 F6
Highcroft Tas.   67 E5, 69 N11, 71 O9
Highett Vic.   40 F11
Highgate WA   87 F2
Highgate Hill Qld   109 B11
Highlands Vic.   47 Q2, 48 C2, 58 I12
High Range NSW   16 I5, 24 I8, 30 G3
Highton Vic.   44 E7, 63 B4
Highvale Qld   110 I8
Hilgay Vic.   50 E4
Hillcrest Vic.   51 P4
Hill End NSW   24 G4
Hill End Vic.   53 M7
Hillgrove NSW   29 M8
Hillman WA   95 J3
Hillmanville SA   79 N4, 81 N13

Hillsdale NSW 11 O9
Hillston NSW 23 L5
Hilltop NSW 17 K4
Hilltown SA 80 I9
Hillview NSW 27 M11
Hillview Qld 113 K9
Hillwood Tas. 73 L6
Hinchinbrook Island Qld 118 G6
Hincks Recreation Park SA 84 F10
Hindmarsh SA 75 A3, 76 D7
Hindmarsh Island SA 79 J9
Hinnomunjie Vic. 54 E2, 62 F11
Hinton NSW 18 G2
Hirstglen Qld 117 O11
HMAS Albatross NSW 17 M13
Hobart Tas. 67 F9, 68 I7, 71 M7
Hobart Airport Tas. 69 K6
Hobbys Yards NSW 24 F6, 30 E1
Hoddle Vic. 53 M12
Hoddles Creek Vic. 48 E13, 53 J5
Hoffmans Mill WA 94 G2
Holbrook NSW 23 Q12, 62 D2
Holder SA 79 N3, 81 N13
Holey Plains State Park Vic. 53 Q8, 54 A10
Holgate NSW 15 R1, 18 E13
Holloways Beach Qld 126 F6
Hollow Tree Tas. 68 E1, 71 K4
Hollywell Qld 113 P4
Holly WA 95 M6
Holmesville NSW 18 F5
Holmwood NSW 24 E6, 30 D1
Holts Flat NSW 30 E10
Holwell Tas. 73 K6
Homebush NSW 10 G5
Homebush Qld 127 G13
Homecroft Vic. 57 J6
Home Hill Qld 118 I8
Homerton Vic. 50 F8
Homestead Qld 118 F9
Homewood Vic. 47 P4, 48 B4, 52 I1, 58 I12
Hooker Creek NT 102 D7
Hooker Creek Aboriginal Res. NT 102 C6
Hook Island Qld 119 K9
Hopetoun Vic. 22 E13, 56 I2, 60 I13
Hopetoun WA 90 I12
Hopevale Vic. 56 H3
Hope Vale Mission Qld 120 H9
Hordern Vale Vic. 51 P12
Hornsby NSW 12 F5, 25 K6
Hornsdale SA 80 I6
Horse Lake NSW 22 D1, 26 D13
Horseshoe Creek NT 100 G8
Horsham Vic. 56 H9
Horsley Park NSW 15 L8
Hoskinstown NSW 24 G11, 30 E6
Hotham Heights Vic. 62 C11
Hotspur Vic. 50 E6
Howard Qld 117 P7
Howard Island NT 101 M4
Howard Springs NT 100 E4
Howden Tas. 71 M8
Howder Tas. 68 I9
Howes Valley NSW 25 J3
Howley NT 100 E6
Howlong NSW 23 O13, 59 P4, 64 G1
Howqua Vic. 53 M1, 59 M13
Howrah Tas. 69 J7
Hoxton Park NSW 15 L10
Hoyleton SA 78 I2, 80 I11
Huddleston SA 80 H8
Hughenden Qld 118 D10
Hughes SA 82 B9
Hume Park NSW 24 E10, 30 D4
Hume Range Vic. 47 N7
Humevale Vic. 47 O8, 52 H3
Hume Weir NSW & Vic. 23 P13, 24 A13, 59 R5, 62 B5
Humpty Doo NT 100 E5
Humula NSW 23 R11, 24 C11, 30 A6
Hunchy Qld 115 J10, 123 C9
Hungerford NSW 26 I3, 116 E13
Hunter Vic. 58 E7
Hunter Island Tas. 72 A1
Hunters Hill NSW 11 J2, 13 J13
Hunterston Vic. 53 Q11, 54 A13
Hunter Valley NSW 25 M3
Huntly Vic. 58 D9
Huon Vic. 59 R5, 62 B5

Huon Valley Tas. 68 G8-F9
Huonville Tas. 68 F9, 71 L8
Hurdle Flat Vic. 59 Q7, 62 A7
Hurlstone Park NSW 11 J7
Hurstbridge Vic. 47 O10, 48 A10, 52 H4
Hurstville NSW 10 I11
Hurstville Grove NSW 10 I12
Huskisson NSW 25 J10, 30 H5
Hyams Beach NSW 25 J10, 30 H5
Hyden WA 90 H10
Hynam SA 56 A11, 77 H7
Hythe Tas. 71 L11

I

Icy Creek Vic. 53 M6
Ida Bay Tas. 71 K11
Iguana Creek Vic. 54 D7
Ilbilbie Qld 119 L12
Ilford NSW 24 H4
Ilfracombe Qld 116 E3
Illabarook Vic. 51 P5
Illabo NSW 24 C9, 30 A4
Illalong Creek NSW 24 E9, 30 C4
Illawarra NSW 17 K8
Illawarra Vic. 57 K12
Illawarra Coast NSW 25 L10
Illilliwa NSW 23 K8
Illowa Vic. 51 J9
Iluka NSW 29 Q4
Image Flat Qld 115 J9, 123 C7
Imbil Qld 114 G7, 117 P9
Impimi NSW 22 H9
Indented Head Vic. 44 I7, 52 F7
Indigo Vic. 59 P4
Ingalta SA 60 A4
Ingebyra NSW 30 C10, 31 E12
Ingham Qld 118 G6
Ingleburn NSW 15 M10
Inglegar NSW 27 R10, 28 C10
Inglehope WA 94 G1
Ingleside NSW 13 O2
Ingleside Qld 113 P8
Inglewood Qld 29 K1, 117 N12
Inglewood SA 56 A6, 79 Q12, 77 H3
Inglewood Vic. 57 Q8, 58 A8
Ingliston Vic. 46 E10, 52 D4
Ingoldsby Qld 110 B13, 112 B1
Injune Qld 117 J7
Inkerman SA 78 H3, 80 H12
Inkerman Qld 118 I8
Innamincka SA 83 R4, 122 F10
Innes National Park SA. 84 G13
Inneston SA 78 C8, 84 H13
Innisfail Qld 118 G4
Innisplain Qld 113 J8
Innot Hot Springs Qld 118 F5, 120 I13
Intaburra Qld 127 A3
Interlaken Tas. 71 M2, 73 M12
Inveralochy NSW 24 G10, 30 F5
Inverell NSW 29 K5
Invergordon Vic. 59 J5
Inverleigh Vic. 44 B7, 52 B7
Inverloch Vic. 53 K11
Invermay Vic. 46 A9
Inverramsay Qld 112 B5
Iona NSW 18 F2
Iona Vic. 53 K7
Ipswich Qld 110 H12, 117 P11
Iraak Vic. 60 I4
Irishtown Tas. 72 C4
Irishtown NSW 14 A3
Iron Baron SA 80 D6, 83 L13, 84 H8
Irondale NSW 14 A3
Iron Knob SA 80 C5, 83 M13, 84 H7
Iron Range Qld 120 E4
Irrewarra Vic. 51 P9
Irrewillipe Vic. 51 O10
Irymple Vic. 60 H3
Isabella NSW 24 G7, 30 F2
Isisford Qld 116 E4
Island Bend NSW 30 C9, 31 E7
Isle of Capri Qld 124 G10
Ivanhoe NSW 22 I3
Ivanhoe Vic. 39 K6
Ivory Creek Qld 110 C3

J

Jabiru NT 100 H5
Jabuk SA 79 N9
Jackadgery NSW 29 O5
Jackeys Marsh Tas. 73 J9
Jack River Vic. 53 P11
Jackson Qld 117 L9
Jacobs Well Qld 113 P2
Jallukar Vic. 51 K1, 57 K13
Jallumba Vic. 56 G11
Jaloran WA 95 L3
Jamberoo NSW 17 O8, 25 J9, 30 I4
Jambin Qld 117 M4
Jamestown SA 80 I7
Jamieson Vic. 53 M2, 59 M13
Jancourt Vic. 51 N9
Jandowae Qld 117 N9
Jan Juc Vic. 44 E10
Jardee WA 94 G9
Jarklin Vic. 57 R6, 58 B6
Jarrahwood WA 90 D12, 94 E6
Jarvis Creek Vic. 62 C5
Jaspers Brush NSW 17 N11
Jaurdi WA 90 I8
Jay Creek Aboriginal Reserve NT 104 I8
Jeebrapilly Qld 110 G12
Jeerlang North Vic. 53 O9
Jeffcott Vic. 57 M6
Jeffries Vic. 56 G12
Jemalong NSW 24 C5
Jenolan Caves NSW 14 B10, 30 G1
Jeogla NSW 29 N8
Jepant Vic. 56 G5
Jericho Tas. 71 M4
Jerangle NSW 30 E7
Jericho Vic. 53 N4
Jericho Qld 116 G3
Jerilderie NSW 23 M11
Jerramungup WA 90 H12, 95 R7
Jerrara NSW 17 O9
Jerrawa NSW 24 F9, 30 D4
Jerrys Plains NSW 25 J2
Jerseyville NSW 29 P9
Jervis Bay ACT 25 J10, 30 H5
Jervois SA 79 L8
Jessie SA 56 B11
Jetsonville Tas. 73 N5
Jigalong Aboriginal Reserve WA 93 J12
Jiliby NSW 18 E11
Jil Jil Vic. 57 L3
Jimboomba Qld 113 K3
Jimbour Qld 117 N9
Jimenbuen NSW 30 D10
Jimna Qld 114 D10
Jindabyne NSW 30 C9, 31 G9
Jindera NSW 59 Q3, 62 A3
Jindivick Vic. 53 L7
Jindong WA 94 C6
Jingalup WA 95 K7
Jingarry Qld 112 A9
Jingellic NSW 23 Q13, 30 A7, 62 F3
Jingili NT 98 C2
Jip Jip National Park SA 77 F5
Jitarning WA 95 O1
Joadja NSW 16 H6, 24 H8, 30 G3
Joanna SA 50 B1, 56 A12, 77 H8
Joel Joel Vic. 57 M11
Joel South Vic. 57 M12
Johanna Vic. 51 O12
Johnberg SA 80 I3
Johnsonville Vic. 54 F8
Jondaryan Qld 117 O10
Josbury WA 95 J2
Josephville Qld 113 J6
Joslin SA 75 I2
Joyces Creek Vic. 46 B2, 57 R12, 58 B12
Judbury Tas. 68 E9, 71 K8
Jugiong NSW 24 D9, 30 C4
Julatten Qld 126 A3
Julia SA 79 K2, 81 K12
Julia Creek Qld 118 A10, 121 G8
Jumbuk Vic. 53 O10
Jumbunna Vic. 53 K10
Junction View Qld 112 A2
Jundah Qld 116 C6, 122 I5
Jung Vic. 56 I8
Junee NSW 23 Q9, 24 B9, 30 A4
Junortoun Vic. 58 D9

K

Kaarimba Vic. 58 I5
Kadina SA 78 F2, 80 F11, 84 I10
Kadnook Vic. 50 D1, 56 D12
Kadungle NSW 23 Q3, 24 B3
Kagaru Qld 113 J3
Kain NSW 30 F7
Kainton SA 78 F3, 80 F12
Kairi Qld 126 D12
Kajabb Qld 121 D7
Kakadu National Park NT 100 H6
Kalangadoo SA 50 A4, 77 H10
Kalangara Qld 110 H1
Kalannie WA 90 F8
Kalbar Qld 112 F4
Kalbarri WA 90 C5
Kalbarri National Park WA 90 C5
Kaldow SA 84 E10
Kaleen ACT 34 C1
Kaleentha Loop NSW 22 F3
Kalgan WA 95 O12
Kalgoorlie WA 91 J8
Kalimna West Vic. 54 G8
Kalkadoon Qld 122 H1
Kalkallo Vic. 47 L9, 52 G3
Kalkee Vic. 56 H8
Kallangur Qld 111 K6
Kallista Vic. 45 E9
Kallora SA 78 H3, 80 H12
Kalorama Vic. 45 E5
Kalpienung Vic. 57 N2
Kalpowar Qld 117 N5
Kalumburu Aboriginal Reserve WA 93 P1
Kalyan SA 79 N6
Kamarah NSW 23 O8
Kamarooka Vic. 58 D7
Kambalda WA 91 J9
Kamballup WA 95 O10
Kamber NSW 28 E11
Kamona Tas. 73 O5
Kanagulk Vic. 56 G12
Kanangra National Park NSW 24 H7, 30 G2
Kanawalla Vic. 50 H4
Kancoona Vic. 59 R8, 62 B8
Kandanga Qld 114 G6
Kandanga Creek Qld 114 G6
Kandos NSW 24 H3
Kangaloon NSW 17 L7
Kangarooby NSW 24 D6, 30 C1
Kangaroo Flat NSW 29 N10
Kangaroo Flat Vic. 58 C10
Kangaroo Ground Vic. 39 Q1, 48 A11
Kangaroo Hill Vic. 46 B6
Kangaroo Hills Qld 118 F7
Kangaroo Island SA 78 A11
Kangaroo Point Qld 109 G8
Kangaroo Valley NSW 17 L10, 24 I9, 30 H4
Kangawall Vic. 56 D10
Kaniva Vic. 56 C7
Kanni SA 79 N3, 81 N12
Kanumbra Vic. 48 F2, 59 K11,
Kanwal NSW 18 F11
Kanya Vic. 57 M9
Kanyapella Vic. 58 G4
Kaoota Tas. 68 G9, 71 L8
Kapinnie SA 84 E11
Kapooka NSW 24 B10
Kapunda SA 79 J4, 81 J13
Karabeal Vic. 50 I4
Karadoc Vic. 60 H3
Karanja Tas. 68 D4
Karara Qld 117 O11
Karatta SA 78 C12
Karawinna Vic. 60 E4
Karcultaby SA 84 D7
Kariah Vic. 51 N8
Karingal Vic. 41 P4
Kariong NSW 15 P1, 20 B5
Karkarook SA 84 F9
Karkoo SA 84 E10
Karlgarin WA 90 H10
Karlo Creek Vic. 55 N6
Karmona Qld 122 H10
Karn Vic. 59 M8
Karnak Vic. 56 D10
Karook Vic. 58 G7
Karoola Tas. 73 L6

Karoonda SA 79 N7
Karramomus North Vic. 59 J8
Karratha WA 92 F9
Karridale WA 94 C8
Kars Springs NSW 29 J12
Karte SA 79 Q7
Karuah NSW 25 M3
Karumba Qld 120 A13, 121 E2
Karumbul Qld 29 J2
Karween Vic. 60 C4
Karyrie Vic. 57 L3
Katamatite Vic. 23 M13, 59 K4
Katandra Vic. 59 J5
Katanning WA 90 G12, 95 M6
Katherine NT 100 G9
Katherine Gorge National Park NT 100 G8
Katoomba NSW 14 E7, 24 I6, 30 G1
Kattabul Qld 119 K10
Kattyoong Vic. 60 F9
Katunga Vic. 23 L13, 59 J4
Katyil Vic. 56 H6
Kawarren Vic. 51 P10
Kearsley NSW 18 D5
Keera NSW 29 J6
Keilor Vic. 38 B3, 52 F4
Keils Mountain Qld 115 K10, 123 E8
Keinbah NSW 18 D3
Keiraville NSW 19 B9
Keith SA 77 F3, 79 P12
Kellalac Vic. 56 I7
Kellerberrin WA 90 G9
Kellevie Tas. 69 O5, 71 O6
Kellidie Bay Conservation Park SA 84 D12
Kellys Creek NSW 24 D7, 30 C2
Kelsey Creek Qld 127 C5
Kelso Tas. 73 K5
Kelville NSW 15 M6
Kelvin NSW 28 I8
Kelvin View Vic. 59 K10
Kembla Grange NSW 17 O6
Kembla Heights NSW 17 N5
Kemps Creek NSW 15 K9
Kempsey NSW 29 O10
Kempton Tas. 68 H1, 71 M4
Kendall NSW 29 O11
Kendenup WA 90 G13, 95 M10
Kenebri NSW 28 F8
Kenilworth Qld 114 H9, 117 P9
Kenley Vic. 61 N7
Kenmare Vic. 56 H3
Kenmore NSW 16 C11, 24 G9, 30 F4
Kennedy Qld 118 G6
Kennedys Creek Vic. 51 N11
Kennett River Vic. 51 Q11, 52 A11
Kenny Hill NSW 15 L12
Kennys Creek NSW 24 E8, 30 D3
Kensington NSW 11 O7
Kensington WA 87 H10
Kentbruck Vic. 50 D8
Kent Dale WA 95 K12
Kenthurst NSW 12 A3, 15 M5
Kentish West Tas. 72 H7
Kentlyn NSW 15 L12
Kenton WA 95 K12
Kent Town SA 75 H6
Kentucky NSW 29 L8
Kentville Qld 110 D10
Keppel Sands Qld 117 N3
Kerang Vic. 22 I12, 57 Q2, 58 A2, 61 Q13
Kerein Hills NSW 23 P3
Kergunyah Vic. 59 R6, 62 B6
Kernot Vic. 53 J10
Kerrabee NSW 24 I2
Kerrie Vic. 46 I7, 52 F2
Kerrisdale Vic. 47 P3, 48 A3, 58 I12
Kerriwah NSW 23 Q2, 24 B2, 27 Q13, 28 B13
Kerrs Creek NSW 24 F4
Kerry Qld 113 K7
Kersbrook SA 79 J6
Keswick SA 75 A10
Kettering Tas. 68 H11, 71 M8
Kevington Vic. 53 M2
Kew NSW 29 O11
Kew Vic. 39 J8, 52 H5
Kewell Vic. 56 I8
Keyneton SA 79 K5
Keysborough Vic. 40 I5

Khancoban NSW 30 B8, 31 A6, 62 H6
Kiah NSW 30 F11, 55 P3
Kialla NSW 24 G8, 30 E3
Kialla Vic. 59 J7
Kiama NSW 17 O8, 25 J9, 30 I4
Kiamal Vic. 60 I8
Kiamba Qld 115 J9, 123 C6
Kiandra NSW 30 C7, 31 E1
Kianga NSW 30 G8
Kiata Vic. 56 F7
Kibbleup WA 95 M6
Kidamann Creek Qld 114 H9
Kielpa SA 84 F9
Kiewa Vic. 59 R6, 62 B6
Ki Ki SA 79 N9
Kikoira NSW 23 O6
Kilcara Heights NSW 15 Q3
Kilcoy Qld 110 F2, 117 P9
Kilcunda Vic. 53 J10
Kilfeena Vic. 59 M8
Kilkerran SA 78 E4, 80 E13
Kilkivan Qld 114 B1, 117 P8
Killara NSW 13 J8
Killarney Qld 29 N1, 112 B10
Killarney Vic. 50 I9
Killarney Heights NSW 13 M9
Killarney Vale NSW 18 F12
Killawarra Vic. 59 N6
Killingworth NSW 18 F6
Killingworth Vic. 47 Q4, 48 C4, 59 J12
Kilmany Vic. 53 Q7
Kilmore Vic. 47 L5, 52 G1, 58 G13
Kilpalie SA 79 O6
Kilsyth Vic. 45 C4, 48 B13
Kimba SA 80 A7, 84 G8
Kimberley Tas. 72 I7
Kimberley Downs WA 93 M5
Kimbriki NSW 25 N1
Kinalung NSW 22 D1, 26 D13
Kinchega National Park NSW 22 D2
Kinchela Creek NSW 29 P9
Kincumber NSW 15 R2
Kindred Tas. 72 H6
Kingaroy Qld 117 O9
King Island Tas. 70 A1
Kinglake Vic. 47 P9, 48 B9
Kinglake National Park Vic. 47 P9, 52 I3
Kingoonya SA 83 J10, 84 D3
Kingower Vic. 57 P8, 58 A8
King River WA 90 G13, 95 N12
Kingsbury Vic. 39 K3
Kings Canyon NT 104 F9
Kingscliff NSW 29 R1, 113 R9
Kingscote SA 78 F10
Kings Cross NSW 8 I8, 11 N4
Kingsdale NSW 16 B11, 24 G9, 30 F4
Kingsford NSW 11 N7
Kingsgrove NSW 10 H10
King Sound WA 93 L4
Kings Park WA 87 A5
Kingston ACT 34 E13
Kingston Qld 111 M13
Kingston Tas. 68 I9, 71 M7
Kingston Vic. 46 B7, 51 R2, 52 B2
Kingston Beach Tas. 68 I9
Kingston-on-Murray SA 79 P3, 81 P12
Kingston S.E. 77 E6
Kingstown NSW 29 K7
Kingsvale NSW 24 D8, 30 C3
Kingswood NSW 15 J7
Kingswood SA 80 G3
King Valley Vic. 59 O9
Kinimakatka Vic. 56 E7
Kin Kin Qld 115 J4
Kinnabulla Vic. 57 K3
Kioloa NSW 30 H7
Kipper Qld 110 B6
Kirkleigh Qld 110 F3
Kirkstall Vic. 50 I9
Kirra Qld 113 Q8, 125 Q4
Kirrawee NSW 15 O11
Kirribilli NSW 9 G11, 11 N2
Kirup WA 94 F6
Kissing Point NSW 12 H8
Kitchener NSW 18 D5
Kithbrook Vic. 59 K10
Klimpton NSW 24 I10, 30 H5
Knebsworth Vic. 50 G7

Knockrow NSW   29 Q2
Knockwood Vic.   53 N3
Knowsley Vic.   58 E10
Knoxfield Vic.   40 C1
Koah Qld   126 C6
Koallah Vic.   51 N9
Kobble Qld   110 I6
Kobyboyn Vic.   47 Q2, 48 C2, 58 I11
Koetong Vic.   62 E5
Kogan Qld   117 N9
Kogarah NSW   11 K11
Koimbo Vic.   61 L8
Kohonup WA   90 G12, 95 K6
Koloona NSW   29 J5
Kolora Vic.   51 L8
Komungla NSW   24 G9, 30 F4
Konanda SA   84 F9
Kondinin WA   90 G10
Kongal SA   77 G4, 79 P13
Kongorong SA   77 G12
Kongwak Vic.   53 K10
Konong Wootong Vic.   50 F3
Kookaburra NSW   29 N9
Kooloonong Vic.   22 G10, 61 M7
Koolewong NSW   15 Q2, 20 C3
Koolunga SA   80 H9
Koolyanobbing WA   90 I8
Koolywurtie SA   78 F5
Koonagaderra Springs Vic.   47 K9
Koonda Vic.   59 K7, 60 D9
Koondrook Vic.   22 I12, 57 R1, 58 C1, 61 R13
Koongamia WA   96 I11
Koonoomoo Vic.   59 J3
Koonwarra Vic.   53 L10
Koonya Tas.   69 N10, 71 O8
Koorack Koorack Vic.   57 P2, 61 P13
Koorawatha NSW   24 E7, 30 C2
Koorda WA   90 G8
Kooreh Vic.   57 O8
Koorkab Vic.   61 M7
Koorlong Vic.   60 G3
Kooroocheang Vic.   46 C5
Koo-Wee-Rup Vic.   53 J8
Kooyong Vic.   39 J10
Kopi SA   84 E9
Koppamurra SA   56 A12, 77 H8
Koraleigh NSW   61 N9
Koriella Vic.   160 F3, 167 K12, 173 K1
Korobeit Vic.   46 F10, 52 D4
Koroit Vic.   51 J9
Korong Vale Vic.   57 P6
Koroop Vic.   57 R2, 58 B2
Korora NSW   29 P7
Korumburra Vic.   53 L10
Korweinguboora Vic.   46 D8
Korweinguboora Reservoir Vic.   52 C3
Koscuisko National Park NSW   24 D13,
   30 C6, 31, 54 I1, 62 I9
Kotta Vic.   58 E5
Kotupna Vic.   58 H5
Koumala Qld   119 L11
Kowat Vic.   55 M4
Koyuga Vic.   58 G5
Krambach NSW   25 N1, 29 N12
Kringin SA   79 Q7
Krongart SA   77 H10
Krowera Vic.   53 K10
Kudardup WA   94 C9
Kuender WA   95 Q2
Kukerin WA   90 G11, 95 O3
Kulangoor Qld   115 K9
Kulde SA   79 M7
Kulgera NT   104 I12
Kulgun Qld   112 G4
Kulikup WA   94 I6
Kulkami SA   79 O7
Kulkyr Vic.   60 I5
Kulnine Vic.   60 D3
Kulnura NSW   18 C11, 29 K5
Kulpara SA   78 G2, 80 G11
Kulwin Vic.   22 F10, 61 J9
Kumarl WA   91 J11
Kumbarilla Qld   117 N10
Kumbia Qld   117 O9
Kumorna SA   77 F2, 79 O11
Kunama NSW   23 R12, 30 B6, 62 H1

Kunat Vic.   61 O12
Kundabung NSW   29 O10
Kungala NSW   29 P6
Kunghur NSW   29 Q1, 113 N13
Kunkala Qld   110 F12
Kunlara SA   79 N5
Kunmunya Aboriginal Reserve WA   93 M3
Kununurra WA   93 R3
Kunwarara Qld   117 M2
Kuranda Qld   126 E6
Kureelpa Qld   115 J9, 123 C7
Kuridala Qld   121 E9
Ku-ring-gai Chase National Park NSW
   15 P4, 21, 25 K6
Kuringup WA   95 P5
Kurlana SA   79 O3
Kurmond NSW   15 J4
Kurnbrunin Vic.   56 F3
Kurnell NSW   11 O13
Kurnwill Vic.   60 D5
Kurraca Vic.   57 P8
Kurrajong NSW   14 I4, 25 J6, 30 I1
Kurrajong East NSW   15 J3
Kurrajong Heights NSW   14 I4
Kurri Kurri NSW   18 E4, 25 L3
Kurting Vic.   57 Q8, 58 A8
Kurumbul Qld   117 M12
Kuttabul Qld   127 F11
Kwinana WA   90 E10
Kwobrup WA   95 O5
Kyabram Vic.   58 H6
Kyalite NSW   22 H10, 61 O8
Kyancutta SA   84 E8
Kybeyan NSW   30 E9
Kybong Qld   114 H5
Kybunga SA   78 I2, 80 I11
Kybybolite SA   56 B11, 77 I7
Kydra NSW   30 E9
Kyeamba NSW   23 Q11, 24 B11, 30 A6
Kyeemagh NSW   11 L10
Kyndalyn Vic.   61 L6
Kyneton Vic.   46 G5, 52 D1, 58 D13
Kynuna Qld   118 A11, 121 G10
Kyogle NSW   29 P2, 117 Q12
Kyup Vic.   50 H4
Kyvalley Vic.   58 G6
Kywong NSW   23 O10

L

Laanecoorie Vic.   57 Q10, 58 A10
Laanecoorie Reservoir Vic.   58 A10
Laang Vic.   51 L9
Labertouche Vic.   53 L7
Labrador Qld   113 P5, 124 B12
Lachlan Tas.   68 F6, 71 L7
Lady Bay Tas.   71 L10
Lady Julia Percy Island Vic.   50 H10
Ladysmith NSW   23 Q10, 24 B10, 30 A5
Ladys Pass Vic.   58 F10
Laen Vic.   57 K7
Laggan NSW   24 G8, 30 F3
Lagoon Pocket Qld   114 G4
Lagoons Tas.   73 R9
Laguna NSW   18 A7
Lah Vic.   56 I5
Lah-Arum Vic.   56 I11
Laheys Creek NSW   28 F13
Laidley Qld   110 D12
Lake Albacutya Park Vic.   60 G13
Lake Albert SA   79 L10
Lake Alexandrina SA   79 K9
Lake Argyle WA   93 R4
Lake Barrine National Park Qld   126 E12
Lake Bathurst NSW   24 G10, 30 F5
Lake Bellfield Vic.   57 J13
Lake Boga Vic.   22 H11, 61 P12
Lake Bolac Vic.   51 L5
Lake Buloke Vic.   57 L6
Lake Burragorang NSW   14 G11, 16 I1
Lake Burrumbeet Vic.   51 P3
Lake Cargelligo NSW   23 N5
Lake Charm Vic.   22 I12, 57 Q1, 58 A1, 61 Q13
Lake Clarendon Qld   110 C10
Lake Clifton WA   94 E1
Lake Condah Vic.   50 G8
Lake Corangamite Vic.   51 O8
Lake Cowal NSW   24 B6

Lake Dumbleyung WA   95 M4
Lake Eacham National Park Qld   126 E12
Lake Echo Tas.   73 J12
Lake Eildon Vic.   48 H3
Lake Eppalock Vic.   58 E10
Lake Eucumbene NSW   30 C8, 31 G4
Lake Eyre SA   83 M5
Lake Frome SA   83 P10
Lake Fyans Vic.   57 K12
Lake Gairdner SA   83 K11
Lake George NSW   24 G10, 30 E5
Lake George SA   77 E9
Lake Gilles Conservation Park SA   83 L13
Lake Goldsmith Vic.   51 O3
Lake Gordon Tas.   70 H6
Lake Grace WA   90 H11, 95 Q2
Lake Hindmarsh Vic.   56 F4
Lake Illawarra NSW   17 O6
Lake Jindabyne NSW   30 C9, 31 G8
Lake Leake Tas.   71 O1, 73 O11
Lake Lonsdale Vic.   57 K11
Lake MacFarlane SA   80 B1
Lake Mackay Aboriginal Reserve NT   104 B4
Lake Macleod WA   90 C1
Lake Macquarie NSW   18 G7
Lake Margaret Tas.   70 E1
Lake Marmal Vic.   57 O5
Lakemba NSW   10 G8
Lake Meering Vic.   57 Q3, 58 A3
Lake Menindee NSW   22 D2
Lake Moogerah Qld   112 E6
Lake Mountain Vic.   53 L3
Lake Mundi Vic.   50 B4
Lake Pedder Tas.   70 H7
Lake Powell Vic.   61 L6
Lake Rowan Vic.   59 L6
Lake Sorell Tas.   73 L12
Lake St Clair Tas.   70 H1
Lakes Entrance Vic.   54 G8
Lakesland NSW   17 K1
Lake Tinaroo Qld   126 D11
Lake Torrens SA   80 E1, 83 N10
Lake Tyers Vic.   54 G8
Lake Victoria NSW   60 C1
Lake View NSW   18 G8
Lake View SA   80 H9
Lake Wallawalla Vic.   60 B3
Lalbert Vic.   22 G12, 57 N1, 61 N13
Lalbert Road Vic.   61 O12
Lal Lal Vic.   46 C11, 52 B4
Lal Lal Reservoir Vic.   52 B4
Lallat Vic.   57 K9
Lambton NSW   18 H5, 19 A6
Lameroo SA   79 P8
Lamington Qld   113 K9
Lamington National Park Qld   29 P1, 113 M9
Lamplough Vic.   57 O12
Lancaster Vic.   58 H6
Lancefield Vic.   47 J5, 52 F1, 58 F13
Lancelin WA   90 E9
Landers Shoot Qld   115 J11, 123 C10
Landsborough Qld   115 K12, 123 E12
Landsborough Vic.   57 M11
Lane Cove NSW   13 K12
Lang Lang Vic.   53 J8
Langhorne Creek SA   79 K8
Langi Kal Kal Vic.   52 O2
Langi Logan Vic.   51 M2
Langkoop Vic.   50 B1, 56 B12, 77 I8
Langley Vic.   46 G4, 58 E12
Langlo Crossing Qld   116 F8
Langloh Tas.   68 D1
Langshaw Qld   114 F4
Langville Vic.   57 Q3, 58 A3
Langwarrin Vic.   43 M1
Lankeys Creek NSW   23 Q12, 30 A7
Lannercost Qld   118 G6
Lansdowne NSW   10 B8, 29 O12
Lansvale NSW   10 A8
La Perouse NSW   11 O12
Lapoinya Tas.   72 E4
Lara Vic.   44 F5, 52 D7
Lara Lake Vic.   44 F5, 52 D7
Larpent Vic.   51 P9
Laravale Qld   113 J7
Largs NSW   18 F2
Lark Hill Qld   110 F11
Larrakeyah NT   99 O12

Larras Lee NSW 24 E4
Larrimah NT 100 I11, 102 I1
Lascelles Vic. 22 F12, 57 J1, 61 J13
Latham WA 90 F7
Latrobe Tas. 72 I6
Lauderdale Tas. 69 K7, 71 N7
Laughtondale NSW 15 M2
Launceston Tas. 73 L7
Launching Place Vic. 48 E12, 53 J5
Laura SA 80 H7
Laura Qld 118 E1, 120 G10
Laurel Hill NSW 23 R12, 30 B7
Laurence Road NSW 29 P4
Laurier WA 95 P7
Laurieton NSW 29 O11
Lauriston Vic. 46 F5, 52 D1, 58 D13
Lavender Bay NSW 9 B9
Lavers Hill Vic. 51 O12
Laverton Vic. 52 F6
Laverton WA 91 K6
Lavington NSW 23 P13, 59 R4, 62 B4
Lawes Qld 110 C11
Lawgi Qld 117 M5
Lawler Vic. 57 K7
Lawloit Vic. 56 D7
Lawrence Vic. 46 A6, 51 R2, 52 B2, 57 Q13
Lawrenny Tas. 68 C1
Lawson NSW 14 G7, 24 I6, 30 H1
Layard Vic. 52 C9
Leadville NSW 28 G12
Leaghur Vic. 57 Q4, 58 A3
Learmonth Vic. 51 Q2, 52 A2
Learmonth WA 92 C11
Leawarra Vic. 43 L1
Lebrina Tas. 73 M6
Leeton NSW 23 O8
Leets Vale NSW 15 L2
Leeville NSW 29 P3
Lefroy Tas. 73 L5
Legana Tas. 73 L7
Legerwood Tas. 73 O6
Legume NSW 29 N1, 112 B11, 117 P12
Legunia Tas. 73 P6
Leichardt Vic. 57 R9, 58 B9
Leichhardt NSW 11 K5
Leigh Creek SA 83 N9
Leigh Creek Vic. 46 B9
Leighton SA 81 J9
Leightonfield NSW 10 B6
Leinster WA 91 J5
Leitchville Vic. 23 J13, 58 C3
Leith Tas. 72 H5
Lemana Tas. 73 J8
Lemnos Vic. 59 J6
Lemon Springs Vic. 56 C9
Lemont Tas. 71 O3, 73 O13
Lemon Tree NSW 18 D9
Lenah Valley Tas. 67 B6
Leneva Vic. 59 Q5, 62 A5
Leonards Hill Vic. 46 D7, 52 C2
Leongatha Vic. 53 L10
Leonora WA 91 J6
Leopold Vic. 44 G8, 52 E8
Leppington NSW 15 L10
Leprena Tas. 71 K11
Lerderderg Gorge Vic. 46 G9
Le Roy Vic. 53 O9
Leslie Manor Vic. 51 O8
Leslie Vale Tas. 68 H8, 71 M7
Lessingham SA 78 I2, 80 I11
Lethbridge Vic. 44 C5, 52 C6
Lethebrook Qld 127 D6
Letts Beach Vic. 54 D11
Leumeah NSW 15 L11
Leura NSW 14 F7
Levendale Tas. 69 L2, 71 N5
Lewana Park WA 94 F6
Lewisham NSW 11 K6
Lewisham Tas. 69 L6, 71 O7
Lexton Vic. 51 P1, 57 O13
Leyburn Qld 117 O11
Liamana NSW 28 G12
Liapootah Tas. 70 I2
Licola Vic. 53 P4
Lidcombe NSW 10 D5
Liddell NSW 25 K2
Lidsdale NSW 14 B3
Lietpar Vic. 61 J9

Liena Tas. 72 H8
Lietinna Tas. 73 N5
Liffey Tas. 73 K9
Lightning Creek Vic. 62 D9
Lightning Ridge NSW 27 R4, 28 C4, 117 J13
Light Pass SA 85 G2
Lileah Tas. 72 C4
Lillimur Vic. 56 B7, 77 I4, 79 R13
Lillimur South Vic. 56 C7
Lilli Pilli NSW 15 P11
Lilliput Vic. 59 O5, 64 C6
Lilydale Tas. 73 M6
Lilydale Vic. 45 D2, 48 B12, 52 I5
Lilyfield NSW 11 K4
Lilyvale NSW 15 N13, 17 P1
Lima Vic. 59 L9
Lime Lake WA 95 L4
Limestone Vic. 47 R5, 48 D5, 53 J1, 59 J13
Limestone Ridge Qld 112 H3
Limerick NSW 24 G7, 30 E2
Limevale Qld 29 K2, 117 N12
Limpinwood NSW 113 N10
Lincoln National Park SA 84 F13
Lincolnfields SA 78 G1, 80 G10
Linda Downs Qld 122 A1
Lindeman Island Qld 119 K9
Linden NSW 14 H7
Lindenow Vic. 54 D8
Lindfield NSW 13 K9
Lindisfarne Tas. 67 H4, 69 J6
Lind National Park Vic. 30 D13, 55 L6
Lindsay Vic. 50 B4
Lindsay Creek NSW 112 F11
Lindsay Point Vic. 60 A2
Lindsay View NSW 29 P1, 112 I11
Linga Vic. 60 E10
Linley Point NSW 11 J1, 13 J13
Linton Vic. 51 P4
Linville Qld 114 B13
Lipson SA 84 F11
Liptrap Vic. 53 L13
Lisarow NSW 18 E13
Lisle Tas. 73 M6
Lismore NSW 29 Q3, 117 Q12
Lismore Vic. 51 O6
Liston NSW 29 N2
Litchfield Vic. 57 L6
Lithgow NSW 14 C4, 24 H5
Little Bay NSW 11 Q11
Little Billabong NSW 62 E1
Little Desert National Park Vic. 56 F8
Little Hampton Vic. 46 E6
Little Hartley NSW 14 D5
Little Jiliby NSW 18 D11
Little River Vic. 44 G4, 52 E6
Little Snowy Creek Vic. 62 C8
Little Topar NSW 26 D12
Little Swanport Tas. 71 P3, 73 P13
Liverpool NSW 15 M9, 25 J7, 30 I2
Lizard Island Qld 120 I8
Llandillo NSW 15 K6
Llangothlin NSW 29 M6
Llanelly Vic. 57 Q9, 58 A9
Llewellyn Siding Tas. 73 N10
Llowalong Vic. 53 R6, 54 B8
Loadstone NSW 113 K11
Lobethal SA 79 J6
Lochabar SA 77 G7
Lochiel SA 78 G2, 80 G11
Lochiel NSW 30 F11
Lochiel Qld 122 H5
Lochinvar NSW 18 D2
Loch Lomond Qld 29 N1
Lochnagar Qld 116 F3
Loch Sport Vic. 54 E9
Loch Valley Vic. 53 M5
Lock SA 84 E9
Lockhart NSW 23 O11
Lockhart River Mission Qld 120 E5
Lockington Vic. 58 E6
Lockridge WA 96 C10
Lockrose Qld 110 D10
Locksley Vic. 58 I10
Lockwood Vic. 58 C10
Loddon Vale Vic. 57 Q4, 58 B4
Logan Vic. 57 O8
Loganholme Qld 111 M13, 113 M1
Loganlea Qld 111 M13, 113 L1

Logan Reserve Qld 113 L1
Logan Village Qld 113 L2
Lombardina Aboriginal Reserve WA 93 L4
Londonderry NSW 15 J6
Londrigan Vic. 59 O6
Longerenong Vic. 56 I9
Longford Tas. 71 L8
Long Flats Qld 114 G4
Longford Vic. 54 B10
Longford Creek Qld 119 J9, 127 B3
Long Island Qld 127 F5
Long Jetty NSW 18 F12
Longlea Vic. 58 D9
Longley Tas. 68 H8, 71 M7
Long Plains SA 78 H4, 80 H13
Long Plains Vic. 61 L11
Longreach Qld 116 D3
Longueville NSW 11 K2, 13 K13
Longwarry Vic. 53 K7
Longwood Vic. 58 I9
Lonnavale Tas. 68 D8, 71 K7
Looma WA 93 M6
Loongana WA 91 O9
Lorinna Tas. 72 H8
Lorne NSW 29 O11
Lorne Vic. 44 A13, 51 R10, 52 B10
Lorquon Vic. 56 F5
Lostock NSW 25 L2, 29 L13
Lotta Tas. 73 Q6
Louth NSW 27 K8
Louth Bay SA 84 F12
Loveday SA 79 P3, 81 P12
Lowaldie SA 79 N7
Lowanna NSW 29 P7
Lowan Vale SA 77 H3, 79 Q12
Lowbank SA 79 N3, 81 N12
Lowden WA 94 F5
Lowdina Tas. 69 J3, 71 N5
Lower Acacia Creek NSW 29 N1
Lower Bucca NSW 29 P7
Lower Creek NSW 29 N8
Lower Gellibrand Vic. 51 N12
Lower Glenelg National Park Vic. 50 D8
Lower Hawkesbury NSW 15 M2
Lower Mangrove NSW 15 O1
Lower Mookerawa NSW 24 F3
Lower Mount Hicks Tas. 72 F5
Lower Norton Vic. 56 H10
Lower Portland NSW 15 L2
Lower Sandy Bay Tas. 67 G13
Lower Wilmot Tas. 72 H6
Lowesdale NSW 23 N13, 59 O3
Low Head Tas. 73 K5
Lowlands NSW 15 J4, 23 L4
Lowmead Qld 117 O5
Lowood Qld 110 F10
Lowther NSW 14 C6
Loxton SA 79 P4, 81 P13
Loyetea Tas. 72 G6
Loy Yang Vic. 53 P8
Lubeck Vic. 57 J9
Lucas Heights NSW 15 N11
Lucaston Tas. 68 F9, 71 F9
Lucinda Qld 118 G6
Lucindale SA 77 G7
Lucknow NSW 24 F5
Lucknow Qld 122 F1
Lucknow Vic. 54 E8
Lucky Bay SA 84 H10
Lucky Flat NSW 28 G8
Lucyvale Vic. 62 E6
Luddenham NSW 15 J9
Ludlow WA 94 D5
Ludmilla NT 98 H5
Lue NSW 24 H3
Lugarno NSW 10 F13
Luina Tas. 72 D7
Lulworth Tas. 73 L4
Lumeah WA 95 L7
Lunawanna Tas. 71 M10
Lune River Tas. 71 K11
Lurg Vic. 59 M8
Lurnea NSW 15 M10
Lutana Tas. 67 D4
Lyal Vic. 46 G1, 58 E11
Lyalls Mill WA 94 G4
Lymington Tas. 68 F12, 71 L9
Lynchford Tas. 70 E2

Lynchs Creek NSW   29 P1, 113 K12
Lyndbrook Qld   118 D5
Lyndhurst NSW   24 F6, 30 D1
Lyndhurst SA   83 N9
Lyndhurst Vic.   41 K1, 52 I7
Lyndoch SA   79 J5, 85 B9
Lyneham ACT   34 D3
Lyons SA   82 H9, 84 B2
Lyons Vic.   50 E7
Lyonville Vic.   46 E7, 52 C2.
Lyrup SA   79 Q3, 81 Q12
Lysterfield Vic.   45 B12
Lysterfield Reservoir Vic.   45 B13

M

Maaoope SA   77 H8
Mablac WA   95 P2
McAlinden WA   94 H5
McAllister NSW   24 G8, 30 F3
Macarthur Vic.   50 H7
Macclesfield SA   79 J8
Macclesfield Vic.   45 I8, 53 J6
McCoys Bridge Vic.   58 H5
McCrae Vic.   42 G7
McCullys Gap NSW   25 K1
Macedon Vic.   46 H7, 52 E2
Macgillivray SA   78 E11
McGraths Hill NSW   15 K5
Machans Beach Qld   126 F7
McIntyres Vic.   57 P9
Mackay Qld   119 L11, 127 H11
McKees Hill NSW   29 Q3
McKenzie Creek Vic.   56 H10
McKillop Vic.   45 F4
McKillops Bridge Vic.   54 I3
McKinlay Qld   121 F9
McKinnon Vic.   40 D11
Macks Creek Vic.   53 P10
Macksville NSW   29 P8
McLachlan SA   84 E9
McLaren Vale SA   78 I8, 85 G13
Maclean NSW   29 Q5
Maclean Bridge NSW   113 K2
McLeay SA   84 H4
Macleod Vic.   39 L4
McMahons Creek Vic.   48 H11, 53 L4
McMahons Point NSW   9 C11
McMahons Reef NSW   24 D9, 30 C4
McMasters Beach NSW   15 R2
McMillans Vic.   58 C3
McMinns NT   100 E4
Macorna Vic.   57 R3, 58 B3
McPhail NSW   24 D3
Macquarie Fields NSW   15 M10
Macquarie Harbour Tas.   70 D3
Macquarie Plains Tas.   68 E4, 71 K6
Macrossan Qld   118 H9
Madalya Vic.   53 O10
Madura WA   91 O10
Mafeking Vic.   51 K2
Maffra NSW   30 D9
Maffra Vic.   53 R6, 54 B9
Maggea SA   79 N4, 81 N13
Magnetic Island Qld   118 H7
Magpie Vic.   46 A10
Magra Tas.   68 F5, 71 L6
Magrath Flat SA   77 C2, 79 L11
Mahaikah Vic.   59 N11
Maharatta NSW   30 E11
Maiala National Park Qld   110 H7
Maianbar NSW   15 O11
Maiden Gully Vic.   58 C9
Maidenwell Qld   117 O9
Maidstone Vic.   38 D7
Mailors Flat Vic.   51 J9
Maimura NSW   24 D8, 30 B2
Main Beach Qld   113 P5, 124 E9
Maindample Vic.   48 I1, 59 L11
Main Ridge Vic.   42 I9
Maitland NSW   18 F3, 25 L3
Maitland SA   78 F4, 80 F13, 84 I11
Majorca Vic.   57 Q12, 58 A12
Major Plains Vic.   59 L6
Majors Creek NSW   30 F7
Majors Line Vic.   58 G10
Malabar NSW   11 P10
Malabar Qld   110 F11

Malagarga Qld   122 H8
Malanda Qld   122 H4
Malbina Tas.   68 G6, 71 L6
Malbon Qld   121 E9
Malbooma SA   82 H9, 84 B2
Malcolm WA   91 J6
Maldon NSW   17 L2
Maldon Vic.   46 C1, 57 R11, 58 B11
Maleny Qld   114 I11, 117 Q9, 123 B11
Malinong SA   79 L9
Mallacoota Vic.   30 F13, 55 O6
Mallacoota National Park Vic.   30 F12
Mallala SA   78 I4, 80 I13
Mallanganee NSW   29 O3
Malmsbury Vic.   46 F4, 52 D1, 58 D12
Malmsbury Reservoir Vic.   52 D1, 58 D12
Malpas SA   79 Q5
Maltee SA   84 B6
Malvern Vic.   39 K12, 40 B11
Mambray Creek SA   80 F5
Mambray Creek National Park SA   80 G5
Manangatang Vic.   22 F10, 61 L9
Manara NSW   22 G3
Mandagery NSW   24 D4
Mandalong NSW   18 E9
Mandemar NSW   16 I6
Mandorah NT   100 D4
Mandurah WA   90 E10
Mandurama NSW   24 F6, 30 D1
Mangalo SA   80 B9
Mangalore NSW   27 O11
Mangalore Tas.   68 H3, 71 M5
Mangalore Vic.   58 H11
Mangana Tas.   73 P8
Mangerton NSW   19 B12
Mangoplah NSW   23 P11, 24 A11
Mangrove Creek NSW   18 B13
Mangrove Mountain NSW   18 B12
Manildra NSW   24 E4
Manilla NSW   29 J8
Maningrida NT   101 K3
Manjimup WA   90 F12, 94 G8
Manly NSW   13 Q9
Manly Beach Vic.   43 K9
Manly Vale NSW   13 O9
Mannahill SA   81 N3, 83 P12
Mannanarie SA   80 I6
Mannerim Vic.   44 H8
Mannering Park NSW   18 F9
Mannibadar Vic.   51 P5
Manns Beach Vic.   53 Q11
Mannum SA   79 L6
Manoora SA   79 J2, 81 J11
Manor Vic.   44 H4, 52 E6
Manorina National Park Qld   110 H8
Mansfield Vic.   59 M11
Mantung SA   79 O5
Manumbar Qld   114 B6, 117 P8
Manumbar Mill Qld   114 C6
Manya Vic.   60 B10
Manypeak WA   95 O12
Mapleton Qld   115 J9, 123 B7
Mapoon Mission Qld   120 C3
Maralinga SA   82 E8
Marama SA   79 O8
Marananga SA   85 D3
Maranboy NT   100 H9
Marathon Qld   118 C10
Maraylya NSW   15 L4
Marble Bar WA   92 I9
Marburg Qld   110 F11
Marcoola Beach Qld   123 H7
Marcus Beach Qld   123 H3
Marcus Hill Vic.   44 H8, 52 E8
Mardan Vic.   53 M10
Mareeba Qld   118 F3, 120 I12, 126 B8
Marengo Vic.   51 P12
Margaret River WA   90 E12, 94 C7
Margate Qld   111 M6
Margate Tas.   68 H9, 71 M8
Margooya Vic.   61 K7
Maria Island Tas.   69 R4, 71 Q6
Maria Island National Park Tas.   71 Q5
Maribyrnong Vic.   38 D6
Marine National Park Qld   126 H1
Marino SA   85 G7
Marion SA   76 D11
Marion Bay SA   78 C8, 84 H13

Marion Downs Qld   122 D2
Markdale NSW   24 F8, 30 E2
Marks Point NSW   18 G7
Markwood Vic.   59 O7, 64 H12
Marla SA   82 H3
Marlbed Vic.   57 L3
Marlborough Qld   117 L2, 119 L13
Marlee NSW   29 N12
Marlin Waters Qld   125 O8
Marlo Vic.   30 C13, 55 J8
Marma Vic.   57 J9
Marmong Point NSW   18 G6
Marmor Qld   117 N4
Marnoo Vic.   57 L9
Marong Vic.   57 R9, 58 C9
Maroochydore Qld   115 L10, 117 Q9, 123 H8
Maroochy River Qld   115 K9, 123 F6
Maroon Qld   112 G8
Maroona Vic.   51 L3
Maroondah Reservoir Vic.   48 E10, 53 J4
Maroota NSW   15 L3
Maroubra NSW   11 Q9
Maroubra Junction NSW   11 O9
Marp Vic.   50 C6
Marrabel SA   79 J3, 81 J12
Marracoonda WA   95 L5
Marradong WA   94 H1
Marrangaroo NSW   14 B3
Marrar NSW   24 B9
Marrawah Tas.   72 A4
Marraweeny Vic.   59 K9
Marree SA   83 N7
Marrickville NSW   11 K7
Marsden NSW   23 Q6, 24 B6, 30 A1
Marsden Park NSW   15 K6
Marsfield NSW   12 H10
Marshall Vic.   44 F8
Martindale NSW   25 J2
Martins Creek Vic.   55 J5
Martinsville NSW   18 E8
Martin Walker Park Vic.   53 O9
Marulan NSW   16 F11, 24 H9, 30 G4
Marungi Vic.   59 J5
Marvel Loch WA   90 I9
Marwood Qld   127 H13
Maryborough Qld   117 P7
Maryborough Vic.   57 P11, 58 A11
Mary Burts Corner SA   78 H3, 80 H13
Mary Creek Qld   114 F3
Maryfields NSW   15 K12
Mary Kathleen Qld   121 D9
Marysville Vic.   48 G8, 53 K3
Maryvale NSW   24 E2, 28 F13
Maryvale Qld   112 B6
Maryvale WA   94 E6
Mascot NSW   11 M8
Massey Vic.   57 L5
Matakana NSW   23 M4
Mataranka NT   100 I10
Matcham NSW   15 R1, 18 E13
Matheson NSW   29 L5
Mathiesons Vic.   58 G8
Mathinna Tas.   73 P8
Mathoura NSW   23 K13, 58 G2
Matlock Vic.   53 N4
Matong NSW   23 P9
Matraville NSW   11 P10
Maude NSW   22 I8
Maude Vic.   44 C4, 52 C6
Maudsland Qld   113 N5
Mawbanna Tas.   72 D4
Mawson NSW   18 H8
Maxwellton Qld   118 B10, 121 I8
Mayanup WA   94 H7
Mayberry Vic.   72 I8
Maydena Tas.   68 B5, 71 J6
Mayfield NSW   18 H5, 19 D4
Mayfield Tas.   71 P3, 73 P13
Maylands WA   96 B13
Mayneside Qld   122 I2
May Reef Vic.   58 E7
Mead Vic.   57 R2, 58 C2
Meadowbank NSW   10 F1, 12 G12
Meadow Flat NSW   24 H5
Meadows SA   79 J8
Meandarra Qld   117 L10
Meander Tas.   73 J9
Meatian Vic.   57 N1, 61 N12

Meckering WA   90 F9
Medindie SA   75 F2
Medindie Gardens SA   75 F1
Medlow Bath NSW   14 E7
Meekatharra WA   90 H3
Meelup WA   94 C5
Meeniyan Vic.   53 M11
Meereek Vic.   56 B12
Meerlieu Vic.   54 D9
Meerschaum Vale NSW   29 Q3
Megalong NSW   14 E8
Megan NSW   29 O7
Melawondi Qld   114 G6
Melba Gully State Park Vic.   51 O12
Melbourne Vic.   37-41, 45, 52 G5
Melbourne Airport Vic.   38 C1, 47 K11
Mella Tas.   72 C3
Mellis Vic.   57 J6
Melrose NSW   23 P3
Melrose SA   80 G5, 83 N13
Melrose Tas.   72 H6
Melrose Park NSW   10 F1, 12 F12
Melton SA   78 G2, 80 G11
Melton Vic.   46 I11, 52 E4
Melton Mowbray Tas.   68 H1, 71 L4
Melton Reservoir Vic.   44 G1, 52 E5
Melville Caves Vic.   57 P8
Melville Forest Vic.   50 G3
Melville Island NT   100 D2
Mena Tas.   71 J1
Menangle NSW   15 K13
Menangle Park NSW   15 K12
Mena Park Vic.   51 O3
Mendooran NSW   28 F11
Mengha Tas.   72 C4
Menia NSW   15 N11
Menindee NSW   22 E2, 26 E13
Meningie SA   77 C1, 79 L10
Mentone Vic.   40 H10, 52 H6
Menzies WA   91 J7
Menzies Creek Vic.   45 F12
Mepunga East Vic.   51 K10
Mepunga West Vic.   51 K10
Merah North NSW   28 G6
Merbein Vic.   22 D8, 60 G2
Mercunda SA   79 N5
Merebene NSW   28 F8
Meredith Vic.   44 B3, 46 C13, 52 B5
Merewether NSW   18 H6
Meribah SA   60 A6, 79 Q5
Merildin SA   79 J1, 81 J11
Merilup WA   95 O3
Merimal Qld   117 M2
Merimbula NSW   30 F10, 55 P2
Merinda Qld   119 J9
Meringur Vic.   60 C4
Merino Vic.   50 E5
Mermaid Beach Qld   113 P6, 124 I9
Mermaid Waters Qld   124 I10
Mernda Vic.   47 N10, 52 H4
Meroo Meadow NSW   17 M11
Merredin WA   90 G9
Merriang Vic.   52 G3, 59 P8
Merricks Vic.   43 K9, 52 H9
Merrigum Vic.   58 H6
Merrijig Vic.   59 N12
Merrimac Qld   113 P6
Merrinee Vic.   60 F4
Merriton SA   80 G8
Merriwa NSW   28 I13
Merriwagga NSW   23 M6
Merrygoen NSW   28 F11
Merrylands NSW   10 B3
Merrywinebone NSW   28 E5
Merseylea Tas.   72 I7
Merton NSW   23 N13
Merton Vic.   48 F1, 59 K11
Messent National Park SA   77 D3, 79 M12
Metcalfe Vic.   46 G3, 58 D12
Methul NSW   23 P9, 24 A9
Metricup WA   94 C6
Metung Vic.   54 F8
Meunna Tas.   72 E5
Miallo Qld   118 F2, 120 I11
Miami Qld   113 P7, 125 J9
Mia Mia Vic.   46 H1, 58 E11
Miami Keys Qld   124 H10
Miandetta NSW   27 P11, 28 A11

Michael Creek Qld   118 G7
Michelago NSW   30 E7
Mickleham Vic.   47 L9, 52 G3
Middleback P.O. SA   84 H8
Middle Camp NSW   18 G9
Middle Cove NSW   13 M10
Middle Creek Vic.   51 N2
Middle Indigo Vic.   59 P5
Middle Island Qld   119 M11
Middle Park Vic.   38 H11
Middle River SA   78 D10
Middle Swan WA   96 H8
Middleton Qld   121 G11
Middleton Tas.   68 H13, 71 M9
Middlingbank NSW   30 D8, 31 H6
Midgeton Qld   119 K10, 127 E7
Midginbil NSW   113 N13
Midland WA   96 F10
Midvale WA   96 G10
Midway Point Tas.   69 K6, 71 N6
Miena Tas.   73 J11
Miepoll Vic.   59 J8
Miga Lake Vic.   56 E11
Mila NSW   30 D11
Milang SA   79 J9
Milawa Vic.   59 O7, 64 F12
Milbrulong NSW   23 P11
Milchomi NSW   28 E7
Mildura Vic.   22 D8, 60 H2
Mile End SA   75 A7
Miles Qld   117 M9
Milford Qld   112 G6
Milguy NSW   28 I4, 117 M13
Miling WA   90 F8
Milingimbi NT   101 L4
Millaa Millaa Qld   118 F4
Millbong Qld   112 H4, 117 P11
Millbrook Vic.   46 C10, 51 R4, 52 B4
Mil Lel SA   77 H11
Millendon WA   96 H4
Millers Forest NSW   18 H3
Millers Point NSW   8 A2
Millfield NSW   18 B6, 25 K4
Millgrove Vic.   48 F12
Millicent SA   77 G10
Millie NSW   28 G5
Millmerran Qld   117 N11
Millner NT   98 C5
Milloo Vic.   58 D6
Millstream National Park WA   92 F10
Millthorpe NSW   24 F5
Milltown Vic.   50 F7
Millwood NSW   24 A10
Milman Qld   117 M3
Milparinka NSW   26 C5
Milperra NSW   15 C10
Milsons Point NSW   9 D11
Miltalie SA   80 B9
Milton NSW   24 I11, 30 H6
Milvale NSW   23 R8, 24 C8, 30 B3
Mimosa NSW   23 Q9, 24 B8
Minbrie SA   80 C9
Mincha Vic.   57 R4, 58 B4
Mindarie SA   79 O6
Minden Qld   110 E11
Mindiyarra SA   79 N7
Miners Rest Vic.   51 Q3, 52 A3
Mingary SA   81 Q2, 83 R12
Mingay Vic.   51 O5
Mingela Qld   118 H8
Mingenew WA   90 E7
Mingoola NSW   29 L3
Minimay Vic.   56 C9
Minimbah NSW   18 B2
Mininera Vic.   51 M4
Minjilang NT   100 H1
Minlaton SA   78 E6, 84 I12
Minmi NSW   18 G5
Minmindie Vic.   57 P4, 58 A4
Minnamurra NSW   17 O8
Minnie Water NSW   29 Q5
Minniging WA   95 K1
Minnipa SA   83 J13, 84 D7
Minore NSW   24 D1, 28 D13
Mintaro SA   79 J1, 80 I11
Minto NSW   15 M11
Mintos Hills Vic.   47 P5
Minvalara SA   80 I6

Minyip Vic.   57 J7
Miowera NSW   27 Q11, 28 B11
Miralie Vic.   61 N9
Miram Vic.   56 D7
Miranda SA   122 E8
Mirani Qld   119 K11, 127 F12
Mirannie NSW   25 L2, 29 L13
Mirboo Vic.   53 N10
Miriam Vale Qld   117 O5
Mirrool NSW   23 P8, 24 A8
Missabotti NSW   29 O8
Mission Beach Qld   118 G5
Mistake National Park Qld   112 C3
Mitcham SA   76 E11
Mitcham Vic.   39 Q9
Mitchell Qld   117 J8
Mitchell River Mission Qld   120 B10
Mitchells Flat NSW   18 B1
Mitchells Hill Vic.   57 L8
Mitchellstown Vic.   58 H10
Mitchellville SA   84 H9
Mitiamo Vic.   58 C5
Mitre Vic.   56 F9
Mittagong NSW   17 J6, 24 I8, 30 H3
Mitta Mitta Vic.   62 D8
Mittyack Vic.   22 F11, 61 J9
Moama NSW   23 K13, 58 F4
Moana Qld   124 H10
Moana SA   85 F12
Mockinya Vic.   56 H11
Modella Vic.   53 K8
Modewarre Vic.   44 C9
Moe Vic.   53 N8
Moe River NSW   117 O13
Moffatt Beach Qld   115 M12, 123 I12
Mogil Mogil NSW   28 E4, 117 K13
Moglanemby Vic.   59 J8
Mogo NSW   30 G7
Mogriguy NSW   28 E12
Moina Tas.   72 G8
Mokine WA   94 I2
Mole Creek Tas.   72 I8
Mole River NSW   29 M3, 117 O13
Molesworth Vic.   48 D3, 53 J1, 59 J12
Moliagul Vic.   57 P9
Molka Vic.   59 J9
Mollongghip Vic.   46 C8
Mollymook NSW   24 I11
Mologa Vic.   58 C5
Molong NSW   24 E4
Molterna Tas.   72 I7
Molyullah Vic.   59 M8
Mona SA   78 G1, 80 F11, 85 F12
Monak NSW   22 E8, 60 H3
Mona Park Vic.   50 H3
Monash SA   79 P3, 81 P12
Monash University Vic.   40 D6
Mona Vale NSW   13 P1, 21 P3, 25 K6
Mona Vale Tas.   71 N2, 73 N12
Monbulk Vic.   45 F8, 53 J6
Monbulk State Forest Vic.   45 D9
Monea Vic.   58 I10
Monegeeta Vic.   47 J7, 52 F2
Mongans Bridge Vic.   62 B8
Mongarlowe NSW   24 H11, 30 F6
Monkira Qld   122 F5
Monkland Qld   114 G3
Mons Qld   115 L10, 123 F9
Monsildale Qld   114 D10
Montagu Tas.   72 B3
Montagu Bay Tas.   67 G7
Montana Tas.   73 J8
Monteagle NSW   24 D7, 30 C2
Montebello Islands WA   92 D9
Montgomery Vic.   53 R7, 54 B9
Montmorency Vic.   39 N3
Monto Qld   117 N6
Montrose Vic.   45 D5, 48 B13
Montumana Tas.   72 E4
Montville Qld   115 J10, 123 C9
Monument Qld   121 D11
Mooball NSW   29 Q1, 113 Q12
Moockra SA   80 H4
Moodiarup WA   95 J5
Moodlu Qld   111 J4
Moody SA   84 F11
Moodys Valley Qld   112 H7
Moogara Tas.   68 E5, 71 K6

Moogerah Qld 112 E7
Moojebing WA 95 M5
Mookarra Qld 127 A3
Moolap Vic. 44 F8, 52 D8
Moolerr Vic. 57 N8
Moolert Vic. 46 B2, 57 Q12, 58 B12
Mooloo Qld 114 F4
Mooloolaba Qld 115 M10, 123 H9
Mooloolah Qld 115 K12
Mooloolah River National Park Qld 115 L11
Moolpa NSW 61 P8
Moombooldool NSW 23 O8
Moombra Qld 110 E7
Moonah Tas. 67 C5, 68 I6
Moonambel Vic. 57 N11
Moonan Flat NSW 25 K1, 29 K12
Moona Plains NSW 29 M9
Moonaran NSW 29 J8
Moonbah NSW 30 C9, 31 F10
Moonbi NSW 29 K9
Moondarewa Qld 113 P4
Moondarra Vic. 53 O7
Moondarra Reservoir Vic. 53 O7
Moonee Beach NSW 29 P7
Moonee Ponds Vic. 38 F6, 52 G5
Mooney Mooney NSW 15 O3
Mooney Mooney Creek National Park NSW
  18 C13
Moongulla NSW 117 J13
Moonie Qld 117 M11
Moonta SA 78 E2, 80 E11, 84 I10
Moonta Bay SA 78 E2, 80 E11
Moora WA 90 E8
Moorabbin Vic. 40 E11, 52 H6
Moorabbin Airport Vic. 40 G8
Mooraberree Qld 122 F6
Moorabool Vic. 44 E6
Moorabool Reservoir Vic. 46 C8, 52 B3
Mooralla Vic. 50 H2
Moora Moora Reservoir Vic. 51 J1, 57 J13
Moorang Qld 112 D4
Moorbel NSW 24 E5
Moore Qld 110 B1, 114 B13
Moorebank NSW 10 A10
Moore Creek NSW 29 K9
Moorefields NSW 10 H9
Moore Park NSW 11 O6
Moore River National Park WA 90 E9
Moores Flat Vic. 57 P12
Moorilim Vic. 58 I8
Moorina Tas. 73 P5
Moorland NSW 29 O12
Moorlands SA 79 M8
Moorleah Tas. 72 E4
Moormbool Vic. 58 G9
Moorna NSW 22 C8
Moornaming WA 95 O5
Moorngag Vic. 59 M9
Moorooduc Vic. 43 L4
Moorook SA 79 O3, 81 O12
Mooroolbark Vic. 45 C4, 48 B12
Mooroopna Vic. 58 I7
Moorowie SA 78 E7
Moppin NSW 28 H3, 117 L13
Moranbah Qld 119 J12
Moranding Vic. 47 L4
Morang Vic. 47 N10
Morangarell NSW 23 Q7, 24 C7, 30 A2
Moran Group Qld 115 J3
Morans Crossing NSW 30 F10
Morans Rock NSW 15 K2
Morawa WA 90 E7
Morayfield Qld 111 K4
Morchard SA 80 H5
Mordalup WA 94 I9
Mordetta WA 95 Q1
Mordialloc Vic. 40 I8, 52 H7
Morea Vic. 56 D9
Moree NSW 28 H4
Moree Vic. 50 E1, 56 E13
Moreenia SA 84 F11
Morella Qld 116 D2
Moreton Bay Qld 111 N7
Moreton Island Qld 111 P4
Morgan SA 79 M2, 81 M11
Morlac Vic. 44 D9
Morisset NSW 18 F9, 25 L4
Morkalla Vic. 60 B4

Morley WA 96 A10
Morney Qld 122 G6
Mornington Vic. 43 J3, 52 H8
Mornington Island Qld 121 C1
Mornington Mills WA 94 F3
Mornington Peninsula Vic. 42-3, 52 G10
Morongla Creek NSW 24 E7, 30 C2
Morpeth NSW 18 G2
Morphett Vale SA 78 I7, 85 G10
Morri Morri Vic. 57 L10
Morrisons Vic. 44 C2, 46 D12, 52 C5
Mortana SA 84 C8
Mortat Vic. 56 D9
Mortchup Vic. 51 P4
Mortdale NSW 10 H12
Mortigallup WA 95 M10
Mortlake Vic. 10 H3
Mortlake NSW 51 L7
Morton Nat. Park NSW 16 I12, 24 H10, 30 G4
Morton Plains Vic. 57 L4
Morundah NSW 23 N10
Moruya NSW 30 G8
Moruya Heads NSW 30 G8
Morven NSW 23 P12, 62 C1
Morven Qld 116 H8
Morwell Vic. 53 O8
Mosman NSW 11 O1, 13 O12
Mossiface Vic. 54 F7
Mosquito Creek NSW 28 I4
Mossgiel NSW 23 J5
Mossman Qld 118 F3, 120 I11
Mossman Gorge National Park Qld 126 A1
Moss Vale NSW 24 I9, 30 H4
Mossy Point NSW 30 G7
Mothar Mountains Qld 114 H4
Mouingba Qld 114 B1
Moulamein NSW 22 I10, 61 R9
Moule SA 84 A5
Moulyinning WA 95 N3
Mount Adrah NSW 24 C10, 30 A5
Mountain River Tas. 68 G8, 71 L7
Mount Aitken Vic. 46 I9
Mount Alexander Vic. 46 F1
Mount Alford Qld 112 F6
Mount Alfred Vic. 62 E4
Mount Anakie Vic. 44 D3
Mount Arthur Tas. 73 M6
Mount Barker SA 79 J7
Mount Barker WA 90 G13, 95 M11
Mount Barney Nat. Park Qld 29 O1, 112 G10
Mount Barrow National Park Tas. 73 N6
Mount Battery Vic. 59 M11
Mount Baw Baw Vic. 53 N5
Mount Beauty Vic. 62 C9
Mount Beckworth Vic. 51 P2, 57 P13
Mount Benambra Vic. 62 E8
Mount Benson SA 77 D8
Mount Beppo Qld 110 D5
Mount Berryman Qld 110 C13, 112 C1
Mount Best Vic. 53 N11
Mount Bindi Vic. 54 G3
Mount Blackwood Vic. 46 F9
Mount Bogong Vic. 62 D9
Mount Boothby Nat. Park SA 77 D2, 79 N11
Mount Bryan SA 81 J9
Mount Buangor Vic. 57 N13
Mount Buffalo Vic. 57 Q10, 62 A9
Mount Buffalo Chalet Vic. 59 Q9
Mount Buffalo Nat. Park Vic. 59 Q9, 62 A9
Mount Buller Vic. 59 O12
Mount Burr Vic. 77 G10
Mount Bute Vic. 51 O6
Mount Camel Vic. 58 F9
Mount Carbine Qld 118 F3, 120 H11
Mount Cavenagh SA 82 G1
Mount Charlton Qld 119 K10
Mount Clear Vic. 46 A10
Mount Colah NSW 12 G2
Mount Cole Vic. 51 N1, 57 N13
Mount Colliery Qld 112 B10
Mount Compass SA 78 I8
Mount Consultation Vic. 46 D3
Mount Coolangatta NSW 17 N11
Mount Coolon Qld 118 I11
Mount Coolum Qld 115 L8
Mount Cooper SA 84 C8
Mount Cooper Vic. 62 E9
Mount Cooroy Qld 123 D3

Mount Cotterill Vic. 52 E5
Mount Cotton Qld 111 N12
Mount Cottrell Vic. 44 H2, 46 H13
Mount Cougal National Park Qld 113 O9
Mount Crosby Qld 110 I11
Mount Cudgewa Vic. 62 E6
Mount Dandenong Vic. 45 E6, 52 I5
Mount David NSW 24 G6, 30 F1
Mount Difficult Vic. 57 J11
Mount Disappointment Vic. 47 N7
Mount Donna Buang Vic. 53 K4
Mount Doran Vic. 44 B1, 46 C12, 52 B5
Mount Druitt NSW 15 K7
Mount Drummond P.O. SA 84 D11
Mount Drysdale NSW 27 M10
Mount Dundas Vic. 50 G3
Mount Duneed Vic. 44 E9, 52 D8
Mount Dutton SA 83 K4
Mount Eccles Vic. 53 L9
Mount Eccles National Park Vic. 50 G7
Mount Edwards Qld 112 E6, 117 P11
Mount Egerton Vic. 46 D10, 52 C4
Mount Elgin Vic. 56 D7
Mount Eliza Vic. 41 R8, 43 K2, 52 H8
Mount Emu Vic. 51 O4
Mount Esk Pocket Qld 110 E5
Mount Evelyn Vic. 45 F3, 48 B13, 52 I5
Mount Evins Vic. 56 F12
Mount Fairy NSW 24 G10, 30 F5
Mount Feathertop Vic. 54 C1, 62 C10
Mount Field National Park Tas. 68 A3, 71 J5
Mount Flora NSW 17 J5
Mount Forbes Qld 112 F2
Mount Franklin Vic. 46 D5, 52 C1, 58 C13
Mount Gambier SA 50 A6, 77 H11
Mount Garnet Qld 118 F5, 120 G13
Mount Glorious Qld 110 H8
Mount Gorong Vic. 46 E10
Mount Hallen Qld 110 D7
Mount Helen Vic. 46 A10
Mount Hill SA 84 F10
Mount Hope NSW 23 M3
Mount Hope SA 84 E11
Mount Horeb NSW 24 C10, 30 B5
Mount Hotham Vic. 54 B2, 62 C11
Mount Howitt Qld 122 H8
Mount Howitt Vic. 59 P12
Mount Hunter NSW 15 J12
Mount Isa Qld 121 C8
Mount Kaputar National Park NSW 28 I6
Mount Keira NSW 17 O5, 19 A9
Mount Kembla NSW 17 N5
Mount Kilcoy Qld 110 F1, 114 F13
Mount Kosciusko NSW 30 B9, 31 C9, 62 I7
Mount Ku-ring-gai NSW 12 H1, 21 O13
Mount Larcom Qld 117 N4
Mount Lawley WA 87 E1
Mount Lewis NSW 10 F8
Mount Lloyd Tas. 68 E6, 71 K7
Mount Lofty SA 76 H10, 79 J7
Mount Lofty Vic. 46 G1
Mount Lonarch Vic. 51 O1, 57 O13
Mount Lyon Qld 113 J12
Mount Macedon Vic. 46 I7, 52 E2
Mount McIntyre SA 77 G10
Mount McLeod WA 95 L12
Mount Magnet WA 90 G5
Mount Maroon National Park Qld 112 G9
Mount Marshall NSW 17 N7
Mount Martha Vic. 42 I5, 52 G8
Mount Mary SA 79 L2, 81 L11
Mount Mee Qld 110 H4
Mount Mellum Qld 115 J12
Mount Mercer Vic. 46 A13, 51 Q5, 52 A5
Mount Misery Vic. 46 I10
Mount Molloy Qld 118 F3, 120 I12, 126 A4
Mount Morgan Qld 117 M3
Mount Moriac Vic. 44 D8, 52 C8
Mount Mort Qld 112 D2
Mount Muirhead SA 77 G10
Mount Mulligan Qld 118 E3, 120 H12
Mount Murray NSW 17 M7
Mount Murray Vic. 54 B2, 59 R12, 62 B12
Mount Napier Vic. 50 H6
Mount Nebo Qld 110 H9
Mount Nelson Tas. 67 E13
Mount Olga NT 104 D11
Mount Olive NSW 25 K2, 29 K13

Mount Ossa Qld 119 K10, 127 F10
Mount Pelion Qld 127 E10
Mount Perry Qld 117 O6
Mount Pleasant Qld 110 H5
Mount Pleasant SA 79 K6
Mount Pleasant Vic. 46 A10
Mount Pollock Vic. 44 B7
Mount Prospect Vic. 46 C7
Mount Rae NSW 16 B7
Mount Rat SA 78 E5
Mount Remarkable National Park SA 80 G5
Mount Rescue Nat. Park SA 77 F2, 79 O11
Mount Richmond Vic. 50 D8
Mount Richmond National Park Vic. 50 E9
Mount St Bernard Vic. 54 B2, 59 R11, 62 B11
Mount St Thomas NSW 19 B13
Mount Samaria Vic. 59 M10
Mount Samaria State Park Vic. 59 M10
Mount Samson Qld 110 I7
Mount Schank SA 50 A7, 77 H12
Mount Seaview NSW 29 M10
Mount Selwyn Vic. 54 A2
Mount Seymour Tas. 71 N4
Mount Slide Vic. 52 I3
Mount Sonder NT 104 H8
Mount Stanley Qld 114 A10
Mount Stanley Vic. 59 Q7, 62 A7
Mount Steiglitz Vic. 46 E9
Mount Stuart Tas. 67 C8
Mount Sturgeon Vic. 50 I4
Mount Sturt Qld 112 A8
Mount Surprise Qld 118 D6
Mount Sylvia Qld 112 A1
Mount Tamborine Qld 113 M5
Mount Tarampa Qld 110 E9
Mount Tarrengower Vic. 46 C1
Mount Taylor Vic. 54 E7
Mount Toolong Vic. 62 I5
Mount Towrang NSW 16 D12
Mount Victoria NSW 14 E6, 24 I6, 30 G1
Mount Victoria Vic. 48 F11
Mount View NSW 18 C5
Mount Vincent NSW 18 E6
Mount Walker Qld 112 E2
Mount Walker Lower Qld 110 E13, 112 E1
Mount Wallace Vic. 44 D1, 46 E12, 52 C5
Mount Waverley Vic. 39 N13, 40 B6
Mount Wedge P.O. SA 84 D9
Mount Wellington Tas. 68 H7, 71 M7
Mount White NSW 15 O2
Mount Whitestone Qld 117 O11
Mount William Vic. 57 J13
Mount Willoughby SA 82 H4
Mount Wilson NSW 14 F4
Mount Windsor Qld 122 G3
Mount Worth State Park Vic. 53 M9
Moura Qld 117 M5
Mourilyan Qld 118 G5
Moutajup Vic. 50 I4
Mowbray Park NSW 17 K1
Mowen WA 94 C7
Mowo Qld 127 D7
Moyhu Vic. 59 O8
Moyston Vic. 51 L2, 57 J13
Muckadilla Qld 117 J8
Muckatah Vic. 59 K4
Muckleford Vic. 46 D2
Mudamuckla SA 84 B6
Mudgee NSW 24 G3
Mudgeeraba Qld 113 O7
Mudgegonga Vic. 59 Q7, 62 A7
Mudjimba Qld 115 L9, 123 H7
Muggleton Qld 117 K8
Muja WA 94 H4
Mukinbudin WA 90 G8
Mulbring NSW 18 E5
Mulcra Vic. 60 B10, 79 R7
Mulgoa NSW 15 J9
Mulgowie Qld 112 C1
Mulgrave NSW 15 K5
Mulgrave Vic. 40 D4
Mulkirri SA 78 I2, 80 I11
Mullaley NSW 28 H9
Mullalyup WA 94 F6
Mullaway NSW 29 P6
Mullengandra NSW 23 P13, 62 C3
Mullengudgery NSW 27 Q11, 28 B11
Mullet Creek Qld 117 P5

Mullewa WA 90 E6
Mullindolingong Vic. 62 C8
Mullion Creek NSW 24 F4
Mullumbimby NSW 29 Q2, 117 Q12
Mulpata SA 79 P7
Mulwala NSW 23 N13, 59 M4
Mumballup WA 94 G5
Mumbannar Vic. 50 C6
Mumbel Vic. 57 N1, 61 N12
Mumbil NSW 24 F3
Mumblin Vic. 51 M9
Mummell NSW 16 A11
Mummulgum NSW 29 P3
Munbilla Qld 112 G3
Munbura Qld 127 H13
Mundalla SA 77 H4, 79 Q13
Mundoona Vic. 58 I5
Mundoora SA 80 G9
Mundoora National Park SA 80 G9
Mundrabilla WA 91 P10
Mundubbera Qld 117 N7
Mungallala Qld 116 I8
Mungana Qld 118 D4, 120 G12
Mungeriba NSW 27 R13, 28 D12
Mungerup WA 95 P8
Mungery NSW 23 R2, 24 C2
Mungindi NSW 28 F3, 117 K13
Munglinup WA 91 J12
Mungungo Qld 117 N6
Munmorah Lake NSW 18 G10
Munro Vic. 54 C8
Muradup WA 95 K6
Murbko SA 79 M3, 81 M12
Murchison Vic. 58 H8
Murdinga SA 84 E10
Murdong WA 95 M6
Murdunna Tas. 69 O8, 71 P7
Murga NSW 24 E5
Murgenella NT 100 H2
Murgenella Wildlife Sanctuary NT 100 H3
Murgheboluc Vic. 44 C7, 52 C7
Murgon Qld 117 O8
Murmungee Vic. 59 P7
Muronbung NSW 28 F13
Murphys Creek Vic. 57 Q9, 58 A9
Murrabit Vic. 22 I12, 61 Q12
Murrawal NSW 28 G10
Murra Warra Vic. 56 H7
Murray Bridge SA 79 L7
Murray Town SA 80 H6, 83 N13
Murrayville Vic. 60 C10, 79 R8
Murrindal Vic. 54 H5
Murrindindi Vic. 47 R6, 48 D6, 53 J2
Murringo NSW 24 D8, 30 C3
Murroon Vic. 51 Q10, 52 A10
Murrumba Qld 110 E6
Murrumbateman NSW 24 F10, 30 D5
Murrumbeena Vic. 39 L13, 40 C10
Murrumburrah NSW 24 D8, 30 C3
Murrungowar Vic. 55 K6
Murrurundi NSW 29 J11
Murtoa Vic. 57 J8
Murwillumbah NSW 29 Q1, 113 P11, 117 Q12
Musk Vic. 46 D6, 52 C2
Muskerry West Vic. 58 E9
Musk Vale Vic. 46 D7
Musselboro Tas. 73 N6
Muston SA 78 F11
Muswellbrook NSW 25 J2, 29 J13
Mutarnee Qld 118 G7
Mutchero Inlet National Park Qld 126 I12
Mutdapilly Qld 112 G2
Muttaburra Qld 116 E2, 118 E13
Muttama NSW 24 D9, 30 B4
Myall Vic. 61 R12, 57 R1, 58 B1
Myalla Tas. 72 E4
Myall Lakes National Park NSW 25 N2
Myall Mundi NSW 27 R12, 28 C12
Myall Plains NSW 23 M11
Myalup WA 94 E2
Myamyn Vic. 50 F7
Myaring Vic. 50 D5
Myers Flat Vic. 58 C9
Mylestom NSW 29 P8
Myola Vic. 58 E8
Myphree SA 78 G2, 80 G11
Mypolonga SA 79 L7
Myponga SA 78 I9

Myra Vale NSW 17 L8
Myrla SA 79 O4, 81 O13
Myrniong Vic. 46 F10, 52 D4
Myrrhee Vic. 59 N9
Myrtle Bank Tas. 73 M6
Myrtle Bridge Vic. 58 D11
Myrtleford Vic. 59 Q8
Myrtle Scrub NSW 29 M10
Myrtleville NSW 16 C7, 24 H8, 30 F3
Mysia Vic. 57 Q5, 58 A5
Mystic Park Vic. 57 P1, 61 P12
Mywee Vic. 59 J3

N

Nabageena Tas. 72 C4
Nabawa WA 90 D6
Nabiac NSW 25 N1, 29 N13
Nabilla Qld 127 G12
Nabowla Tas. 73 N5
Nackara SA 81 K5
Nadda SA 79 Q5
Nadgee Fauna Park NSW 30 F12, 55 P5
Nagambie Vic. 58 H9
Nagoorin Qld 117 N5
Nairne SA 79 J7
Nala Tas. 71 N3, 73 N13
Nalangil Vic. 51 O9
Nalbaugh National Park NSW 55 O3
Nalinga Vic. 59 K7
Nambour Qld 115 K9, 117 Q8, 123 E8
Nambrok Vic. 53 Q7, 54 A9
Nambucca Heads NSW 29 P8
Nammuldi SA 80 A7, 84 G8
Nana Glen NSW 29 P7
Nanango Qld 117 O9
Nanarup WA 95 O12
Nandaly Vic. 22 F11, 61 K10
Nandroya Qld 115 J6, 123 D2
Nanga WA 94 G1
Nangana Vic. 53 J6
Nangari SA 79 Q4, 81 Q13
Nangiloc Vic. 60 I5
Nangri SA 60 A5
Nangus NSW 23 R10, 24 C10, 30 B5
Nangwarry SA 50 A4, 77 H10
Nanneella Vic. 58 F6
Nannine WA 90 G4
Nannup WA 90 E12, 94 F7
Nantabibbie SA 81 K5
Nantawarra SA 78 H2, 80 H11
Napier WA 95 O12
Napoleons Vic. 46 A11, 51 Q4, 52 A4
Nappa Merry Qld 122 G10
Napperby SA 80 G7
Naracoorte SA 56 A11, 77 H7
Naracoorte Caves National Park SA 77 H7
Naradhan NSW 23 N6
Narangba Qld 111 K6
Narara NSW 15 Q1, 18 E13
Narbethong Vic. 48 F9, 53 K3
Nareen Vic. 50 E2
Narellan NSW 15 K12
Narembeen WA 90 H10
Naremburn NSW 13 M12
Nariel Creek Vic. 62 F7
Naringal Vic. 51 L10
Narioka Vic. 58 H4
Narlingup WA 95 J6
Nar-Nar-Goon Vic. 53 J7
Naroghid Vic. 51 M8
Narooma NSW 30 G9
Narrabarba NSW 30 F12, 55 P4
Narrabeen NSW 13 Q4, 21 R4
Narrabri NSW 28 H7
Narracan Vic. 53 N8
Narrandera NSW 23 O9
Narraport Vic. 57 M4
Narrawa NSW 24 F8, 30 E3
Narraweena NSW 13 P7
Narrawong Vic. 50 F9
Narrewillock Vic. 57 O5
Narridy SA 80 H8
Narrikup WA 95 M11
Narrogin WA 90 G11, 94 K2
Narromine NSW 24 D1, 28 D13
Narrows NT 98 I4

Narrung SA   79 K9
Narrung Vic.   61 N7
Narwee NSW   10 G11
Naryilco Qld   122 H12
Nashdale NSW   24 F5
Nashville Qld   114 G3
Nathalia Vic.   23 L13, 58 H4
Natimuk Vic.   56 G9
National Park Tas.   68 C4, 71 J6
Natone Upper Tas.   72 G6
Nattai NSW   24 I7, 30 H2
Nattai River NSW   14 H13
Natte Yallock Vic.   57 O11
Natural Bridge National Park Qld   113 N9
Naturi SA   79 M8
Natya Vic.   61 N8
Navarre Vic.   57 M10
Navigators Vic.   46 B10
Nayook Vic.   53 L6
Neales Flat SA   79 K3, 81 K12
Neath NSW   18 D4
Nebo Qld   119 K12
Nectar Brook SA   80 F5
Neds Corner Vic.   60 C2
Needaling WA   95 P3
Needilup WA   95 R7
Needles Tas.   73 J8
Neeralin Pool WA   95 L3
Neerim Junction Vic.   53 L6
Neerim South Vic.   53 L7
Neeworra NSW   28 F3, 117 K13
Neika Tas.   68 H8
Neilborough Vic.   58 C8
Neilrex NSW   28 G11
Nelia Qld   118 A10, 121 H8
Nelligen NSW   30 G7
Nelshaby SA   80 G7
Nelson SA   77 I12
Nelson Vic.   50 C7
Nelson Bay NSW   25 M3
Nelsons Plains NSW   18 H2
Nelungaloo NSW   23 R4, 24 C4
Nerang Qld   113 O5
Neranwood Qld   113 O7
Nerriga NSW   30 G5
Nerrigundah NSW   30 F8
Nerrina Vic.   46 A9
Nerring Vic.   51 O3
Nerrin Nerrin Vic.   51 M5
Netherby Vic.   56 E5
Nethercote NSW   30 F11
Netherdale Qld.   127 C11
Netherwood WA   95 N4
Neuarpurr Vic.   56 B10, 77 I6
Neurea NSW   24 F3
Neuroodla SA   80 G1
Neurum Qld   110 G2
Neusa Vale Qld   114 I3
Neutral Bay NSW   11 N1, 13 N13
Nevertire NSW   27 R12, 38 C11
Neville NSW   24 F6, 30 E1
New Angledool NSW   27 R3, 28 C3
New Beith Qld   113 J2
Newborough Vic.   53 N8
Newbridge NSW   24 G6, 30 E1
Newbridge Vic.   57 Q9, 58 B9
New Brighton NSW   29 R2, 113 R13
Newbury Vic.   46 E7, 52 D2
Newcastle NSW   15 I5, 19 J6, 29 L4
Newcastle Waters NT   102 I4
Newcomb Vic.   63 I4
Newdegate WA   90 H11
Newell Qld   126 B1
New England National Park NSW   29 N8
New Farm Qld   109 H2
Newfield Vic.   51 M11
Newham Vic.   46 I6, 52 E2, 58 E13
Newhaven Vic.   43 Q13, 52 I10
Newington Vic.   63 C12
New Koreela NSW   112 C13
Newlands WA   94 F5
Newlyn Vic.   46 B7, 51 R2, 52 B2
Newman WA   92 I12
Newmerella Vic.   54 I7
New Mollyann NSW   28 F11
Newnes NSW   24 I4
Newnes Junction NSW   14 D4
New Norcia WA   90 F9

New Norfolk Tas.   68 F5, 71 L6
Newport NSW   21 O4
Newport Vic.   38 D10
Newport Beach NSW   15 Q5
New Residence SA   79 P4, 81 P13
Newry Vic.   53 Q6, 54 A8
Newrybar NSW   29 Q2
Newry Island Qld   127 F9
Newstead Vic.   46 C3, 57 R12, 58 B12
Newton Boyd NSW   29 N5
Newtown NSW   11 L6, 15 K5
New Town Tas.   67 D5, 68 I7
Newtown Vic.   63 C4
New Well SA   79 N4, 81 N13
Ngallo Vic.   60 B11, 79 R8
Ngapala SA   79 J2, 81 J11
Ngukurr NT   101 L9
Nhill Vic.   56 E6
Nhulunbuy NT   101 P4
Niagara Park NSW   18 E13
Niangala NSW   29 L10
Nicholls Rivulet Tas.   68 G11, 71 L9
Nicholson Vic.   54 F8
Nierinna Tas.   68 H9
Nietta Tas.   72 G7
Nightcap National Park NSW   29 Q1
Nightcliff NT   98 B6
Nildottie SA   79 M5
Nile Tas.   73 M9
Nillahcootie Vic.   59 M11
Nilma Vic.   53 L8
Nimbin NSW   29 Q2
Nimmitabel NSW   30 E9
Ninda Vic.   61 K12
Ninderry Qld   115 L9, 123 H8
Nindigully Qld   28 F1, 117 K1
Nine Mile Vic.   57 O7
Ninety Mile Beach Vic.   54 C11
Ningana SA   84 E11
Ni Ni Vic.   56 F6
Ninnes SA   78 G2, 80 G11
Ninyeunook Vic.   57 O4
Nipan Qld   117 M5
Nippering WA   95 M3
Nirranda Vic.   51 L10
Noarlunga SA   85 G12
Nobby Creek NSW   113 O10
Nobby Glen Qld   114 G6
Noble Park Vic.   40 G4
Nockatunga Qld   122 I10
Noggerup WA   94 G5
Nomans Lake WA   95 M1
Nonda Qld   118 B10, 121 H8
Nondiga Qld   114 C1
Noojee Vic.   53 L6
Nookanellup WA   95 L6
Noonamah NT   100 E5
Noonbinna NSW   24 E6, 30 C1
Noondoo Qld   28 E1, 117 J12
Noora SA   60 A5, 79 Q4, 81 Q13
Nooramunga Vic.   59 L6
Noorat Vic.   51 M8
Noorinbee Vic.   55 M6
Noorlah Qld   119 K10
Noorongong Vic.   62 C6
Noosa Head National Park Qld   115 M6
Noosa Heads Qld   115 L6, 117 Q8, 123 H1
Noosaville Qld   115 L6, 123 G1
Nora Creina Bay SA   77 E9
Noradjuha Vic.   56 G10
Norah Head NSW   18 G11, 25 L5
Norahville NSW   18 G11
Noranda WA   96 A9
Nords Wharf NSW   18 G9
Normanby Qld   109 A1
Normanhurst NSW   12 F6
Normanton Qld   121 F3
Normanville SA   78 H9
Normanville Vic.   57 P2
Nornalup WA   95 J13
Norong Vic.   59 O5
Norseman WA   91 K10
North Adelaide SA   75 D3
Northam WA   90 F9
Northampton WA   90 D6
North Arm Qld   115 K8, 123 D4
North Balgowlah NSW   13 O9
North Berry Jerry NSW   24 B9

North Blackwood Vic.   46 F7
North Bondi NSW   11 R5
Northbridge NSW   13 M11
Northbrook Qld   110 F8
North Bruny Island Tas.   71 M9
Northcliffe WA   90 F13, 94 G11
Northcote Vic.   38 I7
North Curl Curl NSW   13 Q7
North Deep Creek Qld   114 G1
North Haven NSW   29 O11
North Hobart Tas.   67 E7
North Manly NSW   13 P8
Northmead NSW   12 B11
North Motton Tas.   72 H6
North Muckleford Vic.   46 D2
North Parramatta NSW   10 C1, 12 C12
North Rocks NSW   12 C10
North Ryde NSW   12 I10
North Shields SA   84 F12
North Star NSW   28 I2, 117 M13
North Strathfield NSW   10 G4
North Sydney NSW   11 M2, 13 M13
Northville NSW   18 G6
North West Aboriginal Reserve SA   82 B3,
   104 D13
North Wollongong NSW   17 O5
Northwood Vic.   58 H11
North Wollongong NSW   19 F9
Norval Vic.   51 L1, 57 L13
Norwell Qld   113 O2
Norwood NSW   16 C11
Notley Hills Tas.   73 K7
Notting Hill Vic.   40 C6
Notts Well SA   79 M4, 81 M13
Nourlangie NT   100 H5
Nowa Nowa Vic.   54 G7
Nowendoc NSW   29 M11
Nowie North Vic.   61 N10
Nowingi Vic.   60 H5
Nowley NSW   28 F6
Nowra NSW   17 M12, 24 I10, 30 H5
Nowra Hill NSW   24 I10, 30 H5
Nubba NSW   24 D8, 30 B3
Nubeena Tas.   67 E4, 69 N11, 71 O8
Nugent Tas.   69 N4, 71 O6
Nulkaba NSW   18 C4, 32 H10
Nullagine WA   92 I10
Nullan Vic.   57 J7
Nullarbor Plain WA   82 A9, 91 M8
Nulla Vale Vic.   47 J4, 52 F1, 58 F12
Nullawarre Vic.   51 L10
Nullawil Vic.   57 M3
Numbla Vale NSW   30 D10, 31 I12
Numbugga NSW   30 F10
Numbulwar NT   101 N8
Numeralla NSW   30 E8
Numinbah NSW   113 N10
Numinbah Valley Qld   113 N8
Numurkah Vic.   23 L13, 59 J4
Nunamara Tas.   73 M7
Nunawading Vic.   39 Q9
Nundle NSW   29 K11
Nunga Vic.   60 I9
Nungatta National Park NSW   30 E11, 55 N3
Nungurner Vic.   54 F8
Nunjikompita SA   82 I12, 84 B6
Nunkeri SA   79 N7
Nurina WA   91 O9
Nurinda Qld   110 C1
Nuriootpa SA   79 K4, 81 K13, 85 F2
Nurom SA   80 G8
Nurrabiel Vic.   56 G11
Nurrondi SA   80 G9
Nutfield Vic.   47 O10
Nyabing WA   90 G12, 95 O5
Nyah Vic.   22 G11, 61 N9
Nyallo Vic.   57 J2
Nyamup WA   90 F13, 94 H9
Nyarrin Vic.   61 K11
Nymagee NSW   23 N1, 27 N12
Nymboida NSW   29 O6
Nymbool Qld   118 E5, 120 G13
Nyngan NSW   27 P11, 28 A11
Nyora Vic.   53 K9
Nypo Vic.   56 G2, 60 G13

O

Oakdale NSW 14 H13
Oakenden Qld 127 G13
Oakey Qld 117 O10
Oakey Creek NSW 28 H11
Oak Flats NSW 17 O7
Oakhampton NSW 18 F2
Oaklands SA 78 F7, 84 I13
Oaklands NSW 23 N12
Oakleigh Vic. 40 D9, 52 H6
Oak Park Vic. 38 F3
Oaks Tas. 73 L8
Oakvale Vic. 57 P3
Oakview Qld 114 C1
Oakwood Tas. 69 O11, 71 P8
Oaky Flats Qld 111 J5
Oatlands Tas. 71 M3, 73 M13
Oatley NSW 10 H12
Oberlin Tas. 71 L6
Oberne NSW 23 R11, 24 C11, 30 A6
Oberon NSW 24 H6, 30 F1
O.B. Flat SA 50 A6, 77 H12
O'Bil Bil Qld 117 N7
Obi Obi Qld 114 I9, 123 A8
Obley NSW 24 E3
O.B.X. Creek NSW 29 O6
Ocean Grove Vic. 44 G9, 52 E8
Ocean View NSW 17 M7
Ockley WA 95 L1
O'Connell NSW 24 G6
O'Connor ACT 34 D4
Oenpelli Mission NT 100 I4
Ogmore Qld 117 L2, 119 L13
Olangalah Vic. 51 P11
Olary SA 81 O3, 83 Q12
Old Adaminaby NSW 31 G3
Old Bar NSW 25 O1, 29 O12
Old Beach Tas. 68 I5, 71 M6
Old Bonalbo NSW 29 O2
Old Bowenfels NSW 14 C5
Old Cannidah Qld 117 N6
Old Cork Qld 122 H2
Oldina Tas. 72 F5
Old Junee NSW 23 Q9, 24 B9, 30 A4
Old Koreelah NSW 112 D11
Old Rothbury NSW 32 G4
Old Sydney Town NSW 20 A6, 25 K5
Old Warrah NSW 29 J11
Olga, Mount NT 104 D11, 107
Olgas, The NT 107
Olinda NSW 24 H3
Olinda Vic. 45 D8, 48 B13, 52 I5
Olinda Reservoir Vic. 45 D3
Olinda State Forest Vic. 45 E7
Olio Qld 118 C12
Ombersley Vic. 51 Q8, 52 A8
Omega NSW 17 O9
Omeo Vic. 54 E3, 62 E12
Ondit Vic. 51 P8
One Tree NSW 23 J7
One Tree Hill Vic. 44 G3
Ongerup WA 90 H12, 95 Q7
Onoto Qld 122 H4
Onslow WA 92 D10
Oodla Wirra SA 81 K5
Oodnadatta SA 83 J4
Ooldea SA 82 E9
Ooma Creek NSW 24 C6, 30 B1
Oonah Tas. 72 E6
Oondooroo Qld 116 C1, 118 C12
Oorindi Qld 121 F8
Ootha NSW 23 Q4, 24 B4
Opalton Qld 116 B3, 121 I13, 122 I2
Opossum Bay Tas. 69 J9, 71 N8
Orange NSW 24 F5
Orangeville NSW 14 I12
Oranmeir NSW 30 F7
Oraparinna SA 83 O10
Orbost Vic. 30 C13, 54 I7
Orchard Hills NSW 15 J8
Ord River WA 93 R3
O'Reillys Green Mountains Qld 113 M9
Orford Tas. 69 O2, 71 P5
Orford Vic. 50 H8
Organ Pipes National Park Vic. 47 K11
Orielton Tas. 69 K5, 71 N6
Orientos Qld 122 G11
Ormeau Qld 113 N2

Ormesby Qld 114 I3
Ormiston Qld 111 N10
Ormley Tas. 73 P9
Ormond Vic. 40 D11
Orpheus Island Qld 118 H6
Orroroo SA 80 I5, 83 O13
Orrvale Vic. 59 J7
Osborne SA 76 A3
Osbornes Flat Vic. 59 P6, 62 A6
Osbourne NSW 23 O11
O'Shannassy Reservoir Vic. 53 L4
Osmington WA 94 C7
Osterley Tas. 71 K3, 73 K13
Otford NSW 17 P1
Ottaba Qld 110 D5
Otway Ranges Vic. 51 Q11, 52 A11
Ourimbah NSW 18 E13, 25 K5
Ournie NSW 23 R13, 30 A8, 62 G3
Ouse Tas. 68 C1, 71 J4
Ouyen Vic. 22 E10, 60 I9
Ovens Vic. 59 Q8, 62 A8
Overland Corner SA 79 O2, 81 O12
Ovingham SA 75 C2
Owanyilla Qld 117 P7
Owen SA 78 I3, 80 I12
Owens Gap NSW 25 J1, 29 J12
Oxenford Qld 113 O4
Oxford Falls NSW 13 N6
Oxley NSW 22 I8
Oxley Vic. 59 O7
Oyster Bay NSW 15 O10
Oyster Cove Tas. 68 H11, 71 M8
Oyster Point SA 84 I13
Ozenkadnook Vic. 56 D10

P

Paaratte Vic. 51 M10
Pacific Palms NSW 25 N2
Packsaddle NSW 26 C8
Paddys River NSW 30 G4
Padstow NSW 10 E11
Padthaway SA 77 G5
Pagewood NSW 11 O9
Paignie Vic. 60 G9
Painswick Vic. 57 P10, 58 A10
Pakenham Vic. 53 J7
Palen Creek Qld 112 I9
Palgarup WA 94 G8
Pallamallawa NSW 28 I4
Pallarang Vic. 60 C9
Pallinup WA 95 N7
Palm Beach NSW 15 Q4, 21 L3, 25 K6
Palm Beach Qld 113 Q7, 125 N7
Palm Dale NSW 18 E12
Palmer SA 79 K6
Palmers Island NSW 29 Q4
Palmerston Gardens NT 99 M10
Palmerville Qld 118 D2, 120 F10
Palm Grove NSW 18 D12
Palm Islands Qld 118 H6
Palm Valley NT 104 H9
Palm View Qld 123 F11
Palmwoods Qld 115 K10, 123 D9
Paloona Tas. 72 H6
Palparara Qld 122 G5
Paluma Qld 118 G7
Pambula NSW 30 F11, 55 P2
Panania NSW 10 C11
Pandie Pandie SA 122 D8
Panitya Vic. 60 B10, 79 R8
Panmure Vic. 51 L9
Pannawonica WA 92 E10
Panton Hill Vic. 47 O10, 48 A10
Pappinbarra NSW 29 O10
Papunya NT 104 F7
Paraburdoo WA 92 F12
Parachilna SA 83 N10
Paradise Tas. 72 I7
Paradise Vic. 57 M10
Paradise Point Qld 113 P4
Paradise Waters Qld 124 E10
Parap NT 99 L7
Paraparap Vic. 44 D9
Paratoo SA 81 L5, 83 P13
Parattah Tas. 71 N3, 73 M13
Para Wirra National Park SA 79 J5
Parilla SA 79 Q8

Paringa SA 79 Q3, 81 Q12
Parkdale Vic. 44 H8
Parkes ACT 34 E10
Parkes NSW 24 D4
Parkham Tas. 73 J7
Park Orchards Vic. 39 R7, 48 A12
Park Ridge Qld 113 K1
Parksbourne NSW 16 A12
Parkside SA 75 G10
Parkville NSW 25 J1, 29 J12
Parkwood Vic. 50 G4
Parndana SA 78 D11
Parragundy Gate NSW 27 J3
Parrakie SA 79 O9
Parramatta NSW 10 C2, 12 C13, 25 J6, 30 I1
Parrawe Tas. 72 E6
Parryville WA 95 K13
Paruna SA 79 Q5
Parwan Vic. 44 G1, 46 G11, 52 D4
Paschendale Vic. 50 F4
Pascoe Vale Vic. 38 F4
Paskeville SA 78 F2, 80 F11
Pastoria Vic. 52 E1, 58 E13
Pata SA 79 P5
Patchewollock Vic. 60 H11
Paterson NSW 18 F1, 25 L3
Patersonia Tas. 73 M7
Patho Vic. 58 D4
Patonga NSW 15 P3, 20 I6
Patonga NT 100 H5
Patrick Estate Qld 110 F9
Patyah Vic. 56 C10
Pauls Range Vic. 47 R9
Paupong NSW 30 C10, 31 H11
Pawleena Tas. 69 L5, 71 N6
Pawtella Tas. 71 N3, 73 N13
Paxton NSW 18 B6
Payneham SA 76 F7
Paynes Crossing NSW 29 K4
Paynes Find WA 90 G7
Paynesville Vic. 54 E8
Paytens Bridge NSW 24 D5
Peachester Qld 115 J13, 123 C13
Peaceful Bay WA 95 J13
Peachna SA 84 E10
Peak Crossing Qld 112 H2
Peake SA 79 N8
Peake Creek SA 83 K5
Peak Hill NSW 24 D3
Peakhurst NSW 10 G11
Peak View NSW 30 E8
Pearcedale Vic. 43 O3, 52 I8
Pearlah SA 84 E12
Pearl Beach NSW 15 Q3, 20 H4
Peats Ridge NSW 18 C12
Pebbly Beach Qld 126 C2
Pedirka SA 83 J2
Peebinga SA 60 A8, 79 R6
Peebinga National Park SA 79 Q6
Peechelba NSW 59 N5
Peel NSW 24 G5
Peelwood NSW 24 G7, 30 E2
Peep Hill SA 79 K3, 81 J12
Pekina SA 80 I5, 83 N13
Pelaw Main NSW 18 E4
Pelham Tas. 68 F2, 71 L5
Pelican Flat NSW 18 G8
Pella Vic. 56 F3
Pelton NSW 18 C5
Pelverata Tas. 68 G10, 71 L8
Pemberton WA 90 F13, 94 G9
Pembroke NSW 29 O10
Penarie NSW 22 H8, 61 O4
Penguin Tas. 72 G5
Penguin Island National Park SA 77 E10
Penna Tas. 71 N6
Pennant Hills NSW 12 F7
Penneshaw SA 78 G10
Pennyroyal Vic. 51 Q10, 52 A10
Penola SA 50 A3, 77 H9
Penong SA 82 G11
Penrice SA 85 H3
Penrith NSW 15 J7, 25 J6, 30 I1
Penrose NSW 16 H10
Penshurst NSW 10 H11
Penshurst Vic. 50 I6
Pental Vic. 61 O11
Pentland Qld 118 F9

Pentland Hills Vic. 46 F10
Penwortham SA 78 I2, 80 I11
Penzance Tas. 67 H2
Peppers Plain Vic. 56 H5
Percydale Vic. 57 O11
Peregian Beach Qld 115 M7, 123 H4
Perekerten NSW 22 H10
Perenjori WA 90 F7
Perenna Vic. 56 F4
Pericoe NSW 30 E11, 55 O3
Perillup WA 95 L10
Peringillup WA 95 M7
Perisher NSW 30 C9, 31 D9
Perponda SA 79 N7
Perkins Reef Vic. 46 C1
Perronne Vic. 56 D9
Perroomba SA 80 H5
Perry Bridge Vic. 54 C9
Perth Tas. 73 M8
Perth WA 87-9, 90 E10
Perthville NSW 24 G5
Perwillowent Qld 115 J10, 123 D8
Petcheys Bay Tas. 68 F12
Peterborough SA 81 J6, 83 O13
Peterborough Vic. 51 L11
Petermann Ranges Aboriginal Reserve NT 104 B10
Petersham NSW 11 K6
Petersons Vic. 47 P6, 52 I2, 58 I13
Petersville SA 78 F4, 80 F13
Petford Qld 118 E4, 120 G13
Petrie Terrace Qld 109 A2
Pettavel Vic. 44 D8
Pheasant Creek Qld 117 M4
Pheasant Creek Vic. 47 P8, 48 B8, 52 I3
Phegans Bay NSW 15 Q2
Phillip Bay NSW 11 P11
Phillip Island Vic. 52 I10
Phils Creek NSW 24 E8, 30 D3
Pia Aboriginal Reserve WA 90 E4
Pialba Qld 117 Q6
Piallaway NSW 29 J10
Piamble Vic. 61 N7
Piangil Vic. 22 G10, 61 N9
Pichi Richi Pass SA 80 G3
Pickettaramoor NT 100 D3
Picnic Point NSW 10 D13
Picola Vic. 58 H4
Picton NSW 17 L1, 24 I7, 30 H2
Picton Junction WA 94 E4
Pier Millan Vic. 61 K10
Piesseville WA 95 L3
Pigeon Ponds Vic. 50 F2, 56 F13
Piggabeen NSW 113 Q8
Piggoreet Vic. 51 P5
Pikedale Qld 117 O12
Pilchers Bridge Vic. 58 D10
Pillar Valley NSW 29 P5
Pilliga NSW 28 F7
Pillinger Tas. 70 E3, 72 E13
Pimba SA 83 L10, 84 G3
Pimbaacla SA 84 C6
Pimpama Qld 113 N3
Pimpinio Vic. 56 H8
Pinbarren Qld 115 J5
Pindi Pindi Qld 127 E9
Pine Creek NT 100 F7
Pine Gap NT 105 J8
Pine Hill Qld 116 H3
Pine Lodge Vic. 59 J6
Pine Point SA 78 F5
Pinery SA 80 H13
Pingaring WA 95 Q1
Pingelly WA 90 F10
Pingrup WA 90 H11, 95 Q5
Pinjarra WA 90 E11
Pinkawillinie Conservation Park SA 83 J13
Pink Lakes State Park Vic. 60 F7
Pinnacle Qld 127 E11
Pinnaroo SA 60 A10, 79 R8
Pioneer Tas. 73 P5
Pipers Brook Tas. 73 M5
Pipers Creek Vic. 46 H5, 52 E1, 58 E13
Pipers Flat NSW 14 A3
Pipers River Tas. 73 L5
Pira Vic. 61 N10
Piries Vic. 59 M12
Pirlta Vic. 60 F4

Pirron Yallock Vic. 51 O9
Pittong Vic. 51 O4
Pittsworth Qld 117 O11
Pitt Town NSW 15 K4
Pittwater NSW 15 Q4, 21 L4
Plainland Qld 110 D11
Planet Downs Qld 122 F7
Platts NSW 30 E11
Pleasure Point NSW 10 C12
Plenty Tas. 68 E5, 71 K6
Plenty Vic. 39 N1
Plevna Downs Qld 122 I8
Pleystowe Qld 127 G11
Plumpton NSW 15 L7
Plunkett Qld 113 M3
Plush Corner SA 85 H2
Plympton SA 76 C10
Poatina Tas. 73 L10
Point Arkwright Qld 115 L8, 123 H5
Point Clare NSW 15 Q1, 20 B3
Point Cook Vic. 52 F6
Point Lonsdale Vic. 44 H9, 52 E9
Point Lookout Qld 111 R9
Point Pass SA 79 K2, 81 K11
Point Perry Qld 115 L8
Point Piper NSW 11 P3
Point Samson WA 92 F9
Point Stuart NT 100 F4
Pokataroo NSW 28 E4
Pokolbin NSW 18 B4, 32 C8
Policemans Point SA 77 D3, 79 M12
Police Point Tas. 68 F13, 71 L9
Polkemmet Vic. 56 G9
Pomborneit Vic. 51 O9
Pomona Qld 115 J5, 117 Q8
Pomonal Vic. 51 K1, 57 K13
Pompapiel Vic. 57 R6, 58 B6
Pondooma SA 80 C9
Pontville Tas. 68 I4, 71 M5
Pontypool Tas. 71 P3
Poochera SA 82 I13, 84 D7
Pooginagoric SA 56 A7
Poolaigelo Vic. 50 C1, 56 C13, 77 I8
Pooncarie NSW 22 E5
Pootenup WA 95 M8
Pootilla Vic. 46 B9, 51 R3, 52 B3
Poowong Vic. 53 K9
Poppet Head Vic. 46 A9
Porcupine Flat Vic. 46 C1
Porcupine Ridge Vic. 46 D5
Porepunkah Vic. 59 Q9, 62 A9
Porlock Qld 112 C2
Porongurup National Park WA 95 N11
Porongurups WA 95 N11
Port Adelaide SA 76 B5
Port Albert Vic. 53 P11
Port Alma Qld 117 N3
Portarlington Vic. 44 I7, 52 F7
Port Arthur Tas. 67 G5, 69 O11, 71 O9
Port Augusta SA 80 F4, 83 M12, 84 I7
Port Broughton SA 80 F9
Port Campbell Vic. 51 M11
Port Campbell National Park Vic. 51 N11
Port Clinton SA 78 G3, 80 G12
Port Davis SA 80 F7
Port Denison WA 90 D7
Port Douglas Qld 118 F3, 120 I11, 126 B1
Port Elliot SA 78 I9
Porters Retreat NSW 16 B1, 24 G7, 30 F2
Port Fairy Vic. 50 I10
Port Franklin Vic. 53 N12
Port Germein SA 80 G6, 83 N13
Port Gibbon SA 78 B1, 80 B10, 84 G10
Port Hedland WA 92 G8
Port Hughes SA 78 E2, 80 E12
Port Huon Tas. 68 E11, 71 K9
Port Julia SA 78 F5
Port Keats NT 100 B8
Port Kembla NSW 17 P5, 25 J8, 30 I3
Port Kenney SA 84 C8
Portland Vic. 50 F9
Portland Roads Qld 120 E4
Port Latta Tas. 72 D3
Port Lincoln SA 84 F12
Port MacDonnell SA 50 A7, 77 H12
Port Macquarie NSW 29 P11
Port Melbourne Vic. 38 G10
Port Minlacowie SA 78 E6

Port Neill SA 78 A3, 80 A12, 84 F11
Port Noarlunga SA 78 I7, 85 F11
Port Pirie SA 80 G7
Port Rickaby SA 78 E5
Portsea Vic. 42 B6, 44 I10, 52 F9
Port Sorell Tas. 73 J5
Port Stephens NSW 25 N3
Port Victoria SA 78 E4, 84 I12
Port Vincent SA 78 F6
Port Wakefield SA 78 G3, 80 G12
Port Welshpool Vic. 53 O12
Pothana NSW 18 B2
Potts Point NSW 8 I4, 11 N4
Pottsville NSW 29 R1, 113 R12
Pound Creek Vic. 53 L11
Powelltown Vic. 48 G13, 53 K6
Powers Creek Vic. 50 D1, 56 D13
Powlett Plains Vic. 57 Q7, 58 A7
Powranna Tas. 73 M9
Prahran Vic. 38 I11, 40 A13
Prairie Qld 118 E10
Prairie Vic. 58 C6
Pranjip Vic. 58 I9
Premaydena Tas. 67 E3, 69 N10, 71 O8
Premer NSW 28 H10
Preolenna Tas. 72 E5
Preston Tas. 72 G6
Preston Vic. 38 I5
Preston South Tas. 72 G6
Pretty Beach NSW 15 Q3, 20 G1
Pretty Gully NSW 29 O2
Prevelly Park WA 94 C7
Price SA 78 G3, 80 G13
Primbee NSW 17 P6
Primrose Sands Tas. 69 M7, 71 O7
Princetown Vic. 51 N12
Priory Tas. 73 Q6
Prooinga Vic. 61 L8
Propodollah Vic. 56 E6
Proserpine Qld 119 K9, 127 D5
Prospect SA 76 D7
Proston Qld 117 O8
Puckapunyal Vic. 47 M1, 58 H11
Pudman Creek NSW 24 E9, 30 D4
Pullabooka NSW 23 R6, 24 C6, 30 A1
Pullut Vic. 56 G4
Pumicestone Qld 111 L3
Pumpenbill NSW 113 M11
Punchbowl NSW 10 F9
Punchmirup WA 95 L6
Pungonda SA 60 A5
Puntable SA 84 B6
Puralka Vic. 50 C6
Pura Pura Vic. 51 M5
Purfleet NSW 25 N1
Purga Qld 110 H13, 112 H1, 117 P11
Purlewaugh NSW 28 G10
Purnim Vic. 51 K9
Purnong Landing SA 79 M6
Purrumbete South Vic. 51 N9
Putney NSW 10 H1, 12 H13
Putty NSW 29 J4
Pyalong Vic. 47 K3, 58 G12
Pyap SA 79 P4, 81 P13
Pyengana Tas. 73 P6
Pygery SA 84 E8
Pykes Creek Reservoir Vic. 46 E10, 52 D4
Pymble NSW 12 I7
Pyramid Vic. 58 C4
Pyramid Hill Vic. 22 I13, 57 R4
Pyramul NSW 24 G3
Pyree NSW 17 N12
Pyrmont NSW 8 A8, 11 M4
Pyrton WA 96 D10

Q

Quaama NSW 30 F9
Quail Island Vic. 43 P4
Quairading WA 90 G10
Quakers Hill NSW 15 L6
Qualco SA 79 N2, 81 N11
Qualeup WA 95 J6
Quambatook Vic. 22 H13, 57 O3
Quambone NSW 27 R9, 28 C9
Quamby Qld 121 E8
Quamby Brook Tas. 73 J8
Quandary NSW 23 Q8, 24 B8

Quandialla NSW   23 R7, 24 C7, 30 A2
Quangallin WA   95 L4
Quantong Vic.   56 G9
Queanbeyan NSW   24 F11, 30 E6, 35 G4
Queenscliff NSW   13 Q9
Queenscliff Vic.   42 A5, 44 I9, 52 F8
Queenstown Tas.   70 E1, 72 E11
Quilergup WA   94 E6
Quilpie Qld   116 D8
Quindalup WA   94 C5
Quindanning WA   94 I2
Quininup WA   94 H9
Quirindi NSW   29 J11
Quobba WA   92 C13
Quorn SA   80 G3, 83 N12
Quorrobolong NSW   18 D6

R
Raby Bay Qld   111 N11
Radium Hill SA   81 P3
Radnor Tas.   69 N11
Raglan Qld   117 N4
Raglan Vic.   51 O2
Railton Tas.   72 I7
Rainbow Vic.   56 G3
Raleigh NSW   29 P8
Raluana Vic.   57 K9
Ramco SA   79 N3, 81 N12
Raminea Tas.   71 K10
Ramingining NT   101 M4
Ramsgate NSW   11 K12, 18 F9
Rams Head Corner WA   95 Q9
Ranceby Vic.   53 L9
Rand NSW   23 O12, 59 P1
Randell WA   91 K8
Randwick NSW   11 P7
Ranelagh Tas.   68 F9, 71 L8
Rankins Springs NSW   23 N6
Rannes Qld   117 M4
Rannock NSW   23 P9, 24 A9
Rapid Creek NT   98 A4
Rappville NSW   29 P3
Rathdowney Qld   29 P1, 112 I9
Rathmines NSW   18 G7
Rathscar Vic.   57 O11
Ravensbourne Qld   117 P10
Ravensdale NSW   18 C10
Ravenshoe Qld   118 F5, 120 I13
Ravensthorpe WA   90 I11
Ravenswood Qld   118 H9
Ravenswood Vic.   58 C10
Ravensworth NSW   25 K2
Rawdon Vale NSW   25 L1, 29 L12
Raymond Island Vic.   54 F8
Raymond Terrace NSW   18 H3, 25 L3
Raymore Qld   122 I7
Raywood Vic.   58 C8
Razorback Mountain NSW   17 L1
Recherche Archipelago WA   91 K12
Redbank Vic.   57 N11, 62 C9
Redbank Plains Qld   110 I12
Redbanks SA   81 K9
Redbourneberry NSW   18 A1
Redcastle Vic.   58 F9
Redcliffe Qld   111 M6, 117 Q10
Redcliffe WA   96 C13
Red Cliffs Vic.   22 D8, 60 H3
Redesdale Vic.   46 H1, 58 E11
Redfern NSW   11 M6
Redhead NSW   18 H7
Redhill SA   80 G9
Red Hill Vic.   42 I8
Red Hill South Vic.   43 J8
Red Island Point Qld   120 C1
Red Jacket Vic.   53 N4
Redland Bay Qld   111 O12
Redlynch Qld   126 E7
Redmans Bluff Vic.   57 J13
Redmond WA   95 M12
Redpa Tas.   72 A4
Red Range NSW   29 M5
Red Rock NSW   29 Q6
Reedy Creek Qld   113 P7, 125 L12
Reedy Creek SA   77 E7
Reedy Creek Vic.   47 N5, 52 H1, 58 H13
Reedy Dam Vic.   57 J4
Reedy Flat Vic.   54 F5

Reedy Marsh Tas.   73 J7
Reefton NSW   23 Q8, 24 B7
Reefton Vic.   48 H11
Reesville Qld   114 I11
Regatta Point Tas.   70 D2, 72 D12
Regents Park NSW   10 D6
Regentville NSW   15 J8
Reid ACT   34 F8
Reid WA   91 Q8
Reid River Qld   118 H8
Reids Creek Vic.   59 P6
Reids Flat NSW   24 F7, 30 D2
Rekuna Tas.   69 J4, 71 M5
Relbia Tas.   73 M8
Remine Tas.   72 C10
Rendelsham SA   77 F10
Renison Bell Tas.   72 D10
Renmark SA   22 A8, 79 Q3, 81 Q12
Renner Springs NT   103 J6
Rennie NSW   23 N12, 59 M2
Research Vic.   39 Q3
Reservoir Vic.   39 J3
Retreat Tas.   73 M5
Revesby NSW   10 E11
Reynella SA   78 I7, 85 G9
Rheban Tas.   69 P3, 71 P5
Rheola Vic.   57 P8
Rhyll Vic.   43 P11, 52 I10
Rhymney Reef Vic.   51 L1, 57 L13
Rhyndaston Tas.   69 J1, 71 M4
Rhynie SA   78 I3, 80 I12
Riachella Vic.   57 K10
Rialto Qld   124 G11
Riana Tas.   72 G6
Richardson Hill Vic.   43 N12
Rich Avon Vic.   57 L7
Richlands NSW   24 H8, 30 F4
Richmond NSW   15 J5, 25 J6, 30 I1
Richmond Qld   118 C10, 121 I8
Richmond Tas.   69 J5, 71 N6
Richmond Vic.   37 I8, 38 I9
Ricketts Sanctuary Vic.   45 D6
Riddell Vic.   46 I8, 52 F3
Ridgelands Qld   117 M3
Ridgeway Tas.   68 I8
Ridgewood Qld   114 I7, 123 A3
Ridgley Tas.   72 F5
Ridleyton SA   75 A1
Riggs Creek Vic.   59 K8
Ringarooma Tas.   73 O6
Ringtail Qld   115 J5
Ringwood Vic.   39 R9, 48 A13, 52 I5
Rio Vista Qld   124 G10
Ripley Qld   110 I13, 110 F12
Ripplebrook Vic.   53 K8
Risdon Tas.   67 E2
Risdon Vale Tas.   67 G1, 69 J6, 71 M6
River Glen Qld   125 P8
Riversdale WA   95 J9
Riverside North Tas.   73 L7
Riverstone NSW   15 L6
Riverton SA   79 J3, 81 J12
Rivervale WA   87 I3
Riverview NSW   11 K1, 13 K12
Riverwood NSW   10 F11
Roadvale Qld   112 G4
Robbins Island Tas.   72 B2
Robe SA   77 D8
Robertson NSW   17 L8, 24 I9, 30 H4
Robertstown SA   79 K2, 81 K11
Robigana Tas.   73 L6
Robinvale Vic.   22 F9, 61 K5
Rocherlea Tas.   73 L7
Rochester SA   80 H10
Rochester Vic.   58 F6
Rochford Vic.   47 J6, 52 F2, 58 F13
Rockbank Vic.   44 I1, 46 I11, 52 F5
Rockbrae Qld   112 A8
Rockdale NSW   11 K10
Rock Flat NSW   30 E9
Rockhampton Qld   117 M3
Rockingham WA   90 E10
Rocklands Reservoir Vic.   50 H1
Rockley NSW   24 G6, 30 F1
Rocklyn Vic.   46 C7, 51 R2, 52 C3
Rocksberg Qld   110 I4
Rockton NSW   30 E11, 55 N3
Rockvale NSW   29 M7

Rocky Cape National Park Tas.   72 E3
Rocky Creek NSW   28 I6
Rocky Dam NSW   28 J3
Rocky Glen NSW   28 G9
Rocky Gully WA   90 F13, 95 K10
Rocky Hall NSW   30 E11
Rocky Hill Vic.   46 B5
Rocky River NSW   29 L8
Rocky Valley Reservoir Vic.   54 D1
Rodinga NT   105 K10
Rodney NSW   30 D10
Roebourne WA   92 F9
Roelands WA   94 F3
Rogans Hill NSW   12 C7
Roger Corner SA   78 E6
Roger River Tas.   72 C4
Rokeby Tas.   69 K7, 71 N7
Rokeby Vic.   53 L7
Rokewood Vic.   51 Q6, 52 A6
Rokewood Junction Vic.   51 P5
Roland Tas.   72 H7
Rollands Plains NSW   29 O10
Rolleston Qld   117 K5
Rollingstone Qld   118 G7
Roma Qld   117 K8
Romsey Vic.   47 J6, 52 F2, 58 F13
Rookwood NSW   10 E5
Rooty Hill NSW   15 L7
Ropely Qld   110 B12
Rosa Glen WA   94 C7
Rosanna Vic.   39 L5
Rose Bay NSW   11 Q3
Rose Bay Tas.   67 H6
Roseberry NSW   113 J13
Roseberth Qld   122 D7
Rosebery NSW   11 N7
Rosebery Tas.   72 E9
Rosebery Vic.   56 I3
Rosebrook NSW   18 E2
Rosebrook Qld   122 H2
Rosebrook Vic.   50 I9
Rosebud Vic.   42 G8, 52 G9
Rosedale NSW   30 D8, 31 I2
Rosedale Qld   117 O5
Rosedale Vic.   53 Q8, 54 A10
Rosegarland Tas.   68 E4
Rosehill NSW   10 D2
Roseneath Vic.   50 D3
Roses Tier Tas.   73 O8
Rosevale Qld   112 E3
Rosevale Tas.   73 K7
Rose Valley NSW   17 O9
Rosevears Tas.   73 L6
Roseville NSW   13 K9
Rosewhite Vic.   59 Q8, 168 A8
Rosewood NSW   23 R12, 30 A7, 62 G2
Rosewood Qld   110 F12
Roslyn NSW   17 A8, 24 G8, 30 F3
Roslynmead Vic.   58 E4
Rosny Tas.   67 G8
Ross Tas.   71 N1, 73 N11
Rossarden Tas.   73 O9
Ross Bridge Vic.   51 L3
Ross Creek Vic.   51 Q4, 52 A4
Rossi NSW   24 G11, 30 E6
Rosslynne Reservoir Vic.   52 E3
Rossmore NSW   15 K10
Ross Mount Qld   114 H1
Ross River NT   105 K8
Rossville Qld   118 F1, 120 I10
Rostrevor SA   76 G7
Rostron Vic.   57 M9
Rothbury NSW   18 C3, 32 G5
Roto NSW   23 L4
Rottnest Island WA   90 E10
Rouchel Brook NSW   25 K1
Roughit NSW   18 A1
Round Corner NSW   12 B4, 15 M6
Round Mountain NSW   113 R11
Rouse Hill NSW   15 M6
Rowella Tas.   73 K5
Rowena NSW   28 F5
Rowes NSW   30 D11, 55 M2
Rowland Vic.   57 R3, 58 C3
Rowland Flat SA   85 C8
Rowsley Vic.   44 F1, 46 G12, 52 D5
Rowville Vic.   40 E1, 52 I6
Roxborough Downs Qld   122 C1

152

Royal George Tas. 73 P10
Royalla NSW 24 F11, 30 E6
Royal National Park NSW 15 O11, 25 K7
Rozelle NSW 11 K4
Rubicon Vic. 48 H6, 53 L2, 59 L13
Ruby Vic. 53 L10
Rubyvale Qld 116 I3
Rudall SA 84 F10
Ruffy Vic. 47 R1, 48 D1, 59 J11
Rufus River NSW 22 B7, 60 C2
Rugby NSW 24 F8, 30 D3
Rukenvale NSW 29 P1, 113 J13
Rumbalara NT 105 K11
Rum Jungle NT 100 E6
Rumula Qld 126 A3
Runaway Bay Qld 124 A10
Rundall River National Park WA 93 K11
Running Creek Qld 117 P8
Running Creek Vic. 59 R8, 62 B8
Running Stream NSW 24 H4
Runnymede Tas. 69 L3, 71 N5
Runnymede Vic. 58 E8
Rupanyup Vic. 57 J8
Rushcutters Bay NSW 11 O4
Rushworth Vic. 58 G8
Rushy Pool WA 95 L2
Russell ACT 34 G10
Russell Lea NSW 11 J4
Russell River Qld 126 I12
Russell River National Park Qld 126 I12
Rutherford NSW 18 E3
Rutherglen Vic. 23 O13, 59 O4, 64 C3
Rutland Tas. 71 M3, 73 M13
Ryanby Vic. 61 M10
Ryans Creek Vic. 59 N8
Rydal NSW 14 B4
Rydalmere NSW 10 D2, 12 D13
Ryde NSW 10 H1, 12 H12
Rye Vic. 42 E8, 52 F9
Rye Park NSW 24 E8, 30 D3
Ryhope NSW 18 F7
Rylstone NSW 24 H3
Ryton Vic. 53 O10

S

Sackville North NSW 15 L3
Sackville Reach NSW 15 L3
Saddleworth SA 79 J2, 81 J11
Safety Beach Vic. 42 I6
St Albans NSW 25 J5
St Albans South Vic. 38 A6
St Andrews Vic. 47 P10, 48 A10
St Anthonys NSW 17 M8
St Arnaud Vic. 57 N8
St Clair NSW 25 K2, 29 K13
St Fillans Vic. 48 F9, 53 K3
St George Qld 117 J11
St Germains Vic. 58 H5
St Helens Qld 127 F9
St Helens Tas. 73 R7
St Helens Vic. 50 H9
St Ives NSW 13 J6
St Ives Chase NSW 13 J4, 21 R12
St James Vic. 59 L6
St Kilda Vic. 38 H12, 52 G6
St Lawrence Qld 117 L1, 119 L12
St Leonards NSW 11 L1, 13 L12
St Leonards Tas. 73 M7
St Leonards Vic. 42 B2, 44 I7, 52 F8
St Marys NSW 15 K7
St Marys Tas. 73 Q8
St Peters NSW 11 M7
St Peters SA 75 H4, 76 E8
St Peter's Island SA 82 H12, 84 A6
Saints SA 78 H3, 80 H12
Salamander Bay NSW 25 M3
Sale Vic. 53 R7, 54 B10
Salisbury NSW 25 L2, 29 L13
Salisbury SA 76 F2, 78 I6
Salisbury Vic. 56 F7
Salisbury West Vic. 57 Q8, 58 B8
Sallys Flat NSW 24 G4
Salmon Gums WA 91 K11
Salt Creek SA 77 D3, 79 M12
Salters Springs SA 78 I3, 80 I12
Saltwater River Tas. 67 D2, 69 M9, 71 O8
Salvator Rose National Park Qld 116 H5

Samaria Vic. 59 M9
Sandalwood SA 79 O6
Sandfire Flat Roadhouse WA 93 J8
Sandfly Tas. 68 H9, 71 M8
Sandford Tas. 69 K8, 71 N7
Sandford Vic. 50 E4
Sandgate NSW 18 G5
Sandgate Qld 111 L7, 117 Q10
Sandhill Lake Vic. 57 P2
Sandigo NSW 23 O10
Sandilands SA 78 F4, 84 I12
Sandon Vic. 46 C4, 51 R1, 57 R12, 58 B12
Sandown Park Vic. 40 F5
Sandringham Qld 122 C4
Sandringham Vic. 40 F12
Sandsmere Vic. 56 D6
Sandstone WA 90 H5
Sandy Bay Tas. 67 F11
Sandy Creek Vic. 62 C6
Sandy Flat NSW 29 M4
Sandy Hill NSW 29 N3
Sandy Hollow NSW 25 J2, 29 J13
Sandy Point NSW 10 C13
Sandy Point Vic. 53 M13
San Remo Vic. 43 R13, 52 I10
Sans Souci NSW 11 K13
Sapphire NSW 29 L5
Sapphire Qld 116 I3
Sapphiretown SA 78 F11
Sarah Island Tas. 70 E4
Saratoga NSW 15 Q2, 20 D2
Sardine Creek Vic. 55 J6
Sarina Qld 119 L11
Sarina Beach Qld 119 L11
Sarsfield Vic. 54 E7
Sassafras NSW 30 G5
Sassafras Tas. 73 I6
Sassafras Vic. 45 D8
Savage River Tas. 72 D8
Savernake NSW 23 N12, 59 M2
Sawtell NSW 29 P7
Sawyers Gully NSW 18 D4
Sayers Lake NSW 22 G3
Scamander Tas. 73 R8
Scarborough NSW 17 P2
Scarborough Qld 111 M6
Scarsdale Vic. 51 P4
Schofields NSW 15 L6
School Hill Vic. 42 H10
Schouten Island Tas. 73 R13
Scone NSW 25 J1, 29 J12
Scoresby Vic. 40 D1
Scotsburn Vic. 46 B11, 51 R4, 52 B4
Scott National Park WA 94 D9
Scotts Creek Vic. 51 M10
Scotts Flat NSW 18 B1
Scotts Head NSW 29 P9
Scottsdale Tas. 73 N5
Scottsville Qld 118 I10
Scrubby Creek Qld 114 F3
Scrub Creek Qld 110 D3
Seacombe Vic. 54 D10
Seaford SA 85 F11
Seaford Vic. 41 N7, 52 H7
Seaforth NSW 13 O10
Seaforth Qld 127 G9
Seaham NSW 18 H1, 25 L3
Seahampton NSW 18 F5
Sea Lake Vic. 22 F12, 61 L12
Seal Rocks NSW 25 N2
Seaspray Vic. 54 C12
Seaton Vic. 53 P6
Seaview Vic. 53 L9
Sebastian Vic. 58 C8
Sebastopol NSW 23 Q9, 24 B8, 30 A3
Sebastopol Vic. 46 A10, 51 Q4, 172 A4
Second Valley SA 78 H9
Sedan SA 79 L5
Sedgwick Vic. 58 C10
Sefton NSW 10 C7
Selbourne Tas. 73 K7
Selby Vic. 45 E11
Sellheim Qld 118 H9
Selwyn Qld 121 E10
Seppeltsfield SA 85 C3
Serpentine Vic. 57 R7, 58 B7
Serviceton Vic. 56 B7, 77 I4, 79 R13
Sevenhill SA 78 I1, 80 I10

Seven Mile Beach Tas. 69 K7, 71 N7
Seville Vic. 45 I3, 53 J5
Seymour Tas. 73 R9
Seymour Vic. 47 N1, 58 H11
Shady Creek Vic. 53 M7
Shakeshaft NSW 18 B12
Shannon Tas. 71 K1, 73 K11
Shannon River Mill WA 94 H10
Shannons Flat NSW 30 D8
Shannonvale Vic. 54 D1, 62 D11
Shark Bay WA 90 B2
Sharps Well SA 80 G9
Shaw Island Qld 119 K9
Shay Gap WA 92 I9
Shays Flat Vic. 57 M11
Sheans Creek Vic. 59 K9
Sheep Hills Vic. 57 J6
Sheffield Tas. 72 I7
Shelbourne Vic. 57 R10, 58 B10
Shelford Vic. 44 A5, 51 R7, 52 B7
Shelley Vic. 30 A8, 62 E5
Shelley Beach NSW 18 F13
Shellharbour NSW 17 P7, 25 J9, 30 I4
Sheoaks Vic. 44 C4, 52 C6
Shepherds Flat Vic. 46 C5
Shepparton Vic. 59 J6
Sherbrooke Vic. 45 D9
Sherbrooke Forest Park Vic. 45 E10
Sheringa SA 84 D10
Sherlock SA 79 N8
Sherwin Ranges Vic. 47 O8
Shirley Vic. 51 N2
Shoalhaven Heads NSW 17 O11, 25 J9, 30 I4
Shoal Point Qld 127 H10
Shooters Hill NSW 14 A11, 24 H7, 30 F2
Shoreham Vic. 43 J10, 52 H10
Shorncliffe Qld 111 L8
Shotts WA 94 H4
Shute Harbour Qld 127 E4
Sidmouth Tas. 73 K6
Sidonia Vic. 46 H3, 58 E12
Silvan Vic. 45 G6, 48 C13, 53 J5
Silvan Reservoir Vic. 45 G7, 48 C13
Silver Creek Vic. 59 P6
Silverdale NSW 14 I10
Silverdale Qld 112 F4
Silverspur Qld 29 L2
Silverton NSW 22 B1, 26 B12
Silverwater NSW 10 E3, 18 F8
Simmie Vic. 58 F6
Simmonds Reef Vic. 46 E8
Simpson Vic. 51 N10
Simpson Desert National Park SA 83 N1,
  105 P13, 122 B7
Simpsons Bay Tas. 68 I13, 71 M10
Simpsons Gap National Park NT 105 J8
Singleton NSW 18 A1, 25 K3
Sir Edward Pellew Group NT 101 P11
Sisters Beach Tas. 72 E4
Sisters Creek Tas. 72 E4
Skenes Creek Vic. 51 Q12, 52 A12
Skipton Vic. 51 O4
Skye Vic. 41 O3
Slacks Creek Qld 111 M12
Slade Point Qld 127 I11
Slaty Creek Vic. 57 N8
Smeaton Vic. 46 B6, 51 R2, 52 B2, 57 R13,
  58 B13
Smiggin Holes NSW 30 C9, 31 E8
Smithfield Qld 29 K2
Smithton Tas. 72 C3
Smithville SA 79 P8
Smoko Vic. 54 B1, 59 R10, 62 B10
Smoky Bay SA 82 H12, 84 B6
Smythesdale Vic. 51 P4
Snake Bay NT 100 D2
Snake Valley Vic. 51 P4
Snobs Creek Vic. 48 H5, 53 L1, 59 L13
Snowtown SA 78 H1, 80 G10
Snowy Mountains NSW 31 C8
Snowy River National Park Vic. 54 I3
Snug Tas. 68 H10, 71 M8
Snuggery SA 77 G11
Sodwalls NSW 14 A5
Sofala NSW 24 G4
Soldiers Point NSW 25 M3
Somers Vic. 43 M9, 52 H9
Somersby NSW 18 D13

Somerset Tas.   72 F5
Somerset Dam Qld   110 F4
Somerton NSW   29 J9
Somerton Vic.   47 L10
Somerville Vic.   43 M3, 52 H8
Sommariva Qld   116 H8
Sorell Tas.   69 L6, 71 N6
Sorrento Vic.   42 C7, 52 F9
Sorrento Qld   124 G11
South Arm Tas.   69 J9
South Bexley NSW   11 J11
South Bowenfels NSW   14 C5
South Brisbane Qld   109 A8
South Bruny Island Tas.   71 M11
South Coogee NSW   11 Q8
South End SA   77 F10
Southern Cross WA   90 H9
Southern Vales SA   85
South Forest Tas.   72 D3
South Galway Qld   122 H6
South Granville NSW   10 C4
South Guildford WA   96 E12
South Gundagai NSW   24 C10, 30 B5
South Hobart Tas.   67 C11
South Hummocks SA   78 G2, 80 G11
South Island Qld   119 M12
South Kerang Vic.   57 Q2, 58 B2
South Riana Tas.   72 G6
South Kilkerran SA   78 E4, 80 E13, 84 I11
South Kincumber NSW   15 Q2
South Melbourne Vic.   37 B11
South Molle Island Qld   127 F4
South Mount Cameron Tas.   73 P5
South Perth WA   87 D9
Southport NT   100 E5
Southport Qld   113 P5, 117 Q11, 124 D12
South Stradbroke Island Qld   113 P3
South West Nat. Park Tas.   68 A13, 70 H8
South West Rocks NSW   29 P9
South Yarra Vic.   37 H12, 38 I10
Sovereign Hill Vic.   46 A10
Spa Vic.   46 F8
Spalding SA   80 I9
Spalford Tas.   72 H6
Spargo Creek Vic.   46 D8, 52 C3
Speed Vic.   22 E11, 60 I11
Speers Point NSW   18 G6
Speewa Vic.   61 O10
Spencer NSW   15 O2
Spicers Creek NSW   24 F2, 28 F13
Spit Junction NSW   13 O12
Spotswood Vic.   38 E10
Sprent Tas.   72 H6
Spreyton Tas.   72 I6
Springbank Vic.   46 C9
Spring Beach Tas.   69 P2, 71 P5
Springbrook Qld   29 Q1, 113 N9
Springdale NSW   24 C8, 30 A3
Springfield Tas.   67 A5, 73 N6
Springfield Vic.   47 K6, 52 F2, 58 F13
Springfield South Tas.   73 N6
Spring Gully National Park SA   78 I1, 80 I11
Spring Hill Qld   109 D2
Spring Hill Vic.   46 F6
Springhurst Vic.   59 O5, 64 C8
Springmount Vic.   46 B7, 51 R2, 52 B2
Spring Ridge NSW   24 G2, 28 G13
Spring Ridge NSW   28 I10
Springsure Qld   117 J4
Springton SA   79 K5
Springvale Qld   122 F3
Springvale Vic.   40 F6
Springwood NSW   14 H7, 24 I6, 30 H1
Stanborough NSW   29 K6
Stanhope NSW   18 C1
Stanhope Vic.   58 G7
Stanley Tas.   72 D3
Stanley Vic.   59 Q7, 62 A7
Stanmore NSW   11 L6
Stanmore Qld   110 H1, 114 H13
Stannifer NSW   29 K6
Stannum NSW   29 M4
Stansbury SA   78 F6, 84 I13
Stanthorpe Qld   29 M2, 117 O12
Stanwell Qld   117 M3
Stanwell Park NSW   17 P2, 25 J8, 30 I3
Stapleton NT   100 E6
Stapylton Qld   113 N2

Staughton Vale Vic.   44 E3, 46 E13, 52 D5
Stavely Vic.   51 K4
Stawell Vic.   57 K12
Steels Creek Vic.   47 Q9, 48 B10, 52 I4
Steiglitz Vic.   44 C3, 52 C6
Stenhouse Bay SA   78 C8, 84 H13
Stephens Creek NSW   28 B12
Steppes Tas.   71 K2
Stewarts Range SA   77 G7
Stieglitz Tas.   73 R7
Stirling Vic.   54 F5
Stirling North SA   80 F4
Stirling Range Nat. Park WA   90 G13, 95 O10
Stockdale Vic.   54 C8
Stockinbingal NSW   23 R8, 24 C8, 30 A3
Stockmans Reward Vic.   53 M3
Stockton NSW   18 I5, 19 I3, 25 L4
Stockyard Creek SA   78 I3, 80 I12
Stockyard Hill Vic.   51 O3
Stokers NSW   113 P12
Stokers Siding NSW   29 Q1
Stokes Bay SA   78 D10
Stonefield SA   79 L3, 81 L13
Stonehaven Vic.   44 D7, 52 C7
Stonehenge NSW   29 M5
Stonehenge Qld   116 C5
Stonehenge Tas.   71 O4
Stone Hut SA   80 H7
Stoneyford Vic.   51 O9
Stonor Tas.   71 M4
Stony Creek Vic.   53 M11
Stony Crossing NSW   22 H10, 61 O9
Stony Point Vic.   43 N8, 52 H9
Stoodley Tas.   72 I7
Store Creek NSW   24 F3
Storeys Creek Tas.   73 O9
Stormlea Tas.   67 E6, 69 N12, 71 O9
Stow SA   78 H2, 80 H11
Stowport Tas.   72 G5
Stradbroke Qld   111 Q10
Stradbroke Vic.   53 R9, 54 B11
Stradbroke Island North Qld   111 Q10
Strahan Tas.   70 D2, 72 D12
Strangways SA   83 L7
Strangways Vic.   46 C3, 57 R12, 58 B12
Stratford NSW   25 M1, 29 M13
Stratford Qld   126 F7
Stratford Vic.   54 B9
Strathaird NSW   16 B7
Strathalbyn SA   79 J8
Strathallan Vic.   58 F6
Stratham WA   94 E4
Strathblane Tas.   71 K10
Strathbogie NSW   29 L4
Strathbogie Vic.   59 K10
Strath Creek Vic.   47 O4, 48 A4, 52 I1, 58 H13
Strathdownie Vic.   50 C5
Strathelbiss Qld   122 E1
Strathewen Vic.   47 P9, 48 A9, 52 I3
Strathfield NSW   10 G5
Strathfieldsaye Vic.   58 D10
Strathgordon Tas.   70 G6
Strathlea Vic.   46 B3, 57 R12, 58 B12
Strathmerton Vic.   23 L13, 59 J3
Streaky Bay SA   82 I13, 84 B7
Streatham Vic.   51 M4
Strickland Tas.   71 J3
Stroud NSW   25 M2
Stroud Road NSW   25 M2, 29 M13
Struan SA   50 A1, 56 A12, 77 H8
Strzelecki Vic.   53 L9
Strzelecki Track SA   83 N9-R4
Stuart Mill Vic.   57 N10
Stuart Park NT   99 N7
Stuart Town NSW   24 F3
Sturt National Park NSW   26 B3
Sturts Stony Desert SA   83 Q2
Sue City NSW   30 C7
Suggan Buggan NSW   30 B11, 54 I2, 62 I11
Sulphur Creek Tas.   72 G5
Summerfield Vic.   58 C7
Summerhill NSW   11 J6
Summerholm Qld   110 D12
Summervale NSW   27 P10, 28 A10
Sunbury Vic.   47 J9, 52 F3
Suncoast Qld   115 L9
Sunday Creek Vic.   47 M5, 52 H1, 58 H13

Sunny Cliffs Vic.   60 H3
Sunshine NSW   18 G8
Sunshine Beach Qld   115 M6, 123 H2
Sunshine Coast Qld   123
Sunnyside NSW   29 M3
Sunnyside Vic.   54 E1, 62 E10
Sunnyvale SA   78 F3, 80 F12
Sunset Vic.   60 A9
Sunshine Vic.   38 B8
Surat Qld   117 K10
Surfers Paradise Qld   113 P6, 117 Q11, 124 F9
Surges Bay Tas.   68 E12, 71 L9
Surrey Hills Vic.   39 M9
Surry Hills NSW   8 E12, 11 N5
Sussex Inlet NSW   30 H5
Sussex Mill WA   94 E7
Sutherland NSW   15 N11
Sutherlands SA   79 K3, 81 K12
Sutherlands Creek Vic.   44 D5
Sutton NSW   24 F10, 30 E5
Sutton Vic.   57 L2
Sutton Forest NSW   16 I8, 25 I9, 30 G4
Sutton Grange Vic.   46 F1, 58 D11
Suttons SA   77 H11
Suttontown SA   77 H11
Swanfels Qld   112 B8
Swan Hill Vic.   22 H11, 61 O11
Swan Marsh Vic.   51 O9
Swanpool Vic.   59 M9
Swan Reach Vic.   54 F8
Swan Reach SA   79 M5
Swansea NSW   18 G8, 25 L4
Swansea Tas.   71 Q2, 73 Q12
Swan View WA   96 I9
Sweetmans Creek NSW   18 B6
Swifts Creek Vic.   54 F4, 62 F13
Switzerland Ranges Vic.   47 Q3
Sydenham NSW   11 L7
Sydenham Vic.   52 F4
Sydney NSW   8-15, 25 K7
Sydney Airport NSW   11 M9
Sydney Cove NSW   11 N3
Sylvania NSW   15 O11
Sylvaterre Vic.   58 C5

T

Tabbara Vic.   55 J7
Tabberabbera Vic.   54 D6
Tabbimoble NSW   29 Q4
Tabbita NSW   23 M7
Tabilk Vic.   58 H10
Tabooba Qld   113 J7
Tabor Vic.   50 I6
Tabragalba Qld   113 L5
Tabulam NSW   29 O3, 117 P13
Tacoma NSW   18 F11
Taggerty Vic.   48 F6, 53 K2, 59 K13
Tahara Vic.   50 F5
Tahara Bridge Vic.   50 F5
Tahmoor NSW   17 L2
Tailem Bend SA   79 L8
Takone Tas.   72 E5
Talawah Tas.   73 O6
Talbingo NSW   30 B7, 62 I1
Talbot Vic.   51 Q1, 52 A1, 57 P12
Taldra SA   60 A4, 79 Q3, 81 Q13
Talgarno Vic.   62 C4
Talia SA   84 D9
Tallageira Vic.   56 B9
Tallanalla WA   94 G2
Tallandoon Vic.   62 C7
Tallangalook Vic.   59 L10
Tallangatta Vic.   62 C5
Tallangatta Valley Vic.   62 D6
Tallarook Vic.   47 N2, 58 H12
Tallebudgera Qld   113 P8
Tallegalla Qld   110 F12
Tallimba NSW   23 P7
Tallong NSW   16 G11, 30 G4
Tallygaroopna Vic.   59 J5
Talmalmo NSW   23 Q13
Talmoi Qld   118 B10, 121 I8
Talwood Qld   28 G1, 117 I12
Tamarang NSW   28 H10
Tamaree Qld   114 G2
Tambar Springs NSW   28 H10
Tambellup WA   90 G12, 95 M7

Tambo Qld 116 G6
Tambo Crossing Vic. 54 F6
Tamborine Qld 117 Q11
Tamborine Mountain Nat. Park Qld 113 M5
Tamborine North Qld 113 M4
Tamborine Village Qld 113 M4
Tambo Upper Vic. 54 F7
Tamboy NSW 25 N3
Taminick Vic. 59 N7, 64 A11
Tamlengh Vic. 59 K8
Tamrookum Qld 113 J7
Tamworth NSW 29 K9
Tanami NT 102 B10
Tanami Desert Wildlife Sanctuary NT
  102 D12, 104 D1
Tanbar Qld 122 H7
Tandarra Vic. 166 C7
Tanderra Qld 116 I5
Tandur Qld 114 H4
Tangalooma Qld 111 P5
Tangmangaroo NSW 24 E9, 30 D4
Tangorin Qld 118 D12
Tanina Tas. 68 F3, 71 L5
Tanja NSW 30 F10
Tanjil Bren Vic. 53 N5
Tanjil South Vic. 53 N7
Tankerton Vic. 52 I9
Tannymorel Qld 29 N1, 112 B10
Tansey Qld 117 O8
Tantanoola SA 77 G11
Tanti Park Vic. 43 K3
Tanunda SA 79 J4, 81 J13, 85 E5
Tanwood Vic. 57 O11
Tanybryn Vic. 51 Q11, 52 A11
Tapitallie NSW 17 L11
Taplan SA 79 Q4, 60 A6
Tara Qld 117 M10
Taradale Vic. 46 F3, 58 D12
Tarago NSW 24 G10, 30 F5
Tarago Reservoir Vic. 53 L7
Taragoro SA 84 F10
Taralga NSW 16 C6, 24 H8, 30 F3
Tarampa Qld 110 E10
Tarana NSW 24 H6
Taranna Tas. 67 G3, 69 O10, 71 P8
Tarcombe Vic. 58 I11
Tarcoola SA 82 I9, 84 C2
Tarcoon NSW 27 O7
Tarcowie SA 80 I6
Tarcutta NSW 23 R11, 24 C11, 30 A6
Taree NSW 25 N1, 29 N12
Taren Point NSW 15 P10
Targa Tas. 73 N6
Tarin Rock WA 95 P3
Tarita Vic. 46 D4
Tarlee SA 79 J3, 81 J12
Tarlo NSW 24 G9, 30 F4
Tarnagulla Vic. 57 Q9, 58 A9
Tarneit Vic. 44 I3, 46 I13
Tarnma SA 79 J3, 81 J12
Tarnook Vic. 59 L7
Tarombe Vic. 47 Q1, 48 C1
Tarome Qld 112 D5
Taronga Park Zoo NSW 11 O2
Taroom Qld 117 L7
Taroona Tas. 68 I8, 71 M7
Tarpeena SA 50 A4, 77 H10
Tarragal Vic. 50 E9
Tarraleah Tas. 70 I3, 72 I13
Tarranginnie Vic. 56 E6
Tarrango Vic. 60 E5
Tarranyurk Vic. 56 G5
Tarra Valley National Park Vic. 53 O10
Tarraville Vic. 53 P11
Tarrawarra Vic. 47 Q10, 48 C10
Tarrawingee Vic. 59 O7, 64 G10
Tarrayoukyan Vic. 50 E2
Tarrenlea Vic. 50 G5
Tarrington Vic. 50 H5
Tarrion NSW 27 O6, 28 A6
Tarro NSW 18 G4
Tarwin Vic. 53 L11
Tarwin Meadows Vic. 53 L12
Tarwonga WA 95 J3
Tascott NSW 20 C4
Tatham NSW 29 P3
Tathra NSW 30 F10
Tatong Vic. 59 M9

Tatura Vic. 58 H7
Tatyoon Vic. 51 M3
Tawonga Vic. 62 C9
Tayene Tas. 73 N6
Taylors Arm NSW 29 O9
Taylors Flat NSW 24 F8, 30 D3
Taylorville SA 79 N2, 81 N11
Tea Gardens NSW 25 M3
Teal Flat SA 79 L6
Teal Point Vic. 61 R13, 57 R2, 58 B1
Teasdale Vic. 44 B5
Tea Tree Tas. 68 I4, 71 M6
Tea Tree Well NT 105 A4
Tecoma Vic. 45 D11
Teddington Reservoir Vic. 57 N10
Teddywaddy Vic. 57 N5
Teesdale Vic. 51 R7, 52 B7
Telangatuk Vic. 56 G12
Telarah NSW 18 E3
Telegraph Point NSW 29 O10
Telford Vic. 59 L4
Telita Tas. 73 O5
Telopea NSW 12 D11
Telopea Downs Vic. 56 B5, 77 I3, 79 R12
Telowie Creek SA 80 G6
Temma Tas. 72 A6
Temora NSW 23 Q8, 24 B8
Tempe NSW 11 L8
Templestowe Vic. 39 O6
Templin Qld 112 G5
Tempy Vic. 60 I11
Ten Mile Vic. 53 N2
Ten Mile Hollow NSW 18 A13
Tennant Creek NT 103 K9
Tennyson NSW 10 I2, 12 H13, 15 J4
Tennyson Vic. 58 D6
Tenterden WA 95 M9
Tenterfield NSW 29 N3, 117 O13
Tenthill Qld 110 B12
Tepko SA 79 K7
Teralba NSW 18 G6
Terang Vic. 51 M8
Teridgerie NSW 28 E9
Terip Terip Vic. 48 D1, 59 J11
Terka SA 80 G5
Termeil NSW 24 I11, 30 G6
Terowie NSW 23 R2, 24 C2, 28 C13
Terowie SA 81 J7
Terrace Creek Qld 112 I12
Terragon NSW 113 N12
Terranora NSW 113 Q9
Terrara NSW 17 M12
Terrey Hills NSW 13 M2, 21 P9
Terrick Terrick Vic. 58 C4
Terrigal NSW 15 R1
Terry Hie Hie NSW 28 I5
Tewantin Qld 115 L6, 117 Q8, 123 F1
Tewinga NSW 29 P8
Tewkesbury Tas. 72 F6
Texas Qld 29 K2, 117 N12
Thagoona Qld 110 F12
Thalaba NSW 24 G8, 30 E3
Thalia Vic. 57 M4
Thallon Qld 28 F2, 117 K12
Thangool Qld 117 M5
Thargomindah Qld 116 D11
Tharwa ACT 24 F11, 30 D11
Thebarton SA 75 A5, 76 D8
The Basin Vic. 45 C7
The Bluff Vic. 44 D1
The Brothers Vic. 54 F1, 62 F11
The Cascade Vic. 62 D6
The Caves Qld 117 M3
The Cove Vic. 51 K10
The Entrance NSW 18 F12, 25 L5
The Falls Qld 112 C10
The Glen Tas. 73 L5
The Gold Coast Qld 124, 125
The Grampians Vic. 51 J1, 57 J13
The Granites NT 102 D11, 104 D1
The Gurdies Vic. 53 J9
The Head Qld 112 D10
The Heart Vic. 54 C10
The Jim Jim Vic. 46 H5
The Lakes National Park Vic. 54 E9
The Leap Qld 127 G11
The Meadows NSW 14 A7
The Oaks NSW 14 I12, 28 I7, 30 H2

Theodore Qld 117 M6
The Patch Vic. 45 F9
The Pinnacles Vic. 42 I12
The Pocket Qld 113 Q13, 114 G5
The Point SA 79 L8
Theresa Park NSW 14 J11
The Risk NSW 29 P1, 113 J3
The Rock NSW 23 P11, 24 A11
The Rocks NSW 8 D2
The Sisters Vic. 51 L8
The Slopes NSW 15 J4
The Spit NSW 13 O11
The Summit Qld 110 H8
The Vale NSW 22 H6
Thevenard SA 84 A6
The Yea Spur Vic. 47 P4
Thirlmere NSW 17 K2, 24 I8, 30 H3
Thirlstane Tas. 73 J6
Thirroul NSW 17 P3
Thistle Island SA 84 F13
Thologolong NSW 62 D4
Thomas Plains SA 78 F2, 80 F11
Thomastown Vic. 39 J1
Thomson Vic. 63 H5
Thoona Vic. 59 M6
Thoopara Qld 127 C6
Thora NSW 29 O7
Thornlands Qld 111 N11
Thornleigh NSW 12 E7
Thornton NSW 18 G3
Thornton Qld 112 C3
Thornton Vic. 48 G5, 53 L1, 59 L13
Thorpdale Vic. 53 N9
Thowgla Vic. 62 G6
Thredbo NSW 30 B9
Thredbo Village NSW 31 C10
Three Bridges Vic. 48 F13
Three Hummock Island Tas. 72 B1
Three Springs WA 90 E7
Thrington SA 78 F2, 80 F11
Thuddungra NSW 23 R7, 24 D7, 30 B2
Thule NSW 58 D1
Thulloo NSW 23 O6
Thurla Vic. 60 G4
Thursday Island Qld 120 C1
Tia NSW 29 M10
Tibbuc NSW 29 M12
Tiberias Tas. 71 M4
Tibooburra NSW 26 C4, 116 A13, 122 H13
Tichborne NSW 24 D4
Tickera SA 80 F10, 84 I10, 96 F1
Tidal River Vic. 49 E10, 52 G13
Tlega Vic. 60 H9
Tilba Tilba NSW 30 G9
Tilpa NSW 26 I9
Timbarra Vic. 54 G4
Timbillica NSW 30 F12
Timber Creek NT 100 D11, 102 D1
Timberoo NSW 60 H9
Timboon Vic. 51 M10
Timmering Vic. 58 G6
Timor NSW 29 K12
Timor West Vic. 57 P11
Tinamba Vic. 53 Q6, 54 A9
Tinana Qld 117 P7
Tinaroo Falls Qld 126 C11
Tinbeerwah Qld 115 K6, 123 E1
Tin Can Bay Qld 117 Q8
Tincurrin WA 95 N2
Tingha NSW 29 K6
Tingiringi NSW 55 K1
Tingoora Qld 117 O8
Tinonee NSW 25 N1
Tintaldra Vic. 30 B8, 62 G4
Tintenbar NSW 29 Q3
Tintinara SA 77 E2, 79 O11
Tipton Qld 117 N10
Tirannaville NSW 16 B13, 24 G9, 30 F4
Tittybong Vic. 57 N2
Tocal Qld 116 C4
Tocumwal NSW 23 M12, 59 J2
Togari Tas. 72 B4
Toggannoggera NSW 30 F7
Toiberry Tas. 73 L8
Tolga Qld 126 C12
Tolmie Vic. 59 N10
Tomago NSW 18 H4
Tomahawk Tas. 73 O4

Tomboy NSW   24 H11
Tomerong NSW   24 I10, 30 H5
Tomewin Qld   113 P9
Tom Groggin NSW   30 B9, 31 A10, 62 H8
Tomingley NSW   24 D2
Tom Price WA   92 G11
Tone River Mill WA   94 H9
Tongala Vic.   58 G5
Tongarra NSW   17 N7
Tonghi Creek Vic.   55 L6
Tongio Vic.   54 F3, 62 F13
Tonimbuk Vic.   53 K7
Tonkoro Qld   122 H3
Tooan Vic.   56 F10
Toobeah Qld   28 H1, 117 L12
Tooborac Vic.   47 K2, 58 F11
Toodyay WA   90 F9
Toogong NSW   24 E5
Toogoolawah Qld   110 C4, 117 P10
Tookayerta SA   79 P4, 81 P13
Toolamba Vic.   58 I7
Toolangi Vic.   47 R9, 48 D9, 53 J3
Toolbrunup WA   95 N7
Toolern Vale Vic.   46 I10, 52 E4
Tooleybuc NSW   22 G10, 61 N8
Toolibin WA   95 M2
Tooligie SA   84 E10
Toolijooa NSW   17 O10
Toolleen Vic.   58 F9
Toolondo Vic.   56 G11
Toolong Vic.   50 I9
Tooloom NSW   29 O2, 112 D13
Tooloon NSW   28 D9
Tooma NSW   23 R13, 30 B8, 62 H4
Toombullup Vic.   59 N10
Toomcul Qld   114 C5
Toompine Qld   116 E9
Toompup WA   95 P7
Toongabbie Vic.   53 P7
Toongi NSW   24 E2, 28 E13
Toonumbar NSW   29 O2
Toora Vic.   53 N11
Tooradin Vic.   43 R3, 52 I8
Toorak Vic.   39 J11, 40 A11
Toorale East NSW   27 L7
Tooraneedin Estate Qld   113 P3
Tooraweenah NSW   28 F10
Toorbul Qld   111 L3
Toorbul Point Qld   111 M4
Toorongo Vic.   53 M5
Toorourrong Reservoir Vic.   47 O8, 52 H3
Tootgarook Vic.   42 F8
Toowoomba Qld   117 O10
Toowoon Bay NSW   18 F12
Top Springs NT   100 F13, 102 F3
Torbanlea Qld   117 P7
Torbay WA   95 M13
Toronto NSW   18 G7, 25 L4
Torquay Vic.   44 E10, 52 D9
Torrens Creek Qld   118 E10
Torrington NSW   29 M4, 117 O13
Torrita Vic.   48 G9
Torrumbarry Vic.   58 E4
Tostaree Vic.   54 H7
Tottenham Vic.   38 C8
Tottenham NSW   23 Q1, 24 B1, 27 Q13, 28 B13
Tottington Vic.   57 M9
Toukley NSW   18 G11
Towallum NSW   29 P6
Towamba NSW   30 F11, 55 O3
Towan Vic.   61 N9
Towaninny Vic.   57 N3
Tower Hill Tas.   73 P8
Tower Hill Vic.   51 J9
Townson Qld   112 C4
Townsville Qld   118 H7
Towong Vic.   23 R13, 30 B8, 62 G5
Towradgi NSW   17 P4
Towrang NSW   16 D11, 24 H9, 30 F4
Trafalgar Vic.   53 M8
Tragowel Vic.   57 R3, 58 B3
Trangie NSW   23 R1, 27 R12, 28 C12
Traralgon Vic.   53 P8
Traveston Qld   114 I5
Trawalla Vic.   51 O3
Trawool Vic.   47 O2, 48 A2, 58 H12
Trayning WA   90 G9
Traynors Lagoon Vic.   57 M8

Traysurin WA   95 N1
Trebonne Qld   118 G6
Treesville WA   94 H3
Treeton WA   94 C6
Tregeagle NSW   29 Q3
Tregony Qld   112 C6
Tremont Vic.   45 C9
Trenah Tas.   73 O6
Trentham Vic.   46 N7, 52 D2
Tresco Vic.   61 P12
Trevallyn NSW   25 L2
Trewalla Qld   122 I5
Trewilga NSW   24 D3
Trewalla Vic.   50 E9
Triabunna Tas.   69 P1, 71 P4
Trida NSW   23 K4
Trida Vic.   53 L9
Trinita Vic.   60 H7
Trinity Bay Qld   126 D3
Trinity Beach Qld   126 E6
Trowutta Tas.   72 C4
Trueman Qld   127 D11
Truganina Vic.   44 I2, 47 J13
Trundle NSW   23 R4, 24 C3
Trunkey Creek NSW   24 F6, 30 E1
Truro SA   79 K4, 81 K13
Tubbul NSW   23 R8, 24 C7, 30 B2
Tubbut Vic.   55 J3
Tuckanarra WA   90 G4
Tucklan NSW   28 G13
Tudor Vic.   61 M9
Tuen Qld   27 M1, 116 F12
Tuena NSW   24 F7, 30 E2
Tuggerah NSW   18 E12
Tuggerah Lake NSW   18 F12
Tuggerawong NSW   18 F11
Tuglow NSW   14 B12,24 H7, 30 G2
Tugun Qld   113 Q8, 125 O5
Tulkara Vic.   57 M11
Tullamarine Vic.   38 D1
Tullamore NSW   23 Q3, 24 B3
Tullanaringa Qld   120 C3
Tullaroop Reservoir Vic.   46 A3, 57 Q12, 58 A12
Tullibigeal NSW   23 O5
Tullis WA   94 H1
Tully Qld   118 G5
Tulmur Qld   122 H1
Tulum Vic.   43 L9
Tumbarumba NSW   23 R12, 30 B7, 62 H2
Tumbi Umbi NSW   18 F12
Tumbling Waters NT   100 D5
Tumblong NSW   23 R10, 24 C10, 30 B5
Tumbulgum NSW   29 Q1, 113 Q10
Tumby Bay SA   84 F11
Tumorrama NSW   24 D10, 30 C5
Tumut NSW   24 D11, 30 B6
Tunart Vic.   60 C5
Tunbridge Tas.   71 N2, 73 N12
Tuncurry NSW   25 N2, 29 N13
Tungamah Vic.   59 L5
Tungkillo SA   79 K6
Tunnack Tas.   71 N4
Tunnel Creek National Park WA   93 N5
Tunney WA   95 L8
Tuppal NSW   23 L12
Turill NSW   28 H12
Turner ACT   34 D6
Turners Marsh Tas.   73 L6
Turondale NSW   24 G4
Tuross Head NSW   30 G8
Turramurra NSW   12 H6
Turrawan NSW   28 H7
Turrella NSW   11 K9
Turriff Vic.   61 J12
Turton SA   78 E7
Turtons Creek Vic.   53 N11
Tutunup WA   94 E5
Tutye Vic.   60 D10
Tweed Heads NSW   29 R1, 113 R8, 117 Q12, 125 Q3
Twelve Mile NSW   24 F2
Twin Lakes Vic.   44 D2, 46 E12, 56 C5
Two Mile Flat NSW   24 G2, 28 G13
Two Wells SA   78 I5
Tyaak Vic.   47 N4, 52 H1, 58 H13
Tyabb Vic.   43 N5, 52 H8
Tyagarah NSW   29 R2

Tyagong NSW   24 D7, 30 B2
Tyalgum NSW   29 Q1, 113 M11
Tyalla Vic.   60 D10
Tycannah NSW   28 H5
Tyenna Tas.   68 B4, 71 J6
Tyers Vic.   53 O8
Tyers Junction Vic.   53 N6
Tylden Vic.   46 G6, 52 D2, 58 D13
Tylerville Qld   112 H10
Tynong Vic.   53 K7
Tyntynder Central Vic.   61 O10
Typo Vic.   59 O10
Tyrendarra Vic.   50 G8
Tyringham NSW   29 O7
Tyrrell Downs Vic.   61 L11

U

Uarbry NSW   28 H12
Ubobo Qld   117 N5
Ucolta SA   81 J6
Uki NSW   29 Q1, 113 O12
Ulamambri NSW   28 G10
Ulan NSW   24 G2, 28 H13
Ulidia NSW   29 O2
Ulinda NSW   28 G11
Ulladulla NSW   24 I11, 30 H6
Ullina Vic.   51 R1, 52 B1, 57 Q13, 58 B13
Ullswater Vic.   56 D11
Ulmarra NSW   29 P5
Ulong NSW   29 P7
Ulooloo SA   81 J8
Ultima Vic.   22 G12, 61 N12
Ultimo NSW   8 B11
Ulupna Vic.   58 I3
Uluru National Park NT   104 E11, 107
Ulverstone Tas.   72 H5
Umbakumba NT   101 P7
Umina NSW   15 Q3, 20 G3
Unanderra NSW   17 O5, 25 J8, 30 I3
Una Voce NSW   15 L2
Undalya SA   78 I2, 80 I11
Undandita NT   104 G8
Undera Vic.   58 I6
Underbool Vic.   60 F10
Undercliffe NSW   11 K8
Ungarie NSW   23 P6
Ungarra SA   84 F11
Union Reef NT   100 F7
Unley SA   75 E10, 76 E9
Unumbar NSW   112 H12
Upper Cedar Creek Qld   110 I8
Upper Coliban Reservoir Vic.   52 D1, 58 D13
Upper Colo NSW   15 J2
Upper Ferntree Gully Vic.   45 B10, 52 I6
Upper Horton NSW   28 I6
Upper Kangaroo River NSW   17 M9
Upper Laceys Creek Qld   110 H6
Upper Maffra West Vic.   53 Q6, 54 A8
Upper Mangrove Creek NSW   18 B12
Upper Mount Hicks Tas.   72 F5
Upper Myall NSW   25 N2, 29 N13
Upper Nariel Vic.   62 G7
Upper Plenty Vic.   47 M7, 52 H2
Upper Swan WA   96 G2
Upper Yarra Reservoir Vic.   48 I11, 53 L4
Upwey Vic.   45 C10
Uralla NSW   29 L8
Urana NSW   23 N11
Urandangi Qld   105 R3, 121 B10
Urangan Qld   117 Q7
Urangeline East NSW   23 O11
Urania SA   78 E4
Uranno SA   84 F11
Uranquinty NSW   23 P10
Urbenville NSW   29 O1, 112 E13
Urunga NSW   29 P8
Uxbridge Tas.   68 D5, 71 K6

V

Vacy NSW   25 L3
Valdora Qld   115 K8, 123 F5
Valencia Creek Vic.   53 R5, 54 B8
Valentine NSW   18 G7
Valley Heights NSW   14 I7
Vasey Vic.   50 G2
Vasse WA   94 D5

Vaucluse NSW 11 Q3
Vaughan Vic. 46 D3, 58 C12
Vectis Vic. 56 G9
Veitch SA 79 P5
Ventnor Vic. 52 H10
Venus Bay SA 84 C8
Veresdale Qld 113 K4
Vergmont Qld 122 I3
Vermont NSW 18 E10
Vermont Vic. 39 R11, 40 A3
Verran SA 84 F10
Vesper Vic. 53 M6
Victor Harbor SA 78 I9
Victoria Desert SA 82 B5
Victoria Park WA 87 I9
Victoria Point Qld 111 O12
Victoria River Crossing NT 100 E11, 102 E1
Victoria River Downs NT 100 E13, 102 E2
Victoria Valley Tas. 71 J3, 73 J13
Victoria Valley Vic. 50 I4
Victory Downs NT 104 I13
Villawood NSW 10 B7
Villeneuve Qld 110 G2
Vimy Qld 117 M4
Vincentia NSW 25 J10, 30 H5
Vineyard NSW 15 L5
Vine Vale SA 85 F4
Vinifera Vic. 61 N10
Violet Town Vic. 59 K8
Violet Valley Aboriginal Reserve WA 93 Q5
Virginia SA 78 I5
Vite Vite Vic. 51 N6
Viveash WA 96 F9
Vivonne Bay SA 78 D12

W

Waaia Vic. 58 I4
Wabba Vic. 62 F6
Wabonga Plateau State Park Vic. 59 O10
Waddamana Tas. 71 K2, 73 K12
Waddikee SA 84 F9
Wagait NT 100 D4
Wagait Aboriginal Reserve NT 100 C5
Wagant Vic. 61 J19
Wagerup WA 94 F1
Waggarandall Vic. 59 L5
Wagga Wagga NSW 23 Q10, 24 B10
Waggs Range Vic. 47 P1
Wagin WA 90 G11, 95 L3
Wagonga NSW 30 G9
Wagoora Qld 127 E9
Wagstaffe NSW 15 Q3, 20 G2
Wahgunyah Vic. 59 O4, 64 A2
Wahring Vic. 58 H9
Wahroonga NSW 12 H5
Waikerie SA 79 N3, 81 N12
Wail Vic. 56 H8
Wairewa Vic. 54 H7
Waitara NSW 12 G5
Waitchie Vic. 59 M11
Wakefield NSW 18 F6
Wakool NSW 23 J11
Walbundrie NSW 23 O12, 59 Q2
Walcha NSW 29 L9
Walcha Road NSW 29 L9
Walgett NSW 27 R6, 28 D6
Walhalla Vic. 53 O6
Walkamin Qld 126 B10
Walker Flat SA 79 M6
Walkerston Qld 127 G12
Walkerville SA 75 H1, 76 E7
Walkerville Vic. 53 M13
Wallabadah NSW 29 J11
Wallabrook SA 56 A9, 77 H6
Wallace Vic. 46 C9, 51 R3, 52 B3
Wallacedale Vic. 50 G6
Wallacia NSW 14 I9, 25 J7, 30 H1
Wallalong NSW 18 G2
Wallaloo Vic. 57 L9
Wallan Vic. 47 M7, 52 G2
Wallangarra Qld 29 M3, 117 O13
Wallangra NSW 29 K4, 117 N13
Wallara Ranch Tourist Chalet NT 104 G10
Wallaroo Qld 117 L4
Wallaroo SA 78 E2, 80 E11, 84 I10
Wallaville Qld 117 O6
Walla Walla NSW 23 P12, 59 R2, 62 A2

Wall Creek SA 82 I1
Wallendbeen NSW 24 D8, 30 B3
Wallerawang NSW 14 B3, 24 H5
Walli NSW 24 E6, 30 D1
Wallinduc Vic. 51 P6
Wallington Vic. 44 G8, 52 E8
Walloon Qld 110 G12
Walloway SA 80 I4
Wallsend NSW 18 H5, 25 L4
Wallumbilla Qld 117 K9
Wallup Vic. 56 H6
Walmer NSW 24 E3
Walmer Vic. 46 D1
Walpa Vic. 54 D8
Walpeup Vic. 60 G9
Walpole WA 90 F13, 94 I12
Walpole-Nornalup National Park WA 94 I13
Walsh Qld 118 D3, 120 F12
Waltowa SA 77 C1, 79 L10
Walwa Vic. 23 R13, 30 A8, 62 F4
Wal Wal Vic. 57 J10
Wamberal NSW 15 R1, 18 F13
Wambidgee NSW 24 D9, 30 B4
Wamboyne NSW 24 B5
Waminda NSW 28 D6
Wamoon NSW 23 N8
Wampoony SA 77 G4, 79 P13
Wamuran Qld 111 J3
Wanaaring NSW 26 I5
Wanalta Vic. 58 G8
Wanappe SA 78 H2, 80 H11
Wanbi SA 79 O6
Wandana SA 84 A5
Wandandian NSW 24 I10, 30 H5
Wandearah SA 80 G8
Wandering WA 90 F10
Wandiligong Vic. 59 R10, 62 B9
Wandilo SA 77 H11
Wandin Vic. 45 G3, 48 C12
Wandin East Vic. 45 I5
Wandin Yallock Vic. 45 H4
Wandoan Qld 117 L8
Wando Bridge Vic. 50 D3
Wandong Vic. 47 M6, 52 G2
Wando Vale Vic. 50 E3
Wandsworth NSW 29 L6
Wanganella NSW 23 K11
Wangarabel Vic. 30 E12
Wangaratta Vic. 59 N6, 64 D9
Wangary SA 84 E12
Wangerrip Vic. 51 O12
Wangianna SA 83 M7
Wangi Wangi NSW 18 G8
Wangoon Vic. 51 K9
Wang Wauk NSW 25 N1, 29 N13
Wanilla SA 84 E12
Wannon Vic. 50 G4
Wanora Qld 110 G12
Wantabadgery NSW 23 R10, 24 C10, 30 A5
Wantagong Qld 122 I3
Wantirna Vic. 40 A2
Wanwin Vic. 50 C7
Wapengo NSW 30 F10
Waraga NT 101 N4
Waranga Vic. 58 H8
Waranga Reservoir Vic. 58 H8
Waratah NSW 18 H5, 19 B4
Waratah Tas. 72 E7
Waratah Bay Vic. 53 M12
Waratah North Vic. 53 M12
Warbreccan Qld 122 I4
Warburton Vic. 48 F12, 53 K5
Warby Range State Park Vic. 59 N6
Wardell NSW 29 Q3
Wareek Vic. 57 P11
Wareemba NSW 10 I4, 11 J4
Warenda Qld 122 E1
Wargeila NSW 24 E9, 30 D4
Warge Rock NSW 23 R2, 24 C2
Warialda NSW 29 J4
Warilla NSW 17 O7
Warkton NSW 28 F10
Warmur Vic. 57 K5
Warnambool Downs Qld 122 I1
Warncoort Vic. 51 Q9, 52 A9
Warne Vic. 57 M2
Warneet Vic. 43 P3, 52 I8
Warner Glen WA 94 C8

Warners Bay NSW 18 G6
Warnertown SA 80 G7
Warnervale NSW 18 E11
Warooka SA 78 E7, 84 I13
Waroona WA 90 E11, 94 F1
Warra NSW 25 M2, 29 M13
Warra Qld 117 N9
Warrabri NT 103 K12, 105 K2
Warrabri Aboriginal Reserve NT 103 K12, 105 K2
Warrabrook Vic. 50 H6
Warrachie SA 84 E9
Warracknabeal Vic. 56 I6
Warraderry NSW 24 D6, 30 B1
Warragamba NSW 14 I9
Warragamba Vic. 58 E6
Warragamba Dam NSW 24 I7, 30 H2
Warragul Vic. 53 L8
Warrain Beach NSW 30 I5
Warrak Vic. 51 N1, 57 M13
Warrambine Vic. 51 Q6, 52 A6
Warramboo SA 84 E8
Warrandyte Vic. 48 A12, 52 H5
Warranook Vic. 57 K9
Warrawee NSW 12 H6
Warrawee Qld 114 E4
Warra Yadin Vic. 51 M1, 57 M13
Warrayure Vic. 50 I5
Warrell Creek NSW 29 P9
Warren NSW 27 R11, 28 C11
Warrenbayne Vic. 59 L9
Warrenheip Vic. 46 B10
Warrenmang Vic. 57 N11
Warren National Park WA 94 F10
Warrentinna Tas. 73 O5
Warrick Park NSW 113 R12
Warrie National Park Qld 113 O9
Warriewood NSW 13 P2
Warri House NSW 122 H13
Warrill View Qld 112 F3
Warrimoo NSW 14 I7
Warrina SA 83 K5
Warrion Vic. 51 P8
Warri Warri Gate NSW 26 C3
Warrnambool Vic. 51 J9
Warrong Vic. 50 I8
Warrow SA 84 E11
Warrumbungle NSW 28 E10
Warrumbungle National Park NSW 28 F10
Wartaka P.O. SA 84 H7
Wartook Vic. 56 I11
Warunda SA 84 E11
Warup WA 95 K4
Warwick Qld 29 N1, 117 O11
Wasleys SA 78 I4, 80 I13
Watchem Vic. 57 L5
Watchman SA 78 H2, 80 H11
Watchupga Vic. 57 K2
Waterfall NSW 15 N12
Waterford Qld 111 M13, 113 M1
Waterford Vic. 54 C6
Waterholes Vic. 54 E7
Waterhouse Tas. 73 O4
Waterloo NSW 11 N6
Waterloo SA 79 J2, 81 J11
Waterloo Vic. 51 O2
Waterloo WA 94 F4
Watervale SA 78 I2, 80 I11
Wathe Vic. 56 I1, 60 I12
Watheroo WA 90 E8
Watson ACT 34 H2
Watson SA 82 E9
Watsonia Vic. 39 M3, 47 N11
Watsons Bay NSW 11 Q1, 13 Q13
Watsons Creek NSW 29 K8
Watsonville Qld 118 F4, 120 I13
Wattagan NSW 18 B8
Wattamolla NSW 15 P12, 17 M10
Wattamondara NSW 24 E7, 30 C2
Wattle Flat NSW 24 G4
Wattle Flat Vic. 46 B8
Wattle Grove Tas. 68 F11, 71 L9
Wattle Hill Tas. 69 M5, 71 O6
Wattle Hill Vic. 51 N12, 59 J12
Wattle Range SA 77 G9
Wattle Tree Vic. 54 H4
Wattle Vale Vic. 58 H10
Waubra Vic. 51 P2

157

Waubra Junction Vic. 46 A8, 51 Q3, 52 A3
Wauchope NSW 29 O11
Wauchope NT 103 K12, 105 K1
Waukaringa SA 83 P12
Wauraltee SA 78 E5
Waurn Ponds Vic. 44 E8, 52 D8
Wave Hill NSW 27 O7
Wave Hill NT 102 D5
Waverley NSW 11 P6
Waverney Qld 122 H6
Waverton NSW 11 L2, 13 L13
Wayatinah Tas. 70 I3
Waygara Vic. 54 I7
Wayville SA 75 D10
Weavers NSW 15 M2
Webbs NSW 24 D1, 28 D13
Webbs Creek NSW 15 L1
Webster Hill Vic. 51 P11
Wedderburn NSW 15 L13
Wedderburn Vic. 57 P7
Wedderburn Junction Vic. 57 P7
Weddin Mountains National Park NSW
  23 R7, 24 C7, 30 B1
Wedge Island SA 84 G13
Weeaproinah Vic. 51 P11
Wee Elwah NSW 23 L4
Weegena Tas. 72 I7
Wee Jasper NSW 24 E10, 30 C5
Weemelah NSW 28 G3
Weeragua Vic. 55 M5
Weerite Vic. 51 N8
Weetah Tas. 73 J7
Weetaliba NSW 28 G11
Weethalle NSW 23 O6
Weetulta SA 78 E3, 80 E12, 84 I11
Wee Waa NSW 28 G7
Wee-Wee-Rup Vic. 58 D3
Wehla Vic. 57 P8
Weilmoringle NSW 27 P3, 28 A3, 117 H13
Weimby NSW 22 G9
Weipa Qld 120 C4
Weja NSW 23 O5
Welaregang NSW 30 B8, 62 G4
Welby NSW 17 J6
Weldborough Tas. 73 P6
Wellingrove NSW 29 L5
Wellington NSW 24 F2
Wellington SA 79 L8
Wellington Mills WA 94 F4
Wellington Point Qld 111 N10
Wellsford Vic. 58 E8
Welshmans Reef Vic. 46 C2, 57 R11, 58 B11
Welshpool Vic. 53 O11
Wemen Vic. 22 F9, 61 J7
Wendouree Vic. 46 A9, 63 B8
Wensleydale Vic. 44 B10
Wentworth NSW' 22 D8, 60 F2
Wentworth Falls NSW 15 F7
Wentworthville NSW 10 A1, 12 A13
Weonawarri Qld 122 I2
Wepar SA 77 H10
Werneth Vic. 51 P6
Werombi NSW 14 I11
Werona Vic. 51 R1, 52 B1, 57 R13, 58 B13
Werrap Vic. 56 G4
Werri Beach NSW 17 O9
Werribee Vic. 44 I4, 52 F6
Werribee Gorge Vic. 46 F11
Werrimull Vic. 60 E4
Werrington NSW 15 K7
Werris Creek NSW 29 J10
Wesburn Vic. 48 E12
Wesley Vale Tas. 72 I6
Wessel Islands NT 101 O2
West Beach SA 76 A9
West Burleigh Qld 125 M9
Westbury Tas. 73 K8
Westbury Vic. 53 N8
Westby Vic. 57 B1, 58 B1, 61 R13
Westdale NSW 29 J9
Western Creek Tas. 72 I9
Western Flat SA 77 H5
Western Hill Vic. 43 M9
West Hobart Tas. 67 C9
Western Junction Tas. 73 M8
Westerton Qld 122 I4
Westerway Tas. 68 C4, 71 K5
Westleigh NSW 12 E6

Westmar Qld 117 L11
Westmead NSW 10 B1, 12 B13
Westmeadows Vic. 38 E1
Westmere Vic. 51 M4
Weston NSW 18 E4
Westons Flat SA 79 N2, 81 N11
West Perth WA 87 A3
West Pymble NSW 12 H8
West Ridgley Tas. 72 F5
West Ryde NSW 12 G12
West Swan WA 96 E7
West Wallsend NSW 18 F5
West Wollongong NSW 19 A10
Westwood Qld 117 M3
Westwood Tas. 73 L8
West Wyalong NSW 23 P7, 24 A7
Wexcombe WA 96 H9
Weymouth Tas. 73 L4
Whale Beach NSW 15 Q4
Wharminda SA 84 F10
Wharparilla Vic. 58 E4
Wheatsheaf Vic. 46 E6
Wheeler Heights NSW 13 P4
Wheelers Hill Vic. 40 D3
Wheeo NSW 24 F8, 30 E3
Whetstone Qld 29 K1
Whim Creek WA 92 G9
Whiporie NSW 29 P4, 117 Q13
Whirily Vic. 57 L3
White Cliffs NSW 26 F9
White Flat SA 84 F12
Whitefoord Tas. 71 N4
Whiteheads Creek Vic. 47 O2, 48 A2, 58 I11
White Hills Tas. 73 M8
White Hut SA 78 C7
Whitemore Tas. 73 K8
White Rock Qld 126 F8
Whitewood Qld 118 C11
Whitfield Vic. 59 O9
Whitlands Vic. 59 O9
Whitsunday Group Qld 127
Whitsunday Island Qld 119 K9
Whittingham NSW 18 A1
Whittington Vic. 63 I5
Whittlesea Vic. 47 N8, 52 H3
Whitton NSW 23 N8
Whitwarta SA 78 H2, 80 H12
Whoorel Vic. 51 Q9, 52 A9
Whorouly Vic. 59 P7
Whroo Vic. 58 G8
Whyalla SA 80 E6, 83 M13, 84 I8
Whyalla Conservation Park SA 83 M13
Whyte Yarcowie SA 81 J7
Wialki WA 90 G8
Wiangaree NSW 29 P2, 113 J13
Wickepin WA 90 G11, 95 M1
Wickham NSW 19 E5
Wickham WA 92 F9
Wickliffe Vic. 51 K4
Widgee Upper Qld 114 D3
Widgiemooltha WA 91 J9
Widgiewa NSW 23 N10
Wihareja Tas. 71 K1, 73 K11
Wilberforce NSW 15 K4
Wilby Vic. 59 M5
Wilcannia NSW 26 G11
Wildeloo SA 84 E11
Wildes Meadow NSW 17 L8
Wild Horse Plains SA 78 H4, 80 H13
Wiley Park NSW 10 G9
Wilga WA 94 H6
Wilgena SA 82 I9, 84 C2
Wilkatana SA 80 F2, 83 N12
Wilkawatt SA 79 P8
Wilkur Vic. 57 J4
Willa Vic. 60 H11
Willamulka SA 78 F2, 80 F11
Willandra National Park NSW 23 K4
Willaring NSW 57 L10
Willatook Vic. 50 I8
Willaura Vic. 51 L3
Willawarrin NSW 29 O9
Willbriggie NSW 23 N8
Willenabrina Vic. 56 H4
William Creek SA 83 L6
Williams WA 90 F11, 95 J2
Williamsdale NSW 30 D7
Williamsford Tas. 72 E10

Williamstown SA 79 J5
Williamstown Vic. 38 E12, 52 G6
Williamtown NSW 18 I3, 25 M3
Willigam NSW 16 A8
Willina NSW 25 N2
Willis Vic. 30 C10, 54 I1
Willochra SA 80 G2
Willoughby NSW 13 M11
Willow Grove Vic. 53 N7
Willowie Qld 113 N8
Willowie SA 80 H5, 83 N13
Willowmavin Vic. 47 L5
Willows Qld 116 I3
Willow Spring WA 94 F7
Willow Tree NSW 29 J11
Willow Vale NSW 17 O10
Willowvale Vic. 51 O5
Willung Vic. 53 Q8, 54 A11
Willunga SA 78 I8
Willyabrup WA 94 C6
Wilmot Tas. 72 H7
Wilmington SA 80 G4, 83 N13
Wilpena SA 83 O13
Wilpena Pound SA 83 O11
Wilson Qld 127 E6
Wilson SA 80 H1
Wilsons Downfall NSW 29 N2
Wilsons Pocket Qld 114 I2
Wilsons Promontory Vic. 53 N13
Wilsons Promontory National Park Vic. 49,
  52 G12, 53 O13
Wilton NSW 17 M2
Wiltshire Junction Tas. 72 D3
Wiluna WA 90 I3
Wimba Vic. 51 P11
Winchelsea Vic. 44 B9, 51 R8, 52 B8
Windale NSW 18 H6
Windang NSW 17 P6
Windellama NSW 24 H10, 30 F5
Windermere Vic. 51 Q3, 52 A3
Windeyer NSW 24 G3
Windjana Gorge National Park WA 93 N5
Windomal NSW 22 G9
Windorah Qld 116 B7, 122 I6
Windsor NSW 15 K5, 25 J6, 30 I1
Windsor SA 78 H4, 80 H13
Windurong NSW 28 E11
Windy Harbour WA 94 G11
Wingamin SA 79 N7
Wingeel Vic. 51 Q7, 52 A7
Wingello NSW 16 H10, 30 G4
Wingham NSW 29 N12
Winiam Vic. 56 E7
Winjallock Vic. 57 N10
Winkie SA 79 P3, 81 P12
Winkleigh Tas. 73 K6
Winnaleah Tas. 73 P5
Winnambool Vic. 61 K8
Winnap Vic. 50 D7
Winnellie NT 99 K1
Winnindoo Vic. 53 Q7
Winninowie SA 80 F4
Winnunga NSW 23 P5
Winslow Vic. 51 J8
Winston Hills NSW 12 A10
Winton Qld 116 B1, 118 B13, 121 I11
Winton Vic. 59 M7
Winulta SA 78 F3, 80 F12
Winwill Qld 110 A12
Winya Qld 110 F2
Wirha SA 79 P7
Wirrabara SA 80 H6
Wirraminna SA 83 K10, 84 F3
Wirrappa SA 83 L11, 84 H4
Wirrega SA 77 G3, 79 P12
Wirrimah NSW 24 D7, 30 C2
Wirrinya NSW 23 R6, 24 C6, 30 A1
Wirrulla SA 82 I12, 84 C6
Wisemans Ferry NSW 15 M1, 25 J5
Wishbone WA 95 N3
Witchcliffe WA 94 C7
Witchelina SA 83 N8
Witheren Qld 113 M6
Withersfield Qld 116 I3
Witta Qld 114 I10, 123 A9
Wittenbra NSW 28 F9
Wittenoom WA 92 G11
Wittenoom Gorge WA 92 G11

158

Wittitrin NSW 29 O10
Wivenhoe Pocket Qld 110 F9
Wiyarra Qld 112 A9
Wodonga Vic. 23 P13, 59 Q5, 62 A5
Wokalup WA 94 F2
Wokurna SA 80 G10
Wolf Creek Crater National Park WA 93 P7
Wolffdene Qld 113 M2
Wollar NSW 24 H2, 28, H13
Wollert Vic. 47 M10
Wollombi NSW 18 A7, 25 K4, 29 M8
Wollongong NSW 17 P5, 19 F11, 25 J8, 30 I3
Wollstonecraft NSW 11 L1, 13 L13
Wollun NSW 29 L9
Wolseley SA 56 A7, 77 H4, 79 Q13
Wolumla NSW 30 F10, 55 P1
Wolvi Qld 114 I2
Womalilla Qld 116 I8
Wombarra NSW 17 P2
Wombat NSW 24 D8, 30 B3
Wombat Vic. 46 C7
Wombelano Vic. 56 E11
Wombeyan Caves NSW 16 E5, 24 H8
Womboota NSW 23 J13, 58 E3
Wonboyn Lake NSW 30 F12, 55 P4
Wondabyne NSW 15 P2, 20 E7
Wondai Qld 117 O8
Wondalga NSW 23 R11, 24 D11, 30 B6
Wongabel Qld 126 C13
Wonga Lower Qld 114 E1
Wongan Hills WA 90 F8
Wonga Park Vic. 48 A12
Wonga Upper Qld 114 D2
Wongarbon NSW 24 E2, 28 E13
Wongarra Vic. 51 Q12, 52 A12
Wongawilli NSW 17 N6
Wonglepong Qld 113 M5
Wongulla SA 79 M5
Wonnerup WA 94 D5
Wonning P.O. SA 84 G7
Wonthaggi Vic. 53 J11
Wonuarra SA 79 Q3, 81 Q12
Wonwondah East Vic. 56 H10
Wonwondah North Vic. 56 H10
Wonwron Vic. 53 P10
Wonyip Vic. 53 O11
Woocalla SA 83 M11, 84 H5
Woodanilling WA 90 G11, 95 L5
Woodbine Qld 112 A2
Woodbridge Tas. 68 H11, 71 M9
Woodburn NSW 29 Q3, 117 Q13
Woodburn WA 95 N11
Woodburne Vic. 44 A3, 46 B13, 51 R5, 52 B5
Woodbury Tas. 71 M2, 73 M12
Woodchester SA 79 J8
Woodenbong NSW 29 O1, 112 F11, 117 P12
Woodend Vic. 46 H6, 52 E2
Woodfield Vic. 48 G1, 59 L11
Woodford NSW 14 G7
Woodford Qld 110 H2, 117 P9
Woodgate Qld 117 P6
Wood Hill NSW 17 N9
Woodhill Qld 113 K4
Woodhouselee NSW 16 A9, 24 G9, 30 F3
Woodlands Qld 110 B12
Woodlands WA 94 C6
Woodleigh Vic. 53 K9
Woodridge Qld 111 L12
Woods SA 78 I3, 80 I12
Woodsdale Tas. 69 L1, 71 N4
Woodside SA 79 J6
Woodside Vic. 53 Q10, 54 A13
Woods Point Vic. 53 N3
Woods Reef NSW 29 J7
Woodstock NSW 24 E6, 30 D1
Woodstock Qld 116 A1, 118 H8
Woodstock Tas. 68 F10, 71 L8
Woodstock Vic. 47 M9, 52 G3, 57 R9, 58 B9
Woodstock WA 92 H10
Woods Well SA 77 C3, 79 M12
Woodvale Vic. 58 C8
Woodville NSW 18 F2, 25 L3
Woodville SA 76 B7
Wood Wood Vic. 61 N9
Woogenellup WA 95 N10
Woohlpooer Vic. 50 H2
Woolamai Vic. 53 J10
Wool Bay SA 78 F7, 84 I13

Woolbrook NSW 29 L9
Woolgoolga NSW 29 P7
Wooli NSW 29 Q6
Woollahra NSW 11 P5
Woolloomooloo NSW 8 G7
Woolloongabba Qld 109 G11
Woolner NT 99 K6
Woolomin NSW 29 K10
Woolooga Qld 114 D1
Woolshed Vic. 59 P6
Woolsthorpe Vic. 51 J8
Woolwich NSW 11 K2
Woolwonga Wildlife Sanctuary NT 100 H5
Wool Wool Vic. 51 O8
Woomargama NSW 23 P12, 62 D3
Woombye Qld 115 K10, 123 E8
Woomelang Vic. 22 F12, 57 K2, 61 K13
Woomera SA 83 L10, 84 G3
Woomera Prohibited Area SA 82 F7
Woompah NSW 122 H13
Woondum Qld 114 H4
Woongoolba Qld 113 O2
Woonona NSW 17 P3
Wooragee Vic. 59 Q6
Woorak Vic. 56 F6
Woorarra East Vic. 53 O11
Wooreen Vic. 53 M9
Woorim Qld 111 N4
Woorinen Vic. 61 O10
Woori Yallock Vic. 47 R12, 48 D12, 53 J5
Woornack Vic. 61 J9
Woorndoo Vic. 51 L6
Wooroonook Vic. 57 N6
Woosang Vic. 57 O6
Wootha Qld 114 I12, 123 A12
Wootong Vale Vic. 50 F3
Wootoona P.O. SA 84 D8
Wootton NSW 25 N2, 29 N13
Wooyong NSW 113 R13
World's End Creek SA 79 K1, 81 K10
Worongary Qld 113 O6
Woronora Reservoir NSW 15 N13
Worrigee NSW 17 M12
Worsley WA 94 G3
Wowan Qld 117 M4
Woy Woy NSW 15 Q2, 20 E3
Wrattonbully SA 50 B1, 56 B13, 77 I8
Wrightley Vic. 59 M10
Wroxham Vic. 55 N4
Wubin WA 90 F8
Wudinna SA 84 E8
Wulgulmerang Vic. 54 H3, 62 I12
Wundowie WA 90 F10
Wunghnu Vic. 59 J5
Wunkar SA 79 O4, 81 O13
Wuraming WA 94 H1
Wurdiboluc Vic. 44 B9
Wurdiboluc Reservoir Vic. 52 B9
Wurruk Vic. 53 R8, 54 B10
Wutul Qld 117 O9
Wyadup WA 94 C6
Wyalkatchem WA 90 G9
Wyalong NSW 23 P7, 24 B7
Wyan NSW 29 P3
Wyandra Qld 116 G10
Wyanga NSW 23 R2, 24 D2, 28 D13
Wyangala Dam NSW 24 F7, 30 D2
Wybong NSW 25 J1, 29 J13
Wycarbah Qld 117 M3
Wycheproof Vic. 22 G13, 57 N4
Wychitella Vic. 57 P6
Wyee NSW 18 F10, 25 L4
Wyeeboo Vic. 62 D6
Wyelangta Vic. 51 O11
Wye River Vic. 51 R11, 52 B11
Wylie Creek NSW 29 N2
Wymah NSW 23 P13, 62 D4
Wymlet Vic. 60 G8
Wynarka SA 79 M7
Wynbring SA 82 G9, 84 A2
Wyndham NSW 30 F11, 55 O2
Wyndham WA 93 Q3
Wynnum Qld 111 M9
Wynyard Tas. 72 F4
Wyong NSW 18 E11, 25 L5
Wyongah NSW 18 F11
Wyong Creek NSW 18 D11
Wyperfeld National Park Vic. 56 G1, 60 F12

Wyuna Vic. 58 H5
Wyuna Downs NSW 27 N7
Wy Yung Vic. 54 E8

Y

Yaamba Qld 117 M3
Yaapeet Vic. 56 G2
Yabba North Vic. 59 K5
Yabba South Vic. 59 K6
Yabba Vale Qld 114 H6
Yabba Valley Vic. 62 C6
Yabmana SA 78 B1, 80 B10
Yacka SA 80 H9
Yackandandah Vic. 59 Q6
Yagobie NSW 28 I4
Yagoona NSW 10 E8
Yahl SA 50 B6, 77 H12
Yalboroo Qld 119 K10, 127 D9
Yalbraith NSW 16 B5, 24 G8, 30 F3
Yalca Vic. 58 I4
Yalgogrin North NSW 23 O6
Yalgogrin South NSW 23 O7
Yalgoo WA 90 F6
Yallah NSW 17 O7
Yallambie NSW 18 A8
Yallaroi NSW 29 J3, 117 M13
Yalla-y-poora Vic. 51 M3
Yalleroi Qld 116 G4
Yallingup WA 90 E12, 94 C6
Yallingup Caves WA 94 C5
Yallourn Vic. 53 N8
Yallunda Flat SA 84 F11
Yalwal NSW 17 K13, 30 G5
Yamba NSW 29 Q4
Yamba SA 22 A8, 60 A3, 81 Q12, 79 Q3
Yambuk Vic. 50 H9
Yambuna Vic. 58 G5
Yanac Vic. 56 D5
Yanakie Vic. 49 B2, 53 N12
Yanco NSW 23 O9
Yanderra NSW 17 L4
Yandiah SA 80 H6
Yandilla Qld 117 N11
Yandina Qld 115 K8, 123 D6
Yandina Creek Qld 115 K8, 123 E5
Yando Vic. 57 Q4, 58 A4
Yandoit Vic. 46 C4, 52 C1, 57 R12, 58 B13
Yangan Qld 112 A8
Yaninee SA 84 D8
Yanipy Vic. 56 C7
Yankalilla SA 78 H9
Yanko Qld 122 H12
Yanmah WA 94 G8
Yantabulla NSW 27 K4, 116 E13
Yantanabie SA 84 C7, 82 I12
Yan Yean Vic. 47 N9, 52 H3
Yan Yean Reservoir Vic. 52 H3
Yaouk NSW 30 D7
Yapeen Vic. 46 D3, 58 C12
Yaraka Qld 116 D6
Yarck Vic. 48 E2, 59 K12
Yardaring WA 93 C7
Yardea P.O. SA 84 E6
Yarloop WA 94 F2
Yarra NSW 16 B12, 24 G9
Yarrabah Aboriginal Community Qld 126
Yarrabandai NSW 23 Q4, 24 B4
Yarrabin NSW 24 F3
Yarraby Vic. 61 N10
Yarra Glen Vic. 47 Q10, 48 B11, 52 I4
Yarragon Vic. 53 M8
Yarra Junction Vic. 48 E12, 53 K5
Yarralena WA 95 L9
Yarralumla ACT 34 B11
Yarram Vic. 53 P11
Yarramalong NSW 18 C11
Yarraman Qld 117 O9
Yarraman North NSW 28 I11
Yarrambat Vic. 47 N10
Yarrangobilly NSW 30 C7
Yarrara Vic. 60 D4
Yarras NSW 29 N11
Yarraville Vic. 38 D9
Yarrawalla Vic. 57 R5, 58 B5
Yarrawonga Vic. 23 N13, 59 M4
Yarrie Lake NSW 28 G7
Yarrock Vic. 56 C6

Travel Diary

Date	Kilometres	Petrol costs	Destination	Accommodation	General comments

Travel Diary

Date	Kilometres	Petrol costs	Destination	Accommodation	General comments

Published by George Philip and O'Neil Pty Ltd
for Faber and Faber, Inc.
This revised edition first published 1986
© Publication and concept
George Philip and O'Neil Pty Ltd
© Maps copyright as designated
BP Australia Ltd or
George Philip and O'Neil Pty Ltd

All rights reserved
Wholly designed and set up in Australia
Printed in Hong Kong through Bookbuilders Ltd

Care has been taken to ensure the
accuracy of this publication but the
publishers do not accept responsibility
for any errors or omissions.

Distributed by Faber and Faber, Inc.
50 Cross Street
Winchester, MA 01890

ISBN 0 571 12962 5

If you value views more than speed, take the meandering Princes Highway (1048 km from Melbourne to Sydney). In parts the road narrows and winds, making progress slow, but what you gain in panoramic views and delightful stopping places more than makes up for the extra driving time. The scenery — particularly along the lovely rugged Illawarra coast — is unsurpassed; and the whole area is dotted with enticing fishing and resort towns. These include Eden, Bega, Narooma and Batemans Bay. You will need to book accommodation well ahead during holiday periods.

If you are in a hurry, you will save a good two hours by taking the excellent Hume Highway (885 km from Melbourne to Sydney). A word of warning: many trucks favour this well-maintained highway, which can be frustrating to the motor car driver, and demands the utmost concentration. Suggested stop-overs are Albury-Wodonga, Gundagai, Yass or Goulburn. If your schedule allows, stop for a stroll through the charming historic village of Berrima.

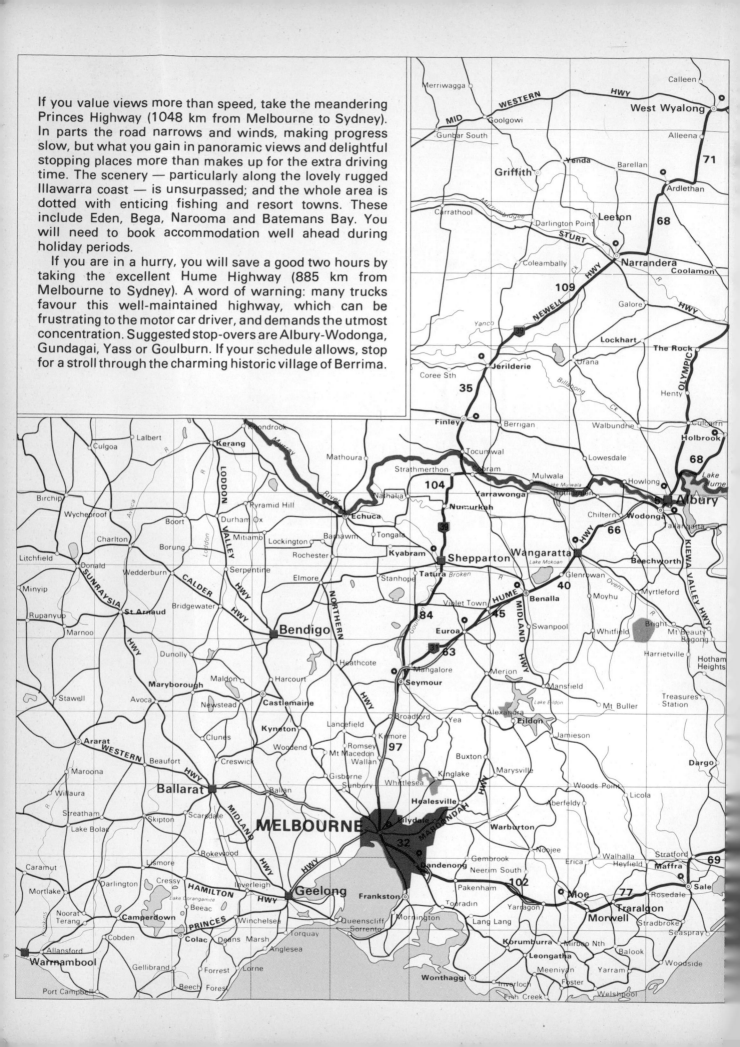